LITERATURE
AMONG THE
PRIMITIVES

John Greenway

LITERATURE AMONG THE PRIMITIVES

FOLKLORE ASSOCIATES
HATBORO, PENNSYLVANIA

1964

First printing, March, 1964

LIBRARY OF CONGRESS CATALOG CARD NUMBER: 64-13289

To MacEdward Leach, dear friend and revered teacher, but for whose inspiration, advice, and encouragement, I would today be in a more profitable line of work.

Contents

Introduction

Neither illiteracy nor adversity, poverty of mind nor penury of culture, can deprive people of literature. Song and story, myth and *Märchen*, are universals among mankind, and indeed have been taken as criteria whose possession separates man from the beasts.

"These two things endure," a great teacher said a generation ago, "poetry and pottery." The treasures of the past are gone, destroyed or transmuted into the wealth of strangers, and the people who made them we know mostly by what they threw away—pieces of broken pottery in midden heaps—or what they scratched on rock walls. Poetry is far older than pottery; thousands of years before man burned clay into culinary ware, the Paleolithic people of Ariège painted a ritual dance on the walls of the cave of Les Trois Frères, a dance that certainly was accompanied by singing. And poetry is far more important than pottery; many peoples get along well without kitchen ware but none is without some form of literature.

Yet judging by the scholarship of anthropologists today, one is likely to imagine that the situation is quite different. Current textbooks give ten times as much space to potsherd analysis as they do to literature, though it may be suspected that literature is at least as important to some of the earth's inhabitants as broken pots. No professional student of man would be able to hold up his head if he were to confuse a Lino Gray sherd with a La Plata Black-on-White, but within the last four years a distinguished Fellow of the American Anthropological Association repeated Schoolcraft's century-old error of calling Hiawatha an Indian culture hero; a year earlier another spoke of poetry (which is almost never found separate from song) as a world-wide possession. The few general works that even briefly consider literature apart from myth disdainfully label it "folklore." As one of the few scholars who are interested in this aspect of culture put it, "readers of non-Western oral literature are, I suppose, about as rare as nuclear physicists who read Bulgarian poetry" (Jacobs, 1959: 1).

It is a pity that anthropologists are not more concerned with the literature of the world's little known people, for of all the arts and crafts, it is the most valuable for their analysis, being the least bound by external function. A chair is function-bound to the purpose of holding the human body in a sitting position; pottery is function-bound to the purpose of holding liquids. One can proliferate legs on the former and handles on the latter, and paint both with designs drawn from all of nature, but their primary utility limits their developmental possibilities. Nevertheless, both pot and chair and thousands of other artifacts are exhaustively studied by anthropologists to trace cultural evolution and meaning while literature is left to the esthetes—literature, which has no function except to communicate the immaterial culture of its tellers: attitudes, emotions, prejudices, biases, ideals, vices, virtues, and, occasionally, art.

Very often art: the exquisite imagery of the Australian myth of the Old Man Nagacork's farewell, with the smoke of his campfire drifting across the night into the Milky Way; the Shakespearean eloquence of the Tongan rejected lover ("Well may the thunder crash and the rains descend, the earth quake and tremble with double shocks"); the Cambodian morning star "drinking on the edge of the misty sky"; and from the "primitive" period of our own literature, the Anglo-Saxon demon Grendel, who "comes in the wan night, stalking, the shadowgoer." As Shelley and the Navaho priest said, literature "walks in beauty," and in religious intensity, and in humor. Television this week will offer no story so hilarious as the Ashanti "Talk" (Chapter Four) nor any so cleverly satirical as the Kikuyu tale about the man and the elephant (Chapter Six).

Why the anthropologists continue to ignore literature is hard to say. One reason is that this discipline, like most others, takes its fashions from powerful personalities, and since Boas, no such dominant male has risen to lead us into literature as Radcliffe-Brown led us into Social Organization. Another is that many anthropologists, untrained in literary appreciation, are afraid of it—almost as much as professors of English literature are afraid of anthropology. C. P. Snow has lamented the steady alienation of the humanists from the scientists; anthropology was once a happy meeting ground for humanists and scientists, but as the *Fellow Newsletter* of the American Anthropological Association acknowledged in September of 1960,

Our profession is becoming more and more like a giant
spiral nebula, and those of us on one edge seem to have
little in common with our colleagues on the opposite side,
several light years away.

Margaret Mead summed it up more briefly when she said anthropology is an overly-extended family without any parents. It need not
be thus; there is room for all in our house, for a hundred flowers to
bloom, and there are many areas where the scientist and the human-
ist can assist and supplement each other. Philology joined ethnology to become ethnolinguistics, and even closer to our area anthropology joined music to become ethnomusicology; it is long past
time for cooperation of two important interpreters of the works of
man to combine in ethnoliterature. It can be a happy and genetic-
ally compatible union; professors of literature need not go to such
extremes as speaking of the Tubatulabal and Pitjandjara in the same
breath with T. S. Eliot, nor professors of anthropology to discuss
Beowulf when examining the archaeology of the Late Scratched Ware
culture. One thing they both will have to come to a pre-nuptial
agreement on, however, is what we all are talking about.

A WORD ON DEFINITIONS

"When *I* use a word," said Humpty Dumpty just before he fell
off the wall, "It means just what I choose it to mean—neither more
nor less." A reviewer of a previous work of mine compared me to
Humpty Dumpty, a comparison that did not annoy me overmuch,
since I always believed that Humpty Dumpty was right. When
using words it is indeed a question of who is to be master. I was
pleased later to find that Lewis Carroll felt the same, for in a less
well known book, *Symbolic Logic*, he stated frankly,

> I maintain that any writer of a book is fully authorised
> in attaching any meaning he likes to any word or phrase he
> intends to use. If I find an author saying, at the beginning
> of his book, "Let it be understood that by the word '*black*'
> I shall always mean '*white*,' and that by the word '*white*'
> I shall always mean '*black*,'" I meekly accept his ruling,
> however injudicious I may think it.

I should like to acknowledge here the kindness of my friends in
anthropology who, learning that I was working on a book to be
titled PRIMITIVE LITERATURE, pointed out to me, all of them,

that the two terms were contradictory (my friends in English called the phrase an "oxymoron"). In deference to their advice I have changed the title to *Literature Among the Primitives*.

I was very glad to learn from my friends in both disciplines that "literature" is derived from the Latin *literatura*, by which the Romans meant learning, grammar, and writing, none of which is characteristic of the people whose literature this book considers. The word should not, accordingly, be used. But the history of English etymology shows that words mean what people want them to mean, and having a Ph.D. in this area, I claim as much right to make "literature" mean unwritten as well as written writing as Warren G. Harding had to impose his invented term "normalcy" upon the English language.

The alternatives were considered and not found attractive. Professor William Bascom went through this agonizing reappraisal (1955: 246) and decided not to fall off the semantic wall:

> The terms "unwritten literature," "popular literature," "folk literature," "primitive literature," and "oral literature" emphasize the relation of these forms to literature, but all are based upon the irreconcilable contradiction that literature is based upon letters and writing, whereas folklore is not.

Professor Bascom went on to suggest the term *verbal art*, which is all right, I suppose, except no one uses it other than Professor Bascom.

Nor can I in conscience allow this material to be called "folklore." Though the overwhelming majority of anthropologists use the term to include primitive literature, correctness in this matter is not determinable by democracy. The term "folk" is an irreplaceable one in describing the processes by which a society evolves from primitiveness to integrated civilization, and loose usage of the word to refer to primitive peoples and their culture entirely deprives us of a way to name those enclaves of unsophisticated people that are within but not wholly a part of an advanced culture. To borrow Lewis Carroll's phrase, let it be understood that by the word *folk* I shall always mean an unsophisticated, homogeneous group living in a politically-bounded advanced culture but isolated from it by such factors as topography, geography, religion, dialect, economics, and race. It is thus proper to speak of the murder ballad which goes

> You brought disgrace upon Whitesville
> By taking me to the old oil mill;

You cut me up there, slice by slice,
For which I blame Squire Avery Rice

as "folk," for it emanated from an obviously unsophisticated frontier
society in the early 19th century. But to call the metaphysically
complex Polynesian myths "folklore" is like calling the culinary ware
of the Mochica "folk pottery."

Similarly the English literature scholars who describe the changes
that occur in ballads the result of "folk processes" are perpetuating
a misconception. What happens to ballads, lyric songs, and tales as
they move freely among the folk is precisely what happens to everything else in any culture, folk or sophisticated, subject to the molding
effects of diffusion, pottery as well as poetry, except that it is more
noticeable in folk literature because there the calcifying force of print
does not interfere. The difference is not qualitative, but quantita-
tive. Not only diffusion, but all the other processes of culture change
(discussed in Chapter Six) are detectable in poetry and pottery.

Still another danger lies in becoming sentimentally attached to the
customs and culture of the folk without understanding clearly that
in so doing we are making a metaphor into reality. The folk enclaves do preserve as living traditions the ideas and ideals obsolete
or obsolescent in the advanced surrounding culture, ideas and ideals
which are nostalgically accepted as the best forces behind the civilization and the essence of the national character.

Because folk literature is an enormous subject that has received
far more than its fair share of attention (some 700 folk ballad collections alone have been published in English during the last fifty
years), while the literature of the primitives has been almost totally
ignored, "folklore" in the sense of the preceding definition will not
be considered in this book, except occasionally to make a point clear,
as in the discussion of Heroes in Chapter Three.

My definition of "literature" may possibly survive criticism. Its
adjective "primitive" will have harder going. Anthropologists are
good people, probably because of their heritage (two generations ago
anthropologists were missionaries), and they are violently repelled by
any adjectives applied to their charges that in the least suggest an
inferiority. There is in fact no difference in cultural capacities among
the several races of the world; this matter was settled by vote of the
Council of Fellows of the American Anthropological Association in
November, 1961. Unfortunately this news has not reached many
persons outside the Association, and since many of the earth's less
favored inhabitants marry their first cousins, make trophies out of

their neighbors' heads, run around naked, eat one another, and engage in other conduct that non-anthropologists find reprehensible, adjectives of any kind quickly pick up invidious connotations. The anthropologists have a hard time keeping up with these distasteful terms, but at the moment they seem to have overtaken the word "primitive." When this book was drafted I had the support in precedent of Elman R. Service's *A Profile of Primitive Culture*, but the second edition of this work abandoned me by coming out under the title *Profiles in Ethnology*, explaining in the preface that the word "primitive" had become "pejorative," presumably since the first edition.

I thought at one time of using the word "preliterate," but was advised that this was also "resoundingly ethnocentric, because it implies that somehow the invention of writing comes after and is hence 'higher' than unwritten oral expression." I do believe this, but I certainly am not going to admit it as long as my colleagues feel so strongly about "writing being merely a recording technique invented by societies who discover a need for it." The acceptable adjective now is "nonliterate," but unless this has been approved by the Third Edition of Webster's New International Dictionary, a source I refuse to consult, good usage requires for this denotation the word "illiterate." And to me at least the title ILLITERATE LITERATURE does not sound very fetching.

A friend versed in neither anthropology nor literature suggested the word "savage"; but this connotes ebony-skinned people with minstrel lips, grass skirts, and soup bones through their septa, hopping around great iron pots full of missionaries. And so we will speak of the material of this book as "primitive literature," trusting that those who are offended by either word will have the charity to willingly suspend their objections, since I mean them no harm.

ACKNOWLEDGEMENTS AND FURTHER EXPLANATIONS

An Introduction is an unnecessary part of a book in which the author presumes to enter briefly into an uninvited intimacy with his readers, to use for a few pages the first personal pronoun before retreating into the anonymity of synonyms like "the writer" and "the author" by which he thinks to evade responsibility for his errors and absurdities or to imply a detached objectivity that reviewers perversely fail to appreciate. Here the writer tells who has suffered to read his manuscript, and thanks these people with the admission that they are to have the credit for what is good in his book but of course are not to be blamed for the errors, which are always the writer's own. Here he hopes to cut the ground from under his reviewers, as I have tried to do in the foregoing paragraphs. For myself and my work, I acknowledge with thanks the financial help given me by the University of Colorado to coordinate my research; the workers of the Human Relations Area Files in making available to all in my profession many sources that otherwise would be impossible to consult; and the generosity of my colleague Omer Stewart in lending me his microfilming camera which greatly simplified the correlation of many more works than are referred to in my bibliography.

The bibliography, incidentally, follows the current anthropological practice of including only works that are specifically referred to in the text. These are the authors from whom I have consciously drawn material; and since many of the ideas and, I fear, even some expressions in this book have come from as far back as my college lecture notes, there may be some material represented as my own that I ought to have acknowledged by footnoting; to such readers as recognize any of their own words here, I beg forgiveness and offer them the compensation that like Shakespeare and the Bible, their phrases have now achieved the immortality of the common domain.

John Barrymore was reputed to have said, and I believe it to be true, that reading footnotes is like running downstairs on one's wedding night to answer the doorbell. Understanding if not sympathizing with this feeling, I have abandoned the system of documentation used by my friends in literary studies for what might be called the unobtrusive documentation that the *American Anthropologist* requires its contributors to use. I have, however, simplified the latter style so that instead of repeating an author's name in the parentheses following the borrowed statement or idea, I give the barest information that will lead the reader to the source; if the man's name is mentioned previously in unambiguous context, and if only one of his works is in the bibliography, the number in the terminal parentheses is the page from which the material was taken. If he is the author of several works cited, then the year of the pertinent source appears before the page number. True footnotes giving additional information are used perhaps too freely, but some concession must be made to the affliction which I share with *my Uncle Toby* in *Tristram Shandy* —the mental aberration that prevents its victim from staying logically on the subject. It is to be hoped that the information therein contained will outweigh the inconvenience of answering the doorbell.

As for catching errors, my wife read only the first two paragraphs of the section entitled "Götterdämmerung" in Chapter Seven, and discovered that I had confused John the Baptist with John the Divine. At that point I took the manuscript away from her.

JOHN GREENWAY

University of Colorado

Special gratitude is expressed to the American Folklore Society, the Bernice P. Bishop Museum, and Edwards & Shaw for their gracious permission to quote extensively from material in their copyright possession, as follows:

The American Folklore Society, for excerpts from the following articles in *Journal of American Folklore:* M. Astrov, "The Concept of Motion as the Psychological Leitmotif of Navaho Life and Literature"; W. R. Bascom, "Literary Style in Yoruba Riddles" and "Verbal Art"; V. Barnouw, "A Psychological Interpretation of a Chippewa Origin Legend"; F. Boas, "Stylistic Aspects of Primitive Literature"; W. H. Davenport, "Marshallese Folklore Types"; F. Densmore, "The Words of Indian Songs as Unwritten Literature"; E. Dozier, "The Role of the Hopi-Tewa Migration Legend in Reinforcing Cultural Patterns and Prescribing Social Behavior"; A. Espinosa, "Notes on the Origin and History of the Tar-Baby Story"; D. Olmsted, "Korean Folklore and Attitudes toward China"; E. Parsons, "Nativity Myth at Laguna and Zuni"; G. Reichard, "Individualism and Mythological Style"; E. Sapir, "Song-Recitative in Paiute Mythology"; and W. Wallace, "The Dream in Mohave Life."

The Bernice P. Bishop Museum, for excerpts from its *Bulletins:* P. Buck, *Ethnology of Tongareva* and *Ethnology of Mangareva;* E. E. V. Collocott, *Tales and Poems of Tonga;* K. P. Emory, *The Legends of Maui and Takahi;* E. S. C. Handy, *Polynesian Religion, History and Culture of the Society Islands,* and *Marquesan Legends;* and K. Luomala, *Oceanic, American Indian, and African Myths of Snaring the Sun,* and *Maui of a Thousand Tricks.*

Edwards & Shaw, for the following tales from R. Robinson's books *Legend & Dreaming* and *The Feathered Serpent:* "Nagacork's Good-Bye," "The Fire-Bird," "Jabbor the Native Cat," "Tjigarit the Billabong-Bird," "Yoola and the Seven Sisters," "The Spirit Children," and "Koopoo the Red Plain-Kangaroo."

Thanks are due also to the following publishers and authors for permission to use the material indicated:

CHAPTER ONE—Angus and Robertson, for the message to Tommy Hairyarse from *Medicine Man,* by F. B. McCann, and the aboriginal oath from *Adam in Ochre,* by Colin Simpson; the Elektra Corporation for the synopsis of *The Golden Apple,* by Edward Jablonski; Farrar & Rinehart for the valedictory of Nurunderi and the description of the Nullarbor city from *Myths and Legends of the Australian Aborigines,* by W. Ramsay Smith; the Yale University Press for the stanza from *Omar Khayyam,* translated by Arthur J. Arberry; the Viking Fund Publications in Anthropology for the Coyote and Skunk episode from *The Content and Style of an Oral Literature,* by Melville Jacobs; the journal *Mankind,* for the children's song from "A Selection of Children's Songs from Ooldea, Western South Australia," by Ronald M. and Catherine Berndt; Faber and Faber, for the Bemba Chisingu song from *Chisingu, a Girls' Initiation Ceremony among the Bemba of Northern Rhodesia,* by Audrey I. Richards; and Score Record Company, for the song on the "god men," by Bill Harney.

CHAPTER TWO—Whitcombe and Tombs, Ltd., for the Maori cosmogony from *The Coming of the Maori*, by Peter H. Buck; the Government Printer at Lagos, for "Why the Tortoise is Dented," from *The Tiv People*, by Roy C. Abraham; Harper & Bros., for the tale of the Porcupine from *A Black Civilization*, by W. Lloyd Warner; Houghton Mifflin Company, for the hornbill curse from *Patterns of Culture*, by Ruth Benedict; the American Book Company, for the Trobriand spell from *Coral Gardens and Their Magic*, by Bronislaw Malinowski; the Human Relations Area Files for the translation of the Jivaro Spell from *The Headhunters of Western Amazonia*, by Rafael Karsten; Henry Holt and Company, for the Anglo-Saxon charm from *Bright's Anglo-Saxon Reader*, edited by James R. Hulbert; the American Museum of Natural History, for the Chukchee love charm from *The Chukchee*, by Waldemar Bogoras; Folkways Record Co., for the Bambala litigation text from *Folk Music of the Western Congo*, by Leo A. Verwilgen; the American Book Company, for the Tikopian funeral verse from *We, the Tikopia*, by Raymond Firth; and the *Journal of the Polynesian Society*, for the samples of Samoan oratory from "Proverbial Expressions of the Samoans," by E. Schultze.

CHAPTER THREE—Routledge and Kegan Paul, for the Trickster episodes from *The Trickster*, by Paul Radin; W. W. Norton, for the Clitoris Watcher tale from *Myth in Primitive Psychology*, by Bronislaw Malinowski; Harper & Brothers, for the Bamapama tale from *A Black Civilization*, by W. Lloyd Warner; Thomas Y. Crowell Company for the basic items in the list of animal symbols from *The Reader's Encyclopedia*, edited by William Rose Benet; Humphrey Milford for the Tar Baby story from *Nuer Customs and Folk-Lore*, by Ray Huffman; and Oxford University Press, for the list of heroic characteristics from *The Hero*, by Lord Raglan.

CHAPTER FOUR—Harcourt, Brace & World, for one of Carl Sandburg's "Ten Definitions of Poetry"; E. J. Brill, for the Bedouin litany from *Hadramaut, Some of Its Mysteries Unveiled*, by Daniel van der Meulen and H. von Wissman; the American Anthropological Association for the discussion of literary parallelism from "American Indian Poetry," by Eda Lou Walton and T. T. Waterman, which appeared in *American Anthropologist; American Speech*, for the Coeur d'Alêne imagery from "Imagery in an Indian Vocabulary," by Gladys A. Reichard; Henry Holt & Company, for "Talk" from *The Cow-Tail Switch and Other West African Stories*, by Harold Courlander and George Herzog, and for "Dust of Snow" from *Collected Poems of Robert Frost;* the University of Melbourne Press, for the explanation of Aranda myth sterility from *Aranda Traditions*, by T. G. H. Strehlow; and Hutchinson and Company, for the Cambodian festive song from *Little Vehicle*, by Alan H. Brodrick.

CHAPTER SIX—the Macmillan Company, for the illustrations of a narrator's contamination of traditional material from *My Life with the Eskimo*, by Valhjalmur Stefansson; the Human Relations Area Files for the translation of the Jivaro fire-stealing myth from *The Head Hunters of Western Amazonia*, by Rafael Karsten; the University of Michigan, for the Atayal Origin of Death story from *Folklore of the Atayal of Formosa and the Mountains of Luzon*, by Edward Norbeck; Oxford University Press, for the song about the Portuguese from *Chopi Musicians*, by Hugh Tracey; Martin Secker and Warburg, for the Mau Mau story from *Facing Mount Kenya*, by Jomo Kenyatta; George Allen & Unwin, for the Kuwait Bedouin song from *The Arab of the Desert*, by H. R. P. Dickson; the University of Arizona, for the story of San Pedro and Jesucristo from *Yaqui Myths and Legends*, by Ruth W. Giddings; and the Carnegie Institution of Washington, for the *ejemplos* from *The Folk Literature of a Yucatecan Town*, by Margaret Redfield.

CHAPTER SEVEN—Macmillan and Co., for the conclusions on the historical unreliability of Thonga tales from *The Life of a South African Tribe,* by Henri Junod; Funk & Wagnalls Company, for the remarks on the gospels by Charles F. Potter in *Funk & Wagnalls Standard Dictionary of Folklore Mythology and Legend,* edited by Maria Leach; W. W. Norton & Co., for the conclusions on the historicity of myth from *Myth in Primitive Psychology,* by Bronislaw Malinowski; Seekyl Service & Co., for the Ngonde tale of the Hedgehog from *The Spirit-Ridden Ngonde,* by D. R. Mackenzie; Oxford University Press, for the song about Badiemaal from *The Web of Kinship among the Tallensi,* by Meyer Fortes, and for the Nuer lyric from *The Nuer,* by E. E. Evans-Pritchard; the Bureau of American Ethnology, Smithsonian Institution, for the Trickster story from *Chippewa Customs,* by Frances Densmore; the Carnegie Institution of Washington for the *ejemplo* about the selfish son from *The Folk Literature of a Yucatecan Town,* by Margaret Redfield; and the University of Michigan Press, for the song from *Social Singing Among the Mapuche,* by Mischa Titiev.

Chapter One / THE BARRIERS OF CULTURE AND LANGUAGE

Some few years ago during the reign of King George the Fifth, the Crown had occasion to communicate with one of the Empire's humbler subjects in the Northern Territory of Australia. The recipient of the message was a young man whose legal identity derived from a physical characteristic that would have been concealed had he worn clothes, but since he was an Old Stone Age aboriginal, he had neither trousers nor shame. Because the matter was a serious affair, concerning what the Commonwealth held was murder and the natives called a tribal execution, the message delivered to the aboriginal began with a salutation of regal dignity:

> George V, by the Grace of God, of Great Britain, Ireland, and the British Dominions beyond the seas, King, Defender of the Faith, Emperor of India, by our trusty and well-beloved servant, Sir Isaac Alfred Isaacs, Knight Commander of our noble order of St. Michael and St. George, Governor General and Commander-in-Chief in and over our Commonwealth of Australia, to our trusty and well-beloved servant, Tommy Hairyarse, greetings . . . .

Squatting in the red dust of central Australia surrounded by all his worldly possessions—two or three fire-sharpened spears, a spear-thrower, and a couple of boomerangs—poor Tommy of the hirsute bottom understood this missive about as well as he would have done had it begun with $E = MC^2$. He was fortunate in that the message went on to offer him a Royal and gracious pardon for turning the Crown's evidence in the premature demise of a clumsy fellow named Billy Arseoverhead (McCann: 197), but if he had been like hundreds of other natives who displeased their white masters, he would have had a chain fastened around his neck and been dragged hundreds of miles to the court at Darwin, unimaginably bewildering to an aboriginal, where an oath like the one quoted by Colin Simpson (195) would have been administered to him:

> Now some proper-fella trouble bin come up longa Oenpelli. Orright. I wantim you tell us all about that trouble. No

1

more gammon, no more lie, no more humbug, but tellim
true-fella alla time. No more what that nother-fella boy he
talk-talk or that nother lubra yabba-yabba longa you, but
what you bin seeim longa your own eye and hearim longa
your own ear. Now talk out loud-fella, allabouts bim
wantim hear about this trouble.

Though this is stiff and difficult pidgin, befitting the formality of
the occasion, Tommy would have understood it well enough to know
something his fellows had done annoyed in some vague way the
Court, and he would have responded with the answers he thought the
white men wanted, obsequious but untruthful, and he would have
been summarily thrown into jail (or in that land, gaol), from which
he would emerge some months later to return to his tribal country
and tell his naked companions of the wonderful little house with the
soft bed where he was fed thrice daily and supplied with the luxurious
comforts of the whitefellow.

Ten thousand years of cultural evolution separate Tommy from
ourselves. He lives as our Paleolithic ancestors must have lived,
scratching in the dirt for ants to eat, fighting nature with sticks and
stones, placating the vast Unknown with futile ceremonies and explaining it with simple myths. In our intellectual evolution of a
hundred centuries he shared not at all; Einstein in his tribe might
have used his fingers to count to four. While it is possible with
ingenuity, imagination, and disregard for accuracy to make a rough
equation between the functional and semantic components of Tommy's language and ours, there is no equation to be made between
the two cultures.

In view of what is required to make a good translation, the persons
who have labored at what Ezra Pound called "this desolate undertaking" are the most maligned of all intellectual workers. Alexander Pope's friend Mr. Lintott called them "the saddest pack of
rogues in the world," and the Italian slander *traduttore—traditore*
reverberates even among the Coeur d'Alêne Indians, who literally
regarded interpreters as traitors. A bilingual poet might attain the
echo that Borrow said was the ultimate achievement in translation;
more than this the cultural barrier makes impossible. T. G. H.
Strehlow was born and reared among the Aranda tribe of central
Australia, he was educated at the University of Sydney in anthropology and English, yet he admits that he can converse adequately
only with aboriginal children, who themselves know only the play-
parts of their culture.

The dulling force of repetition deludes us into believing that some great stories of other civilizations bridged the cultural gulf. Homer seems as much a part of English tradition as Shakespeare, for we read from episode to episode, not realizing as Lord Raglan did in his iconoclastic book *The Hero* that the ravishing Helen must have been nearly a hundred years old at the time of her elopement, judging by internal evidence. But even in Homer we can be brought sharply up against reality by so simple a thing as this synopsis of the American stage version of the story, *The Golden Apple* (Jablonski):

> The book tells the story of a returned soldier, Ulysses, just after the Spanish-American war. He has come home to his wife, Penelope, in the small town of Angel's Roost, nestling at the foot of Mount Olympus in the state of Washington. The trouble begins when the town is visited by a traveling salesman, Paris, who proves to be most attractive to farmers' daughters, and especially so to one of the liveliest, Helen. She and Paris run off to the Big City together and Ulysses goes off in pursuit. He is gone for ten years, while Penelope patiently sits at home. The Big City is filled with temptations, such as might be found in the offices of the firm of Scylla and Charybdis, Brokers. Finally, Ulysses and Paris meet in a boxing ring, Paris is defeated and Ulysses brings the none-too-willing Helen back to Angel's Roost.

Even when the translated cultures are as alike as English and American the barrier of culture is seldom cleared. H. L. Mencken (256) quotes a passage from one of E. W. Hornung's "Raffles" stories, in which an American prizefighter is made to say, "Blamed if our Bowery boys ain't cock-angels to scum like this . . . . By the holy tinker! . . . Blight and blister him! . . . I guess I'll punch his face into a jam pudding." And many an American soldier stationed in England during World War II was shocked to hear his date ask to be taken home early because she expected to be "knocked up" at dawn.

TRANSLATION WITHIN A CULTURE: FROM ANGLO-SAXON TO MODERN ENGLISH

Since one cannot appreciate the difficulties of translation without being both bilingual and bi-cultural, perhaps the best way to show the problems of artistic communication is to examine briefly a number of attempts by eminent scholars and poets to convey a literary classic within our own culture. Though we have changed a lot since Harold

Godwinsson got an arrow in his eye at Senlac and the French swarmed in upon us, we are under the surface patina of technological advancement closer to the Anglo-Saxons than we are to many contemporary Europeans. Whatever we are that is not Puritan is Anglo-Saxon, from our language to our view of the world. An Anglo-Saxon poem, therefore, so long as it deals with material familiar to ourselves, should offer little more than linguistic difficulties to the translator. Of course the prosody of the Anglo-Saxons, incorporating such devices as alliteration, kennings, enjambment, caesuras, decorative insets, Homeric similes, runic symbols, homiletic inserts, ecphrasis, anaphora, appositional descriptions, macaronic devices, anacrusis, "Sievers' Types," and incremental-, envelope-, parallel-, and rhythmical-patterns, is strange to a generation that prefers to play its poetic tennis with the net down, but these things are unintelligible to most readers in any language; it is the meaning and the mood that our translators strove to communicate.

With minor transliterations, the original manuscript of the greatest Anglo-Saxon poem, the *Beowulf*, begins (the first eleven of 3182 lines):

HWÆT, WĒ GĀR-DEna in gēardagum,
þēodcyninga þrym gefrūnon,
hū ða aeþelingas ellen fremedon!
  Oft Scyld Scēfing sceaþena þrēatum,
monegum mǣgþum meodosetla oftēah,
egsode eorlas, syððan ǣrest wearð
fēasceaft funden; hē þas frōfre gebād,
wēox under wolcnum weorðmyndum þāh,
oð þæt him ǣghwylc ymbsittendra
ofer hronrāde hȳran scolde,
gomban gyldan; þaet was gōd cyning!

Just as the Romans distrusted the permanency of Latin, preferring Greek for important inscriptions, Englishmen for centuries distrusted the permanency of English. So as late as 1815 one G. J. Thorkelin preserved the poem in Latin:

Quomodo Danorum In principio
Populus Regum Gloriam auxerit
Quomodo principos Vertute promoverit
Soepe Scyldus Scefides Hostes turmis
Multis nationibus Dignas sedes auferens
Terruit, Dux Postquan fiebat
Miseris abviis Solatiuum mansit

Crevit sub nubibus	Honore viguit
Donec illi quilibet	Accolarum
Ad cetorum vias	Suum cognetur
Tributum solvere	Ille fuit bonus Rex

—an effort which, if translated from this translation into modern English, would remind us of the Anglican churchman in Gilbert's *Close Quarters* who translated *The Book of Common Prayer* into Eskimo, and, persuaded that the work would not create a great demand in England, translated it back again into English, achieving what the publisher believed to be a better job than the original.

The English translations of *Beowulf* begin their disagreements with the first word. Literally translated "What," "Hwaet" not only was equated with various archaic and modern expressions, but with non-semantic acts like the poet's striking a chord on his harp, clearing his throat, and banging the table with his fist in the noisy meadhall —interpretations substantiated by the fact that this word was used throughout the Old and Middle English periods (450–1150 and 1150–1450) as an onomatopoeic equivalent of a sharp noise.

The greatest linguistic difficulty in translating Anglo-Saxon poetry into modern English is the conveyance of the numerous poetic devices, most of which have long since disappeared in our literature. It would seem, therefore, that the prose translations, requiring only syntactic alteration and some concession to euphony, would be nearly identical. This is not the case. Perhaps the most nearly literal rendering is that of B. J. Whiting:

> Behold, we have heard of the glory in former years of the Spear-Danes, of the kings of the people, how the heroes did brave deeds!
>
> Often Scyld Scefing deprived crowds of foes, many tribes, of their seats in the mead-hall; he frightened heroes, after the time when he was first found in poverty. He lived to see solace for that, he flourished on earth, prospered in honors, until each of the neighboring peoples across the whale road had to obey him and pay tribute—that was a good king!

The earliest prose translation that still finds its way into college anthologies is that of John Earle in 1892, which does not go too badly when one gets past the first two words:

> What ho! We have heard of the grandeur of the imperial kings of the spear-bearing Danes in former days, how those

ethelings promoted bravery. Often old Scyld of the Sheaf
wrest from harrying bands, from many tribes, their con-
vivial seats; the dread of him fell upon warriors, whereas he
had at the first been a lonely founding;—of all that (humilia-
tion) he lived to experience solace; he waxed great under the
welkin, he flourished with trophies, till that every one of
the neighboring peoples over the sea were constrained to
obey him, and pay trewage:—that was a good king!

The chief fault of Earle's translation and that of R. K. Gordon
(1916) is that both scholars introduce archaic expressions so that the
reader will understand that this is pretty old stuff—something like
the monolingual Englishman who is sure foreigners will understand
him if he only shouts loud enough:

Lo! We have heard the glory of the kings of the Spear-
Danes in days gone by, how the chieftains wrought mighty
deeds. Often Scyld Scefing wrested the mead-benches
from troops of foes, from many tribes; he made fear fall
upon the earls. After he was first found in misery (he received solace for that) he grew up under the heavens, lived
in high honor, until each of his neighbors over the whale
road must needs obey him and render tribute. That was a
good king!

For scholarship and reliability the standard prose translation is
that of Chauncey B. Tinker (1902), who set about his work like his
no-nonsense ancestors:

Lo! We have heard of the glory of the kings who ruled
the Spear-Danes in the olden time, how those princes
wrought mighty deeds. Oft did Scyld of the Sheaf wrest
the mead-benches from bands of warriors, from many a
tribe. The hero bred awe in them from the time when
first he was found helpless and outcast; for this he met with
comfort, waxed great beneath the sky and throve in honors,
until all the neighboring tribes beyond the ocean-paths were
brought to serve him and pay him tribute. That was a
good king!

In 1896 J. Lesslie Hall wrote what he claimed was "a modest effort
to reduce approximately in modern measures, the venerable epic,
Beowulf. Approximately, I repeat; for a very close reproduction of
Anglo-Saxon would, to a large extent, be prose to a modern ear."

William Ellery Leonard was well known in Germanic scholarship as an eminent poet, Anglo-Saxon authority, and enemy of the locomotive (a traumatic experience with a locomotive in his infancy embedded in him a psychosis that prevented him from being able to leave the Wisconsin campus until he psychoanalyzed himself with *The Locomotive God*), but less well known was his almost irrational impatience with people like J. Lesslie Hall. He once addressed to them an open letter which, with slight modification, might well be retained as a permanent guide to poetic translators in any language; for this reason we will spare the room to quote it. Of those people who maintain that there is neither rhythm, meter, or plan to Old English poetry, he said (1929),

> I wish devoutly that some one or another of them would examine the following line:
>
> > Over yonder afar in Morocco's domains where the roofs
> > of the mosques are ashine
>
> Let him repeat it, tapping to the eight beats with pencil on the arm of his chair, not forgetting the rest beat at the end, till he has fixated its recitation in a given tempo:
>
> > Over yónder afár in Morócco's domaíns where the róofs
> > of the mósques are ashíne '
>
> Then let him chant, to the tap of the pencil continuously in the same tempo, down through these ten lines:
>
> > Over yónder afár in Morócco's domaíns where the róofs
> > of the mósques are ashíne '
> > They're féaring nów alréady ' Some níght attáck of míne '
> > Yónder afár in Morócco ' Where róofs of mósques do shíne'
> > Yónder ín Morócco ' Where róofs of mósques shíne '
> > They're féaring alréady ' Some níght attáck of míne '
> > Afár ín Morócco ' Where mósque roófs shíne '
> > Fár dówn soúth ' The mósque roófs shíne '
> > Where they're féaring féaring féaring ' Some
> > níght attáck of míne '
> > Fár dówn soúth ' Mósque roófs shíne '
> > Over yónder afár in Morócco's domáins In the
> > kíngdom so sóon to be míne '
>
> He will find that each successive tap has coincided with each successive metrical beat (speech beat or rest beat) in spite of a syllabic variation of from six to 21 syllables, and that the 80th tap of his pencil synchronizes with the rest beat

after the last line. And he will find too that he has rendered
the lines quite in accord with their intrinsic metrical pattern. Or, if he is unsuccessful in the experiment (after,
say, a third trial), he should realize that *der lieber Gott*
destined him for other things than Germanic versification.

Hall's translation is certainly vulnerable to Leonard's strictures;
he seems to be one of those innocents in literary artistry who think
poetry is any printing that does not reach all the way to the right
margin of the page:

> Lo! the Spear-Danes' glory through splendid achievements,
> The folk-kings' former fame we have heard of,
> How princes displayed then their prowess-in-battle,
> Oft Scyld the Scefing from scathers in numbers
> From many a people their mead-benches tore,
> Since first they found him friendless and wretched
> The earl had had terror; comfort he got for it,
> Waxed 'neath the welkin, world-honor gained,
> Till all his neighbors o'er sea were compelled to
> Bow to his bidding and bring him their tribute:
> An excellent atheling!

Edwin Morgan, who essayed the effort himself in 1952, wrote of
Beowulf (ix), "the only poet to turn his hand to it has been William
Morris, and this translation is disastrously bad, being uncouth to
the point of weirdness, unfairly inaccurate, and often more obscure
than the original (hardly, in fact, a translation at all, since Morris
'worked up' a prose paraphrase passed to him with increasing mis-
giving by the scholarly A. J. Wyatt)." Unless Morgan was freely
exercising his right to define "poet" as I have done with "literature"
and "primitive," he was in error on the history of translations of
this poem, but Morris would generally be taken as the most capable
poet—in other things—to try a modern translation of *Beowulf*. The
translation is, as Morgan says, blighted by its archaisms, but then
Morris was born in a time out of joint, and like Miniver Cheevy,
wished himself and his century back in the Middle Ages:

> What! We of the Spear-Danes of yore days, so was it
> That we learn'd of the fair fame of kings of the folks
> And the Athelings a-faring in framing of valour.
> Oft then Scyld the Sheaf-son from the hosts of the scathers
> From hundreds a many the mead-settles tore;

It was then the earl fear'd them, sithence he was the first
Found bare and all-lacking; so solace he bided
Waxed under the welkin in worship to thrive,
Until it was so that the round-about sitters
All over the whale-road must hearken his will
And yield him the tribute. A good king was that.

Leonard himself translated *Beowulf*, using the "Sing a Song of Sixpence" meter, which is defensible logically but esthetically abominable. Morgan said it was "damned at the outset":

What ho! We heard the glory
Of Spear-Danes, clansmen-kings,
Their deeds of olden glory,
How fought the aethelings!
Often Scyld-Scefing
Reft his foemen all,
Reft the tribes at wassail
Of bench and mead in hall.
Smote the jarls with terror,
Gat good recompense
For that he came a foundling
A child with no defense.
He waxed beneath the welkin,
Grew in honors great,
Till each and every people
Of those around who sate
Off beyond the whale-road
To him was underling,
To him must tender toll-fee;
That was a goodly king!

Another scholar, J. Duncan Spaeth (1921) tried similarly to convey the rhythm of Anglo-Saxon poetry by a jogging meter, in this case anapestic:

List to an old time lay of the Spear-Danes,
Full of the prowess of famous kings,
Deeds of renown that were done by the heroes;
Scyld the Sheaf-Child from scourging foemen,
From raiders a-many their mead halls wrested.
He lived to be feared, though first as a waif,
Puny and frail he was found on the shore.

> He grew to be great, and was girt with power
> Till the border tribes all obeyed his rule,
> And sea-folk hardy that sit by the whale-path
> Gave him a tribute, a good king was he.

Alliteration is the most obvious characteristic of Anglo-Saxon verse, and several translators let that device carry what feeling of antiquity the poem needed to go well in modern parlors. Charles W. Kennedy's alliterative version (1940), he said, was in "authentic modern verse," whatever that means:

> Lo! We have listened to many a lay
> Of the Spear-Danes' fame, their splendor of old,
> Their mighty princes, and martial deeds!
> Many a mead-hall Scyld, son of Sceaf,
> Snatched from the forces of savage foes.
> From a friendless foundling, feeble and wretched,
> He grew to a terror as time brought change.
> He throve under heaven in power and pride
> Till alien peoples beyond the ocean
> Paid toll and tribute. A good king he!

This translation of Kennedy's is really intolerable, for he sometimes carried the alliteration to the fourth accented syllable, which the Anglo-Saxon *scops* never did. James Joyce made the same mistake in Episode 14 of *Ulysses* where he described the development of Mina Purefoy's fetus with a parallel development of the English language. But that is what happens when you turn two Irishmen loose on Germanic versification.

Morgan had other objections to Kennedy's work; he found too many locutions like "wretched wights" to allow Kennedy either modernity or good taste. Francis B. Gummere's translation (1909) is no happier in this respect:

> Lo, praise of the prowess of people-kings
> Of spear-armed Danes, in days long sped,
> We have heard, and what honor the athelings won!
> Oft Scyld the Scefing from squadroned foes,
> From many a tribe, the mead-bench tore,
> Awing the earls. Since erst he lay
> Friendless, a foundling, fate repaid him:
> For he waxed under welkin, in wealth he throve,
> Till before him the folk, both far and near,

> Who house by the whale-path, heard his mandate,
> Gave him gifts: a good king was he!

Not much mutual tolerance obtained among the various translators of *Beowulf*. C. K. Scott-Moncrieff tried to preserve the dignity of the Anglo-Saxon with poetic diction that plunged him into
grotesqueries, such as "their sarks rattled," and being a Scot did not
help him with the English critics. Augustine Rivers, perhaps inspired by the poetic form, cast his remarks into verse:

> . . . another surly Scot, Moncrieff,
> Who brings the early Saxon songs to grief,
> Who translates *Beowulf*, and then (oh epitaph!)
> Has on the cover his own photograph. . . .

Moncrieff's syntax is chaotic. One wonders if he did not translate
each word on a separate slip of paper, throw the lot into a hat, and
draw out his poem at random:

> What! We of Spear-Danes in spent days,
> Of the Folk-Kings' force have heard,
> How the Athelings excelled in fight,
> Oft Scyld of the Sheaf from scathing hordes
> From many meinies their mead-stools tore.
> Affrighted them the earl, since erst he was
> Found, unwealthy; then friendship he awaited,
> Waxed under the welkin, in worship throve,
> Until each one of those out-dwelling
> Over the whale-road, must hearken to him,
> Gold must give him. That was a good king!

Syntax is the most difficult aspect of the poem to many translators,
and some, confusing Germanic of the tenth century with that of the
19th, run along and drop their verbs at the end of the sentence; a
typical example is James M. Garnett (1882):

> Lo! We of the Spear-Danes, in days of yore,
> Warrior-kings' glory have heard,
> How the princes heroic deeds wrought.
> Oft Scyld, son of Scef, from hosts of foes,
> From many tribes, their mead-seats took;
> The earl caused terror since first he was
> Found thus forlorn; gained he comfort for that,
> Grew under the clouds, in honors throve,

> Until each one of those dwelling around
> Over the whale-road, him should obey;
> Should tribute pay: that was a good king!

The most outspoken critic of all previous translators is Edwin Morgan who, after demolishing his predecessors, showed us how *Beowulf* should go (1952):

> How that glory remains in remembrance,
> Of the Danes and their kings in days gone,
> The acts and valour of princes of their blood!
> Scyld Scefing: how often he thrust from their feast-halls
> The troops of his enemies, tribe after tribe,
> Terrifying their warriors: he who had been found
> Long since as a waif and awaited his desert
> While he grew up and throve in honour among men
> Till all the nations neighboring about him
> Sent as his subjects over the whale-fields
> Their gifts of tribute: king worth the name!

Morgan's effort is an appropriate one to end this survey of translations of *Beowulf*. It is a model of eclecticism, incorporating a fair sampling of all the weaknesses he found in the earlier attempts.

Yet *Beowulf* is the easiest kind of poetry to translate. It does not have to cross a cultural barrier, and, moreover, its material is so timelessly fantastic that the time barrier also fades out of the situation.

THE DIACHRONIC FACTOR IN TRANSLATION

The time barrier poses a problem in translation not often recognized by the translator—the diachronic factor, which affects nearly all translations. Neither in culture nor in poetry does time stand still. *Beowulf* exemplifies the vast transition in prosodic ideas over the centuries; modern poetry, unless deliberately archaic, retains scarcely a single characteristic of Anglo-Saxon prosody. But one need not go so far back in time to prove the point; thirty years is the outside limit of readability for all but the very best in our own literature, and with culture changing even faster, the difficulty is magnified. Even Thomas Wolfe seems sophomoric to those who read him as sophomores and thought his death the greatest and most untimely blow to literature since Keats died young.

Changing fashions in poetry in both the translated and translating cultures likewise create problems that can be resolved only by ad-

mitting that literature among all peoples goes through phases in
which there is nothing worth reading or listening to. Among ourselves, the 15th century was such a period, and for that reason it is
represented in college readers by the folk ballads, nearly all of which
originated in some other century. But what is an anthologist to do
when a major poet (Stephen Hawes in this instance) turns out such
stuff as this?

> Before whom than I dyd knele adowne,
> Sayeng: O sterre of famous eloquence,
> O gylted godesse of hyghe renowne,
> Enspyred with the hevenly influence
> Of the doulcet well of complacence,
> Upon my mynd, with dewe aromatyke,
> Distyll adowne thy lusty rethoryke.

This is even worse than it looks, for many of the rhymed words here
and in other 15th century poems were brand new importations from
Latin.

Shakespeare was a boy when Roger Ascham could still advise poets
to paint the lily—"even so as a faire stone requireth to be sette in
the finest gold, with the best workmanship or else it loseth much of
the grace and price," but within fifty years Francis Bacon stated
the new poetic ideal, and even the simplicity of his phrasing illustrated it: "Vertue is like a Rich Stone—best plaine set." In the
15th century no one wrote readable literature in England, except the
unlettered jailbird Thomas Malory and those bourgeois upstarts, the
Paston family, but in Shakespeare's time everybody could turn out
respectable poetry—witness Sir Walter Raleigh's verses.

This diachronic change in poetic taste accounts for much of the
apparently poor quality of primitive literature as it is found in most
19th century ethnographies and anthologies. The best way to appreciate Walt Whitman is to read some of the poetry he was rebelling
against. What seems to be bad primitive literature in the books of
the early ethnographers is really bad 19th century literature. Take
Henry Rowe Schoolcraft for instance. The Ojibwa children whom
he found gamboling amid the fireflies on the banks of St. Mary's
River cannot fairly be blamed for what he excused as the "wild im-
provisations of children in a merry mood" without "meter . . . or a
regular character" (1853: 230). What the children sang was

> Wau wau tay see!
> Wau wau tay see!

Homer B. Hulbert (375–376) observed a mass interpretation of the same sort among the Koreans. In one of their tales there was a

> boy whose father lay dying of hunger. The youth whetted a knife, went in to his father's presence, cut a generous piece of flesh from his own thigh and offered it to his parent. The story takes no account of the fact that the old reprobate actually turned cannibal instead of dying like a decent gentleman. The Koreans seem quite unable to see this moving episode in more than one light, and they hold up their hands in wondering admiration, while all the time the story is exquisitely ironical.

Though persistent mass misinterpretation is one of the most usual causes of change in folk and primitive literature, Hulbert rashly trod a corpse-strewn path in attributing universal emotions, ideas, and attitudes to exotic literatures. These things must be read in the light of their culture, which is always very much different from our own. The Australian aboriginal languages are exasperatingly laconic, and to make the stories in these tongues go at all in English, the translator must piece out their imperfections with his thoughts. But he must be wary of the presumed universals. W. Ramsay Smith (173) doubtlessly felt safe in having the departing culture hero Nurunderi deliver this valedictory to his people:

> Children, there is a Great Spirit above whose dwelling place is heaven. It is his will that you should know him as the whole spirit of whom you are parts. He is your provider and protector. Live as children of the Great Father. Control your appetites and your desires. . . . Selfishness is not of the Great Spirit. Cultivate everything good. Be moderate in eating and in pleasure. Be generous to others. Cultivate a healthy state of mind and body. Be guided by pure morals.

The natives thus exhorted to Christian virtue had no concept of monotheism, or heaven, or protective deities, or transcendentalism, or "morals"; and as for eating in moderation, one traveller in deepest Australia, H. H. Finlayson, saw two aborigines consume a large kangaroo at a sitting that lasted from noon till dusk—and when the Australian aborigines eat something, they eat all of it. Smith should have been warned by the experience of an earlier translator, Alexander F. Chamberlain (210–211), who imputed the concepts of romantic love and jealousy to the Australoids:

> O where is he who won
> My youthful heart,
> Who often used to bless
> And call me loved one?
> You, Weerang, tore apart
> From his fond caress
> Her whom you now desert and shun;
> Out upon thee, faithless one!
> Oh may the Boyl-las bite and tear
> Her whom you take your bed to share.
> Yang, yang, yang, yoh.

Weerang and her lover, reposing in their habitual nakedness in the Australian bush, innocent of any ideas about romantic love, blessings, Elizabethan imprecations, malevolent spirits, or even beds, would have been puzzled by the poetic environment into which they were thrust by the inflation of a "love" song that in its original expression probably went no further than "yang, yang, yang, yoh" and a few libidinous gestures. But Smith, though a Fellow of the Royal Anthropological Society, was too well inured by habitual error to avoid such subtle pitfalls as the illusion of universal morality. It was he who built in South Australia

> a city surrounded by four white walls, which varied in height from five hundred to a thousand feet. The distance from one corner of the city to the other was a day's journey —about forty miles from sunrise to sunset. Along the top of each wall there were domes and spires (74).

This, on the lunar desolation of the Nullarbor, where no one, white or black, ever saw structures more pretentious than corrugated iron shanties!

George Cronyn's *Path on the Rainbow*, a popular book of Indian poetry published at the end of the first World War, is often cited by folklorists for the numerous errors it managed to incorporate, but one mistake that has escaped previous commentators grew out of Cronyn's thrift. In his preface to "Songs of the Ghost Dance Religion" (62) he says "Unessential repetitions have been omitted for brevity's sake"—but the repetitions he economically deletes are the one fundamental identifying characteristic of all Ghost Dance songs —the repetition of each phrase!

Compilers of bibliographies and anthologies of translated literature rarely acknowledge the errors that seem to be an occupational handicap of their profession. A classic exception is Frederick R. Burton's public confession of his monumental misinterpretation of a three-word Ojibwa song; this story is so instructive to all translators and readers of translations that it deserves reprinting in its entirety after fifty years (154–160):

> It was not long after I had begun my quest for melodies that I chanced upon Tetebahbundung drumming and singing for his little son, Adamosa, to dance. They were quite by themselves, indulging in the diversion for its own sake with no thought of spectators. The boy threw himself into the fantastic and difficult movements of the dance with extravagant enthusiasm, and the father applied himself to his part almost as seriously as if the event signalized an important decision by a council of chiefs—almost, for he was not drumming loudly, and in his grave eyes glowed the light of parental satisfaction. By reason of his comparatively light drumming and the clearness of his voice, I heard the quaint tune distinctly and it caught my fancy at once. I had no difficulty in notating it, for by then I had become accustomed to the alternation of triple and double rhythm, and, moreover, Tetebahbundung sang it over and over until the boy stopped dancing from sheer exhaustion. My next consideration was for the words, and Tetebahbundung slowly dictated them, syllable by syllable: "Mujje mukesin awyawyon."
>
> Three words, the most compact poem discovered up to that moment—I have since found one that is limited to one word. I doubt whether anybody could imagine the intensity of my eagerness to learn what they meant. I was all excitement over the melody, my imagination even then leaping forward to the use I subsequently made of it in orchestral writing; and it was so individual, so perfectly rounded out, so inspiriting, that I suppose I unconsciously forecast a significance in the words that should be worthy, to say the least, of the tune. At all events it was with something like a shock that I heard the Indian's answer to my inquiry as to the meaning.
>
> "I use bad shoes," said he.
>
> I had no distrust of Tetebahbundung's intentions, but there was abundant reason to doubt the accuracy of his

translations, for at that time he knew little English and his pronunciation was most imperfect. So I found occasion to ask another Indian about the words, and from him received identically the same answer. "I use bad shoes."

Then, as in the case of "My Bark Canoe," I withdrew to the solitude of my own thoughts. What possibly could be implied that was not expressed by these words? I asked myself. There was no faint shadow of poetic suggestion in them; they were simply funny, and I came not unwillingly at last to that acceptation of the song, for the tune itself sparkled as with humor. So I undertook to reproduce the Indian humor in English. This was easy enough, for a grotesque, or even a commonplace phrase subjected to incessant iteration becomes irresistibly laughable, and it was merely a question, therefore, of conveying the literal meaning of the sentence in the words that would fit the rhythm.

Very well; the only use to which shoes could be put was for wearing, and bad shoes, from my own cornful experience, were those that pinched; but it was well nigh inconceivable that an Indian should pinch his toes in yielding moccasins, and I readily concluded that from his point of view the only bad shoes would be those that were past repair, worn out; and so a line adjusted itself quickly to the rhythm of the tune:

"Worn out shoes I am a-wearing."

I committed many absurdities that first summer among the Indians, among them being the installation of a machine that in a bygone age had been a pianoforte in my lodge. To it I took my new song, and in my confident enthusiasm I invited two or three whites and such Indians as were in call to listen. The whites responded to the humor of the piece and I was vastly satisfied with myself. Tetebahbundung was there and I asked him what he thought of it, but I am sure that my question was disingenuous. Anybody, red or white, could have seen that I expected commendation. Tetebahbundung politely gave it. Not a hint did he venture that I was in total error. His mental attitude doubtless might have been expressed thus: "It pleases him, it pleases his friends; who am I that I should presume to instruct him in the use of his own language?"

At all events no shadow of suspicion crossed my mind that I had not made a correct interpretation, and, as the song proved popular with all whites who came my way, I sang it many times, eventually to a kindergartner who begged a copy of it that she might teach it to her children. She tried it on, found that the children tackled to it eagerly, spoke to other kindergartners about it, and before long I was in receipt of urgent requests from various parts of the country to print the song. I did so, and "Old Shoes" speedily found its way to kindergartens and primary schools, and even to the concert platform. Meantime I continued to sing it myself whenever I was in company with Indians entertaining white audiences, and for a long time nobody among my Ojibwa friends said a word.

One day, nearly a year after the publication of the song, Obetossoway confronted me. He is the wittiest Indian among my acquaintances, quick to see and to make a joke, but portentously solemn or dignified when he has something of importance to say to one whom he regards as his superior. At that time I was his employer, and I imagine he must have nerved himself mightily to correct me.

"Sir," said he, in his most dignified manner, "you have got that song all wrong. It does not mean that I am wearing worn out shoes at all, sir."

"Well," I responded, "I want to be set right if I have made a mistake. What does it mean?"

"It means 'I use bad shoes,' sir."

This was almost annoying. Obetossoway speaks English fluently, and, with his bright mind, I thought he should have grasped my interpretation and not insist on bald literalness; but I was anxious to encourage just the kind of service he was trying to perform for me, and I went patiently into my argument.

"Worn out shoes are bad shoes, are they not?" I asked, and he admitted that they were. "Well," I proceeded, "in English we do not speak of using shoes, but of wearing them. Don't you understand?"

"I do, sir," said he.

"Then, if I am wearing worn out shoes, I am using bad shoes. Isn't that so?"

"It is," Obetossoway admitted, adding firmly, "but, sir, the song means 'I use bad shoes.' "

In weariness of spirit, I gave it up, silently abusing the Indian for an unsuspected blockhead, and I was so certain of my interpretation that I was disturbed by no doubt about it.

The revelation of my error came a few days after the conversation with Obetossoway. At that time the play "Hiawatha" was being performed daily in the open air. I had notated most of the songs that are introduced into the play but had not paid attention to those that figure in the gambling scene for the very good reason that I never could hear them. The drum is pounded incessantly while all the Indians dance except the few who are directly concerned in the game. Now and again I could hear the singer's voice, but never sufficiently to catch a complete musical phrase, and the words were wholly inaudible. The fact that music entered even into the gambling of the Indians suggested that it must have special significance there; and that was incentive enough for investigation. In order to get some notion of the song, or songs, I concealed myself among bushes close to the stage with music paper on the ground before me. From this vantage I could hear every word and nearly every note. Imagine my bewilderment when the gambling began, to hear Tetebahbundung sing "Mujje mukesin awyawyon!" But I am not altogether blind, or deaf, or stupid. In a moment the significance of the song flashed upon me, for I recalled what was visible from the viewpoint of the audience. The Indians were playing what they call the "Moccasin Game." One player hides a small object, no matter what, under one of three or more moccasins; his opponent tries to select the moccasin that conceals the object. That, in brief, is the whole game, and it is said to be the origin of that infamous swindling device known to whites as the shell game. But it is picturesque and dramatic as the Indians play it. The process of hiding is accompanied by a variety of confusing gestures, and it takes a long time; and while the first player is lifting one moccasin after another, pretending to hide the object, distracting his opponent's attention in every possible way, the singer is industriously warbling "Mujje mukesin awyawyon."

Obetossoway was right. Of course the song means "I use

bad shoes"; it can't mean anything else, but what is implied
and not expressed might be put this way: "I am using be-
witched shoes; they will fool you; you're not smart enough to
get around these wicked shoes of mine." Worn out shoes indeed! O, the superior discernment of the paleface! I felt
some chagrin as I lay there in the bushes with my needless
music paper before me, but presently yielded to the humor
of the event, and at the earliest possible moment after the
performance I sought out Obetossoway and made amends
for my obstinacy.

Very occasionally a mistranslation engenders a literary work incomparably better than the original. The classic example is Edward
Fitzgerald's translations of the quatrains of an outstanding mathe-
matician and astronomer, but negligible poet, of 12th century Persia
named Ghiyathuddin Adulfath Omar Ibn Ibrahim Al-Khayyami.
Omar's *Rubaiyat* was inspired less by the poetic impulse than by his
dissatisfaction at the shift in dominant philosophical thought from
the agnosticism of Avicenna to the orthodoxy of Mahmud of Ghazna,
to which he reacted with poorly articulated, hedonistic, rationalistic,
pessimistic verses leavened with a little wry humor. A greater shift
in philosophical orientation was occurring when Fitzgerald, a classicist who went into retirement in Suffolk after his graduation from
Cambridge, was introduced to Omar's quatrains by a learned neighbor: Alfred Russel Wallace in Borneo and Charles Darwin in England were quietly preparing the greatest intellectual revolution in
Western history. But intellectual England was not to be completely surprised by the proof of evolution; as one writer put it, this
was the great suppressed truth of the early 19th century, and it was
not just coincidence that Darwin's *The Origin of Species* and Fitzgerald's *The Rubaiyat of Omar Khayyam* were both published in
1859. Both Omar and Fitzgerald reacted to their times with "Carpe
diem"—seize the day. Omar blasphemously showed that man's
pleasures were of the earth; in Arberry's (22) literal translation,

> If hand should give of the pith of wheat a loaf,
> And of wine a two-maunder, of a sheep a thigh,
> With a little sweetheart boy seated in a desolation,
> A pleasure it is that is not the attainment of any sultan.

Fitzgerald's England did not appreciate the aristocracy of wheaten
bread and would not admit even poetic homosexuality, so he translated these lines into the most famous stanza of the *Rubaiyat:*

> A Book of Verses underneath the Bough,
> A Jug of Wine, a Loaf of Bread—and Thou
>   Beside me singing in the Wilderness—
> Oh, Wilderness were Paradise enow!

Omar's blasphemy was not consistent; he often lapsed into a whining supplication:

> Oh Thou who knowest the secrets of everyone's mind,
> Who graspest everyone's hand in the hour of weakness,
> Oh God, give me repentance and accept my excuses,
> Oh Thou who givest repentance and acceptest the excuses of everyone.

Fitzgerald would have none of this mawkishness; like Thomas Hardy, who had this stanza read on his deathbed, he persevered in blasphemy:

> Oh Thou, who Man of baser Earth didst make
> And ev'n with Paradise devise the Snake:
>   For all the Sin wherewith the Face of Man
> Is blackened—Man's forgiveness give—and take!

Could this properly be called a translation?

EMBEDDED MEANING

The quatrains of both Omar and Fitzgerald are heavy with embedded meaning that can be extracted only by a reader with a good knowledge of the cultures that produced them. All literature, regardless of primitiveness, is laden with interlinear significance that few translators are able either to recognize or impart. "You see Piuty man singin' sometime," an Indian informant once said to Mary Austin (60–61), "and cryin' when he sing. It ain't what he singin' make him cry. It's what he thinkin' about when he sing make him cry." The music of India sounds to our Western ears no more than exotically dissonant, but to an Indian not only the song but the scale in which it is played conveys such things as a dominant sentiment (tranquillity, valor, compassion, and the like), gender, part of the human body, ruling lunar constellation, color, zodiacal sign, and element (fire, earth, or water); and furthermore, would be chosen by the musician in accordance with the appropriate date and time of day. There is obviously no possibility of translating these connotations into another musical system. Jacobs (1959a: 17 ff) demonstrated the richness of embedded meaning in his explication of a Clackamas Chinook tale, "Coyote and Skunk: He Tied His Musk Sac." To the unwary reader, the first paragraph of this story seems dull and sterile, both in its content and its telling:

> Coyote and Skunk lived there. They would look for something, they would eat it. I do not know how long they did like that. Then he said to him, "Younger brother, Supposing I tie you, and then I summon everyone, they will come to see you." "Oh no!" I do not know how many times he spoke to him, before he permitted him to. Then he went outside, he hallooed and hallooed, "Who will come? Our younger brother might die."

The Chinook show greater understanding and appreciation. They respond to every phrase of the narrator with an emphatic "Annnnn," and take delight in the tale. Jacobs accounts for the audience reaction by revealing that each phrase is a stylized literary mnemonic, which opens great connotational vistas quite beyond the comprehension of persons other than Clackamas Chinook. The first words announce the names and location of the actors who, thus named together, are recognized as a well known pair of incompetent and preposterous hunters, and need no more description than Mutt and Jeff or Amos and Andy would require in our culture. The audience knows the character of the actors, and anticipates the outrageous and probably scatological trickery that must emerge from their association. The audience further knows that Coyote and Skunk live on a river embankment; "a comment about the actors' residence would have been an esthetic irrelevance because emphasis was upon the behavior of Coyote and Skunk and their relationship, not upon architecture and site." The gender inflection of the Chinook words reveals that the actors are male. "They would look for something" is an "equational predication" of a hunting partnership; the kinds of food they hunt need not be named, for everyone knows the diet of these animals. "I do not know how long they did like that" is again a conventionalized expression, providing transition from the introduction to the action proper. "He said to him" is to us ambiguous, but the salutation "Younger brother" identifies the speaker to the Chinook as Coyote, since as a headman in the mythology, he refers to others as his junior siblings. "Let me tie you" is a euphemism that gives the plot away; Coyote plans to make a living cannon out of his companion, tying his scent gland, and "firing" him at the guests who may be lured to visit Skunk on the false announcement

of his illness. Skunk's reluctance and subsequent consent, Jacobs
explains, express "anticipation of suffering, timorousness, dislike of
being forced to retain and then discharge musk because the effort
nearly kills him, and resentment against being used as the handy
implement of the older and more affluent brother. But Skunk is
trapped in the relationship that shackled Clackamas themselves:
one could not say 'no' indefinitely, least of all to a man of wealth."

Most translators put the burden of extracting embedded meaning
upon the reader, since it is easier to translate literally, and since
literal translation reduces the chance of misinterpretation and conse-
quent criticism of reviewers. The most mechanical method of translation is the safest, and many ethnologists therefore employ the
process of bare transliteration, a literal translation, and a paragraph
of explanation for each stanza of a song. Thus the Berndts (424)
translated a children's song from Ooldea in the far west of South
Australia:

walga	*reri reri*	*ngenda*	*dagu*
marks/	shivering with cold/	a big snake/	tell you/
walga	*djuna*		
marks/	put it down		

jara   *walga*   *linda*
a white-blossomed tree/ marks/ to throw sand with
                                            one's hand.

Explanation: A man is shivering with cold; he sees the
tracks (marks) of a big snake. He tells another man; together they follow the edible snake and kill it near a white-
blossomed tree. The last word of the song refers to the
digging of a depression in the sand in which to make a fire
for cooking a snake.

Similarly, Richards (187–188) conveys a song from the cycle of the
chisungu girls' ceremony among the Bemba of Lake Tanganyika:

Twingile shyani? How are we going in?
Twingile mipempe; We are going in as through a tunnel into
                                            a dark place;
Nga bakolwe. We are going in like monkeys.

Interpretation: Mipempe are the grass reeds built to form a
narrow passage into the interior of a fishing weir. Hence it
conveys the idea of a passage into a secret place, i.e., the
secrets of the *mbusa*. It is also a passage concealed from the

outside world as the girls are concealed from the eyes of the
rest of the community under the blankets. Monkeys are
represented throughout the chisungu as being enterprising in
thefts, usually for the sake of the family.

The immediate interpretation given was that the song
meant the hiding of the girls from the village; and that the
crawling was meant to make them look ridiculous. I. A.
Nkonde gives:

"How shall we go into the ceremony? Shall we enter like
monkeys that crawl in in stealth? Thus we show we are for-
saking the normal way of life. But we have to go through
dark and difficult places before we get wisdom."

Kasonde says:

"How shall we enter in? We shall enter in exposing our
buttocks like monkeys. We are free in the house. There is
nothing secret to us."

German scholarly translations too often remind one of a boy
trying to find out what makes a firefly glow; thus Leonhard Schultze
(194) translated a Hottentot tale:

> Girls (/gõati "daughters") went walking (sari narr. pass.)
> to the (//ga)kraal of the Aigamucha woman; and when they
> got there (si, with the personal suff. of the subj.) one (/gui)
> of them ("a persons," kχol's fem.) is pregnant (!gom); this
> one is addressed (mî "to say") like this by (/a) the Aiga-
> mucha woman: "Come (/kχi), let yourself (literally: 'and
> e [imperative], I -ta, massage you -si') be massaged!"
> (!guri, cf. Care of the Skin, pp. 207 and 215). And she is
> massaged. Then her (ã, root of the poss. pron., -sa personal
> suff. of the possessor) front apron (!gäeb) was bound to-
> gether (! gai "to bind," //are "to unite") with (/kχa) the
> front apron of the former (//(e)îs, personal pron.) and the
> others (expressed here only by the personal suff.) went
> home (//aru, vb.).

to which the reader may be constrained to respond like Chaucer's
Host, "Namoore of this, for Goddes dignitee!"

But Schultze, like a good ethnographer, could be relied on for accuracy if not poetic elevation, and he had only contempt for those
who put other considerations before precision, like the man he
criticised (188) for persistently calling a louse a "little animal,"

with what effect on the story's sense one can imagine.*

Frances Densmore (1950: 452–453) well contrasted the two approaches to translation in her stimulating article on these "unwritten" aspects of literature. While transcribing the words of a Tule Indian employed to translate a long poem about a boat race, she suspected that her informant was being too economical in his interpretation. It happened that her most skilful interpreter, Alfred Robinson, was engaged nearby on another assignment; she called him in to put into English a passage which the other man had translated simply as "The boat was going very fast." Robinson responded with

> There are many flags at the top of the mast,
> They make a sound like bright birds.
> The sound of the ropes whistling in the wind is like the sound of many birds.
> The blocks tick together like the ticking of a watch.

Burton, that untiring confessant among translators, tells how he wrote "My Bark Canoe," one of the most popular "Indian" songs ever written (149–153):

> A better example of compactness may be found in the following to which I have previously referred as the song that awakened my interest in Ojibway music and led me to this prolonged investigation. Short as it is, the Indian does not piece it out with "heyah." The entire poem is here given as sung by the Indians, with the meaning of the words under the Ojibway equivalent:

Chekahbay	*tebik*	*ondandeyan*
Throughout	night	I keep awake
Chekahbay	*tebik*	*ondandeyan*
Throughout	night	I keep awake
ahgahmah-sibi	*ondandeyan*	
Upon a river	I keep awake	

> I am quite sure that this literal transfer of meanings from one language to another would convey nothing to the English paleface who knew nothing by direct contact of Indian life.

---

* Writers of Schultze's generation were also apt to revert to Latin when confronted by passages in primitive literature that offended Victorian sensibilities, and since the generality of folk and primitive authors revel in coprophilia and sexual obscenity, translations from this era have a macaronic appearance. Modern ethnography has moved so far away from this delicate avoidance that it is fortunate for scholarly communication that the Watch and Ward Society confines its censorious reading to comic books and the like instead of ethnographic journals.

His poetic fancy might evolve a meaning from it, but it is
hardly likely that it would be in consonance with the Indian's
meaning. I venture to take the reader over the course that
was necessarily mine when I undertook to translate the song.
At that time I knew not one Ojibway word. The intelligent
Indian whom I asked for a translation slowly dictated the
following;

"I am out all night on the river seeking for my sweetheart."

This impressed me as poetic in feeling, but I wished to get
closer to the words themselves which I had carefully spelled
from dictation and written as above, leaving spaces beneath
for the English equivalents. I could see that there were only
four words. By dint of patient, detailed questioning I arrived approximately at the English equivalents above given.
Then I was puzzled and disturbed.

"Where is the word for sweetheart?" I asked.

"It is not there," replied the Indian, tranquilly.

"Then," said I, "how do you make out that the song
means 'I am seeking for my sweetheart'?"

Had he been a paleface he would have smiled pityingly at
my lack of comprehension, but, as he had all the traditional
courtesy and dignity of his race, he put my own patience to
the blush by pointing to the word "ondandeyan" which
occurs three times.

"That mean," said he, " 'I keep awake.' I get tired, yes,
and sleepy, but I no sleep. I keep awake. That word
(tebik) is night. Now you see. Why does a man keep awake
all night when he want to sleep?"

Like the true orator and debater, he paused for reply.

"Well," I suggested, half in weakness, and half in determination to make him work out the meaning, "he might be
hunting for deer, or something else to eat."

"No, no!" he responded gravely, "not this time. See: I
keep awake all night long on the river. Only one reason. I
go to find my sweetheart. The word is not there but we understand it. We know what is meant. Perhaps mebbe her
family has gone away. Perhaps mebbe she said she would
meet me and something happened so she couldn't. I don't
know; but we know that the man who made this song was
looking for his sweetheart, and we do not need the word
there."

With this bewildering light thrown upon the subject, I retired to my own quarters and pondered. It was my eager desire to make the attractive melody available for paleface singers. To this end it was essential that there should be singable verses. Observe this use of the plural. One verse, or one stanza would not do for the demands of civilization. The Indian is content to sing his one line over and over again, but the paleface must have variety in his language even in so short a song as this. I confess that my first impulse was to string together some rhymed lines that would fit the tune, and let it go at that, as the easiest way out of the difficulty, but it seemed a shame to discard the suggestion offered in the Indian verse, and doubly wrong to put forth an Indian song that should not at least reflect the Indian thought; but so much was implied and so little expressed! And that despairing reflection was the key to the problem. So much implied! I set myself to studying how much more might be implied than the search for a sweetheart, and it occurred to me that if an Ojibway were on the river he would necessarily be in his canoe. Here was promise of singable results and of the verbal repetition without which no representation of the original could be regarded as satisfactory. It was with conscious excitement that I hurried to my Indian friend and asked the question—would not the singing lover be in his canoe?

"Of course," said he, and then a ghost of a smile lit up his dark features; "but you don't find the word *chemaun* there, do you?" he asked.

Chemaun means canoe. "No," I answered, "but it's understood, isn't it?"

"Yes," said he, "we understand it so," and he turned away as if that settled it, or as if a continuance of the conversation would lead him to inquire sarcastically if I supposed the lover would be swimming the river all night, or balancing on a perilous, uncomfortable log.

It did settle it, and before I arrived back at my table I was humming the first of the stanzas with which the song has been identified since its publication—

> In the still night, the long hours through,
> I guide my bark canoe,
> My bark canoe, my love, to you.

> While the stars shine and falls the dew
> I seek my love in bark canoe,
> In bark canoe I seek for you.
>
> It is I, love, your lover true,
> Who glides the stream in bark canoe;
> It glides to you, my love, to you.

Though Burton's song may not satisfy everyone's taste, he was a rare translator—acquainted with the culture of his informants, sympathetic toward the material, capable musicologically, and possessing a reasonably good poetic ability. The efforts of mere ethnographers to make poetic translations are frequently so inept that one prefers the unpretentious literalness of Schultze. Poetry is an art that requires skill, careful study under competent teachers, and assiduous practice, yet like another ancient profession, poetry is overrun by amateurs who think all that is necessary for proficiency is a love of the game. As for technique, everyone knows that writing poetry is just a matter of keeping the lines from running to the edge of the page, mixing up the syntax, and sprinkling the text with archaic pronouns, obsolete verb endings, and grammatical incongruities. The great anthropologist Malinowski (1935, II:261) must have thought so when he translated a Trobriand verse as "I kick in bottom thine"—just about as bad as the effort of the high school composer who sang his football team on to victory with "Go ye Tigers around that end." When we insist that translation is fundamentally a matter of conveying the ideas, traits, and emotions of one culture to another, we must not overlook the fact that the medium of conveyance—language—is still the most important single element in the process.

THE BARRIER OF LANGUAGE

Since construction was halted on the Tower of Babel, nothing in man's culture has been more divisive than language difference, and in all the uses of language, nothing has been harder to communicate than poetic style. Edward Sapir said (227):

> It is strange how long it has taken the European literatures
> to learn that style is not an absolute, a something that is to
> be imposed on the language from Greek or Latin models, but
> merely the language itself, running in its natural grooves,
> and with enough of an individual accent to allow the artist's

personality to be felt as a presence, not as an acrobat. We understand more clearly now that what is effective and beautiful in one language is a vice in another. Latin and Eskimo, with their highly inflected forms, lend themselves to an elaborately periodical structure that would be boring in English. English allows, even demands, a looseness that would be insipid in Chinese. And Chinese, with its unmodified words and rigid sequence, has a compactness of phrase, a terse parallelism, and a silent suggestiveness that would be too tart, too mathematical, for the English genius.

English poets who have tried to cram their language into the microforms of the Orient will understand the frustration of Stephen Schlitzer who used the Japanese hokku—a form that consists precisely of three lines with five, seven, and five syllables respectively—to confess his incompetence (in Wood: 33):

> I could reach your heart—
> Perhaps make you immortal—
> But not in three lines!

Not many languages permit such happy translations as "Where are the snows of yesteryear" from "Mais ou sont les neiges d'antan." How would one go about translating Keats' "Ode on a Grecian Urn," with its dominant theme of time, into the language of the Hopi Indians, who have no concept of time?* Reciprocally, how could a Hopi poet convey the idea of precise movement in English, which, unlike his own tongue, has no grammatical devices like the segmentative aspect, which differentiates continued rotative motion by six separate verbs?

The Hopi are not unique in seeing the world differently from ourselves. The Eskimo, living in a watery world, have no concept of water generally; they have a term for drinking water (fresh water), but an entirely different term for sea water. Likewise among the Eskimo there is a word for "snow on the ground," but another for "falling snow," a third for "drifting snow," and a fourth for "snowdrift." These are not merely different terms, but different concepts, as Boas demonstrated (1938b). To equate falling snow and drifting snow would strike an Eskimo as being quite as illogical as equating a tiger with a seal on the ground that both are carnivores.

---

* "Hopi has no words, grammatical forms, constructions, or expressions that refer directly to what we call 'time' . . . . The Hopi language contains no reference to 'time' either implicit or explicit" (B. L. Whorf, quoted in Carroll).

Still another source of confusion in our translating is our assumption that there is but one language for each society, whereas in actual fact numerous peoples have a set of languages whose use is rigorously prescribed for certain occasions and for certain company. The Javanese have three such languages, one used in speaking to equals, another for superiors, and a third for inferiors; an "ugly American" situation resulted from the effort of an American missionary to require the people to use the equal form—as a missionary he was in a high status group, and could use only the language of his class.

Diachronically, this era has a translation problem that previous ages did not have—the necessity to inject or to extract propaganda connotations deliberately for political purposes. Orwell in his appendix to *1984*, "The Principles of Newspeak," brilliantly analyzed this function of language in the hypermodern state, extrapolating from the tendencies apparent in the two great Communist nations. The total efficiency of *1984* has not been achieved yet, but there are a few *doubleplusgood* examples that can be cited: The Chinese, when they rant against "American imperialism," must actually say "American-country-emperor-country-ism" (*Mei-kuo ti-kuo chu-i*), an expression that surely must sound *ungood* to the peasants who know the "United States" as *Meilichien*—"Beauty Sharp Strong" (Wright: 195). The Russians in *prolefeeding* the aboriginal Chukchee translated "Communist Party Card" as "Bearer of the good spirit," which had a real *bellyfeel* for the Chukchee who know the "good spirit" as "gasoline" (Kolarz); but then, what can one expect of a language whose one Nobel Prize novel deals with characters named Maxim Aristarkhovich Klintsov-Pogorevshikh?

There is no refuge for the translator. It would seem that the universal sounds of nature would interact identically with the human auditory system, whether one was a Djaberadjabera or an Iowan, but Nida (13) showed that our "tramp tramp" is "ku ka" in Luvale and "mingodongodona" in Malagasy. The fashionable religious philosophy among mid-century American beatniks is Zen; "Zen" was the way the Japanese heard the Chinese "Ch'an," which was the way the Chinese heard the Indian "Dhyana."

The English translator may find some comfort in knowing that there are languages less conducive to successful translation than his own. Consider the plight of the Melanesian bound to pidgin, who must render "lunar eclipse" as "kerosene lamp bilong Jesus Chrise him bugger up finish altogether" or "I am going to study" as "makem

head bilong me walk about long too much paper yabber." Yet in
this lamest of media a successful literary work is possible. Harney
recorded a poem made by an aboriginal in the Australian variety
of pidgin:

> The god-men say when die that Jesus came
> To save our sins and let us know
> The right from wrong and in his name
> To die and into heaven go—
> Might be, might be; I don't know.
>
> The god-men say when die go sky
> Through Pearly Gates where river flow,
> The god-men say when die we fly
> Just like eaglehawk and crow—
> Might be, might be; I don't know.

And the Australian translation of the mythical dimension known to
the Aranda as the *alchera* is "the Dreaming," a much more accurate
and poetic word than the "Dream Time" found in most anthropology texts mentioning these people.

But all handicaps considered, the translator has chosen a desolate
undertaking indeed. A simple homonym can destroy him, as it destroyed John White, whose construction of a Polynesian supreme
deity, Io, was made out of a muscular twitch, *io*. Be he never so
competent, his printer may stultify him—that is how such immortal
abominations as the "Idle Bible," the "Ears to Ear Bible," the
"Place-Makers' Bible," the "Wife-Hater Bible," the "Unrighteous
Bible," and the "Murderers' Bible" came into being. And even if
everything goes well, there will be some who will find his work intolerable. Chapman's version of Homer is undoubtedly the most
honored translation in the English language, having inspired the
great sonnet of Keats, "On First Looking into Chapman's 'Homer'."
But poet Matthew Arnold thought it an execrable job of translation,
and poet William Cowper, who, like Keats, had received it as a present, wrote his benefactor ungraciously, "I have as yet seen but little
of it, enough, however, to make me wonder that any man, with so
little taste for Homer, or apprehension of his manner, should think it
worth while to undertake the laborious task of translating him."

In reading the translations that make up the material of this book,
one should keep in mind poor Tommy of the opening pages of this

chapter and adopt the charitable attitude of Innequahung Shawani-
benayse, who replied to Burton's indiscreet question about the Indians' opinion of Longfellow's perversion of Ojibwa traditions (113),
"It is not all just as we understand it, but it is very hard for the
white man to understand the Indian's thought and feelings. It does
very well, it is good."

Chapter Two / THE FORMS OF LITERATURE IN THE PRIMITIVE WORLD

When Sister Inez Hilger approached an Araucanian informant for some folktales, he asked her, "Do you want a fox story or the other kind?"

The anthropologist was able later to abstract a more meaningful classification from her collected material, but only by subjecting it to the psychology of her own culture, for the main difference between the folk—primitive mind and the sophisticated mind in the area of literature is the former's unwillingness to abstract. Indeed, even the civilized mind must be educated to classifying before it can deal independently with any evaluation of material more heterogeneous than rating football teams. Probably no student of European literature knows without prior instruction that he has encountered an example of the *Ubi Sunt* theme when he reads Villon's *Ballade des Dames du temps jadis* or the *Carpe Diem* theme when he reads Herrick's *To the Virgins, to Make Much of Time.* Even the folklorist goes well into his profession before he recognizes as significant categories such things as Neck Riddles and ithyphallism.

The collector whose native informants have evolved a literary taxonomy is almost uniquely fortunate. Malinowski's Trobriand Islanders divided their literature (1926: 26 ff) into *kukuwanebu* (entertainment tales), *libwogwo* (legends), and *liliu* (sacred tales)—a remarkably logical classification compared to that of Radin's Winnebago Indians (1956: 118) who recognized two kinds of prose narrative—*worak* (tragically ending stories that could be told any time) and *waikan* (happily ending stories that could be told only when snakes were above ground); or the Navaho chantways ("Enemy Way," "Plume Way," "Male Shooting Way," "Big Star Way," etc.) which do not make much sense to us even when explained. Primitive taxonomies are like the gait of Dr. Johnson's bipedal dog—they are not done well, but one is surprised to find them done at all. Polynesian literature is the usual exception to almost every statement one can make about "primitive" literature; in this case, the Polynesians recognizing such categories as myth, legend, cosmogony, traditional history, folktale, animal tale, *cante fable*, riddle, explanatory tale, proverb, riddling tale, hero saga, charm, oration, and artistic conversation (Luomala in Dorson, 1961: 421); but most pre-literate peoples are quite indiscriminate about their classifications. Many Australian tribes have no word for any artistic endeavor, much less a concept of literary types. Melville Jacobs (1957) more than any other folklorist has tried to elicit meaningful classifications from his native storytellers with what must have been frustrating results. "All informants with whom I worked," he complained (158), "placed slight value upon story headings and at first gave them with patent indifference." One storyteller gave the name "Coyote" to all tales in which Coyote appeared; another titled a story "Badger and Coyote Were Neighbors," though the tale included nearly a dozen other characters acting a drama on the theme of death and everlasting life. Nor is this resistance of some literatures to analysis limited to primitive forms. Brodrick (69) surrendered the effort to classify sophisticated Cambodian drama:

> There are only about thirty dramas in the Royal Library and they have not ten plots between them. It needs an expert to tell one piece from another. It's always the same sort of story. An abducted princess. "Giants" who thwart or favor. A hideous hero who eventually stands revealed as a godlike prince. Animals turned into men. Men turned into animals—twilight—timeless—and when these dramas are acted, that is, mimed by the ballet and sung by chorus and choir, the digressions, the interpolations are so rambling and twisting that as often as not the story changes completely and gathers a new set of characters before you are half-way through.

One wonders what a Cambodian would say about medieval metrical romances or modern television Westerns. We might as well concede that the classifications found in this or any other study dealing with primitive literature are arbitrary, ethnocentric, and often invalid. With few exceptions they are types developed out of Western ideas, needs, and psychological orientations, and are imposed upon materials most of which cannot be forced into any logical order. Stith Thompson gives us the category "Wonder Tales"—"stories filled with incredible marvels" (1951: 21)—but this classification is entirely an analysis of comparative credulity and has nothing really to do with the literary type. The Yahgan of Tierra del Fuego surely would have thought the germ theory of disease a "wonder tale," but measles wiped them out. And Thompson's important study *Tales of the North American Indians* divided this conglomerate literature into Mythological Stories, Mythical Incidents, Trickster Tales, Hero Tales, Journeys to the Other World, Animal Wives and Husbands, Tales Borrowed from Europeans, Bible Stories, and very importantly, Miscellaneous Tales; this, as one of Thompson's students said of another book's organization, "is a little like dividing beans according to whether they are large, small, Navy, white, or red" (Richmond: 97). But a folklorist must devise his chapters somehow (since our culture demands chapter divisions) even if, as Boas said (1925: 329), the only universal forms of literary activity around the world are song and tale.

In studying primitive literature, the Western reader must abandon some of the most self-evident forms of expression which he has been trained to appreciate. Poetry, for example, does not exist as an entity separate from song, and in rhythmically-oriented societies like most of those in Africa, singing, drumming, dancing, acting, clapping, and instrument-playing are combined into what Lord Hailey correctly saw as "one homogeneous art form" (67). To the Ojibwa, whatever was not prose was *nogamon* (song); among the Bambara, the word *fo* meant both "to speak" and "to play a musical instrument." In the matter of poetry and song, literacy comes closest to establishing an absolute difference between its possessors and the peoples who have not attained to writing. Among preliterate and illiterate (that is, folk—not "nonliterate") societies "poetry" is a recitative art, and therefore sound, bypassed in our reading, becomes an essential element which must be made pleasurable by rhythm, melody, and other euphonic devices. To the primitive understanding "eye rhymes" and "free verse" are patent absurdities, and poetry without music is a fatal amputation (though music without poetry is frequent, since it is the sound rather than the sense of the song that is the basis of aural enjoyment). Similarly, our ideas of the duration of primitive song must be corrected. For nearly two generations American ears were trained by music on 78-rpm records to define a song as a piece of music with words that lasted from two minutes and forty-five seconds to three minutes and fifteen seconds. Many Indian songs are short as separate entities (Driver: 213), but almost always these songs are repeated until the singer is exhausted, or they are parts of longer sequences. The Navaho *Yeibechai*, consisting of 24 sequences with 324 songs, runs for nine nights; the Navaho Mountain Chant has 13 sequences with 161 songs. Halfway around the world from the Navaho the Arnhem Landers perform the *kunapipi* cycle of 129 songs and the *djanggawul* cycle of 188 songs (Elkin, 1954: 264), which in Berndt's translation occupies 90 printed pages. Even secular songs and music in this region are apt to ignore reasonable hours; it is common for a *didjeridu* player to drone on and on until someone knocks him silly with a club. Far to the north of Australia the Filipinos take 24 hours to render the *hud hud;* and across the globe to the West, the English folk sang the *Gest of Robyn Hode* in 456 stanzas (Child: 254).

The ballad (narrative folksong), which has kept 1000 of our scholars busy for 100 years, does not exist in preliterate cultures.* Logically, the ballad should have developed out of the *cante fable* (narrative interspersed with song), but no anthropologist expects logic to have much influence on human behavior.

"Folk epics arose spontaneously among primitive peoples," declares an authoritative literary study (Lieder: 1049), citing *The Iliad* and *The Volsunga Saga* as examples, but apart from such dubious cases as the *Walam Olum*** the true epic is a form peculiar to European and Central American literatures.

A number of categories frequently used by folklorists can be seen in primitive literatures if one tenuously extends their definitions, but since their incidence is very much higher in the oral literature of Europe and their connotations inseparably linked to this culture, it would seem better to limit their use to the "folk" as defined in the Introduction. These include:

> *Märchen:* the widely accepted German name for what the English call "fairy tale" and the French *conte populaire;* a long complex story in which characterization is subordinated to incidents of a marvelous nature. If it were not for the specialized connotations of the term, *Märchen* would be more useful in the classification of primitive literature.
>
> *novella:* a more sophisticated, often literary, form of *Märchen*, in which characterization is stronger and the marvelous more credible.

---

* This is as good a place as any to warn the reader that in no anthropological study is an unexceptional statement possible. Here, for instance, one exception is the ballad-like pieces found by Sapir among the Paiutes (1910).

** The *Walam Olum* of the Lenni Lenape or Delaware Indians was an historical song-epic asserted by Brinton to be genuine. Less credulous students find its authenticity doubtful; from its first sentence, which speaks of "Manito" as an extraterrestrial deity, the *Walam Olum* is worrisome. Other alleged primitive epics, like the Ifugao *hud hud* (Malcolm: 425) are even more obviously based upon literate sources, or are conflations assembled by over-enthusiastic collectors.

hero tale: a more unified, less fantastic biography of a super-human archetype of a people than the equivalent characterization of heroes among primitive peoples.

Sage: a term devised for the passably-believable local legend; elements of the marvelous are retained in the *Sage*, but the events are of the improbable-possible rather than the probable-impossible, as in their primitive counterparts. Not to be confused with the Saga, a Scandinavian or Celtic heroic tale.

fabliau: a satirically humorous and lascivious story, originally a sophisticated composition but filtering down to the folk.

merry tale: a humorous anecdote; though this form is often collected among primitive peoples, anthropologists have been content to let the term "merry tale" be applied only to European folk materials.

These are the commonly used terms in folklore scholarship that are less defensible in considering primitive literature; having winnowed them out, we may list some forms which, despite their vulnerability to the criticisms noted above, have been of some use in helping us classify and understand the lore of primitive peoples.*

MYTH**

Myth holds the mirror up to the nature of the mythologist. Like the projective techniques of the psychologist, in defining it he defines himself. To Pythagoras, myth was a didactic allegory. To Euhemerus, myth was the result of human deification. To the Deists of the 18th century, myth was the mischievous invention of corrupt imaginations. To Max Müller, myth was a disease of language. To Gaidoz, Max Müller was a myth. Lang saw myth as a device to create "practically useful ghosts." Jane Ellen Harrison and her myriad followers insisted that myth was the detritus of ritual. To Freud, myth was the daydreaming of the human race. But regardless of the disparity of their exegeses, all the writers on myth over the last 2500 years have agreed that myth is a narrative associated with religion.

That is, until the present time. Now the impiety of our age and culture is driving a sharp wedge into the ancient unanimity. Richard

---

* A few forms, such as legend (Chapter Seven) are examined elsewhere.
** For the function of myth and the reflection of culture by myth, see Chapter Seven; for the scholarship of myth, Chapter Eight.

Chase tells us that *"myth is literature and therefore a matter of aesthetic experience and the imagination,"* (vi), hammering down the assertion with italics. Only an age that has lost its religion can imaginably produce a book like *The Bible Designed to be Read as Living Literature;* only such an age can see mythology as *belles lettres.* From the time when the Neanderthals piled up the first altar of bear skulls in an Ice Age cave until science rudely moved the mountains that prayer and magic had been ineffectually importuning for fifty thousand years, religion was man's universal and only means of controlling nature and supernature, of getting things done. Of all the cultural universals, none has been more unvarying than religion—not social or sexual customs, or food-getting, or communicating, or art, or fighting the environment. All religions have possessed the same basic characteristics—an undefinable but identifiable emotional content, a belief in the supernatural, ritual to recharge the belief, dogma to coerce or to guide conduct, recourse to a transcendent motive power,* practitioners to conduct that power from the spirit world to mankind, and myth, the narrative charter of the religion. Since a cosmogony must be in narrative form and since the events it relates are incredible to the folklorist (who may not feel the same incredulity about his own mythology), the temptation to shovel this independent cultural item into the bin of fiction is irresistible to Western collectors, despite Swanton's warning more than a half-century ago that this is one of the most unfortunate and widespread errors in ethnology (1910: 5). As Malinowski so memorably stated it, "Myth as it exists in a savage society is not merely a story told but a reality lived" (1926: 18). The connotations of deliberate and malicious falsity that we inherited from the Deists are an unsupportable load on the useful words "myth" and "mythical." We even hear sports announcers speaking of "mythical national championships." Since words mean what people want them to, there is nothing we can do about rehabilitating the terms generally, but for this book at least let us use them properly. The old Australian *inkata*, the religious leader of his clan, devoutly tracing his gnarled thumb over the incised path lines of his totemic ancestors on his *tjurunga* or drawing the same lines in the sand and simultaneously reciting the myth of

---

* This power is called *mana* by anthropologists, following R. H. Codrington's identification of the concept among the Melanesians. Best understood as spiritual electricity, only certain people and things and in certain circumstances, could possess it; it was thought to reside in the head and hair—the Samson story in the Bible is the classic example. Among ourselves it is, like other universal religious ideas, a weak and vestigial concept, but can be identified as "grace" and "luck."

the cosmogonic journey, ought to be seen with precisely the same objectivity as a devout Catholic performing the Stations of the Cross, retracing the path lines of Christ to Calvary and meditating the accompanying myth. To the unbeliever both events thus reinacted may be fictitious, but they are not fiction, which is quite a different thing. It is the attitude of the possessor of a myth that determines the only valid classification, and no true believer sees it simply as a story told.

The difficulty here is that most primitive peoples do not distinguish between the sacred and the secular. Although it was Durkheim who first insisted on this distinction, it was also he who propounded its most brilliant refutation—the insight that religion is society sanctified. Ruth Benedict wrote that "myth bolsters a religion, as folklore bolsters other aspects of the culture" (1933: 180), but the bolstering in the primitive cultures is interdependent among culture, folklore, religion, myth, and society. Benedict (1935) herself must have appreciated the difficulty of making a distinction between the sacred and the secular when she arranged her Zuni "myths" into Emergence and other Katchina Tales, Ahaiyute Adventures, Tales of Courtship, Tales of Despised and Unacknowledged Children, Tales of Husbands and Wives, Tales of Conflicts with Witches, Tales of War and Famine, Animal Tales, and Miscellaneous. Swanton's list (1905) of "myth types" among 250 narratives of the Tlingit Indians of the Northwest Pacific Coast is even more chaotic:

1. The Man Captured by the Supernatural Beings
2. The Man Who Married the Grizzly Bear
3. The Woman Who Married the Supernatural Being
4. The Kidnapped Wife
5. The Supernatural Helper
6. Person Rewarded for Giving Food to Animal, or Helping Animal
7. The Supernatural Child
8. The Magic Feather
9. The Boy Who Was Abandoned
10. The Boy and His Grandmother Who Were Banished
11. The Ill-Disposed Mother-in-Law
12. The Goose Wife
13. The Land Otter Sister
14. The Eagle People
15. Beaver and Porcupine
16. The Rival Towns

Attempts to isolate myth chronologically by calling myths "accounts of things as they happened before the world was as it is now" (Reichard 1947: 5-6) also fail since this approach too is that of a society without faith. The translation previously criticized of *alchera* as "the Dream Time" among the Australian aborigines implies that the events of these myths belong to a *time* forever past; the aboriginal himself calls it "the Dreaming," for this is not a time, but a dimension. The *alchera* ancestors still walk the Australian earth, and Heaven still exists for the believing Christian. In Arnhem Land, Parungbar of the Djamunjun tribe told Roland Robinson (1956: 26) of his "Dreaming":

> A blackfellow named Tjigarit had a lot of wives. They came to a billabong. All the women talked: "We are going to sit down here." "Well," said Tjigarit, "I am going out hunting." Tjigarit went out to hunt the rock-wallaby Ngangut. He hunted for a long time but he did not find any wallabies. He came back to the camp empty-handed, tired and hungry. None of his wives had been out looking for food. They were all still sitting down in the camp talking among themselves.
>
> Tjigarit said to his wife Marlwaruk: "I did not find anything. I am hungry. What is the matter? You have sat down here all the time and have not found me any tucker."
>
> Tjigarit lay down and went to sleep. When he woke his wives were still sitting in the camp talking among themselves. "Ah," said Tjigarit, "you will not find me any tucker. What shall I do? Ah, it is better that I hang up my dilly-bag." Tjigarit hung his dilly-bag, Kunurr, in a tree. "It is better," he said, that I put my testicle down here. I do not want it any more. This is my dreaming. Karngut Wahgorah."
>
> Tjigarit said to his wives: "Go on, clear out! I do not want you any more. Go. You can go down into the water now." Tjigarit drove his wives down into the water of the

billabong. There his wives became the lily-tucker, the bulbs Marlwaruk.

Tjigarit changed into the bird you always see about the billabongs among the lilies. He runs about. He is angry. He talks all the time: "Tjig-tjig-tjig-arit!"

When any blackfellows go to a billabong, Tjigarit sees them coming. He runs about. He calls out. When those blackfellows get the lily-bulbs, they cook them and throw some to the bird. When they do this Tjigarit sees that they get good tucker. If you do not do this, you get rubbish all the time.

I say to those blackfellows getting the lily-tucker: "Don't eat my dreaming. I must eat this lily-tucker first. Then you can eat." That bird, and all that lily-tucker are my dreaming.*

As a culture achieves greater control over its environment, as the society moves from primitiveness to sophistication, the sacred recedes from the profane, into the past, into a world apart. In this phase man holds to his weakening ties with the divine, and in his myths (now crumbling into legend) he sends emissaries back—Gilgamesh, Ishtar, Tammuz, Persephone, Orpheus, Izanagi, Christ (the Harrowing of Hell), Dante. This phase of myth is so widespread** that some folklorists set it apart as an autonomous form.

In those rare ecological situations where a people wins the struggle for subsistence but for some reason does not take the final step into civilization, myth, though no longer serving its primary function, may run wild, as if all the society's energy were channelled into its development. The classic example is Polynesian mythology, whose complexity makes the Judeo-Christian eschatology seem meagre. In Genesis the cosmos is illuminated in three verses:

In the beginning God created the heaven and the earth.

And the earth was without form, and void; and darkness was upon the face of the deep. And the spirit of God moved upon the face of the water.

And God said, Let there be light; and there was light.

---

* Blackfellow: common pidgin term for aboriginal; no opprobrious connotations.
Billabong: a flooded river effluent.
Wallaby: a small species of kangaroo.
Tucker: pidgin term for food.
Dilly-bag: a reticule found in northern Australian tribes.
** Ann Gayton compared more than fifty "Orpheus" stories among the American Indians, from the Tlingit in the farthest northwest to the Alibamu on the eastern Gulf Coast.

The Maori, who had only one version of Polynesian cosmogony,* make this a bare synopsis of creation. Void, obviously, must precede any other state, since it is nothingness. But the Maori proliferated even nothingness, grading it into concepts such as The Void-in-which-nothing-could-be-obtained and The Void-in-which-nothing-could-be-done. Long before light there came periods of darkness (*Po*), both physical and mental, whose intensity and length were each identified by many divisions. Still light was withheld until other, to us irrelevant, phases were completed:

> *Te Rapunga*—seeking
> *Te Kukune*—growth
> *Te Pupuke*—swelling
> *Te Hihiri*—energy
> *Te Mahara*—thought
> *Te Hinengaro*—mind
> *Te Manako*—longing

Even moonlight came in slowly:

> *Te Marama-i-whanake*—the waxing moon
> *Te Marama-i-roa*—the lengthened moon
> *Te Marama-i-whiro*—dark night of the moon
> *Te Marama-whakaata*—moon with the faint light
> *Te Marama-waha-roa*—great mouthed moon
> *Te Marama-atua*—moon of the thirteenth day
> *Te Marama-mutu-whenua*—last days of the moon (Buck, 1949: 434–436).

All of this is expressed in language of unexcelled dignity and beauty before which the King James periods, magnificent as they are, stand as bare as the culture from which they were translated:

> From the conception the increase,
> From the increase the swelling,
> From the swelling the thought,
> From the thought the remembrance,
> From the remembrance the consciousness, the desire.
>
> The world became fruitful;
> It dwelt with the feeble glimmering;

---

* Strictly speaking, two versions: a simplified one for the common people and a more complex one for the priests. Some of the doubt about the existence of the supreme deity Io is due to the disappearance of the esoteric cosmogony with its high priests after the coming of the missionaries.

It brought forth night;
The great night, the long night . . .
The night ending in death.

From the nothing the begetting,
From the nothing the increase,
From the nothing the abundance,
The power of increasing, the living breath;
It dwelt with empty space,
It produced the atmosphere which is above us.

Nor can the Bible overpower this cosmology with its "begats"—
the genealogies of Polynesia have no peers anywhere in world mythologies for detailed complexity. Moreover, this dilatation pervades
every aspect of Polynesian mythology—gods, demons, spirit worlds
(Rarotonga had ten overworlds alone), souls—even the lullabies were
saturated with long mythical elements.*

EXPLANATORY TALES

Among cultures more primitive than the Polynesian, myth drains
out into a simplicity that early folklorists separately classified as
"etiological" or "explanatory" tales. The temptation to do so was
strong in the formative era of ethnology, when primitive peoples still
were seen as adult children—and since so many children's tales were
slight stories of "How the Rabbit Got Long Ears," mythic episodes
were viewed in the same light and given the same titles. All narrative
is explanatory, but extracting a minor motif from a complex primitive story and letting it carry the entire thematic burden of the tale
is like calling *Moby Dick* "How Captain Ahab Lost His Leg."

Typical of these so-called explanatory tales is this example Abraham collected among the Tiv of Nigeria (171–172):

The hare and his three children, Atondo ka'an, Abarusu
and Ankagh ashwe built themselves a house at the side of a
lonely road, the very road where Death used to stalk past
on his errands. The hare was wise but he did not know that
this was the haunt of Death and when he came in the early
morning on his rounds, he called saying "Is the hare at
home?"; the hare was still asleep but his son Atondo ka'an
answered and Death replied "He who has answered my call
must die."

---

* See for example the mad mother's lullaby in Chapter Four.

When the hare woke, he saw his son was dead and was mystified and determined to lie awake the following night and listen; so when Death came again on his round and called "Hare! Hare!" he did not reply, but he had forgotten to warn Abarusu, and the latter said "Yes" and fell dead on the spot. The hare now understood who was his enemy and went out to seek some animal to sleep in his hut.

He first invited the cob to sleep at his house and next morning the poor cob answered the call of Death and perished. This went on for a long time, till the animals seeing that whoever went to stay with the hare never returned, refused to have anything to do with him. All this time the hare and his wife were getting fatter and fatter, for they were eating the meat of every animal which was killed by death.

Finally he forced the tortoise to go home with him, and before he retired for the night, he instructed the tortoise, saying, "If you hear someone calling me while I am still asleep, do not wake me up, but answer for me." When dawn was near and Death called "Hare! Hare!" the hare lay awake waiting for the tortoise to reply, but his friend kept silent, and Death becoming impatient called out, "I will come in and find you." The hare whispered to the tortoise, "Come on, answer for me" but the latter replied "There is no need for that now, as you are awake yourself."

The hare was unable to persuade the tortoise to answer and as Death was saying over and over again, "I am coming in," the hare called out "yes" and this was the end of him. The crafty tortoise said to Anjiyeke, the hare's widow, "My wife, we shall have a banquet today," but on hearing this, she caught hold of the tortoise and dashed him against a stone; that is why he is so dented.

This is a story of the biter bit, of death at the door, of death postponed by substitution, and other motifs, themes, and characters all of which are more important in the tale than the tortoise's dented carapace, but Abraham titled the story "Why the Tortoise is Dented."

When one motif in a complex narrative has special interest to the folklorist, either intrinsic or as an example of a process (such as polygenesis or diffusion), the temptation is understandably great to isolate and exaggerate the motif, even to making a title of it. The following story, collected by Roland Robinson (1956: 84–85) from Minyanderri of the Pitjandjara tribe in central Australia, is a typical *alchera* myth in which totemic ancestors move aimlessly and erratically about the land now occupied by the band possessing the myth, creating mountains, valleys, plants, animals, and men; leaving sacred topographical evidence of each halt and action; originating religious ceremonies (here confused with "corroborees," secular dances); and finally disappearing into the ground or rising into the sky:

The old-man Yoola was always wanting women. He was always chasing them through the bush. One day he saw seven women who were seven sisters. Yoola chased after them but he could not catch them. When he got close to them the seven sisters became frightened. They flew up into the sky. The sisters travelled through the sky and came down at the rock-hole Karraloo, close to the Petermann Range.

Yoola started walking after the sisters. They were sitting down at the rock-hole when they turned round and saw him coming. The sisters got up and ran away to the water-hole Puntanbanya. The old-man Yoola went all round this place to surround the sisters. Steep cliffs rose up all round the sisters so that they could not run away. They looked back and saw the old-man Yoola coming through a path in the cliffs. "Ai! Ai!" they shrieked, "our only road is blocked." Together the sisters rushed at Yoola. They ran and swerved past him on every side. Yoola did not know which sister to try and catch. He did not catch one of them.

When the sisters escaped, Yoola sat down and made the corroboree Puntanbanya. The sisters ran away into the desert. At Untjeeworrango, where there is no water, the sisters sat down and made the men's corroboree of knocking out a front tooth. Yoola got up from his place and followed after the sisters. The women looked back from where they were making the corroboree. They saw Yoola coming after them. They got up and ran on into the desert.

In the desert Yoola became tired. He walked along dragging his spear behind him. Where he dragged his spear he made a valley and a sandhill. Yoola camped in the desert Pilanka. Where he camped, a big gum-tree, a dreaming, stands up. Yoola travelled on in the desert. He was still tired and he dragged his spear behind him. Again he made a valley and a sandhill as he walked on. Sometimes Yoola felt good and he carried his spear. All the way he travelled like that.

The sisters looked back and saw Yoola coming. They ran on but Yoola went round them out of sight. The sisters found that they were running up a creek with a range on either side of them. Yoola sat on the top of a red uprearing rock-face and sang his corroboree. The sisters rested at Wattapulka soak. They looked back and saw Yoola coming close behind them. Yoola chased them but the sisters split up and ran away in different directions. When they had left Yoola behind, the sisters came together again.

Yoola still followed after the sisters. As he travelled he left behind himself the mountain range, the dreaming Wankareenga. He camped and laid down his spear. He left behind him in that place the long stone, like a spear, Titjeengunga. Yoola travelled on. He camped and stood his spear up in the ground and left a big gum-tree dreaming standing up into the sky. Still Yoola travelled on from rock-hole to rock-hole, sometimes dragging his spear, sometimes carrying it and thinking all the time about those women he was chasing.

At Karrawalkarntja he sat down. He looked out and saw smoke from the fire of the seven sisters. Yoola travelled up quickly towards the smoke. He sneaked up and saw the sisters sitting down by the big water-hole, Wankarrennga, in a creek. Yoola did not show himself. He went back and sneaked round the sisters. He pulled off and threw down his loin-string in the place Tjani. He was still watching the sisters. As he went round them from place to place he sang many corroborees which belong to one big one.

Yoola had sung up high cliffs all round the sisters. From the water-hole the sisters looked up and knew they were trapped. They saw Yoola coming. They looked and the high cliffs were all round them. There was no way out. As Yoola ran up, the seven sisters jumped into the water-hole. Yoola came running up and jumped in after them. They all went down into the water and Yoola drowned the sisters, swimming down after them in the water-hole.

The spirits of the sisters, Koongarrennga, went up into the sky. They are the stars, the seven sisters. The old-man

Yoola went up into the sky, still chasing them.   He is the
big star, close up to the cluster of the seven little stars
who are frightened and running away from him.

There is no doubt that Minyanderri interpreted this story as the
charter by which his people held their land, for are not the desert
Pilanka, the rock-hole Karraloo, the rock Titjeengunga, the water-
holes Puntanbanya and Wankarrennga, and the mountains Wankareenga all there as testaments to the creation by the *inkata* ancestor Yoola?   But the folklorist is in quite a different prospect; he
knows the Greek myth in which the sisters Electra, Maia, Merope,
Alcyone, Taygete, Sterope, and Celaeno fled Orion and became the
Pleiades, and he may know that the Lapps also see the constellation
as fugitive sisters, as do several tribes in the New World; he is not
much concerned about Minyanderri's title to a patch of savanna, but
he is interested in how this curious idea diffused to the center of an
isolated continent.   Or, more curious still, if it was independently
invented, what psychic drive caused these primitive peoples, scattered themselves like stars, to see the flickering assemblage as sisters?
This is the sort of story that turns up in scholarly journals as "A
Pleiades Tale from Central Australia."

After T. T. Waterman's famous article in 1914 appeared criticiz-
ing the easy classification "explanatory tales" folklorists were more
cautious.   In this article Waterman gave the results of an exhaustive
study of North American Indian tales (in which, incidentally, the explanatory element is stronger than in most literatures), showing that
explanations occurred in only 36 per cent of the stories, and in very
few of these were they prominent components.

Some narratives can properly be set in the etiological category,
but to justify the classification, the explanatory element must be the
primary motivation in the story.   Warner (538) found an example
among the Murngin of Arnhem Land:

> Djir-mung-o, the Porcupine, was in Koparpingo country.
> He belongs to the Yiritja moiety.   While there he saw Long-
> legged Plover's wife.   When Djurt-djur, the Plover, was
> away, Porcupine stole his wife.   Plover said, when he re-
> turned, "All right, I'll get all my relatives and we'll go
> fight Porcupine."   What Porcupine had done was very bad,
> because Plover's wife was Yiritja and belonged to the same
> moiety as he.
>
> Plover and all his brothers marched over to Porcupine's

country. When they arrived Porcupine and Plover's wife
were asleep. She was a young girl. All the Djurtdjur surrounded Porcupine. They had provided themselves with
sting-ray prong spears. They stabbed Porcupine with the
sting-ray prongs and filled him full of barbs. They pulled
his back legs out and put them on front and put his front
legs where the hind ones had been. One can see Porcupine
now, and see him covered with sting-ray prongs. After they
had done this Porcupine sang a little song. He said, "I
am Porcupine now, and I have been hurt with sting-ray
spears."

But even this can be interpreted better as a gnomic story empha-
sizing the incest prohibition within moieties or as a justification for
the Murngin tribes' overwhelming reason for warfare—wife stealing.

The only unequivocal explanatory tales are those products of a
crumbling folklore that are kept alive now only in nurseries. They
are like folk etymologies, superstitions of literature, in which a de-
clining people try to retrieve a lost concept. The peasants of the
Salisbury plain have long forgotten that at Stonehenge the Hele Stone
was named by the Anglo-Saxons who saw it "hiding" (*heland*) the
sun at the summer solstice, so they invented an etiological tale of an
inquisitive friar whose "heel" was struck by the stone which the
Devil threw at him—and see! there is the mark of the heel still on
the stone! This is the worth of most "explanations"—they are tag-
end deceptions feebly offered as evidence for a feeble story.

CURSES, CHARMS, AND IMPRECATIONS*

Every man is his own wizard in the primitive world. A desperate
situation may require the employment of a professional sorcerer, but
dark deeds are best done alone in the dark. In Australia, where all
deaths are attributed to sorcery, open enmity between two men
marks the survivor for fatal revenge, so there it is expedient to be the
smiler with the knife under his cloak. Or, more exactly, the smiler
with the bone in his dilly-bag. Though the Australians are among
the most adroit handlers of spear and club in the world, the most
lethal weapon in their arsenal is the pointing bone, a generic term
for various short rods of bone or wood, variously devised. Among
the Aranda the most dangerous is the *injilla*, made from a notched
human radius or ulna, one end pointed and the other trailing a tail of

* For shamans' songs, see Chapter Five.

braided human hair.   Like nearly all civilian firearms in our society,
the pointing bone is rarely fired at a human being; in fact, it is worth
a man's life to be found in possession of so deadly a weapon.   But
these things happen, and one man may warm his hatred for another
to the point where he makes an *injilla* and sings the killing incantation into it.   Since "boning" is very much alive in Australia today
because of its proved effectiveness (the victim is under irresistible
social and psychic pressure to die)* it is very hard to obtain texts
of the curses sung into the bone.   Warner (207–208) wrote that the
most deadly of all magic to the Murngin were death magic songs,
but he could obtain no texts, since everyone either denied knowledge
of such songs or were afraid to quote them.   Spencer and Gillen cite
one—"May your head and throat be split open"—which is unimaginative but effective enough.

The Australian natives, in spite of their savage visages and the
slanders made upon them by early settlers, are a docile and friendly
people who never got as far as inventing true war and among whom
the per capita murder rate is far lower than that of American cities
today.   The Polynesians, contrariwise, were much further along the
way to full civilization, and consequently devised curses that would
have curdled the blood of a Bluebeard.   And do not be misled by
their good behavior during most of the last two centuries; William
Mariner, who knew them well on Tonga in the old days, quoted a
fine specimen of Tongan hatred:

> Dig up your grandfather by moonlight and make soup of
> his bones; bake his skin to cracknel; devour your mother;
> dig up your aunt and cut her to pieces; feed on the earth
> of your own grave; strike your god; chew the heart of your
> grandfather; swallow the eyes of your uncle; eat the grisly
> bones of your children; suck the brains of your grand-
> mother; dress yourself up in the skin of your father and tie
> it on with the entrails of your mother. . .

which surely must be among the most disrespectful behavior toward
relatives to be found in any literature.   Raymond Firth found the
Tikopia using the imprecation "May your father eat filth" so frequently that it had lost all semantic significance and in fact had
become almost a polite expression of mild annoyance.

---

* Enmity of the degree necessary to cause bone-pointing cannot be kept secret in
such small social groups as those of the Australian aborigines. When a man is "boned,"
therefore, everyone knows of his misfortune and treats him as if he were already dead.
Accordingly, as one white observer said, "I have never seen a boned man refuse to die."

The Tongans might not have approved of the syntax of the following curse which Rivers (259) found the Todas, like the Australians, expediting with a pointed bone, but they surely would have commended the sentiment:

> To him will destroy disease come may;
> To him one incurable sore come may;
> His leg broken may be;
> His hand broken may be;
> His eye destroyed may be;
> His house into his family to all trouble come may;
> He to me troubles did who accordingly to him also troubles
>   occur may;
> His country there is that we shall know,
> Those gods there are that we shall see,
> This bone into the ground what happens
> That man to also happen may.

Allegedly the world's most unpleasant people are the Dobu, who infect a group of islands off the southeast coast of New Guinea. Even anthropologists, dedicated to uncritical description of other peoples, have condemned them as group paranoids. Ruth Benedict (1934: 137–138) repeats from Reo Fortune, their chief student, an incantation used by the fortunate possessor of the curse causing gangosa, the frightful disease often confused with leprosy, in which the malady is exhorted by the sorcerer to tear his victim like the savage hornbill:

> Hornbill dweller of Sigasiga
> in the lowana tree top,
> he cuts, he cuts,
> he rends open,
> from the nose,
> from the temples,
> from the throat,
> from the hip,
> from the root of the tongue,
> from the back of the neck,
> from the navel,
> from the small of the back,
> from the kidneys,
> from the entrails . . .

and so on through the anatomy.

The civilized world is hardly aware of the intense animism of the uncivilized world, where spirits reside in everything—rocks, trees, clouds, and earth—spirits that can be dangerous to man if precautions are not taken to coerce them into good behavior. Therefore the incantations directed against man are a small proportion of the magical directives put to use in the everyday life of the primitive. Every activity is subject to contending psychical forces, and since it can at worst do no harm to attempt the influencing of these forces, magic is as common among primitives as prayer in a clergyman's household. It is, in fact, the equivalent of prayer; the only difference between magic and prayer is in method of handling the spirits: magic coerces and prayer supplicates.

Malinowski filled two large volumes with incantations used by the Trobrianders to help with their gardening, an activity that prospers so well in that fertile land that one would hardly expect any magic at all to be used. Yet the Trobrianders are not neighbors of the Dobu for nothing, and they do not poke a digging stick into the ground without launching into a spell like

> The belly of my garden leavens,
> The belly of my garden rises,
> The belly of my garden reclines,
> The belly of my garden grows to the size of a bush-hen's nest,
> The belly of my garden grows like an ant-hill,
> The belly of my garden rises and is bowed down,
> The belly of my garden rises like the iron-wood palm,
> The belly of my garden lies down,
> The belly of my garden swells,
> The belly of my garden swells as with a child.
> I sweep, I sweep, I sweep away (Malinowski, 1935, II: 98)

Two elements are basic to this kind of magic: the belief that repetition will make it so, and the command to the spirits to inspire the crops. The second element is dominant in this example from the Jivaro, who do not spend all their time shrinking their neighbors' heads (Karsten: 132):

> At night united we sing,
> Being daughters of Nungui, the woman,
> To Nungui, the woman, we sing:
> Multiply the manioc,
> Multiply the camote,
> Multiply the earth-nuts,

> Multiply the potatoes,
> Multiply the sangu,
> Everything multiply!

Magic as an aid to husbandry is universal in time and space. In the primitive period of our own culture, the Anglo-Saxons used a charm almost identical to that of the Jivaro:

> Erce, Erce, Erce, eorðan mōdor,
> geunneþe se alwalda, ecce Drihten.
> æcera wexendra and elniendra,
> scēafta heries, scīre-wæstma
> and ðæra bradan berewæstma
> and ðæra hwitan hwætewæstma
> and ealra eorðan wæstma . . . (James Hulbert: 180–181)*.

Grendon found 22 manuscripts of charms still remaining from Anglo-Saxon times, though the Church, neither mollified nor deceived by the insertions of appeals to God, tried to suppress these vestiges of ancient heathenism. The Anglo-Saxons and the Jivaros, the Lepchas and the Permiaks—all peoples who have not transferred their faith to science use charms to assure the success of an enterprise and to avert disaster. And the habit dies slowly: Peter Buck (Te Rangi Hiroa) tells of seeing two of his Maori countrymen, former chiefs, playing billiards in a Wellington, New Zealand, hotel. They were men of dignity, well educated, grave and restrained—but at a crucial point of the play Buck heard amid the clicking of the balls, the old Maori magical ejaculation, *"kuruki whakataha"* ("lose power, turn aside")!

LOVE SONGS

In all societies except our own and a very few others also infected by the medieval legacy of Courtly Love, the straightest way to a woman's heart is the surest. All cultures provide for prospective lovers to indicate preliterally that like Barkis, they are willin'; all cultures approve masculine boasting for the purpose of seduction— Finck (487–488) quotes a Dyak swain, "I am the comb of the cham-

---

*Great, great, great mother of earth
Grant, you who are omnipotent, eternal Lord,
The waxing of the acres, and their growing,
Increasing and strengthening,
The shafts of the shire-growth,
And there the broad barley-growth,
And there the white wheat-growth,
And the growth of all the earth.

pion fighting cock that never runs away"; all cultures have their
languid lovers who are happy only when they are unhappy and
singing about their unhappiness; but the normal savage lover proceeds to his objective directly and efficiently with a little help from
the spirits. Most primitive "love songs" are wordless, since they are
played upon the universal instrument of love, the flute, but incantations are common. A Chukchee who had a reputation for romantic
conquests confided his method to Bogoras (1909):

> If I want to have this woman, I take out her heart and
> liver, then I go towards the Evening "direction," and hang
> her organs on both sides of the Evening. Then I say,
> "Here is the heart and the liver of that woman. Make
> them entangled in a seal-net! Let her be without her intes-
> tines! Let her pine away with desire for me! This man is
> not your husband. This is a seal's carcass drifted to the
> seashore, rotting up on the pebbles. Every wind blows upon
> it, and its bones are bared. And you are not a woman; you
> are a young reindeer doe. The smell of the carrion comes to
> you, and you flee away, and come into my possession."

If truth is, as some people think, determinable by democracy, we
must transfer the seat of the affections from the heart to the intestines, like the Chukchee Romeo, for the surge of love among peoples
as diverse as the Puritans (see Samuel Sewall's pursuit of Madame
Winthrop) and the Australian aborigines, is "my bowels yearn for
her." Though we move the locus of amorous affection to a more
decorous part of the anatomy, the minds of primitive peoples move
on a lower if more realistic level. Without our multifarious ways of
sublimating the sexual urge, peoples closer to nature are less reticent
about nature's pleasurable enticement for the propagation of the
species. Obscenity saturates their literature to such a degree that
one cannot set it apart as a special form.*

GAMBLING SONGS

Censorship of sexual expression grows from the subconscious recognition of the socially-destructive effect of unregulated sexual activity.

---

* See for example the Trickster stories in Chapter Three. The differentiation implied here is valid only for our own published literature. Every folklorist who has
collected material in the United States knows that obscenity is found in a large per-
centage—perhaps even a majority—of song and narrative. In addition to innumerable private collections, there are deposited in universities and libraries collections of
obscene material that cannot be published.

Similarly in cultures based on productive economic effort, like our own, gambling is subconsciously recognized as subversive and is censored also. For this reason we are astonished to find that gambling songs are a near-universal in primitive literature. Even the desert aborigines of Australia who have almost nothing to gamble with have both the songs and the games. Unaware of its debilitating effects, some preliterate peoples allow gambling and gambling songs to infiltrate their religion. Few ceremonies are more sacred than the Navaho *Yeibechai*, yet the demigod *Yeibechai* himself is a buckskin-garbed gambling figure, who moves with a shuffling step (Matthews: 8):

> He comes to us on toes and feet,
> He comes to us on toes and feet,
> He comes to us on toes and feet,
> With coat upon coat of fine-dressed skin,
> He comes to us on toes and feet,
> He comes to us on toes and feet,
> He comes to us.

And no ceremony was more tragically serious than the Ghost Dance, yet gambling songs were frequent in its ritual also (Lesser). One reason, perhaps, for the compatibility of religious ceremony and gambling songs is the magical and esoteric quality of the latter. Gambling, whether based on chance or skill, implies some help from the supernatural. The American Puritans bolstered the economic motivation against gambling by the argument that gambling made frivolous use of God's providence. Among the primitives, however, the spirits were not as strait-laced as Calvin's Jehovah. Densmore (1936: 76) gives an example of the unity of the sacred and profane in Mad Bull's Hand Game Song:

> My ball is going around three times.
> They are playing over there [in the spirit land].

> Our father above, I have seen.
> The raven says, "There is going to be another judgment day."

WORK SONGS

Since Adam was driven from the Garden to begin his long term at hard labor, mankind has been fulfilling its service grudgingly. Man has not been happy at his work. Work songs, intrinsically considered,

are extremely rare among primitive peoples; several societies, the
Polynesians and Africans especially, sing at their work, but the songs
are seldom regarded by the singers as songs of work. They may be
incantations or spells to augment the productivity of the exertion
they accompany, or a distractive activity, or even a plaint or protest
against the effort, but the type of song that we recognize as a work
song—that is, like the agricultural group labor songs and prison
gang songs of the Negroes of the Southern United States or the
capstan shanties of the wooden-ship sailormen—are characteristic of
folk rather than primitive societies. And even in these groups they
seldom have enough substance to be considered literature under the
broadest definition. The Chinese laborers' chant "Hung Ho Hai
Ho" is a work song, since it is nothing else, but it is hardly literature.*

Carl Bücher, led stray by his profession as an economist, advanced
in his influential book *Arbeit und Rhythmus* the hypothesis that music
originated in rhythmical communal work, and that therefore the work
song was the primal type of literature and music. The most remarkable thing about Bücher's theory is that he was able to assemble
enough discussion on the subject to fill a book, for there is no objective evidence whatsoever to substantiate his idea. True work songs
have about the same incidence among primitive peoples as they do
among ourselves. Except where Euramerican exploitation of native
labor is established, or among Communists, who have elevated work
to a place in their theology, work songs are absent in the Western
Hemisphere; in the Old World, they occur only where there is organized communal labor. The fact that the African social and
economic organization produced communal work songs which transferred so well to the Negro folk group forming on American soil has
greatly exaggerated the importance of this category of literature in
our minds.

An exception more apparent than real to the preceding remarks is
the hunting song, which is found everywhere at this level of subsistence. Hunting-gathering peoples do indeed have songs about their
work apart from magical coercions to the spirit of the animals to
permit themselves to be killed, but as literature they are negligible.

---

* War songs, which are so important in many primitive cultures, are also infra-
literary, being almost always a psychological tension-increasing device in which words,
when they are present, are irrelevant or gratuitous, like the lyrics of an endless Bedouin war song: "I don't like the Shurf, I take the weapon of Mauser" (Leslau).
Lullabies also fall into this category, though an important exception is the Polynesian
oriori, a conventionalized form whose purpose is not merely to lull a child to sleep,
but to educate it to the history, traditions, and knowledge of its tribe (Luomala,
1949: 90).

The desert aborigines of Australia sing for an interminably long time
a song whose lyrics consist wholly of "Rat, come out of your hole"
(Elkin, 1953). On the other side of the world, the Eskimos, as skilful but as unfortunate in their contention against a hard environment as the aboriginal Australians, sing things like

> First they shot a female caribou,
> Then two buck caribou came along,
> Their horns were just beginning to appear
> All velvet as in the spring,

which is rather better than one would expect in a land where so much
effort must be put into bare existence.

SONGS OF CONTENTION AND RIDICULE

While we overestimate the importance of work songs in the uncivilized world, we underestimate the importance of ridicule and contention literature; in fact, only students of folklore and anthropology
know of its existence. It was not always so with us; early English
and Scottish poets used the *flyting* (contention song) as a substantial
literary form—witness the *flyting* of Beowulf and Unferth in *Beowulf*
and the flyting of Dunbar and Kennedie in Middle Scots poetry.
Why our culture should have abandoned this most effective, efficient,
and relatively painless means of discharging disruptive social tension
is an anthropological puzzle, though the abandonment is recent. In
England the Slander of Women Act was not passed until 1891; some
Old Inhabitants can remember the merciless but influential reviewing
of 19th century English journals that retired many a poetaster to
more fitting employment; and many of us can remember sending or
receiving comic valentines. A society that does not make use of
ridicule and verbal contention must make use of more unpleasant
coercive devices to relieve competitive tensions and enforce social
conformity. We have more laws governing torts than any man's
mind can possibly comprehend and more reason for them, yet the
Eskimos, who are psychologically no less contentious than ourselves
enjoy better social behavior though they have no prescribed laws—
but they have the *nith* song.* When mutual dislike ripens into
enmity, two men will meet publicly and belabor each other with
ridicule songs composed for the occasion. The contention, it must

---

* From a Norwegian word meaning "contention." The form was described first
among the Greenland Eskimos, but Boas found it strong among the natives of Baffin
Land and Brinton among the Tlingit. The Eskimo also call the form "song-tying"
and "drum song."

be admitted, is not wholly verbal; the litigant who has the floor is permitted to emphasize his points by head-butting, which his opponent is supposed to ignore. This goes on until the wit or the skull of one of the contenders gives out; the winner is acknowledged by public applause, and the two men part as friends—or so we are told. Day (44) quotes two songs from a *nith* contest:

Savdlat:
The south shore, O yes, the south shore I know it;
Once I lived there and met Pulangit-Sissok,
A fat fellow who lived on halibut, O yes, I know him.
Those south-shore folks can't talk;
They don't know how to pronounce our language;
Truly they are dull fellows;
They don't even talk alike;
Some have one accent, some another;
Nobody can understand them;
They can scarcely understand each other.

Pulangit-Sissok:
O yes, Savdlat and I are old acquaintances;
He wishes me extremely well at times;
Once I know he wished I was the best boatman on the shore;
It was a rough day and I in mercy took his boat in tow;
Ha! Ha! Savdlat, thou didst cry most pitiful;
Thou wast awfully afeared;
In truth, thou wast nearly upset;
And hadst to keep hold of my boat strings,
And give me part of thy load.
O yes, Savdlat and I are old acquaintances.

Though it is to be doubted that Savdlat and Pulangit-Sissok eventually purged themselves of their hostile feelings, one or the other was made the laughing stock of the neighborhood, which, as Hodge (77) said, "is a sweet morsel of revenge for any Eskimo. At any rate the crisis that in other societies leads to violence is usually thus averted, for the laughing-stock has no safe recourse but to accept the decision and learn not to antagonize better men."

Similar song-contentions are widespread among preliterate peoples. Calame-Griaule (5–24) speaks of the settling of disputes among the Dogon of Africa by singing and dancing; the Haitians have a form called the *point*, very like the Eskimos' *nith* song; Surinam Negro women revenge themselves on unfaithful lovers by the public singing

of the *lobi singi;* Arnhem Landers sing the calypso-like *gunborg* to
ridicule the local sinners.   But the most highly developed litigation
singing is that of the western Congo.   When a Bambala fancies himself the victim of a tort, he petitions the chief to convoke a tribunal
at the next assizes.   The court is convened by the chief on a talking
drum, and charge given over to the lawyers, professional representatives of the litigants.   Judging by Verwilgen's published phonograph
recording of such an event, no British wearer of the wig is more adept
at badgering a witness or playing to a jury than the half-naked
Bambala barrister who not only speaks well and rapidly but sings
also, and has the support of his audience who clap, yell, stamp,
whistle, join in the choruses, and generally signify appreciation of
skilful ploys in a manner no civilized jury would be permitted to do.
Verwilgen's example begins with the confrontation of the litigants,
who speak and sing in metaphor and simile the aptness of which we
cannot appreciate:

Defendant:
I was in my house and would have liked to stay.   But he has
come and wants to discuss the matter in public.   So I have
left my house and that is why you see me here.

  Sings: I am like a cricket.   I would like to sing, but the
wall of earth that surrounds me prevents me.   Someone has
forced me to come out of my hole, so I will sing.

  Let us debate the things, but slowly, slowly, otherwise we
will have to go before the tribunal of the white people.   You
have forced me to come.   When the sun has set, we shall
still be here debating.

  Sings: I am like the dog that stays before the door until
he gets a bone.

Plaintiff:
Nobody goes both ways at the same time.   You have told
this and that.   One of the two must be wrong.   That is why
I am attacking you.

  Sings: A thief speaks with another thief.   It is because
you are bad that I am attacking you.

The Bambala type of litigation, fused with carnival dancing
(*calipso*), became the Trinidad *calypso,* which in its pre-popularized
form was a topical song laden with abuse, ridicule, and reproach
against specifically unidentified but well recognized social offenders.
Even in its less well developed African form the public ridicule song

could hardly be surpassed for the "forcefulness of the reprimand conveyed to a wrongdoer when he finds his misdeeds sung about before all the people of the village" (Tracey, 1948: 3). "What better sanction could be brought to bear upon those who outrage the ethics of the community," Tracey continues, "than to know that the poets will have you pilloried in their next composition? No law of libel would protect you from the condemnation conveyed by those concerted voices of the whole village set to full orchestra and danced in public for all to revel in." "Nor is it in the village communities only," he writes elsewhere (1954: 237), "that we find these morality songs. They are particularly in evidence on the Copperbelt, for example, and in Johannesburg. It is tribal education at work using the salutary fear of public opinion. You can say publicly in songs what you cannot say privately to a man's face, and so this is one of the ways African society takes to maintain a spiritually healthy community."

The most heart-warming of these contention and ridicule songs is the Ashanti *apo*, which the chiefs of these people of Ghana used to permit their subjects to rain upon their heads. In the *apo* public resentment that even the best of rulers incurs is discharged through invective, insults, and reproach against the chief, which he accepts humbly in the knowledge that this catharsis will release feelings which if allowed to build up would do spiritual harm to himself and his people.

DIRGES

Most peoples have their *In Memoriam*, their *Lycidas*, their *Seventeenth Devotion upon Emergent Occasions*. Although it is true that all the world fears a ghost and that all funeral rites equivocate sincere hope for the best possible reward for the dead man's soul with equally sincere hope that he will be content to remain wherever he is sent, the finest literary effort of which any people is capable is most likely to be inspired by death.* Nor is the final rite of passage an evocation of literary art alone—death can inspire in the civilized

---

* And also some of the worst. An old American tradition that is happily dying out is the *genre* of newspaper obituary verse, which was bought by the inch by bereaved relatives. Benjamin Franklin satirized this sort of thing with a little stanza commemorating the demise of the pet squirrel of one of his young lady friends:

> Here Skug
> Lies snug
> As a bug
> In a rug

which has given us one of our best known similes.

world such a peerless example of religious, literary, dramatic, and visual art as the solemn requiem mass, and in the primitive world the Polynesian *tangi*.

Dirges—funerary songs—are found among all peoples, though the forms they take and the emotions they inspire are infinitely varied. Our own culture prefers to look upon death lugubriously, to make the worst of it; other peoples, like the Trobrianders (Baldwin) make well of it; but the Polynesians made by far the best of it. An Irish wake is literally funereal compared to the obsequies of the Maori. Huck Finn's factitious King would have been perfectly accurate in describing the rites of the aboriginal New Zealanders as "orgies." While the priests prepared the body of the dead chief for his prolonged exposure, oiling his hair, painting him with red ochre, dressing him in the finest raiment of flaxen linens and fur robes, and decking him with feathers, his female relatives began the keening which would be a continuous background accompaniment for all the activities to follow. This wailing was evidently affective, for Buck tells of attending the funeral of a man he knew only slightly, but the wailing put him in the proper mood quickly, and soon he was weeping as copiously as anyone. Meanwhile visitors by the hundreds came from as far off as the chief was known, for the death of an *ariki* was the call for a political convention. Diplomatic etiquette required the host village to continue the obsequies at its own expense until all possible delegates had time to come, and since this might mean continuation of the ceremonies for several months, the chief often approached over-ripeness and his family bankruptcy before he was finally deposited in his expensive bone-chest. The entertainment that accompanied the public grief was Babylonian: dances, chants, recitation of elegiac poems, *kava* drinking, love making, intellectual games, and even athletic contests—Buck confesses having won the hop-step-jump event at one Maori wake—eliminated any possibility of tedium. We can imagine literary events beginning when the new chief, again like Huck Finn's King, gets up and comes forward a little, and works himself up and slobbers out a speech, all full of tears and flapdoodle. Someone might begin a *haka* (posture dance), leaping about, waggling his pelvis, shaking his fingers, sticking out his tongue, making ferocious faces, and bugging out his eyes while singing a calpyso-like commentary on public affairs. Some of the goings-on were more appropriate to the sobriety of the occasion. Luomala (1949: 88) gives an example of the *tangi*, from which the funerary ceremonies took their general name:

Alas! my grief that gnaws within
For you, O beloved, no longer with me on the wet coast of
    Te Koiti,
Where was the fire for tattooing the lips of your ancestor
    Pawaititi.
Death is not a new weed!
In ancient days death came to Maui because the Patatai
    laughed
And he was severed within.
When twilight came, Tiwaiwaka flew and lighted on the
    refuse bar.
Thus evil came to thee. Knowledge of water,
Knowledge of good, then spread abroad.
Your ancestors in ancient times had no power;
Ka-hae was impotent.
The world went wrong. Farewell!

The interlinear meaning of this is so rich that we cannot begin to appreciate the allusive quality that was apparent to all who heard this chanted in tones of inconsolable sorrow by a priest who quivered his fingers in accompaniment; but even as it stands, it is far superior to the funeral verse that can still be found in some rural American newspapers, or its equivalent in other primitive cultures. Even in the marginal areas of Polynesia the dirge was admirably developed. Firth recorded a fair sample from Tikopia, in the farthest west of the Polynesian waters:

Your sky, father,
Stands in the ocean;
Your canoe will be buried in the sea
Blanketed by the waves
Of the ocean wastes, it will be buried.

Broken is the shelter
Of my father,
Lost to sight.

His mind also,
Nevaianevaia!
His mind
Has become untied, while I
Am living orphaned.

PROVERBS

"The wisdom of many and the wit of one," the proverb is used by all the peoples of the world (except perhaps the American Indian) as a rationalization for all kinds of behavior. Especially in unsophisticated societies the proverbs offered as justification for expedient conduct are unanswerable by logic, for wit turneth away wisdom as a soft answer turneth away wrath; the only possible counter is a contradictory proverb, and every proverb has its antithesis.* Though the proverb is embedded in even civilized jurisprudence (which, significantly, is fonder of precedent than of abstract justice), it is taken seriously by the commonality only in simple societies where black is never gray and the complexities of life are happily unsuspected. A corroboration rather than a refutation of this is found in the indiscriminate use of proverbs by Ralph Waldo Emerson who was speaking to a society that needed self-confidence far more than it needed wisdom.

Having more occasion to use the proverb, primitive peoples are better at making proverbs than ourselves, to whom proverbs are debased wisdom, as superstitions are debased religion. We have little to compare to the Masai "coal laughs at ashes" or the Ngonde "the tongue has no bones" (beware of talkative people) (Mackenzie: 163); our "pat each other on the back" is puny beside the Tiv "the right hand washes the left" (Malherbe: 99) and the Tiv "the horse who arrives early gets good drinking water" (Abraham: 64) does not invite a destructive emendation as our equivalent "the early bird catches the *early* worm." But some, like the Tiv "rash turns into leprosy" we are lucky not to have.

The question of incidence of proverbs among the North American Indians will probably never be satisfactorily resolved now, since their folklore is so thoroughly contaminated by our own. Most folklorists are therefore willing to accept the statement of one of the earliest systematic and competent investigators, Franz Boas, that the form was not characteristic of our aborigines (1938a: 598). Diffusion of proverbs from the Orient, where they are an important literary convention, seems to have frozen at the Arctic Circle, for Hulbert found proverbs few and undeveloped among the Chukchee. The

---

* Archer Taylor, our greatest scholar on the proverb, suggests (in Leach: 903) that the contradictory nature of most proverbs is due to their underlying advice against excess of any kind. A more cynical explanation is that proverbs advise expediency, which obeys no consistent precepts.

distribution of the proverb suggested to Kroeber (1948: 544) that

> there must have been a time when proverbs were unknown anywhere—still 'uninvented' by mankind. Then somewhere in the Old World, they came into use. Perhaps it was a genius that struck off the first sayings, to be repeated first by his associates and then preserved by his more remote environment. At any rate, the custom spread from people to people until it extended over almost all the Eastern Hemisphere. Some cause, however, such as the relative lateness of the invention, or geographical isolation, prevented the extension of the movement to the Western Hemisphere. The American Indians thus remained proverbless because the habit was never transmitted to them.

On the other hand, there is no doubt that the best spawning ground of the primitive world's most superb proverbs is Africa, where they are cited as accompaniment to every action and form the body of precedent and direction in the Africans' highly developed legal systems. Many African peoples could say like the Chaga, "we have four big possessions: land, cattle, water, and proverbs" (Raum: 217).

Proverbial style reflects the cultural *Gestalt*. Africa's teeming animal life is evidenced throughout African culture, but nowhere better than in proverbs: "When a man is away, the monkey eats the maize"; "never sow ground-nuts when the monkey is watching"; "As long as life lasts, the cow never ceases to move its tail"; "A horse has four legs, yet it often falls"; "You have tied a bone around the dog's throat" (you have sent a child to the store for candy); "No horse bargains for itself" (reflecting the courtship customs in which a prospective bride is approached through her guardian); these and others are cited by Abraham (64) as examples of the Tiv's animal-oriented culture. The greater attention to close observation among Oriental peoples gives them proverbs that are either weakly or not at all echoed by our own blunter maxims: "The man who had his face slapped in Tonjagi waits till he gets to Subingo before he makes faces at his insulter"; "You cannot sit in the valley and see the new moon set"; "Even the hedgehog says her young are smooth"; "The blind man stole his own hen and ate it"; "Where there are no tigers, wild-cats will be very self-important"; "He pours instruction into a cow's ear"—all these which Hulbert found in Korea will surprise the American veteran who saw these people as inarticulate "gooks." The Koreans, too, illustrate the Oriental tendency to see beauty even in ugliness: "What looked like blossoms on the dead tree turned out to be only the white mould of decay."

Proverbs are so commonly tied to unique cultural characteristics that their value as guides to behavior often ends at their culture's frontier. "One must not point out the male of the guinea fowl" seems clearly enough to warn against over-extending one's perception, but to the Thonga it means "Don't count your chickens before they are hatched" (Junod: 177). Samoan *arii* (aristocratic) proverbs are the distillation of 60 generations of nobility and so many are unintelligible to the Euramerican and unusable by the Samoan commoner ("Accept trouble as an Arii Nui"; "You will eat of the chest and filet of the boar"), though some are plain talk for any ruler: "The people are like a crying child, easily coaxed with gentle words, easily enraged by ill treatment"; "An Arii's anger must be like the wind Maraamu, not heard but felt"; "Mediate before speaking; your words are flashes of lightning, as mighty as the clap of thunder; they cannot be recalled" (Handy 1930a: 39 ff). The Samoans' most highly developed endeavor is oratory, and the essence of their oratory is proverbs. Schultz, who studied this aspect of Samoan life and literature thoroughly, found that *muagagana* ("embellishment of the language, elevated style") fall into twelve categories:

1. Expressions of respect and courtesy
2. Respect and courtesy in form of self-abasement
3. Laudatory and complimentary remarks
4. Expressions of joy and contentment
5. Expressions of love, compassion, and sympathy
6. Expressions of repentance and remorse
7. Raillery, ridicule, and jests
8. Offensive expressions and insults
9. Encouragement and persuasion
10. Comforting, consolatory expressions
11. Warning, exhortation, appeasement
12. Denial, refusal

Samoan oratory is so highly developed that, like modern poetry, its allusions are quite unintelligible to the uninitiated. "E gase a uluga" is no clearer to us in translation: "The dying of a pair of birds," but to the educated Samoan audience the expression, Schultz explains (141), has this meaning:

> The feathers of certain birds, *e.g.*, the tava'e or tropic bird, are attached to the fish-hook to serve as artificial bait.

Before the introduction of firearms, this bird was caught in
the following way: The hunter searched for a nest with
young and climbed up to it. With a thread pulled through
the young bird's nostrils, he tied up the fledgling's bill in such
a way that it was still able to cry but not to swallow. When
the parents returned they were so terrified at the young one's
inability to eat, that they left all caution aside and could be
caught easily. The Samoans maintain that if the parents
were left undisturbed, they would remain with their young
and allow themselves to starve to death.

So "E gase a uluga" in a speech was *upa alofa*—an expression of love,
compassion, and sympathy.

In Africa proverbs infiltrate not only other forms of art (as for
example wood carving), but the most mundane circumstances of life.
Rattray (223) describes the "proverb weights" used by the Ashanti
to weigh gold, which are inscribed with symbols suggesting, as a
cynic might suspect among such sharp businessmen, several equally
applicable proverbs. Since the design affects the weight, this must
be the most profitable employment of proverbs in the world, as the
goldsmiths admit in the proverbs: "A chief's weights are not the
same as a poor man's weights"; "the bird caught in the trap is the
one to sing sweetly"; "The beetle has fallen among the fowls"; and,
most apt of all, "A man does not rub bottoms with a porcupine."

RIDDLES

The riddle is the reverse of the proverb's coin. Their distribution,
incidence, and development are much the same,* and the main
difference between them is that the riddle requires some form of
dialogue and its purpose is more frankly entertainment—though
these distinctions are a matter of degree. The didactic element is
never wholly lacking, and Thomas Rhys Williams argues strenu-
ously that anthropologists are in error in not assigning primary function to riddles—and, indeed, to other forms of literature. As for the

---

* Archer Taylor critically examined the allegation that the riddle is not found
among the American Indians, the Chinese, and the Hebrews, and concluded that the
American Indians are the only people who did not have the riddle aboriginally, and
even here, as in the case of the proverb, the lack is not entirely proved. Charles T.
Scott in the *Journal of American Folklore*, July-September, 1963 (76: 301) offers
"New Evidence of American Indian Riddles," which as the latest positive word on
the subject actually weakens rather than strengthens the case for pre-Columbian
Indian riddles. The Australian aborigines are also held by some to have been utterly
without riddles. Though the form is not frequent in Australia, it is not entirely absent.
Mrs. Langloh Parker quotes several in her book, *The Euahlayi Tribe*, 132–133.

form of riddles as opposed to that of proverbs, the riddle can also be stated in question-and-answer pattern (Raum: 218).

Riddle scholarship is almost as ancient as myth scholarship; Aristotle, for instance, pointed out a fact still little appreciated, that the riddle is closely related to the metaphor. The ancient attention to riddles may be accounted for by the antiquity of riddles themselves (Frazer had part of the truth at least when he suggested that they might have grown out of situations in which certain words were tabu; Williams shows that for the Dusun of North Borneo riddles may reveal a situation that it is inexpedient to talk about explicitly, thus placing the riddle in function among ridicule and contention literature) and by the fact that the riddle is inherently and by definition a mystery.

In view of the long history of riddling and riddle analysis, it is hard to account for the generally poor methodology and scholarship in contemporary riddle collection. There is hardly a folklorist or anthropologist who tries to extract from a collection even their literary principles.

There are exceptions. Georges and Dundes are attempting to apply the method of structural folklore to riddles, but since their approach requires the use of such classifications as "the privational contradictive opposition," the prognosis of popularity for their method is not good. Their work so far is only theoretical; Bascom's analysis of Yoruba riddles (1949) offers a working example of how riddles can be systematically described. "Of the many forms of folklore," he says, "riddles might seem to offer the fewest possibilities of stylistic variation, yet they illustrated this variation perhaps more clearly than any other form. Riddles, essentially, are briefly stated questions whose answers are to be guessed by the listener, but an interrogation is neither the 'natural' nor the obvious form of statement" (1). He goes on to illustrate 29 formulas used in 55 riddles. The simplest is "Who is X that a?" ("Who is it that drinks maize beer with the king? The fly"); the most complex is "Ya,X; YaX, Xb; ZaX, Xb" ("Ancient well of my father, ancient well of my father; if a child gets into it, it reaches his neck; if an elder gets into it, it reaches his neck. A shirt").* It might be said in defense of the less analytical folklorists that only African riddles (like the African proverbs) have evolved to such complexity, and even in Africa the very common characteristic of riddles—lack of imagina-

---

* An unusual feature of riddles among the Chaga of the Kenya highlands is that those which are recited to warn someone of an imminent but avoidable unpleasant eventuality are sung (Raum: 221).

tion—makes them the dullest form of literature and as offensive to
the artistic sensibility as the pun. Only a Nuer could find anything
clever or entertaining in

> Guess what is a red hornless cow but its horns are of skin?
> It is a dog (Huffman: 104)

or an Mbundu in

> There is a red belt around our field. What is it?
> Red ants (Hambly: 253)

Even the normally reliable Chinese nod when it comes to riddling:

> With a peaked jaw and black coat, here a rive and there a
> bite; when the trouble has been stirred up you make a jump
> and clear out.
> The louse (Hutson: 49)*

Like other forms of literature, the riddle is often a microcosm
of the culture that produced it. The life of the Todas of the Nilgiri
hills of South India is oriented around milk and milking. Typical
riddles collected among these "holy milkmen" by Rivers (599) show
this preoccupation:

> What is it that gives milk without an udder, what is it that
> drinks without a mouth?
> Rain, earth.

> What is it that goes into a village without an udder, what is
> it that goes into the forest without a leg?
> Hen, snake.

The Mexican national character has been called by many impartial
observers, both Mexican and foreign, almost pathologically morbid
(Hewes; see also Chapter Five). Much evidence has been assembled
to prove this trait, to which we can add these riddles as found by
Redfield in the Yucatecan town of Dzitas (49):

> El que la teje, la teje cantando; el que la compra, la compra
> llorando; y el que la ha de comprar nunca la puede menestar
> (He who weaves it, weaves it singing; he who buys it, buys it
> weeping; and he who has to buy it never needs it"—a
> shroud).

---

*In fairness it must be acknowledged that Hutson collected from the same people
this admirable vignette:
> On his head he wears a red button, his body is clothed with a white robe,
> his walk is like an elegant scholar's, but his talk is like a barbarian's.
> The goose.

The Dzitas Indians see death even in a cow; taking the familiar English cow-riddle, "Four stiff standers, four dilly-danders, two lookers, two hookers, and a wig-wag," they make of it

Cuatro pacapacas, dos miradores, dos matagente, y una matamosca (Four stampers, two lookers, two man-killers, and one fly-killer).

Chapter Three / TRICKSTERS, TAR BABIES, & OTHER HEROES

The small child who night after night watches "Popeye the Sailor Man" to see Brutus pursue Olive Oyl across the television screen until that lady's dull witted suitor fortifies himself with canned spinach and rescues her with fisticuffs is not at all concerned with literary forms, not even to the extent of perceiving a fundamental difference between animated cartoons and reality until his harassed parents suggest that there is an element of unreality in the story and characters. If they learned in college literature classes that growing sophistication moves the adult reader from an interest in plot through an evolution of discrimination to an interest in theme, the parents are likely to conclude that it is the story that fascinates their child, unless they watch along with him for a few evenings and discover that one Popeye cartoon is as much like another as one basketball game is like another. The child actually derives his first literary pleasure from the comfortable recognition of familiar characters performing familiar events, and for them to criticize the events and the characters as being foolishly incredible is incompetent, immaterial, and irrelevant. Ontogeny recapitulates phylogeny in literary as well as biological evolution, at least so far as narrative for entertainment is considered, and in this area of literature the primitive is as innocent and unsophisticated as the child. Let us hasten to say that there is nothing biological about this; it is a question of literary sophistication. The bottom would drop out of the comic book market if free, white, Protestant American adults suddenly stopped reading them. The primitive may have the intellectual capabilities of reading and understanding Kafka, but it is a fact that he does not. His chief interest is not in theme or form or plot, as we define these things, but in familiar characters; he exercises no discrimination among the comfortable friends of his literature. To the child, Bugs Bunny needs no more reason for being than Edward R. Murrow; to the primitive, Tar Baby needs no more reason for being than his deified grandfather. It may be that the Tar Baby and the grandfather may both owe their existence in his literature to a brawl between their inventor's id and superego, a totemistic rationalization, a sublimated incest cathexis, or a piece of undigested pork, but to him any such explanations are as incompetent, immaterial, and irrelevant as criticisms of their literary elevation. He may not know anything about psychology or the New Critics, but he knows what he likes.

TRICKSTER

The student of American civilization dismisses the Travelling Salesman as an uncouth and obscene anomaly now razed along with the outhouses and farmers' rear bedrooms where he carried on his scatological and amatory exploits; the student may suspect that a few Travelling Salesmen survived the general destruction and are now carrying on in discreet airport motels disguised in Brooks Brothers suits, but unless he has studied folklore, he has no suspicion that the Travelling Salesman is one of the most familiar characters in world literature, and, after Satan (to whose creation he probably contributed), the most artful shape-shifter. He has an ancient if not honorable ancestry, going back to the oldest written story in the world, the Gilgamesh epic, first inscribed on clay tablets in Mesopotamia 5000 years ago (Gaster: 21–43); Gilgamesh was probably the direct ancestor of Hercules and Mercury and the myriad satyrs in Greece, and later, in the medieval period, became historical as the court jesters. Among the North American Indians he was Coyote, Raven, Mink, Old Man, Sitkonski, Nihansan, Inkotomi, Finished Man, Rabbit, Hare, Nanabozho, and Wisakedjak, to name only his most common forms. He came to this continent again on the slave ships, and set up existence as Compair Lapin, 'Ti Malice, and B'rer Rabbit. There is no form he may not take; among the Apinaye of South America he was the Moon. But wherever and whatever he is, a drummer for Dr. Mundy's Soothing Syrup along Tobacco Road or Maui-tikitiki-a-Taranga in Polynesia, he is the Trickster.

It is inaccurate to call him a "trickster," for this implies intelligence and cleverness; Trickster usually does not play wilful tricks, but blunders into situations that often result in his being rudely discomfited. He is cunning, but that is different from being clever; and he has other bad qualities as well. In fact, to understand his place and purpose, one should know that he has all the bad qualities —both those of deficiencies, like stupidity, and disposition, like cruelty and vanity. To describe him further would be to engage in scandalous name calling; but the stories that follow will make his character clear enough.

Trickster is interesting not only to people who like dirty stories but to anthropologists concerned with the problem of diffusion and polygenesis, which we will look into more thoroughly in Chapter Six. His character and exploits are so nearly identical in all parts of the primitive world that Trickster tales wherever found seem like different variants of the same story, and yet they come from such widely separated places that diffusion or borrowing seems impossible. Consider as an example the motif of the "Buttocks Watcher" in the Wakjunkaga cycle collected by Paul Radin (1956: 16–17) among the Wisconsin Winnebago. In this episode Trickster has just killed and roasted several ducks.

> "I will wait for them to be cooked," he said to himself. "I had, however, better go to sleep now. By the time I awake they will unquestionably be thoroughly done. Now, you, my younger brother, must keep watch for me while I go to sleep. If you notice any people, drive them off." He was talking to his anus. Then, turning his anus toward the fire, he went to sleep.
>
> When he was sleeping some small foxes approached and, as they ran along, they scented something that seemed like fire. "Well, there must be something here," they said. So they turned their noses toward the wind and looked, and, after a while, truly enough, they saw the smoke of a fire. So they peered around carefully and soon noticed many sharp-pointed sticks arranged around a fire with meat on them. Stealthily they approached nearer and nearer and, scrutinizing everything carefully, they noticed someone asleep there. "It is Trickster and he is asleep! Let us eat this meat. But we must be very careful not to wake him up. Come, let us eat," they said to one another. When they came close, much to their surprise, however, gas was expelled from somewhere. "Pooh!" such was the sound made. "Be careful! He must be awake." So they ran back. After a while one of them said, "Well, I guess he is asleep now. That was only a bluff. He is always up to some tricks." So again they approached the fire. Again gas was expelled and again they ran back. Three times this happened. When they approached the fourth time gas was again expelled. However, they did not run away. So Trickster's anus, in rapid succession, began to expel more and more gas. Still they did not

run away. Once, twice, three times it expelled gas in rapid
succession. "Pooh! Pooh!" Such was the sound it made. Yet
they did not run away. On the contrary, they now began to
eat the roasted pieces of duck. As they were eating, the
Trickster's anus continued its "Pooh" incessantly. There the
foxes stayed until they had eaten up all the pieces that were
being roasted under ashes and, in spite of the fact that the
anus was expelling gas, "Pooh! Pooh! Pooh! Pooh!" continuously, they ate all these up too. Then they replaced the
pieces with the meat eaten off, nicely under the ashes. Only
after that did they go away.

The Trobriand Islanders are halfway around the world from the
Winnebago; no contact between these societies can possibly be imagined, unless we construct a continent in the Pacific Ocean like
Churchward's Mu to facilitate their passage, and even thus ac-
comodated, they would have a long walk. Although the Trobriand
character in the story following is female, the watcher her clitoris,
the predator a cockatoo, and the food yams and pigs, these are minor
adaptations of the theme; the problem still remains: how did this
similarity of a complex type come about?

The White Cockatoo and the Clitoris (Malinowski, 1929: 408–409)

A woman named Karawara gave birth to a white cockatoo,
who flew away into the bush. One day Karawata went to
the garden, telling her *kasesa* (clitoris) to look after the
kumkumuri (earth baking oven). The *kasesa* replies confidently: *Kekekeke*. But the white cockatoo has seen
everything from the bush; he swoops down and strikes the
clitoris, who cries out plaintively: *Kikikiki*, and topples
over, while the cockatoo eats the contents of the oven.
(It is necessary to imagine the big, flat mound-like earth
oven, the tiny clitoris standing on guard, and the cruel
white cockatoo watching sardonically for its chance. The
absurdity of the situation appeals to the natives' sense of
the ludicrous.)

Next day, Karawata says again to her *kasesa:* "Let us
catch pig, get some yams, and bake it all in the earth."
Again she takes off her *kasesa*, and leaves it to look after the
oven, and the *kasesa* says confidently as before, *Kekekeke*.
Again the white cockatoo descends from the branch, strikes
the *kasesa*, who, with a plaintive *kikikiki*, topples over; and

again the cockatoo eats the contents of the oven. Next day the woman says, "I shall go to the garden and you look properly after the food." *Kekekeke*, answers the *kasesa*, but all that happened on the two previous days is repeated, and Karawata and her *kasesa* die of hunger.

Despite the lameness of Malinowski's translation which robs this tale of its immediacy, the similarity is striking enough to pose a distributional problem without considering other Trickster adventures. But it is not an isolated parallel; Trickster finds identical exploits of various kinds all over the world. Katherine Luomala (1940) studied the Snaring the Sun motif in Oceania (Polynesia, Micronesia, and Melanesia), North America (Eastern Cree, Tête de Boule, Lake Superior Ojibwa, Menominee, Grand Lake Victoria, Timagami Ojibwa, Montagnais, Fox, Bungi, Assiniboine, Mandan-Hidatsa, Omaha, Iowa, Mackenzie, and Yurok), and Africa (West Africa between the southwest Sudan and the Kasai district of the Congo). Conflating the 26 American variants, Luomala gave this type synopsis:

> The hero is an orphan called Tchkabech who lives with his sister. He is a little boy or pygmy. The sun scorched his cloak as he fasted or lay on a sun trail. In the sky to which he climbed on a magic tree he set a snare of his sister's hair to catch the sun. He told his sister of his deed, or she suspected him when darkness covered the earth. The hero, sometimes aided by animals, failed to free the sun. At last a rodent gnawed the snare and released the sun. The animal received its present peculiarities as the result of its efforts.

Despite the overemphasis given the Polynesian sun deity, Ra, by those who like to trace him back to the Egyptian Ra (the words are pronounced differently), the sun is a minor figure in Oceanic mythology, but the Trickster Maui found time to snare it. The conflate myth is expectedly simpler than in North America:

> Maui decided to snare the sun which went so fast that food could not be cooked before darkness. He went alone to the eastern horizon where the sun rose from its underworld pit and snared the sun. Ordinary ropes proved unsatisfactory but those made of hair held the sun. Maui abused the sun until it was forced to go more slowly ever after.

This myth is so similar all over Polynesia that diffusion is certainly the explanation for its presence. Every island group except Samoa has Maui as the hero; every island group has the complaint that the sun moves too fast; almost every archipelago has the complaint that food was raw because of the short hours of sunlight; and that Maui snared the sun at its underworld source. Where there are deviations from the type tale, they can be accounted for by the interference of stronger forces; the hair rope is absent from New Zealand, Buck argued, because the tabus against use of hair were especially strong there.

In Africa the tale is differently motivated:

> A woman caught a white ram which ate gleanings from her millstone. She told her husband. Endless night followed. Oracle said someone caught a white ram. The couple confessed, released the white ram, and the sun climbed back into the sky.

These are conflations, drawn out of the common stock of elements. When some of the subsidiary motifs are examined, the question of diffusion versus polygenesis is more difficult than ever to resolve. Luomala shows that the curious practice of dilatory travellers retarding the sun by placing a stone in the fork of a tree is known in North Africa, the Transvaal, South Africa, Yucatan, and Australia.

Of all primitive narratives, Trickster tales are most offensive to Euramerican readers because of his habit of committing unnatural sexual acts and wallowing in excrement. Possibly because of our sensitivity on these themes, Trickster's coprophilia and satyromania strike us as his chief identifying characteristics. Primitive peoples, living somewhat closer to nature, are less dainty about these things. One of the most popular Trickster tales among the North American Indians is that of his unfortunate adventure with the laxative bulb. Radin tells it more delicately than most collectors (1956: 25):

> As he went wandering around aimlessly he suddenly heard someone speaking. He listened very carefully and it seemed to say, "He who chews me will defecate!" That was what it was saying. "Well, why is this person talking in this manner?" said Trickster. So he walked in the direction from which he had heard the speaking and again he heard, quite near him, someone saying, "He who chews me, he will defecate; he will defecate!" That is what was said. "Well, why does this person talk in such a fashion?" said Trickster. Then he walked to the other side. So he continued walking

along. Then right at his very side, a voice seemed to say,
"He who chews me, he will defecate; he will defecate!"
"Well, I wonder who it is who is speaking. I know very well
that if I chew it, I will not defecate!" But he kept looking
around for the speaker and finally discovered, much to his
astonishment, that it was a bulb on a bush. The bulb it was
that was speaking. So he seized it, put it in his mouth,
chewed it, and then swallowed it. He did just this and
then went on.

"Well, where is the bulb that talked so much? Why, indeed should I defecate? When I feel like defecating, then
I shall defecate, no sooner. How could such an object make
me defecate!" Thus spoke Trickster. Even as he spoke,
however, he began to break wind. "Well this, I suppose, is
what it meant. Yet the bulb said I would defecate, and I
am merely expelling gas. In any case I am a great man
even if I do expel a little gas!" Thus he spoke. As he was
talking he again broke wind. This time it was really quite
strong. "Well, what a foolish one I am. This is why I am
called Foolish One, Trickster." Now he began to break
wind again and again. "So this is why the bulb spoke as
it did, I suppose." Once more he broke wind. This time
it was very loud and his rectum began to smart. "Well, it
surely is a great thing!" Then he broke wind again, this
time with so much force, that he was propelled forward.
"Well, well, it may even make me give another push, but it
won't make me defecate," so he exclaimed defiantly. The
next time he broke wind, the hind part of his body was
raised up by the force of the explosion and he landed on
his knees and hands. "Well, go ahead and do it again! Go
ahead and do it again!" Then, again, he broke wind. This
time the force of the expulsion sent him far up in the air
and he landed on the ground, on his stomach. The next
time he broke wind, he had to hang on to a log, so high was
he thrown. However, he raised himself up, and, after a
while, landed on the ground, the log on top of him. He was
almost killed by the fall. The next time he broke wind, he
had to hold on to a tree that stood near by. It was a poplar
and he held on with all his might yet, nevertheless, even then,
his feet flopped up in the air. Again, for the second time,
he held on to it when he broke wind and yet he pulled the

tree up by the roots. To protect himself, the next time, he went on until he came to a large tree, a large oak tree. Around this he put both his arms. Yet, when he broke wind, he was swung up and his toes struck against the tree. However, he held on.

After that he ran to a place where people were living. When he got there, he shouted, "Say, hurry up and take your lodge down, for a big war party is upon you and you will surely be killed! Come let us get away!" He scared them all so much that they quickly took down their lodge, piled it on Trickster, and then got on him themselves. They likewise placed all the little dogs they had on top of Trickster. Just then he began to break wind again and the force of the expulsion scattered the things on top of him in all directions. They fell apart from one another. Separated, the people were standing about and shouting to one another; and the dogs, scattered here and there, howled at one another. There stood Trickster laughing at them till he ached.

Now he proceeded onward. He seemed to have gotten over his troubles. "Well, this bulb did a lot of talking," he said to himself, "yet it could not make me defecate." But even as he spoke he began to have the desire to defecate, just a very little. "Well, I suppose this is what it meant. It certainly bragged a good deal, however." As he spoke he defecated again. "Well, what a braggart it was! I suppose this is why it said this." As he spoke these last words, he began to defecate a good deal. After a while, as he was sitting down, his body would touch the excrement. Thereupon he got on top of a log and sat down there, but, even then he touched the excrement. Finally, he climbed up a log that was leaning against a tree. However, his body still touched the excrement, so he went up higher. Even then, however, he touched it so he climbed still higher up. Higher and higher he had to go. Nor was he able to stop defecating. Now he was on top of the tree. It was small and quite uncomfortable. Moreover, the excrement began to come up to him.

Even on the limb on which he was sitting he began to defecate. So he tried a different position. Since the limb, however, was very slippery he fell right down into the ex-

crement. Down he fell, down into the dung. In fact he
disappeared in it, and it was only with very great difficulty
that he was able to get out of it. His raccoon-skin blanket
was covered with filth, and he came out dragging it after
him. The pack he was carrying on his back was covered
with dung, as was also the box containing his penis. The
box he emptied and then placed it on his back again.

Radin collected this tale among the Winnebago Indians of Wisconsin, and if it were peculiar to this tribe, its odiousness could be
accounted for by the alleged odiousness of the Winnebago themselves. Captain Frederick Marryat, who visited them nearly a hundred and twenty five years ago—before they were further besmirched
by white contact—said in his *Diary in America*, the "Winnebago are
considered the dirtiest race of Indians, and with the worst qualities;
they were formerly designated by the French *puans*, a term sufficiently explanatory." The English colonists referred to the Winnebago as "Stinkards," and their own neighbors, the Sauk and Fox,
called them "People of the Filthy Water." No Indians, for that
matter, received any citations for cleanliness, but there were some
tribes that did not actually nauseate European visitors, and these,
too, had tales as nasty as this. An equally coarse use of his anus
was attributed to Bamapama, the Trickster in northern Australia.
As voracious as his American cousin, Bamapama (masquerading as
Ure) surprises two men cooking a turtle. He eats the turtle, its shell,
its excrement, the campfire, the earth oven, and the two men. The
men's companions, attracted by the sound of Bamapama defecating,
start a bush fire to burn him.

> Ure heard them. He raised his buttocks and put his
> hands on his knees and looked back. He defecated as though
> he were throwing spears at them, for he was trying to put
> the fire out. He turned his anus around and around, firing
> at them to prevent the fire from getting to him, but it was
> no use. He could not. Even though he made a wall of
> defecation about him, higher and higher, it was no use.
> The fire came on and on (Warner: 559).

But the Australian aborigines, too, made a poor impression upon
European travellers. Nearly three centuries ago the gentleman
pirate William Dampier wrote the first description made by the outside world of these hapless people, concluding "They all of them
have the most unpleasant Looks and the worst Features of any

People that ever I saw, though I have seen great Variety of Savages."

Though Americans have the reputation in Europe of being nearly out of their minds on the subject of personal cleanliness, we have some inelegant stories. We disapprove of them in our printed literature, but they circulate freely as oral tales—among the male population at least. And our attitudes toward the Travelling Salesman and his alter egos are the same as those of primitive people toward their Trickster: he is outrageously funny, so long as he remains fictitious. Warner (545) says that Bampama tales "always elicit gales of laughter and make the Trickster a figure of derision; at the same time he is liked as an amusing fellow." But in real life the Murngin have a different view of "crazy fellows"—any such habitually asocial person who cannot be disciplined is called *wakinu* —"all the same as Bamapama"—and is either killed by his own tribe or taken out of tribal territory so that the execution can be carried out indirectly at the hands of the tribe's enemies. Similarly, the American Indians are convulsed by Trickster's adventures and may even admire his cunning, but one would be ill-advised to emulate his behavior.

The universal distribution of Trickster stories, the ambivalent attitude toward him, and his flaunting of the mores that preserve the social group have intrigued folklorists with a psychological bent. Victor Barnouw made an intensive analysis of the cycle of Trickster (Wenebojo) stores among the Chippewa (Ojibwa) which his informant, an old Midewiwin priest, remembered in this order:

1. The sun impregnates a girl.
2. The girl gives birth to triplets (Wenebojo and two brothers)
3. Wenebojo kills his stone brother
4. Wenebojo causes his second brother's death
5. Wenebojo's brother makes the road to the other world
6. Wenebojo discovers a laxative
7. Wenebojo assumes the form of a beaver
8. Wenebojo turns his intestines into food
9. Wenebojo kills a moose, but does not eat the meat (the meat is stolen by wolves)
10. Wenebojo gets his head caught in the moose's skull
11. Wenebojo dances with the rushes
12. Wenebojo tricks the water birds and kills some
13. Wenebojo punishes his rear end and creates tobacco.
14. Wenebojo joins a pack of wolves
15. Wenebojo quarrels with the wolves

16. Wenebojo's wolf nephew is killed by the underwater spirits
17. Wenebojo wounds the two underwater kings
18. Wenebojo curses the kingfisher
19. Wenebojo kills the mother of the two kings
20. Wenebojo kills the two kings
21. Wenebojo escapes drowning
22. Wenebojo creates the earth
23. Wenebojo becomes depressed and threatens all the spirits
24. The spirits try to appease Wenebojo
25. The spirits give Wenebojo some parents and establish the medicine dance

Psychological interpretation is all the rage at this moment in anthropological history, and this might be an opportune place to look at the method in action and to suggest respectfully a few cautions in its use for the comfort of those older folklorists who are not entirely convinced of its validity.

Barnouw's approach was to draw deductions from the cycle by three elements—qualities, symbols, and themes—and then to apply these to actual Ojibwa behavior for what agreement or correlation could be established. He abandoned the approach of "qualities" (such things as colors and sounds) since it proved sterile in analysis. Symbols were more rewarding, for symbols after all are as essential to psychologists as spines are to chiropractors. Snakes abounded in the stories, all of them obvious phallic symbols. Trees were even more plentiful and more significant, since they are by nature ithyphallic: "As Ferenczi puts it, 'Originally penis and tree, penis and church-steeple, were consciously equated; but only with the repression of interest in the penis does the tree and the church steeple become invested with inexplicable and apparently ungrounded interest; they become penis symbols" (Barnouw: 353–352).

Writing this in a journal of folklore, Barnouw was conscious of the fact that some of his readers accused psychologists of calling anything longer than it is wide a phallic symbol; he subsequently dropped this element also, saying "the interpretation of *Symbols* is so full of difficulties that some will think it best to discard this method of approach altogether (355). But themes were productive. Duplicity and deception stood out (as they do in all Trickster stories). Barnouw saw oral frustration in Trickster's conduct as indicative of chronic food scarcity among the Ojibwa, a theme reinforced by other tales dealing with cannibalistic *windigos* and children being deprived of milk. Anal themes, it need scarcely be mentioned, were frequent, and these he interpreted as punishment of the rectum, citing evidence that the Ojibwa often complained of constipation; moreover, "the theme of penetration of the rectum may also be related to paranoid fears or unconscious desires" (345). Sexual themes were astonishingly few, though Barnouw did not give any significance to the fact that his informant was seventy years old. Examining these and other themes (aggression, sadism, masochism, etc.) he summed up:

> We get the impression that Chippewa culture fostered an emotionally isolated kind of personality. Social ties were weak and uncertain. Relationships between men and women were lacking in warmth and affection, and the dependency needs of children were not satisfied. The isolated individual anticipated emotional frustration and hostility, so that he became wary and developed paranoid or pseudoparanoid fears of persecution. Ties between men were stronger than those between men and women, but homosexual relations were tabooed and homosexual tendencies were a source of anxiety. Constipation may have been a psychosomatic response to the tense social atmosphere. The anal zone, at any rate, became a focus of attention, and some patterns of the "anal" character developed, particularly a suspicious and "retentive" attitude toward others. This was combined with undercurrent cravings for oral satisfaction and dependency. Such needs, however, generally encountered frustration so that aggressive feelings were generated. These hostile impulses were checked as much as possible, due to fears of retaliation and retribution; but they occasionally broke forth, evoking further repercussions of fear and anxiety (353).

The trouble with this brilliant and plausible analysis is that these personality traits would have to be attributed to the bulk of mankind, since they are universal characteristics of Trickster stories— and Barnouw's analysis requires that they be restricted to the Ojibwa.

Paul Radin's exegesis of the Winnebago Trickster cycle is even more impressive. Radin was a scholar who wrote well on many subjects, but toward the end of his life he became almost obsessively preoccupied with Winnebago psychology, as we shall see in a moment.

In 1912 he collected from Sam Blowsnake, a fullblood Winnebago
Thunderbird, the Trickster cycle composed of the following episodes,
which again are useful to have because they further delineate the
character of the Trickster:

1. Trickster cohabits with woman before war party
2. Trickster wishes to go on warpath alone
3. Trickster discourages his followers from accompanying him
    on warpath
4. Trickster kills buffalo
5. Trickster makes his right arm fight his left
6. Trickster borrows two children from his younger brother
7. Children die because Trickster breaks rules
8. Father of children pursues Trickster
9. Trickster swims in ocean inquiring where shore is
10. Trickster catches fish
11. Trickster mimics man pointing
12. Dancing ducks and talking anus
13. Foxes eat roasted ducks
14. Trickster burns anus and eats his own intestines
15. Penis placed in box
16. Penis sent across water
17. Trickster carried by giant bird
18. Women rescue Trickster
19. Trickster and companions decide where to live
20. Changes into woman, Trickster marries chief's son
21. Last child of union cries and is pacified
22. Trickster visits wife and son
23. Trickster and the laxative bulb
24. Trickster falls in his own excrement
25. Trees mislead Trickster in finding water
26. Trickster mistakes plums reflected in water for plums on tree
27. Mothers seek plums while Trickster eats children
28. Skunk persuaded by Trickster to dig hole through hill
29. Mothers lured in hole by Trickster and eaten
30. Tree teases Trickster, who gets held fast in fork
31. Wolves come and eat Trickster's food under tree
32. Flies in elk's skull lure Trickster, who gets caught in elk's
    skull
33. People split elk's skull off
34. Trickster changes self into deer to take revenge on hawk
35. Bear lured to his death by Trickster

36. Mink outwits Trickster and gets bear meat
37. Trickster pursues mink in vain
38. Chipmunk causes Trickster to lose part of his penis
39. Discarded pieces of penis thrown into lake and turn into plants
40. Coyote leads Trickster to village
41. Trickster imitates muskrat who turns ice into lily-of-the-valley roots
42. Trickster imitates snipe's method of fishing
43. Trickster imitates woodpecker's way of getting bear
44. Trickster imitates pole-cat in getting deer
45. Mink soils chief's daughter as Trickster planned
46. Coyote is duped into being tied to horse's tail
47. Trickster removes obstacles on the Mississippi
48. Waterfall is forced to fall on land by Trickster
49. Trickster eats final meal on earth and retires to heaven

There is some question about the chronological rigidity of the order of these episodes, but since this order is essential to Radin's explanation, no discussion of the explanation can be made without its acceptance. It is further necessary to accept his premise that there is method in both the order and the episodes, built in during the Winnebago Dreaming by a law-giver whose identity has been totally lost, but whose wisdom continues across the years to direct his posterity's behavior by acting upon its subconscious. Thus, Radin maintained, the initial episodes are psychologically placed to shock the Indian audience into a receptive attitude for the lesson that the entire cycle teaches, for nothing that follows, however repulsive it may seem to us, has nearly the effect of outrage upon the Winnebago as the behavior of Trickster here: his violation, as a chief, of the strict prohibition against chiefs' participation in war; his equally fundamental infraction of the rules by engaging in sexual intercourse before going on a war party; and his illegal enterprise of taking war into his own hands. The completely amoral and asocial nature of Trickster is reiterated in the next half-dozen episodes as he compounds his irresponsibility. In the fifth exploit "he is still living in his unconscious, mentally a child, and this is here symbolized by the struggle between his right and left hands in which his left hand is badly cut up." Episode nine finds him "completely unanchored . . . not only isolated from man and society, but—temporarily at least—from the world of nature and from the universe as well. However, there is also another point involved here. Being frightened is, in Winnebago symbolism, generally the indication of an awakening

consciousness and sense of reality, indeed, the beginning of a conscience," which Trickster admits by self-revulsion, not typical of
him: "Yes indeed . . . it is on this account that the people call me
Wakdjunkaga, the foolish one! They are right." Radin sees Trickster evolving subtly in the succeeding five episodes: ". . . for the
first time we are made aware of his sexuality. . . . If . . . it is not
mentioned until now, this is because the author or authors who gave
this cycle its present shape wished to give us not a series of Trickster's adventures as such but the evolution of a Trickster from an
undefined being to one with the physiognomy of man . . . ," though
he is unable to account satisfactorily for Episode 20, where Trickster
becomes a woman: "We have here reached a point where ordinary
words and terms are indeed completely inadequate. Only symbols,
only metaphors, can convey the meaning properly." All this business of snaking his penis across the water, scorching his anus, devour-
ing his own intestines, and changing his sex is a bit unsettling to
Trickster and, says Radin, shocks him into acting like a "good
citizen, as a thoroughly socialized individual," as well it might for
any of us. But then he has another, rather more literally, unsettling
experience with the laxative bulb which also unsettles the exegesis,
for, Radin admits, "from a literary and psychological point of view
our myth-cycle breaks down after the incident 26"—or about halfway through the lesson, which argues a certain inability of the
teacher to communicate effectively or a certain dullness on the part
of his Winnebago students. Dull the students certainly were, for
Radin, probing the Indians' own interpretation of the cycle, elicited
the admission that Trickster was a rascal, surely enough, "yet one
thing he never did: he never went on the warpath, he never waged
war"—an interesting statement in view of that impressing opening
episode. Barnouw's Indians were as obtuse as Radin's or Fenimore
Cooper's—their confusion began immediately at the beginning (78):

> The story that I'm going to tell you won't be about this
> earth. It will be about a different world. There were only
> two people living in this other world: an old lady and her
> daughter.
>
> Look how this world looks around us—trees, flowers, and
> everything. In this other world there was only grass and
> bushes, no timber.
>
> The old lady's daughter used to go every day into the
> woods . . . .

However plausible either may be alone, Barnouw's and Radin's interpretations are mutually incompatible. The validity of Barnouw's explanation depends on the uniqueness of the Trickster cycle, Radin's upon its commonness. Internally, the sexual symbolism supporting Radin's exegesis collapses in Barnouw's, which has none of the typical Trickster adventures in venery. To accept either interpretation, we must accept either of two absurd alternatives: that the human subconscious is incomparably more perceptive than the human conscious mind, or that there existed in the distant Dreaming a higher species of the genus *Homo* that invented the Trickster episodes as a communicative vehicle for ideas utterly beyond the conscious apprehension of its human descendants, red and white alike. Radin states the latter case explicitly in his 1948 analysis: "What were the remote ancestors of the Winnebago trying to convey to us . . . ?" Both alternatives violate a fundamental biological law, the irreversibility of evolution, to say nothing worse about them.

But worse can be said about these and similar depth interpretations of the myths of primitive peoples. Barnouw and Radin are simple—like Edgar A. Guest interpreting Ella Wheeler Wilcox—compared to Claude Lévi-Strauss' three-dimensional structural study of myth. Lévi-Strauss' approach is impossible to summarize, since it deals not only in a three-dimensional view of the material but applies to it formulae like f_x (a): $^f y$ (b) — ^f_x (b) – 1 (y), but some test of its validity can be made by evaluating his basic assumption that Trickster "practically everywhere" (62) is a carrion eater. This works well enough with Coyote and Raven, but falls a bit lame with Bre'r Rabbit, an inveterate eater of carrots, formulae notwithstanding. The intellectual effort expended by these psychological interpreters of Trickster is impressive, but the product of the effort is not. What one Winnebago said in summing up both his own people and Trickster (Radin, 1956: 148) could be applied to the interpreters as well: "We dance and make a lot of noise but in the end we accomplish nothing."

TRICKSTER AS CULTURE HERO

If Trickster were simply an outrageous fellow imposing upon his divinity to violate social rules, he could be explained easily enough, though the explanation would require psychological probing beyond the understanding of most primitive people who vicariously sympathize and empathize with him without having read Freud. But he is more complex: as Hewitt eloquently described him in the character of the Eastern woodlands Nanabozho more than half a century ago (1905a: 19),

> Nanabozho is apparently the impersonation of life, the active quickening power of life—of life manifested and embodied in the myriad forms of sentient and physical nature. . . . He impersonates life in an unlimited series of diverse personalities which represent various phases and conditions of life, and the histories of the life and acts of these separate individualities form an entire cycle of traditions and myths which, when compared one with another, are sometimes apparently contradictory and incongruous, relating, as these stories do to the unrelated objects and subjects in nature. The conception named Nanabozho exercises the diverse functions of many persons and he likewise suffers their pains and needs. He is this life struggling with the many forms of want, misfortune, and death that come to the bodies and beings of nature.

For all his show of ferociousness toward his neighbors and bravado toward his gods, primitive man had so little confidence in himself that we wonder whether this alone kept him from progressing beyond the Paleolithic for nearly all of his history on earth. So long as man believed in myth and its gods he rarely attributed the invention of things to human beings, but to Culture Heroes. The Culture Hero is seldom an unequivocal deity, but in his ideal form a demigod whose nature is corrupted by a love for mankind, a weakness that leads him into treason against the god, from whom he steals such things as fire, daylight, summer, magic, *mana*, game animals, and the like, by means of which man tries to overcome his hostile environment, and who also institutes the social rules by means of which man tries to overcome his own self-destructive nature. When asked for an example of the Culture Hero in this definition, students always respond "Prometheus," thereby denying the Culture Hero of our own society, who should come more immediately to mind if it were not in our nature to overlook our own irrationalities when they are described in terms of other peoples. Our Culture Hero is of course Jesus Christ, who fits very well into the general definition.

It would be easier to understand the roles of the Culture Hero and Trickster if literatures, primitive and sophisticated, kept them separate, but more often than not the Culture Hero is also the Trickster. Even Christ, the least ambiguous of all Culture Heroes,

is worrisome in the apocryphal legends that have persisted for two
thousand years in spite of the penalties that were visited upon heretics
and blasphemers whenever the Church was strong enough to keep
the thinking of its communicants pure. The orthodox mythology
of Christianity retains only one clear vestige of a Trickster nature:
the Disobedience in the Temple; but European folklore and folksong
tell of Christ as a Trickster from before his birth ("The Cherry Tree
Carol") to just before his death (the legend of the Wandering Jew)*.
His tricks were not merely disobedience and mischief, but fatal ones
for his human playmates, just like those of the North American
Indian Trickster. This ambiguity of Trickster and Culture Hero has
worried everyone who has dealt with this area of mythology and
folklore. Radin (1956: 125) asked

> whether Trickster was originally a deity. Are we dealing
> here with a disintegration of his creative activities or with
> a merging of two entirely distinct figures, one a deity, the
> other a hero, represented either as human or animal? Has a
> hero here been elevated to the rank of a god or was Trickster
> originally a deity with two sides to his nature, one construc-
> tive, one destructive, one spiritual, the other material? Or,
> again, does Trickster antedate the divine, the animal and the
> human?

Boas (1898: 7) persuasively accounted for the North American
Indians' retention of the ambiguous Culture Hero-Trickster, who
blunders good things to man without any altruistic motivation, to
accident:

> He is not what we ordinarily understand by the term "cul-
> ture hero," a benevolent being of great power whose object
> it is to advance the interests of mankind, but he is simply
> one of many more or less powerful beings who gave the
> world its present shape. With this conception of the so-
> called culture hero the difficulty disappears of uniting in one
> person the benevolent being and the trickster. He helps
> man only incidentally by advancing his own interests. This
> he tries to do by fair means or foul, just as the Indian will

---

* These are not casual libels invented out of sectarian malice, for some of the stories
are far too complex and widespread to be dismissed as recent inventions. The Wandering Jew story, for example, is itself a complex legend, as shown by the various
identities of the Jew—Ahasuerus, Cartaphilus, Isaac Laquedem, Joseph, John But-
tadeus, Salathiel ben Sadi, and the "Wild Huntsman" of Germanic folklore, which
connects this character with Odin legends.

treat his enemy. When he overcomes his enemies, the result of his labors must accrue to the benefit of his fellow beings or of later generations, while wherever he fails, he necessarily often appears as a foolish trickster. We have a condition corresponding almost exactly to the attitude of medieval Christendom to the devil. The latter was considered as a powerful being, always intent to advance his own interests. Often he succeeds, but often his triumph is defeated by the cleverness of his adversaries. The difference between these two series of myths lies mainly in the fact that the devil in all his adventures had only one object in view, namely, the acquisition of souls, while the Indian transformer struggles with a great variety of enemies who infested the country.*

The disinterest in man's welfare, characteristic of the North American Indian Trickster which Boas attributes to an extension of the Indian personality, is perhaps not to be tied so easily to group selfishness, for it is typical also of the Trickster-Culture Hero in aboriginal Australia where group cooperation is enforced by a bewildering variety of societal devices, though the rough edges have been hewn from the eastern Australian sky heroes (Baiame, Daramulun, Binjil, Goin, Biral, and Nurunderi) by the half-century of missionary influence preceding the first objective collecting of native tales. Bamapama of the north-eastern Arnhem Land Wulamba people (the Balamunu, Barera, Dai, Djinba, Jaernungo, Janginung, and Ritarungo tribes which Warner combined under the arbitrary name "Murngin") is closer to the North American type, engaging in behavior absolutely prohibited to human beings, and accidentally and casually doing some good for mankind.

Trickster has been set upon by the Freudians because his obvious origin is psychological; this has been understood for a long time— since Aristotle explained that people go to see tragedies on the stage because they vicariously empathize with the protagonist and thereby purge themselves of the latent desire to become involved in tragedies. This is why Americans go to see gangster films and Japanese go to see puppet actors committing suicide; this is why primitive peoples enjoy their Trickster. It could be stated as a general rule and defended fairly well by ethnographic evidence that the occurrence of

---

* There is only an apparent contradiction in identifying both Christ and the devil with Trickster, for all complex mythologies are inconsistent in the character and origin of deities and demons. Demons in the higher religions are normally the losers in a jurisdictional dispute between rival deities.

Trickster tales is directly proportional to the degree of oppressiveness of socioreligious restrictions. In such situations Trickster is a cathartic* to purge his audience of tensions built up by incest tabus, avoidance restrictions, and similar regulations of conduct in the area of sexual relations. In medieval Europe the Church for all its power had to allow tension-relieving devices like the Boy Bishop, the Feast of Fools, and the Foolish Pope to make religion's interference in life more nearly tolerable. As with nearly everything else in primitive society and culture, these things reach across the ages into our civilization; not many who attend church on Sunday know the altar rail was constructed first to keep the louts from shooting craps on the altar, not many children who overturn outhouses on Mischief Night or clerks who wear lampshades on their heads at the office Christmas party realize they are reinacting Trickster exploits.

Our contention that the Trickster evolves with sophistication into a Culture Hero who consciously performs altruistic acts for man is well illustrated by the greatest of primitive Tricksters—the Polynesian Maui-tikitiki-a-Taranga ("Maui-topknot-of-Taranga"), who can hold his head up nobly even in the company of Promethus, though his superior sense of humor makes him appear less dignified than the classic Greek Culture Hero. Maui's tricks are the recreation of a creator who works overtime for his mortal wards, snaring the sun, stealing fire, trapping winds, raising the sky, fishing up islands, building topographies, rescuing people from monsters, and inventing artifacts and institutions (Luomala: 1949). He deservedly is known over some 13 million square miles of the Pacific, including nearly all of Polynesia, Melanesia, and Micronesia. In the few places in this vast area where he is not known, it is usually because one of his thousand nicknames has replaced his more common cognomen. On Samoa he is known simply as "Tikitiki-a-Taranga."

Where the Culture Hero appears as a separate entity from Trickster in more primitive cultures his less admirable qualities are incorporated into a separate character. Thus the three brothers Quaqlqal, Kokwe'la, and the Old Man** of the Thompson River Indians of British Columbia walk a more virtuous path. The Australian totemic ancestors are Culture Heroes who cannot be seen as

---

* The word is used in its psychological rather than physiological connotation, and is suggested by Aristotle rather than the Winnebago story of the laxative bulb.
** The Arnhem Land aborigines also have an Old Man Culture Hero, sometimes known as Nagacork.

violators of sanctions, since they are primarily the creators of sanctions.   Throughout South America there are Twin Culture Heroes.
The Wolaro of the Kimberley region of Australia have a creator,
Gwini, who used demiurges (his son Dagubal and the Rainbow Serpent) in his creating.   The infinite variety of man's ways has produced nearly everything imaginable in Culture Heroes, as in other
aspects of culture: Radcliffe-Brown (1922) even found among the
Andamanese a Culture Heroine, Biliku, who made the sun and the
moon, discovered fire, and invented all the things used by mankind.
And there is the renowned Eskimo Sea Goddess, Sedna; but Culture
Heroines are seldom things, appearing in those few societies that permit women to participate equally with men as religious practitioners.
Such Culture Heroines are not to be confused with the mother god-
desses of later agricultural societies, who are so well known as to
require no description here.

ANIMAL HEROES

In primitive literature "talking beasts are common, beasts acting
as men are common; no less common, among savages, is the frame of
mind in which practically no distinction is taken between gods,
beasts, and men.   The more barbaric the people, the more this lack
of distinction marks their usages, myth, and tales" (Lang, Introduction to Cox, 1893: xiii).*   Seventy subsequent years of collection
and scholarship have not much altered Andrew Lang's remarks about
the proximity of the animal world to the world of men in the minds
of unsophisticated peoples, though wagon loads of theory have been
produced to explain the primacy of the animal tale in what Lang was
able to call "savage" societies.   Van Gennep (1910), drawing his
evidence largely from Australia, the homeland of totemism where it
is impossible to see any clear distinction between humans and lesser
animals in the Dreaming myths, offered the theory that animal tales
were vestiges of totemism.   This explanation is reasonable, though
it does not explain the presence of the animal tale in cultures that
have no other evidence of the totemic concept; indeed, it is more
reasonable than it needs to be.   In our own serious literature it is
needful to employ the willing suspension of disbelief to accept sapient

---

* In this same famous Introduction to the first scientific study of a folktale—Cinderella—Lang laid down the rule that the wonder-working character in this story is
more likely to be an animal the closer it is to its primitive origin, and that only in
later, sophisticated versions does the fairy godmother appear.   For a fine corroborative example of a sophisticated variant reverting to the primitive form according to
Lang's rule, the Zuni version of Cinderella is cited in Chapter Seven.

animals, yet few modern fathers are so prosaic that they must rationalize the situation before reading Mother Goose stories to their children, and the children show no bewilderment when first introduced to Donald Duck and Mickey Mouse. In primitive societies, where animals are more intimate acquaintances of human beings, even less mental adjustment is required to have the animals talk and behave like men; there, animals and men meet on terms of equality, and expect to continue their relationship in what poor heavens the savage knows.

As a literary device, the animal is a popular figure in both primitive and sophisticated story. Human actors are distressingly unpredictable as stock characters; Hooton and Lombroso to the contrary, one cannot certainly predict unvarying behavior from anybody's looks. Even actors in Western dramas must be stereotyped into character by arbitrary symbols such as the color of their hats and their horses and the length of their sideburns. Animals are easier to the unsophisticated author; if a fox appears on the scene, cunning behavior inevitably follows. And, as a matter of psychological fact, certain animals seem to personify types of human disposition. Expanded from William Rose Benet's list in *The Reader's Encyclopedia* (36), the following compilation of animals and their symbolic significance is by no means limited to our own literature:

Ant: wisdom, frugality, prevision, resourcefulness
Ape: cunning, malice, lust, uncleanliness, insidiousness
Ass: stupidity, stolidity, obstinacy
Bantam cock: gallinaceousness, pluck, priggishness
Bat: blindness
Bear: ill temper, brutishness, uncouthness
Bee: industry, independence
Beetle: blindness
Bull: strength, straight-forwardness, ill-controlled temper, tyranny
Bulldog: pertinacity
Butterfly: sportiveness, improvidence
Camel: stupidity, submissiveness, ugliness
Cat: deceit, self-indulgence
Calf: lumpishness, cowardice, immaturity
Cicada: poetry
Cock: vigilance, insolence
Cow: stolidity, femininity, placidity
Crow: longevity, expedience, craft
Crocodile: hypocrisy

Cuckoo: cuckoldom
Dog: fidelity
Dove: innocence, harmlessness, fidelity
Duck: deceit
Eagle: majesty, inspiration
Elephant: sagacity, ponderosity, persistence of memory
Fly: feebleness, insignificance
Fox: cunning, artifice
Frog and *Toad:* inspiration, persistence
Goat: lasciviousness
Goose: conceit, folly, gullibility
Grasshopper: old age, improvidence
Gull: gullibility
Hare: timidity
Hawk: rapacity, mercilessness
Hen: maternal care, stupidity
Hog: impurity, gluttony
Horse: speed, grace, reliability
Jackal: obsequiousness, cowardice
Jackdaw: vain assumption, empty conceit
Jay: senseless chatter
Kitten: playfulness, innocence, harmlessness
Lamb: innocence, sacrifice
Lark: cheerfulness
Leopard: sin, unchangeability
Lion: nobility, courage, vigilance
Magpie: garrulity
Mink: insatiability
Mole: blindness, obtuseness
Mouse: timidity
Monkey: trickiness
Mule: obstinacy, stupidity
Nightingale: forlornness, beauty
Ostrich: curiosity, stupidity
Owl: wisdom
Parrot: mocking verbosity
Peacock: pride
Pigeon: cowardice
Pig: obstinacy, filthiness, greed, gluttony
Puppy: empty-headed conceit
Rabbit: fecundity, cowardice

Rat: deceit, cowardice
Raven: malice, ill luck
Robin: confiding trust
Serpent: wisdom, deceit, insidiousness
Sheep: silliness, timidity, servility
Shrew: ill temper, ferocity
Sparrow: lasciviousness, greed
Spider: wiliness, deceit, mercilessness
Stag: cuckoldom
Swallow: untrustworthy friend
Swan: grace, purity
Swine: filthiness, greed, gluttony
Tiger: ferocity, beauty, mercilessness
Tortoise: chastity, stolidity, persistence
Turkey cock: official insolence
Turtle: turgidity, persistence, caution
Turtle dove: conjugal fidelity, affection
Vulture: rapine
Wolf: cruelty, savage ferocity, rapine, deceit
Worm: servility, cringing

Though some of these are patently inaccurate as dispositional characteristics of the animals in question—the domestic habits of the dove, to choose only one example, are disgustingly promiscuous —it is astonishing how the same qualities commended themselves to widely separated peoples. Among the Tiv the spider is the arch-deceiver (Abraham: 64). Culture has a lot to do with apparently aberrant animal symbols: the Bedouin culture, nucleated around the camel, sees this hideous beast as the paragon of beauty; the Watusi culture, based upon cattle pastoralism, sees the bull as the king of beasts in beauty, strength, and courageousness. Tyrannized over by their larger neighbors, the Hottentots rejected the lion as the aris-tocrat of animals, making it instead the object of hate and ridicule because of its cruelty and ferocity, and saw themselves in the jackal, the cleverest of the animals in their bestiary (Schultze: 244–245). In Hottentot tales it is not hard to see the equation

lion:Negro :: jackal:Hottentot.

In a larger view, the incidence of the animal tale is highest among Negro peoples, whether they are the native races of Africa, the aboriginal inhabitants of Melanesia, or the slaves of the southern United States. Why this should be so, no one has satisfactorily explained; the quickest answer to mind, that Negroes and animals both are plentiful in the Tropics, does not hold up in ethnographical examination. Another coincidence in animal tales is their importance where the incidence of proverbs is also high; conversely, where animal tales are unimportant and poorly developed, as among the American Indians, the proverb is a negligible form. The coincidence is probably due to the fact that the stereotyped characterization of animals in these stories leads straight into didacticism. Since many if not most animal tales are fables, an evolution of this genre can be argued: the simple explanatory tale becomes the fable, and the fable becomes the beast epic. The evolution of this form of literature parallels cultural development, with the fable the dividing line between primitive and folk, and the beast epic the dividing line between folk and sophisticated societies.

Animal tales merge imperceptibly into tales about wholly human characters. As in our fairy tales, animals talk to men with no embarrassment on the part of either. As in real life, contact leads to miscegenation, so one widespread form of the animal tale is that in which a human being takes an animal spouse, with a variety of consequences.* Another point of contact is the usefulness of animal tales as explanations for more important phenomena than how the rabbit got long ears—for instance, the origin of death. As Boas described this use (1938: 617).

> One trait of the animal tale has been carried over almost consistently into mythology: the idea that what happened once has determined the fate of the world. Because a certain person died and it was decreed that he should not rise again, all men must die and remain dead, although before this death was unknown.**

The Adam and Eve story in Genesis is a good instance of the merging of the animal and the human world and the mythical and mundane dimensions, as well as an explanatory tale that has had some influence on human belief.

The Tar Baby

The most peripatetic of the animal characters is probably the Tar Baby, pursued around the world for more than forty years by Aurelio Espinosa, who died without convincing all folklorists that he had

---

* See in Chapter Seven how this theme has been used to account for racial differences.
** For examples, see Chapter Seven.

tracked down the elusive stick-fast to its original lair. Just as the
Garden of Eden story, discredited by many as serious evidence for
the origin of anything, nevertheless drew the 19th century search for
the origin of all aspects of civilization to the Tigris and Euphrates,
so the great popularity of the Uncle Remus story pulled the attention
of Tar Baby authorities to Africa. It might be said for the Africanists that at the time of Harris' publication of the Uncle Remus tale
the only other versions known were from Africa—and there was an
imposing number of these—though Espinosa's later search through
the literature turned up several European variants that had been
published and promptly forgotten by 19th century folklorists, just
as Mendel's genetic laws had been published and promptly forgotten
by 19th century biological scholarship.

Essentially the Tar Baby motif relates the Trickster tricked and
trapped through his characteristic violence and stupidity by an ad-
hesive manikin which he successively threatens and strikes with
hands, feet, and head, thus sticking himself fast by all extremities.
Though derivative motifs such as the Grimms' "The Golden Goose"
idea of the thieves stuck together and similar stories of adhesion are
well known in European story, the basic theme is proliferated only
in Africa, taking on special features such as the female Tar Baby,
the mock pea, the water stealing motive, and the live-tortoise trap
(Espinosa, 1930: 194), and often becoming as in this Nuer variant
(Huffman: 100–102), a minor thematic element:

> A long time ago the fox and his mother had a village.
> The fox often went fishing. In the afternoon he would come
> home with his catch. He would put the fish on the ground.
> He would say to his mother, "Prepare this catch of fish; you
> cook it." The mother would prepare the fish and the fox
> would eat it. The same thing would happen next day. When
> the fish were cooked he would say to his mother, "Bring me
> all the fish and the head and the neck. Bring it all." The
> mother would give him all. He ate it. He would leave his
> mother out.
>
> This went on for a month. He himself ate all the fish.
> He went fishing, brought his catch home and said to his
> mother, "Mother, why is the tail of the fish like this?
> Bring the other parts and the head and the neck and the
> gravy. Bring all of it, mother."
>
> The mother was very thin, resembling a very thin fish.
> When he had finished eating he would call to his mother,

"Mother, mother-of-the-fox, bring water. Your son has had enough." The mother would hiss. The fox would hear. The fox would say, "What, mother-of-the-fox, did you hiss at your child?" The mother would say, "Nothing, my son." She would go to the river. She would give him the water.

When the mother grew very thin, she went to a woman called Nyajwani. Nyajwani knew how to plan all kinds of things. The mother-of-the-fox said to Nyajwani, "My sister, my child is killing me. My son has no consideration. Show me what to do." Nyajwani said to her, "Go to the forest. Bring gum from the tree. I will show you a plan. You will surely be healthy after to-day."

Mother-of-the-fox brought the gum. She gave it to Nyajwani. Nyajwani formed a very nice woman, a very red woman, she put beads in her ears and she put anklets on her legs also. She made her out of gum. She was a very good woman who never had children yet. When she was finished Nyajwani created a name for her. She called her Nyaluac.

That day the fox went fishing. They gave Nyaluac to the mother-of-the-fox. The mother brought her to the house. She spread a mat and put her sitting on it. In the afternoon the fox brought in fish. He threw them on the ground and called his mother. "Mother-of-the-fox, cut up this catch of fish." His mother said to him, "Oh, my son, there is a traveller at the village, a woman who refuses to live with her husband. She says, 'My husband is the fox!'" The fox exclaimed, "I told you to hurry with the fish so that the guest may eat." His mother answered, "Oh!" She roasted the catch of fish. She offered it to the fox. The fox refused. He said to his mother, "I know, mother-of-the-fox, that I am ashamed to eat in front of my sweetheart. Give the fish to the guest." Mother-of-the-fox brought the food into the house and ate it herself. Every time the fish was cooked she offered it to the fox, but he refused to have it. Mother-of-the-fox brought it again into the house. Mother-of-the-fox ate it.

Mother-of-the-fox got so fat that her skin was very smooth. When she knew she was fat she said to the fox, "My son, to-day you and your wife may visit. I will tell you one thing, my son. Do not whip the daughter of the

Nuer. This one has a very tender skin. Do not harm her."
The fox answered, "Oh!"

Late that afternoon the fox went into the house. When
he went into the house he said to Nyaluac, "Blow the fire."
She was silent. The fox said, "I will blow the fire in the
house of my mother." When he had blown the fire he said to
the woman, "What is it?" She was silent still.

He pushed her with his club. The club stuck. He tried
to pull it back and thought that the woman had perhaps
caught it. He said to her, "Let my club alone." The woman
was silent. He said, "What! Have you not heard that I always whip a guest? I am the fox." He said again to the
woman, "Do you want to be whipped? Are you not a guest?
Let go of my club." The club fell of its own accord. He
again pushed the woman with the club. "What's the matter?" The club again stuck in the body of the woman.

The fox said to Nyaluac, "But why are you always holding
my club? Let it alone, if you are really like the daughter of
a man." The woman was silent. The fox did not know that
the woman was formed of gum. He took his raw-hide
whip. He struck the woman across the back. Her back
broke.

The fox fled.

In Africa the motif has become so commonplace that its apparently
original function as a demonstration of Trickster's stupidity has been
buried beneath other themes. The Hottentots even permit the incident to happen to their beloved jackal.

By 1930 Espinosa had 152 versions of the story, most from Africa,
but several from Europe and Asia, including a most important variant from the Jātaka (Jātaka Number 55). The Jātaka are a collection of 547 Pali stories dealing with the various incarnations of
Buddha as the Bodhisatta, though the majority of the tales are pre-
Buddhistic or non-Buddhistic (some, for example the Barlaam and
Josephat story, get into Christian myth; others migrate to China;
and several of the best are found in Aesop's *Fables*). Because of its
antiquity the Jātaka tale was taken by Espinosa as the cornerstone
of his theory that the motif came ultimately from India, though in
this telling it is obviously a derivation of an earlier, generalized stick-
fast tale (Espinosa, 1930: 138–140):*

---

* One bit of documentary evidence for this contention is the allusion in the earliest
extant Buddhistic canon, the Samyutta Nikāya, to stick-plasters used by Himalayan
hunters to catch monkeys.

Once upon a time when Brahmadatta was reigning in Benares the Bodhisatta or Buddha was born as his queen's child.

When the prince had come to years of discretion, and was sixteen years old he was sent to study in the town of Taka-sila.   Upon the completion of his education he left for Benares, armed with a set of five weapons which his master had given him.

On his way he came to a forest haunted by an ogre named Hairy-Grip, and, at the entrance to the forest a man who met him tried to stop him, saying, "Young brahmin, do not go through that forest; it is the haunt of the ogre Hairy-Grip, and he kills every one he meets."   But, bold as a lion, the self-reliant Bodhisatta pressed on, till, in the heart of the forest, he came on the ogre.   The monster made himself appear in stature as tall as a palmtree, with a head as big as an arbor and huge eyes like bowls, with two tusks like turnips and the back of a hawk; his belly was blotched with purple, and the palms of his hands and the soles of his feet were blue-black!   "Whither away?" cried the monster. "Halt! You are my prey."   "Ogre," answered the Bodhi-satta, "I knew what I was doing when entering this forest. You will be ill-advised to come near me.   For with a poisoned arrow I will slay you where you stand."   And with this defiance, he fitted to his bow an arrow dipped in deadliest poison and shot it at the ogre.   But it only stuck on to the monster's shaggy coat.   Then he shot another and another, till fifty were spent, all of which merely stuck on to the ogre's shaggy coat.   Whereupon the ogre, shaking the arrows off so that they fell at his feet, came at the Bodhisatta; and the latter, again shouting defiance, drew his sword and struck at the ogre.   But, like the arrows, his sword, which was thirty-three inches long, merely stuck fast in the shaggy hair.   Next the Bodhisatta hurled his spear, and that stuck fast also. Seeing this, he smote the ogre with his club; but, like his other weapons, that too stuck fast.   And thereupon the Bodhisatta shouted, "Ogre, you never heard yet of me, Prince Five-Weapons.   When I ventured into this forest, I put my trust not in my bow and other weapons, but in myself.   Now will I strike you a blow which shall crush you into dust."   So saying, the Bodhisatta smote the ogre with his right hand; but the hand stuck fast upon the hair. Then, in turn, with his left hand, and with his right and left feet, he struck at the monster, but hand and feet alike clave to the hide. Again shouting, "I will crush you into dust!" he butted the ogre with his head, and that too stuck fast.

Yet even when thus caught and snared in fivefold wise, the Bodhisatta, as he hung upon the ogre, was still fearless, still undaunted. And the monster thought to himself, "This is a very lion among men, a hero without a peer, and no mere man. Though he is caught in the clutches of an ogre like me, yet not so much as a tremor will he exhibit. Never since I first took to slaying travellers upon this road have I seen a man to equal him. How comes it that he is not frightened?" Not daring to devour the Bodhisatta off hand, he said, "How is it, young brahmin, that you have no fear of death?"

"Why should I?" answered the Bodhisatta, "Each life must surely have its destined death. Moreover, within my body is a sword of adamant, which you will never digest, if you eat me. It will chop your inwards into mincemeat, and my death will involve yours, too. Therefore it is that I have no fear." (By this, it is said, the Bodhisatta meant the Sword of Knowledge, which was within him.)

Here on, the ogre fell a-thinking. "This young brahmin is speaking the truth and nothing but the truth," thought he. "Not a morsel so big as a pea could I digest of such a hero. I'll let him go." And so, in fear of his life, he let the Bodhisatta go free, saying, "Young brahmin, you are a lion among men; I will not eat you. Go forth from my hand, even as the moon from the jaws of Rahu, and return to gladden the hearts of your kinsfolk, your friends, and your country."

The Bodhisatta makes the ogre the fairy of the forest, returns to Benares and rules the country like a just king.

Thirteen years later Espinosa wrote (1943: 31), "I have now in my possession 267 versions, 115 more than when I published my first article in 1930, but my opinion concerning the origins and general history of the tale have not changed." Now, however, with this great champion of the Indian origin gone, scholars are beginning to be swayed back to Africa by the overwhelming preponderance of

Tar Baby stories on that continent, particularly if, like Melville J. Herskovits, they are Africanists to begin with.* The emotional storm that presently rages over the relations of Negroid peoples with Cascasoids makes objectivity in most aspects of Negro culture study impossible, and while the influence of the racists has been loud and raucous, the gentler influence of the anti-racists overwhelms anthropological scholarship, although so far as scientific evidence in the matter of racial cultural capacity is concerned, neither side has anything but negative arguments. More than we like to admit, therefore, a sentimental benefit of doubt is always cast toward Africa when the origin of a culture trait well developed in Africa has a doubtful origin. Thus the highly evolved music of Africa is taken to be a native development—and indeed, instinctive to Africans until instinctive traits, good and bad, were recognized as racist contentions—though an extremely strong case can be made for the diffusion of this trait from the Dry World. Murdock, on little more than good will, proposed the independent discovery of agriculture by West Africans (17–24). In the present controversy, the evidence offered to offset Espinosa's documentary exhibits supporting a Eurasiatic origin of the Tar Baby consists entirely of distributional weight —which is like arguing that the original homeland of Americans was the United States, since there are so many of them here. All things considered, Espinosa in his grave still has the better of the argument.

OGRES

The ogre with which the Bodhisatta had such a disquieting experience in Jātaka 55 was a nobleman among his kind. More typical of the species was the unpleasant fellow whom Jack found at the top of the beanstalk—a giant in bulk and unprovoked villainy. Stith Thompson's *Motif-Index of Folk-Literature* allows nearly 400 categories of ogre, all of them a bad lot: cannibals, wizards, necrophagous ghouls, unnatural animals, hobgoblins, monsters, werewolves, night- and day-mares, windigos, demons, poltergeists, awl-elbowed witches, bogles, cyclopes, doppelgangers, trolls, djinn and djinniyah, gnomes, kobolds, jenny hanivers, raw heads and bloody bones. Anyone who has ever dreamed has seen one, but this does not satisfy mankind's curiosity—he wants to see real ones, and his innumerable tales of

---

* Herskovits was the most influential of the Africanist folklorists, and although he admitted that African story was part of the general Old World stock of oral literature (1958: 4), he opposed Espinosa's argument as being "scarcely tenable in the light of the weighting of the distribution toward Africa" (in Leach: 1104).

imaginary ogres are unsatisfactory substitutes. Even the most advanced and sophisticated civilization that humankind has ever evolved eagerly deludes itself with romantic names, faked photographs, yak scalps, and wishful thinking to justify expensive expeditions under British knights to hunt the Himalayas for Sherpa bogeymen, much to the amusement of the Sherpa. Sir Edmund Hillary surely must have read about *Beowulf* in school, but evidently the snowy environment of Nepal prevented him from seeing the close resemblance between Grendel and the Abominable Snowman.

The fascination that ogres have for heroes, from Beowulf to Hillary, is a fatal one for the ogre despite the terrifying arsenal of weapons possessed by the monsters, from death ray glances (the Greek Medusa, the Jicarilla Apache Big Owl, and the medieval cockatrice) to what folklorists delicately call *vaginae dentatae*— though heroes who fall foul of the latter device bring trouble on themselves. It is one of the regular duties of the Culture Hero to rid his people of ogres, and curiously enough the literature of people who like the Eskimo have no real Culture Heroes is overrun by ogres. Since the ogre has incomparably more strength than his human adversary, the hero must use man's unique possession, his guile, to overcome his stupid enemy. For cruelty, there is little to choose between the antagonists—witness Odysseus' treatment of Polyphemus. Ogre tales for these reasons are not pleasant stories. The wry wisdom of the giantess in "The Giant's Toy" who admonishes her Glumdalclitch of a daughter who has taken up a plowman and his team as toys, "You must take him back; he will drive us away," is as unusual as the humor of the "Bear Taken for Cat" tale, in which an ogre who has a rough evening in a darkened barn with an itinerant bear retires permanently to safer haunts when he is told that "the big cat" is still there, and has, moreover, had three kittens. Fear is the universal emotion evoked by ogre tales, and since fear is a powerful source of psychic energy, ogres are used to coerce people into proper conduct, whether the situation is a Saracen mother frightening her child with King Richard or an Aranda witch doctor invoking an *eruncha* demon.

There is no task so profitless that some scholar will not devote his intelligence to it, and so we have several theories accounting for the origin of ogres (Naumann suggested that ogres were made out of the dead in primitive ritual), though it would seem almost as productive to account in theory for the origin of eating.

HUMAN HEROES AND OTHER CHARACTERS

There is little doubt that the heroes of sophisticated literature were "lang a-growin'," from unbelievable anthropomorphic animals to equally incredible paragons like King Arthur, and that reality finally overtook them, as it must all of us. The end point of the evolution—or devolution—is Hemingway's Ole Andreson, who finds the work of living not worth the while.

Disillusion sets in at the end of the folk phase of development, when the people get sick to death of even Robin Hood and allow him to be beaten soundly by every tinker, tanner, and curtal friar who has a mind to take a staff to him. Though the height of heroic development is in folk literature—or, more accurately, in that stage of literature which is later preserved in folk culture—the folk hero is made of myriad and often contradictory processes that begin with the earliest primitives. Lancelot is the most sophisticated hero in early English literature, but behind his creation lies Gawain (of whom the French had quite enough by the end of the 12th century) and behind Gawain lies Cuchulain, and behind Cuchulain some forgotten primeval solar deity. An analysis of late folk and early sophisticated heroes, therefore, is profitable in understanding the primitive archetypes. Two of the most valuable studies of common characteristics of heroes are those of Lord Raglan (1937) and Klapp (1949), though both scholars present their findings as syntheses rather than analyses.

Raglan, borrowing heavily from Rank, found 22 thematic characteristics sufficiently common to mythological heroes to construct from them the following type tale:

1. Hero's mother is a royal virgin;
2. His father is a king, and
3. Often a near relative of his mother, but
4. The circumstances of his conception are unusual, and
5. He is often reputed to be the son of a god.
6. At birth an attempt is made, usually by his father or his maternal grandfather, to kill him, but
7. He is spirited away, and
8. Reared by foster parents in a far country.
9. We are told nothing about his childhood but
10. On reaching manhood he returns or goes to his future kingdom.
11. After a victory over the king and/or a giant, dragon, or wild beast,

12. He marries a princess, often the daughter of his predecessor, and
13. Becomes king.
14. For a time he reigns uneventfully, and
15. Prescribes laws, but
16. Later loses favor with the gods and/or his subjects, and
17. Is driven from the throne and city, after which
18. He meets with a mysterious death,
19. Often at the top of a hill.
20. His children, if any, do not succeed him.
21. His body is not buried, but nevertheless
22. He has one or more holy sepulchres.

Raglan gives a spot check of these characteristics among a small sampling of heroes:

Oedipus, 19	Arthur, 19	Sigurd, 11	Elijah, 9
Perseus, 18	Theseus, 20	Robin Hood, 13	Heracles, 17
Asclepios, 12	Jason, 15	Romulus, 18	Pelops, 13
Joseph, 12	Dionysos, 19	Bellerophon, 16	Zeus, 15
Nyikang, 14	Moses, 20	Apollo, 11	Watu Gunung, 18
			Llew Llawgyffees, 17

A sampling, assuredly, but Raglan in his wry manner prods the reader to check the list against the unnamed heroes—Christ as an obvious example.

Klapp's "Cultural Distribution of Hero and Villain Roles" is less rigid and therefore more generally applicable than Raglan's pattern, but less attractive as narrative literature. He identifies four general kinds of heroes—the Conquering Hero, the Clever Hero, Cinderella, and the Martyr, the particular characteristic depending on the characteristic role. The Conquering Hero demonstrates an extraordinary power in performing Feats, in winning Contests, surviving Tests, and accomplishing Quests (the Quest is defined by Klapp as a "prolonged endeavor toward a high goal, usually involving a series of feats, contests, and tests, before final attainment"). Clever Heroes are Tricksters, primarily, who accomplish their goals by clever ruses, and Klapp is astute enough to appreciate that the Clever Hero is perilously close to being a Villain. The Cinderella or Unpromising Hero is "(a) an unpromising person (b) derided or persecuted by rivals (c) before his unexpected, brilliant triumph. By way of contrast to the unexpected victories of the clever hero, the unpromising hero succeeds by some other means than cleverness, usually luck, miraculous assistance, or modest toil." The Martyr is the product of a more sophisticated literary era, an altruistic benefactor who triumphs in death—death caused so often by treachery that "it is almost possible to say that for every hero there should be a villain to betray him." Klapp gives his villains short shrift, disposing of them in two categories, traitors who betray the hero through weakness or cowardice, and powerful persecutors. Because his orientation is ethnocentric, Klapp's table (18) is very sketchy for primitive heroes, but the roles are so nearly universal that the student of ethnoliterature can fill in blank spaces and create many other columns.

The studies of Raglan, Klapp, and other literary scholars assume a cultural environment like our own, a static stage on which only the actors are dynamic, and while their type patterns are valuable as a starting point for the anthropological analyst (who conversely is unfamiliar with the literary method), they do not use the ethnological equipment that would explain the presence or absence of particular kinds of heroes in particular cultures. One would not, for example, expect to find Heracles in an Apollonian culture or Cinderella among the Dionysiacs.*

A compendium of actors in primitive literature is as arbitrary as a compendium of forms, and just as unprofitable. There is an endless diversity of heroes; the Melanesians see Mars inhabited by a great red pig; Géza Róheim, probing Australian myth with a dirty stick, wrote, "the penis is the hero of this drama" (1945: 16). Every man is his own hero—or, to look at it another way, every hero is the projection of each individual who hears his story told.

---

* Cinderella, expectedly, fits well into the Zuni Apollonian environment, as the excellent example in Chapter Seven shows.

Chapter Four / THE ANATOMY OF QUALITY

Beauty is in the ear as well as the eye of the beholder. Western music, especially folk and popular song, is swamping out its native counterparts all over the world, but the primitives came to their appreciation of the unfamiliar as we must, by relentless indoctrination. Though many Australian aborigines now acquire guitars before trousers and the Puka Pukans in the remotest South Pacific have forsaken their own song for American hillbilly tunes, it was not always thus. When one of the first European sea captains to sail into the Pacific regaled a group of Polynesians with his violin, the natives were aswoon with admiration for the white man's digital dexterity, but regretted that the demonstration had to be accompanied by such dreadful noises. Much later, when Raymond Firth whiled away the evening hours on distant Tikopia with recordings of the best music of his culture, he was embarrassed to find that so far as the islanders were concerned, "the finest notes of our most famous European tenors and sopranos appealed to them merely as efforts at humor." Alice Fletcher attained a rare objectivity in appreciating the nature of the esthetic gap between the Indians and ourselves:

> Our difficulty in hearing the music of the Indian is equalled by the trouble he has with our instruments. His attention is engaged by the mechanism. He hears the thud of the hammer, 'the drum inside' the piano, the twanging of the metal strings, and the abrupt, disconnected tones. Until he is able to ignore these noises he cannot recognize the most familiar tune (1900: 118).

Poetry, John Ciardi insists, is a "manner of speaking," and it is also a manner of listening, a manner of understanding. To anyone who has studied ethnoliterature it is hard to understand how so perceptive a person as J. C. Furnas could say of Polynesian poems that they are "dismally dull, relieved only by an occasional obscenity," or that Padraic Colum, who made one of the famous translations of Hawaiian myths, could conclude that "these long and monotonous stories told in the old days must have derived their value as entertainment, not from intrinsic values, but from the extravagant skill in gesture and intonation of the native story teller." With both the beam and the mote figments of our own imagination, who is to say what is good and what is bad in literature? *Lady Chatterley's Lover* means very different things depending on whether the reader is a devotee of indoor or outdoor sport, as the reviewer for the journal *Field and Stream* demonstrated:

> Although written many years ago, this fictional account of the day-by-day life of an English gamekeeper is still of considerable interest to the outdoor minded reader, as it contains many passages on pheasant raising, the apprehending of poachers, ways to control vermin and other duties of the professional gamekeeper.

> Unfortunately, one is obliged to wade through many pages of extraneous material in order to discover and savor these sidelights on the management of a Midlands shooting estate, and in this reviewer's opinion, this book cannot take the place of J. R. Miller's *Practical Gamekeeper.*

The rest of this chapter will be addressed to literary readers, for anthropologists these days deal with value judgments the way the Devil is said to deal with holy water. Never before in their unhappy history have the less successful people in the competition to possess the earth had more good will from their conquerors, who study them with consideration and kindness before they die out. This avoidance pattern of anthropologists is not due to their fear that tomorrow's newspaper will announce one of these people taking a seat in the United Nations, though that is a possibility; it is due to their sensitivity about the status of their discipline. They consider themselves scientists now, and since they are aware that some physicists regard this pretension as impudence, they are not eager to give offense by making any generalizations about comparative values. Ethnography is a dirty word, and whatever cannot be measured does not exist. Many geneticists in the profession insist that races do not exist, except as statistical abstractions. It has been discovered, too, that even to say good things about a foreign culture or its bearers is to suggest instinctive differences, and so the value judgments that follow, whether they praise or dispraise a literature, are not to be used in anthropology classes.

Nineteenth century anthropologists were not much concerned about Emergent Nations, and their academic training nearly always

included a thorough if not sound education in literary standards, so
the books that we must go to for much of our material bristle with
value judgments. Connolly's description of Fanti culture is for the
most part unobjectionable enough, but their literature was too much
for him. His long volume on Fanti ethnography sums up their
"Poetry and Folk Lore" in three invidious paragraphs (141–142):

> It is difficult to arrive, even after lengthened investigation,
> at any success in trying to discover the materials of poetry
> and folk-lore which exist among such a people, so suspicious
> and so vain-glorious. If poetry or verse exists, it is kept
> secret for Fetish purposes, and therefore not to be disclosed,
> and the natives are shy to an extraordinary degree in relat-
> ing one of their own tales before a European, perhaps because
> every detail is nicely exact, and the language, "painful and
> free" like the language of some of the Arabian Nights.
> One of the tales has for subject the faithlessness of the wife
> of Kweku Anansi, or Kweku Spider, who, on his return
> from hunting one day, found his door barred and heard a
> noise inside. On forcing open the window *with his gun*,
> Kweku discovered his deceitful wife and her paramour. A
> *palaver* ensues, during which the lover manages to escape,
> and at the end of which Kweku is compelled to forego any
> demand for compensation *because he saw nothing*. It is very
> popular amongst all carriers and hammockmen, and consists
> of a long recitative broken by refrains, "Oh, Anansi, oh,
> Anansi, you are being tricked," or "your wife's too much
> for you," or some such piece of sparkling wit.
> After many burials a troop of mourners following the
> coffin will sing a song of quite another pattern. It is
> lit. translated,
>
> > Bear him along,
> > He is only a poor body now,
> > Bear him along,
> > Give pity to the poor body,
> > Bear him along.
>
> And when a chief or a great man dies, at the custom,
> held in his honour, his virtues are at first chanted until
> the influence of rum suggests pleasanter topics. But in
> such song there is neither meter, rhyme, or even attempt at
> rhythm; the sole object of the minstrel seems to be to get
> as many words as possible into a single breath, to the ac-

companiment of a very monotonous air, and with the clangour of the equally monotonous tom-toms.

Our own age of egalitarianism is more biased toward the literature of the world's less influential peoples (hence the existence of this book) and dignified scholars like Paul Radin can see the Trickster story in which a polecat kills deer by shooting them with the wind expelled from his anus as "delightful" (1956: 144). If the 19th century translators did primitive literature less than justice, mid-20th century translators are apt to sin in the opposite direction. Ronald Berndt translated 90 pages of the most tedious narrative to get into English writing since the *Ormulum*, the Arnhem Land *Djanggawul* myth, yet he doggedly made poetry of lines which in our culture would be found written on lavatory walls; for example, he has a canoe-load of paddlers speak of "undulating our buttocks," a phrase which would lose something of its elegance had it been translated as "wiggling our behinds" or as the aborigines themselves would have translated it even less gracefully.   Berndt, however, defends the *Djanggawul* songs stoutly as "some of the most beautiful literary efforts of Aboriginal Australia" (1953a: 60). *De gustibus á son gout*, as the German lady said, though most Australianists would feel that Berndt's remark was an unnecessarily unkind one to make about aboriginal song.

Ronald Berndt is only an anthropologist, not a poet, offering like ourselves esthetic valuations of an art whose master practitioners find inexplicable. A. E. Housman admitted "I can no more define poetry than a terrier can define a rat; I only know that when a poem goes by I must run after it," which even as an admission of incapacity is better than what another poet said about the craft—he defined poetry as "a purple feeling in the pit of my stomach." Carl Sandburg offered "Ten Definitions of Poetry" like "Poetry is a theorem of a yellow-silk handkerchief knotted with riddles, sealed in a balloon tied to the tail of a kite flying in a white wind against a blue sky in spring." But the function of a poet is to express feeling, not meaning; meaning can be safely left to lesser folk, like anthropologists.

The anthropologist, dissociated from emotional entanglement with art, can easily divide all poetry into two parts, narrative and lyric. Narrative poetry, universal among primitive peoples, took to its death bed in our culture when printing was invented, and now is so far gone that we cannot evaluate it except by applying the criteria of lyric poetry, which is not in such very good shape itself. Lyric poetry, the attempt to communicate emotion, falls into five general categories:

1. *The simple outcry:* a brief ejaculation of emotion, common in primitive but rare in sophisticated literatures.

2. *The descriptive lyric:* a form in which the poet draws a picture of the thing that evokes emotion in him in order to evoke the same emotion in his audience.

3. *The narrative lyric:* a brief incident communicating the mood of a moment, most successful in poems like Robert Frost's "Dust of Snow":

> The way a crow
> Shook down on me
> The dust of snow
> From a hemlock tree
>
> Has given my heart
> A change of mood
> And saved some part
> Of a day I had rued,

and least successful in the Homeric simile, which has a tendency to get sidetracked away from its original purpose.

4. *The lyrical expression of an idea:* the poetic epigram, a form that inclines to intellectualize itself out of the emotional category, like Pope's famous "quotations."

5. *The euphonic lyric:* in which words are meaningless or nearly so, and which relies on the emotive and onomatopoeic effect of the words on the ear rather than on the brain—Carroll's "Jabberwocky" and Poe's whiffling and piffling of the bells are well known examples.

Appreciating the truth that one cannot apprehend a lyric poem dealing with an emotion one has never experienced, the old psychological texts graphed emotions on a psychical spectrum:

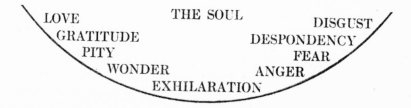

LOVE   THE SOUL   DISGUST
GRATITUDE   DESPONDENCY
PITY   FEAR
WONDER   ANGER
EXHILARATION

These are the nine primary, elemental emotions, which can be combined to form complex psychical states, like HATE, which may range almost anywhere along the spectrum. Some literatures confine their lyricism to one segment; most prefer one chord; all have significant omissions. In our age wonders have come so fast that WONDER has been lost. GRATITUDE, too, has disappeared, though it was frequent in English poetry as recently as the Victorian period.

Though we can profitably apply these criteria to primitive literature in order to test its worth to us, it is doubtful that the primitives had much recognition of what we would call literary standards beyond an unanalyzed appreciation that some pieces were more satisfying than others. Their lack of standards as we understand the term is due to the comparative irrelevance of such standards. In a conscious way their measure of "goodness" is in terms of spiritual power, that is, the song's efficacy in drawing *mana* for the purpose at hand. For this reason accuracy is a widely demanded quality in preliterate singing or narration, a requirement that had a petrifactive effect on primitive literature comparable to the effect of printing on our own literature. Unsophisticated peoples therefore may use in total unawareness language that strikes the sophisticated collector as very beautiful. The University of Pennsylvania's legendary professor of English, Cornelius Weygandt, once heard a back-country woman say of an itinerant peddler of heavy wares, "he came to us on the edge of evening, selling stoves." Weygandt, then an old man, wrote his autobiography under the title *On the Edge of Evening*, as happy a name as any man has given to his life's summing-up.

STYLE

There are nine and sixty ways
Of constructing tribal lays
And every single one of them is right.

Kipling drew this discerning observation from his knowledge of the tribes then nestling within his beloved Empire; had he known more of the earth's tribes, the meter of his poem might have been injured but not the accuracy of his perception. There are at least as many "ways" in primitive literature as there are cultures, each of them as fair to its possessors as ours is to us.

Anthropologists have long suspected that "style" is the most important element of a culture, transcending such comparatively trivial and irrelevant matters as quality, yet because of its intangibility very little has been done with it either in poetry or pottery. The most provincial Westerner can recognize at a glance a Chinese vase, costume, sculpture, food, or poem, but who, regardless of his cosmopolitanism, can define the *Chineseness* of the artifact? We have not even progressed to the point of giving a satisfactory name to this element—we struggle with such inadequate words as "style," "ways," "fashion," "*Gestalt*," and "ethos."

A few good tries have been made to isolate the determinative factor in culture. Ruth Benedict (1934) developed and applied to anthropology Nietzsche's concept of the Apollonian and Dionysian polar attitudes. The Dionysian way of arriving at the values of existence is through excess, which means individualism, competition, aggressiveness, distrust, frenzy, intoxication, preoccupation with sensory experience, discipline, warfare, mysticism, addiction to drugs and stimulants, and the like. The Apollonians on the other hand approach life through moderation, and are therefore cooperative, non-competitive, non-aggressive, friendly, altruistic, societal, quiet, humble, peaceful, permissive, ritualistic, ceremonious, and mannerly. Benedict's classic book *Patterns of Culture* shows these approaches in societies at opposite ends of the spectrum of behavior—the Apollonian Zuni and the Dionysian Dobu. It is a beautiful book, appropriately so for the poet that its author was before she came to anthropology, but the dichotomy she postulates is imaginary. She had to comb the world's cultures for a suitable example of the Apollonians, and neither archaeology nor ethnology will bear up her contention that the Pueblos (to which group the Zuni belong) were so ideally cooperative, peaceful, and non-competitive as she thought. Any tourist who has fallen into the clutches of the mercenary Taos in their colorful pueblo know that these people can hold their own among any Dionysians, including ourselves. By the very terms of her thesis, as a matter of fact, Apollonians cannot exist, for they would long ago have been exterminated by the Dionysians.*

Nietzsche's brilliance contributed another idea elaborated by a poetic philosopher. Spengler used his suggestions to identify the classical Greek ethos as one of containment, exemplified in their architecture, politics, wealth, sculpture, music, drama, mathematics, astronomy, and history; our own culture, at the opposite end of the scale, is one of expansionism.

Studies of national character are promising, the more so in view

---

* But we must report in fairness that in the Keams Canyon, Arizona, jail, run by and for the Pueblo Hopis, an honor system with unlocked doors has worked without incident or abuse for fifty years.

of the great opposition made against them by most anthropologists. Mexican and foreign observers alike, from the time of the Conquistadores to the present, have agreed that the Mexican national character builds upon a sense of insufficiency, manifested in such apparently diverse Iberoamerican traits as the *Jorgenegretismo* of Mexican movies, the national homicide rate, social tendency to "amification," hyperdiminutives in speech, micromania in art, necrolatry in confectionary skulls on the Day of the Dead, veneration of sanguinary *santos*, and the "taurine martyrdom" of the *corrida*. But considering the work that has gone into the analysis of broken pottery, comparatively nothing has been done to perfect the anthropological tool of style detection. Some scholars even deny its existence. Eda Lou Walton, abetted by her silent partner Waterman, forcefully said that "to chatter . . . about *the* Indian's ways, or style of composing, as though all Indians were on one level, is very pointless; very childish and naive. Fancy the absurdity of talking about the way *the* Indian builds his dwelling" (1925: 26). True enough, there are great and presently unaccountable differences between the literature of the Navaho and that of their Pueblo neighbors, but anyone with the slightest knowledge of primitive literature could immediately distinguish any North American Indian song from any one sung by the Australian aborigines, the Polynesians, or even the nearby Eskimos. From the Atlas Mountains 8000 miles eastward to the Gobi Desert there is less stylistic difference in "Dry World" (Russell-Kniffen) singing than there is between the music of any of these nomadic peoples and that of their sedentary acquaintances a few hundred miles north or south. Similarly the cultures of the "Polar World" have a style not approximated elsewhere, and the Polynesian style is only dialectally different over ten million square miles. We may not be able to define style any more than we can define electricity, but when we come into contact with it, we know it is there.

THE DEVICES OF STYLE

Repetition

From wallpaper patterns to sin, repetition is pleasurable to man. Freud even saw repetition—"repetition compulsion"—as a characteristic by means of which all animal organisms prepared against traumatic fright. Whatever the psychological validity of this theory may be, repetition is beyond doubt the most common quality of song and poetry. Rhythm itself, the basis of music and song, is only regular repetition, and rhythm is pre-cultural. As soon as they can stand, babies will respond to rhythm, duplicating (so far as their sense of balance will allow) the tempo of the music. Though repetition is still pleasing to us in literature, the substitution of reading for recitation has intellectualized poetry, with what effect on its popularity it is easy to see. The change has affected our appreciation of primitive song as well, so that the very repetitive nature of this material is likely to annoy rather than to please us. In her study of Zuni myth, Ruth Benedict tells us with apparent disbelief that in one ceremonial narrative forty dancers enter individually, fugue-like, and the same story is repeated to each of them. Forty times also, according to Boas (1925: 331), the same formula is repeated with a description of the ceremonial in Kwakiutl tradition. Boas also cites the tales of the Chinook Indians, which

> are always so constructed that five brothers, one after an-
> other, have the same adventure. The four eldest perish
> while the youngest one comes out successful. The tale is
> repeated verbatim for all the brothers, and its length,
> which to our ear and taste is intolerable, probably gives
> pleasure by the repeated form (1938a: 591).

Primitive literary repetition is by no means always intolerable; very often it affects us as deeply as the audience for which it was constructed. Natalie Curtis (1907: 362) has preserved this beautiful lyric to the horse of the sun, riding on "precious hides" (clouds) across the Navaho sky:

> How joyous his neigh!
> Lo, the Turquoise horse of Johano-ai,
> How joyous his neigh!
> There on precious hides outspread standeth he;
> How joyous his neigh,
> There on tips of fair fresh flowers feedeth he;
> How joyous his neigh,
> There of mingled waters holy drinketh he;
> How joyous his neigh,
> There he spurneth dust of glittering grains;
> How joyous his neigh,
> There in mist of sacred pollen hidden, all hidden he;
> How joyous his neigh,
> There his offspring many grow and thrive for evermore;
> How joyous his neigh!

Polynesian literature is also rich in examples of the repetitive style. Handy (1927:102–103) gives this prayer to Kane (Tane) from the Hawaiian Islands:

> A query, a question,
> I put you:
> Where is the water of Kane?
> At the Eastern Gate
> Where the Sun comes in at Haehae;
> There is the water of Kane.
>
> A question I ask of you:
> Where is the water of Kane?
> Out there with the floating Sun,
> Where cloud-forms rest on Ocean's breast,
> Uplifting their forms at Nihoa,
> This side the base of Lehua,
> There is the water of Kane.
>
> One question I put to you:
> Where is the water of Kane?
> Yonder on the mountain peak,
> On the ridges steep,
> In the valleys deep,
> Where the rivers sweep,
> There is the water of Kane.
>
> This question I ask of you:
> Where, pray, is the water of Kane?
> Yonder, at sea, on the ocean,
> In the driving rain,
> In the heavenly bow,
> In the piled-up mist wraith,
> In the blood-red waterfall,
> In the ghost-pale cloud form,
> There is the water of Kane.
>
> One question I put to you:
> Where, where is the water of Kane?
> Up on high is the water of Kane,
> In the heavenly blue,

In the black-piled cloud,
In the black-black cloud,
In the black-mottled sacred cloud of the gods;
There is the water of Kane.

One question I ask of you:
Where flows the water of Kane?
Deep in the ground, in the gushing spring,
In the ducts of Kane and Loa,
A well-spring of water, to quaff,
A water of magic power,
The water of life!
Life! O give us this life!

There are in all literatures several easily recognized kinds of repetition:

Narrative repetition: in which the same story, part or whole, is reiterated, as in the examples given above by Boas and Benedict from the Zuni, Kwakiutl, and Chinook.

Rhythmic repetition: in which the repetition is a musical rather than a poetic device. American Indian song exemplifies this kind of repetition.

Incremental repetition: most familiar as a frequent rhetorical characteristic of the British folk ballad, in which a partial stanza repetition joins material moving the action forward, as in this American variant of Child ballad 53 ("Young Beichan").

For seven long years I'll keep this vow true,
Then seven more, and two or three;
If you will marry no other maiden,
No other man shall marry me.

For seven long years she kept this vow true,
Then seven more, and two or three;
Then she gathered all her gay fine clothing,
Saying, "Lord Bateman I'll go see."

Primitive use of this device is less frequent, but still widespread. Biddulph gives an illustration from the unpoetic Bard people of the Hindu Kush (326):

This pan belongs to Bair Gul.
I will never let any one place this pan on the hearth.
I will place it there myself.

This pan belongs to Malik, the Chief of Gilgit.
I will never let any one place this pan on the hearth.
I will place it there myself.

This pan is worthy of belonging to kings.
I will never let any one place this pan on the hearth.
I will place it there myself.

and so on, and on, and on.

Sequential repetition: again familiar in our folk literature in tales like "The House that Jack Built"; sequential repetition includes also

Spiral repetition: which carries the action upward rather than forward. Sebeok collected this example among the Cheremis, the native peoples of the Soviet Republic of Marii, in the Tatar area (1958):

> Oh, oh, the Vjatka is very wide,
> The meadow is wider than the Vjatka.
> Hillocks upon the meadow,
> A copse of black alders on each hillock,
> Boughs upon the alders,
> Upon each flower an alder berry,
> That alder berry gathering, gathering,
> My index finger wore off.
> While to you coming, coming,
> My gelding's hoof wore off.

Anaphoric repetition: in which the beginning words of a phrase are repeated in the next; the Old English (Anglo-Saxon) poem on the *Ubi Sunt* theme, *The Wanderer*, with its insistent opening question "Hwaer com" ("What has become of") is an unforgettable illustration.

Litany: the most common kind of repetition among primitive peoples, since it is a religious rather than a literary device. Several examples have already been seen in "Charms, Curses, and Imprecations" in Chapter Two; few are more winsome than the following invocation gathered by Meulen and von Wissman (65) among the ferocious Bedouin of the Hadhramaut in southern Arabia:

> O mighty Chief,
> Swallow the Pagans!
> Tomorrow the Emir rides to war;
> Swallow the Pagans!
> God grant him victory;
> Swallow the Pagans!
> God grant him two hundred slaves;
> Swallow the Pagans!
> God grant him a thousand slaves;
> Swallow the Pagans!
> His concubines rejoice;
> Swallow the Pagans!
> His slave lads rejoice;
> Swallow the Pagans!*

An unclassified and generally unnoticed kind of repetition is that used by the Australian aborigines in pidgin, which gives them little other vocabulary resources to express travelling with cumulative speed. Harney effectively demonstrates this on his record "Talkabout." An aboriginal thus described to him the tracking of a kangaroo; slowly, cautiously, the hunter crept up with his spear set in the *woomera* (spearthrower), then rushed upon his prey—

> I bin gooooooo I bin go I bin go I bin go Ibingo Ibingo Ibingo IbingoIbingo I bin s n e a k i n I bin sneakin I bin sneakin I bin follerin im I bin follerin im follerim follerim follerim CRACK! Capped im dis time by Chrise proper good one no more gammon!

Parallelism

Closely resembling repetition and often accompanying it in the more highly-developed primitive literatures is the device of parallelism. Anglo-Saxon poetry elaborated parallelism far beyond any later use of it, though the Middle English *Sir Gawain and the Green Knight* (which is in its prosody more Old English than Middle Eng-

---

* This kind of simple song may go on for hours to the accompaniment of tension-building percussion instruments until the Bedouins who are infected by the rhythm are ready to swallow someone, pagan or fellow Believer.

lish)* is in its entirety an intertwining series of envelope parallels. Few readers have noticed that the prosody and story lines of the first half of the poem are reversed and echoed in the second half; the poem begins

Siþen ðe sege and ðe assaut watȝ sesed at Troye

2500 lines later the story ends

After ðe sege and ðe assaut watȝ sesed at Troye, iwysse.

Walton and Waterman in their analysis of Navaho prosodic devices give us a useful summary of some common types of parallelism (37–38). Defining parallelism as "a correspondence of terms in one line to those of another in respect of meaning, not in respect of number of syllables . . . based upon a universal biological principle, repetition with variation," they list in addition to the *envelope parallelism* of *Sir Gawain and the Green Knight*,

Chain parallelism: "made up of a succession of clauses so linked that the goal of one clause becomes the starting point of the next:

That which the palmer worm hath left
Hath the locust eaten;
And that which the locust hath left
Hath the canker worm eaten;
And that which the canker worm hath left,
Hath the caterpillar eaten."

Antithetical parallelism: in which the second line is an antithesis of the first;

Incremental parallelism: what we have already described as "incremental repetition";

Parallelism of meaningless syllables; and

Repeating parallelism: in which the "second line repeats the first in slightly different form:

Ada and Zillah, hear my voice,
Ye wives of Lamech, harken unto my saying."

The fact that Walton and Waterman use Biblical examples for these forms incidentally shows the popularity of this rhetorical contrivance

---

* Old English is the language spoken in England from 450 to 1150 A.D.; Middle English, from 1150 to 1450; and Modern English from 1450 to the present.

in Semitic literature (often called the "Biblical style"). In sophisticated literature the writers of the 16th century English school of Euphuism delighted in elaborate parallel constructions like "Instead of a senate of a hundred grave counsellors there is now a synod of a hundred greedy caterpillars." As one might expect from the foregoing examples, conscious parallelism is a rare thing in the least sophisticated literatures.

Structural Economy

A compelling reason for the repetitiousness of primitive literature is the poverty of its texts. Without repetition and other padding devices many peoples would have nothing left to sing.

The songs of the aborigines of the Western Hemisphere from the Eskimo to the Alacaluf are distinguished—if that is the proper word —by a brevity of text that no other area can approach, though translators, understandably enough, have concealed this fact by filling out the original songs. One Eskimo song frankly confesses, "All songs have been exhausted,"* and proves the case for the Eskimo at least by saying nothing more. Most Eskimo songs are like this—a terse statement amounting to little more than a title, followed by the characteristic ululation "aayaa aayaa yaayaa yaayaa." Even the Eskimo tales seldom demand much stamina of their narrators; Bogoras gives the whole of a humorous story among the Eskimos' neighbors across the Bering Strait: "Once the root of *Polygonum viviparum* scratched its head on the ice" (149).

The Eskimos' neighbors to the south are even more taciturn. Frances Densmore (1936) gives four entire songs in as many lines:

> Old age is hard to bear.
>
> The stones are all that last long.
>
> I have medicine power.
>
> I don't care if you're married, I'll get you back again.

Burton, as we have seen, was talented in extending the texts of Ojibwa songs, but on some he abandoned hope—like the following (257–258):

> Ungitched-ah, hey ah   hey ah

---

* It is amusing to remember that John Lydgate the greatest English poet of his time, apologized for the poverty of his work by saying in effect that after all, everything to write about had already been written about—this, a century before Shakespeare!

Hey ah   hey ah   ah ah hey ah   hey ah ah
Hey ah   hey ah   hey   ah hey ah   hey ah   hey ah   hey ah hey.

The only meaningful word here is the first, which Burton extended
300 per cent by translating it "the bravest man."

But Alice Fletcher probably had the champion catch with the
Ponka "Song of the Laugh" (1900: 12–13):

Ha, ha, ha,   ha ha!   hi hi!   ha ha! hi!

It may be that the intellect of the paleface was too unimaginative
to catch the embedded nuances of these songs.   The Indians were
often told of the ridiculous brevity of their songs by tactless collectors whose obtuseness the Indians were too polite to mention.
Natalie Curtis tells a tale on herself (463):

Tuari (Young Eagle) is at work far from his native village.
When asked for a song, he said, "I will sing you my own song
that I sing to my wife."

"But how can you sing to her when she is at home in
Laguna and you are here?"

The Pueblo youth stared at the question, then answered,
quietly, "I sing to her though I am far away, and she, too,
sings to me.   The meaning of my song is this: 'I am here,
working for you.   All the while I work I think of you.   Take
care of yourself, and take care of the horses, and the sheep
and the fields.'"

"But your song has no words!"

"No, but that is what it means.   So when I am far away
we sing to each other, my wife and I."

Perhaps we shall have to re-examine what we thought the Indians
meant when they said "Ugh!"

Other reticent literatures are likewise heavy with allusions not
apparent in the texts.   James Breeks related an incident very much
like that of Natalie Curtis and Tuari, though he sees the fault in
his informant, as most 19th century collectors did (34):

A Pekkan man, Kiniaven, one of my intimate acquaintances, when asked whether his people had any songs like the
Bagadas, said, yes, they had songs, and after entreaties for a
specimen, began a queer monotonous sort of drone through
his nose.   He said there were no words to the song, but when
pressed as to the meaning, and what they thought about

when singing, he replied they thought about the names of
their gods, which he enumerated. After racking his brains
a little more, he discovered that they also thought about
Dirkish the son of En. What did Dirkish say? "Where
have you gone, why have you left us, have you gone to
heaven, what shall I do?" etc., etc. Yes, they sang that
Dirkish made everything, the krals, the buffaloes, the Todas,
the paltchis, etc., etc., with childishly minute enumeration.

Frances Densmore, who had more experience as a collector than
anyone else, insisted (1943) that the "meaningless" syllables of
Indian song were heavily meaningful, quite unlike our own "tra la
las." They might be remains of obsolete words, vowel interpolations
to fit the meter, and, depending on their expression (whether they
are aspirated explosively or breathed out gently), pre-semantic
vocables communicating emotions. In any event, they seem to be
nearly impossible for us to translate properly. As one Ojibwa told
Frances Densmore after she had tried to sing a series of these vocables, "You have the tune all right but you have not an Indian
throat." Something near the ultimate in this sort of thing is the
drum language of the Ashanti and other West African tribes; Rattray (266 ff) translates the whole history of the Mampon clan of the
Ashanti as beaten out on the "male" and "female" talking drums.

Rhyme

The device of rhyme is quickly disposed of in a discussion of
prosody in primitive literature: it is almost never found. Even in
English it came in late and is leaving early; in all Anglo-Saxon verse
there is only one short poem that uses it to any noticeable extent,
and for that reason it is known as the "Rhyming Poem." Where
rhyme occurs among preliterate peoples, it appears to be either a
contribution of the recorder, as with Schoolcraft's (226)

Ne osh im aun	(My sliding stick
Ne way be naun	I send quick quick)

or is induced by the form of the language. Polynesians insulated
one consonant from another with vowels, which produced what some
scholars think is deliberate rhyme. Katherine Luomala gives what
purports to be a rhyming poem from a Maui *fakaniua:*

Langi to fitu, langi tuo valu,	Seventh sky and eighth sky,
Nofo ai a Hina mo Sinalau;	Dwell there Hina and Sinalau;

Koe langi ape e tamutamu	The sky of the thunder
Ha mea e leo lahi ange fau,	With a great loud voice,
Oka ita oka longolongo tau.	When angry or giving omen of war.
Langi tuo hiva, tuo hongofulu,	The ninth sky and the tenth,
Koe langi ni fulufulu mokuku,	The sky feathery like herons,
Koe langi ape oku uulu,	The sky of uncertain rumbling,
Kae fefei e tala tuku.	Perhaps telling of parting.

But there are two things that disqualify this as rhyme: first, when properly pronounced, only two of the couplets rhyme; second, all the other words in the song end in vowels, and if these words were arranged in random fashion, they would rhyme as well as in the meaningful syntax. Some Australian languages produce this automatic rhyme also; the Aranda tongue ends nearly all its words with "-a," so that an Aranda song can hardly avoid rhyme.

Linguistics and Euphony

English resisted rhyme until the 13th century avalanche of French shifted its accent from the front to the back of words, rendering alliteration inconvenient if not impossible. Now we are moving back again to the Germanic pattern of initial accent, which we find more comfortable. The inhospitability of English to rhyme is only one familiar example of the interdependence of prosodic, linguistic, and musical style. None of these styles is free to develop in directions that cannot be followed by the others. Speech patterns are so obvious in African drum tones that even outsiders can understand the talk of the drums without too much trouble after mastering the spoken language; the "sing song" tonal language of the Chinese sounds to Occidental ears like Chinese music, as it should; the glottal trilling that characterizes the singing of Dry World and marginal Oriental peoples is heard in their aerophones also. In a stimulating discussion of the relationship between music and language, William Bright drew inferences from so many cultures both primitive and civilized that he left no doubt about their interdependence. One can hear this conveniently in the United States in the singing of English and Spanish; Spanish songs distort the language, English does not; French sung pronunciation is sufficiently different from spoken pronunciation to make French songs unintelligible to second-year students of the language. Two less familiar examples cited by Bright are the singing of the Twi, which

minimizes the clash between word pitch and song pitch; on

the other hand, the Lushai language of northeastern India permits song pitch to override word pitch completely, so that a word that has rising pitch in speech may have any type of falling or level pitch in singing. This is true not only in modern songs, which often copy European melodies, but in traditional songs. The Lushai claim, however, that they can understand the meanings of song lyrics even when the word pitches are effaced in this way; this provides an interesting measure of the degree to which linguistic communication may take place even under conditions of great distortion.

As a character of language rather than literature, euphony naturally occurs in hospitable tongues, such as the Polynesian with its lubricating vowels. Even the name of Polynesia's Trickster rolls trippingly from the tongue: Maui-tikitiki-a-Taranga. Australian languages, though inclined to encourage a harsher, tenser enunciation, sound attractively euphonic: the song about the little bird that lays a tiny egg and flies off with a triumphant "tau tau tau"—

> Tabo tabo naberi wandinaia jimunguni
> Naberi wandinaia tabida-baii
> Tau tau tau

rapidly chanted by the Yirkalla songman to the fascinating accompaniment of the *didjeridu* drone pipe has a hypnotically euphoric effect on American college students who have heard Elkin's record (1953) of it played. Music everywhere has a dominating effect on the language, often forcing it to be euphonious (Hodge: 271; Bright), or driving it out altogether in wordless songs.

While the purposeful singing of preliterate peoples uses sound merely as a conveyance for spiritually powerful words, belletristic literature is more likely to reverse the situation, using language as "the medium of literature as marble or bronze or clay are the materials of the sculptor" (Sapir, 1921: 263).

Language may even become a subconscious psychological device. Balken and Masserman statistically proved that in our culture at least "a high incidence of verbs denotes a kinetic release in the phantasy of anxious tensions in the narrator" (77), something Benedict suspected for the Hopi also. This may account for the fact that Navaho, a "language of the verb, in contrast to English, which relies chiefly on the use of the noun" (Astrov: 45), is pathologically concerned with sickness and healing. But Americans are as bad as the Navaho so far as hypochondria is concerned, and have been for about a hundred years, according to the remarks made about us by 19th century visitors.

Probably all languages make use of puns, paronomasia, assonance, and similar word play, but such things are hard for the foreigner to detect unless like the Samoan, the literature in question is notorious for the use of these devices. Samoans even tinker with the sacrosanct historical recitations,* inventing ancestors like Tutu and Ila, who first discovered Tutuila, or Sava and I'i, who landed the first canoe on Savai'i. "This punning mythology," says Mead (155), is of never-failing interest to the Samoans; endless incompatible tales are built up by splitting up place names and family names and fabricating myths about the linguistic elements."

Easily overlooked also by the outsider are esoteric and archaic linguistic usages, since often the narrators are equally ignorant of their meaning. Like our own magicians' "hocus pocus" and children's "onerzoll twoerzoll zickerzoll zan," terms that have altered in pronunciation sufficiently to erase their meaningfulness are frequent in unsophisticated literatures. These occur especially when ritualistic inserts are embedded in tales, where they bother their narrators no more than the nonsense choruses of our folk ballads bother us; in either case they sound all right, and no one looks for meaning except analytical scholars. In our culture secret languages are limited to criminals, tramps, teenagers, and other unabsorbed groups who prefer to keep their activities to themselves, but primitives whose societies are more homogeneous use artificial languages for the amusement of all. Handy (1930b: 19) reported trick languages from the Marquesas strikingly like the English argots in structure. *Uhi tua*, once spoken by the inhabitants of Nukuhiva's Haa Paa valley (the cannibalistic Happar Valley of Herman Melville's *Typee*), transposes syllables of words and occasionally inserts gratuitous vowels to confound the chaos: "*pehea oe*" ("Where are you going?") becomes "*hepea oe*." Another Marquesan artificial language is *E'o hu'i* ("Language turned over"), which Handy believes resulted from an effort to imitate the Tahitian dialect; "*pehea oe*" in *E'o hu'i* becomes "*peheiherea ooiroe*." Evidently the Marquesans thought the Tahitians spoke a stuttering dialect of their own language. In the Pacific and adjoining western mainland areas intrasocietal dialects function as status indicators, and as such contaminate the literature.

---

* This point should be kept in mind for the discussion of the historical reliability of these chants in Chapter Seven.

Among the American Indians a vestige of this may be the convention of denying certain sounds to certain characters in animal tales; Boas (1914) said that among his Kwakiutl the Mink cannot pronounce the sound *ts*, and among the Kutenai Coyote cannot pronounce *s*. Similar dialectal lacks characterize Shoshone, Chinook, and Nootka animal narratives. Gladys Reichard noticed that the Coeur d'Alêne showed the Catbird to be tiny and babyish by giving him speeches in babytalk (1947: 25). The Coeur d'Alêne, she reported, are almost unique in their fondness for onomatopoeic sounds, or more precisely, conventionalized sounds that are taken to be onomatopoeic, as in the following list (29):

p'ap'aq: a "bad-sounding" noise made by Skunk
tcisasat'at: a "nice" noise made ordinarily by Fisher
olu'lu'lu: noise made by Fisher when he dives
tsalala: noise made by Kingfisher diving
ona'na'na'n: noise made by Magpie's children eating
ots'ats'at: noise made by Rabbit's children eating
patatsat: noise made by Chipmunk hopping
nalnala: noise made by another squirrel hopping
mu mu mu: noise made by bones being transformed into dentalia
t'a t'a t'a: Cricket's sound
oyurayura: Grizzly's sound
qwar qwar: Crane's sound (very disagreeable-sounding to Coyote)
otcar tcar: Raven's sound
op'axp'axp'ax: sound made by snowshoes on snow
opampam: noise of bow
opatsatsa: sound of Snake's stick hitting Chipmunk
ola'u ola'u: sound of "pans" in Coyote's ear
xuts xuts xuts: sound of bone breaking (sounds "awful")
otsaxtsax: sound of teeth grinding
ludidi ludidi: sound of spiders spinning

The Coeur d'Alêne also have conventionalized sounds to express feeling:

anininin: pain felt by Meadowlark when her legs have been broken
animim: pain felt by Splinter Leg in carving his own leg bones
alilili: feeling of cold water on the body
tsasakaninin: feeling of Catbird passing through Elk's nose
halalas: the phrase with which Mole introduces herself

Formulas and Stereotypes

Once upon a time we were fonder of stereotyped openings and other formulas than we are now, though until very recently an author could not sell a story to a popular magazine unless its first sentence introduced the chief character speaking while doing something. The formulas are still present, but now they are more subtle—one does not begin a story with "Hwaet" or end with "they lived happily ever after," though movies still symbolize the latter pleasant improbability by marching the protagonist and his lady love off into the sunset, hand in hand. Our more delicate authors still indicate the commission of an act of sexual intercourse by starting the next paragraph a bit farther down the page and beginning it with "Later . . . ." Some of these stereotypes are both good and enjoyable in anyone's literature; a cliché is after all only an apt expression worn out. Lady Malaprop's misuses are all the more delightful because they are incessant, and we feel about her just as the Coeur d'Alêne feel about Coyote, who can never use kinship terms correctly. We would not accept Sir Fopling Flutter without his habitual expression "Stap me vitals" nor would the Coeur d'Alêne accept Catbird's grandmother without her habitual expression, "Impossible! Scandalous even to think of it" (Reichard: 27). Neither may attain the highest reaches of literary characterization, but they are great fun all the same.

Formalized openings and endings are found everywhere in primitive literatures. In the Bahamas at the end of the last century every story began with "Once it vwas a time" and ended with "E bo ban, my story's en' " (Edwards). The Hausa story teller announces "gatanan, gatanan," ("a story, a story") and his audience encouragingly responds "Ta ja, ta kō mo" ("Let it go, let it come"). Dahomeans may introduce a tale with statements like "Hyena lives alone," thus announcing another story about the adventures in evil of that notorious character (Herskovits, 1958: 23). With some exceptions (Radin, 1926, said there were no opening-ending stereotypes among the Winnebago), American Indian ritual narratives generally opened with an exclamation signifying the ensuing theme (Hodge: 271). "You shall no longer be a man-eater" is an intriguing formula in Coeur d'Alêne narrative, but Reichard hints that its frequent use as a concluding moral may have taken away much of its former significance. The Trobrianders, morassed in incantation and ritual, carry over the formulas into their tale telling. Malinowski (1935: 156) said that they end every story with the same intoned stanza:

The *kasiyena* yams are breaking forth in clusters; this is the season when crops cut through, when they grow round. I am cooking taro pudding; So-and-So (some important person present is named in a jocular tone) will eat it. I shall break off betel-nut; So-and-So (another notable is named here) will eat it. Thy return payment, So-and-So (and the man to recite next is named).

Herskovits' Dahomeans end the *heho* (legendary tales, distinguished from *hwenhoho*, or myths) with the standard formula, "The words I told, which you now have heard, tomorrow you will hear a bird tell them to you." Reichard's Coeur d'Alêne like to use some variation of the playful conclusion, "the little bird sat on a tree at the end of the road and was shot." Among the folk of the Western world, there is no literature so enchanting as the Irish, and what Matthew Arnold called "Celtic magic" pervades even to the ending of their tales. Thompson (1951: 458) repeats a delectable consummation from a Donegal story:

The marriage lasted nine days and nine nights. There were nine hundred fiddlers, nine hundred fluters, and nine hundred pipers, and the last day and night of the wedding were better than the first.

Allusion and Symbolism

No literature, not even that in the *Congressional Record*, is so prosaic as to say everything it means. Symbolism (in which Thing A stands for Concept B) and allegory (in which Story A stands for Story B) are literary universals, though the richness of these devices depends on the richness of the culture, the elevation of the literature, and no less on the whims of fashion. Medieval English literature was run through with allegory, but now we tolerate it only in editorial page cartoons. Conversely, symbolism has run wild in serious modern literature and has alienated all except an inner circle of initiates. Because of the overbearing attention to symbolism in our own contemporary writing, we try to find it to the same extent in preliterate expression, where in point of fact there is very little of that deliberate obfuscation that makes the work of Kafka and his imitators unintelligible. There is much in primitive literature that we do not and cannot understand—strange imagery, esoteric allusion, secret language, mystical significance, and the like—but except where religious tabus prevent it, the primitive composer is straightforward.

If an Indian makes up a song out of a personal dream, he keeps the meaning to himself—it is not, therefore, symbolic, but secret; he does not append footnotes to his text like T. S. Eliot to let the world in on it. On the contrary, symbolism in graphic and mimetic art is at the very least as common among primitives as among ourselves, but the reason for its frequent occurrence in these art forms is that painting and drama are simply poor conductors of meaning.* Arbitrary symbols must be imposed and agreed upon if these things are to communicate. There is no intrinsic meaning in the color red, but in Church symbolism it means martyrdom; in blazonry, it means magnanimity; among most American Indians it is the symbolism of success and violence (Matthews in Hodge: 325–326); and among ourselves it stands for stop and brothels. So with all kinds of visual symbolism—and literary symbolism as well.

Most of what we call symbolic in other literatures than our own is merely allusive, and the better the literature, the richer the allusions. By this criterion (which agrees with other criteria), Navaho, African, and Polynesian literatures are in the forefront of what the precivilized world has to offer. For the Navaho, Walton and Waterman state the case well (33):

> A conspicuous feature of Navaho poetry is that it consists of a series of statements connected with each other only through their reference to a thread of inner meaning which runs through each song. These songs are often at first glance somewhat obscure, for in them no proper sequence of ideas appears. Apparently the idea of the first day may be quite unrelated to that of the second. Usually no meaning can be discerned in a ceremonial song until a knowledge of its background (that is, of the religious conceptions of the tribe) supplies the relation of each statement to the underground idea. Each predication is woven, as it were, in a warp of mythical significance, the hidden threads of which connect it with the next predication. Such predications are mainly concerned with symbols, and each religious symbol referred to a statement, carries with it in the minds of the Navaho listener, a perfect aura of mystical associations and mystical emotions.

---

* Graphic art is often used as a mnemonic with recited myth. The song drawings of the Ojibwa Midewiwin society (Hoffman, Jenness); the Australian *churinga* and sand drawings; the Navaho sand paintings; the *quipu* of the Inca *quipucamaya;* and the bark roll of the Lenni Lenape are well known examples.

It would be ridiculous to require the Navaho priest to accompany each allusion with a historical and theological glossary, just as it would be to require a Christian minister to summarize the history of Christianity every time he elevates a crucifix. The congregation in both cases know what the symbol stands for.

Polynesian chants and songs are even more esoterically allusive than the Navaho.* Allusion has been so highly developed that it is a vice rather than a virtue, though some of the less skilful usages (less skilful in the Polynesians' view) have the qualities of real literature. In these unromantic and unliterary times a rejected lover might be expected to get drunk and leave town for richer pastures, but a Tongan victim of love unrequited, reacted because of his age and profession as a fisherman with this Shakespearean soliloquy (Collocott: 85):

> Well may the thunder crash and the rains descend,
> The earth quake and tremble with double shocks!
> Thunder rumbles around; I am bandied about in talk,
> They sit in judgment on me,
> On this ill-advised voyage of mine,
> Slanderous talk and cause of reproach.
> Ne'er before have I seen a thing so strange
> Like the "Whisper-in-Manuka."
> Now first I have known
> That the mat is chiefly, forsooth
> Is thy mind foolish?
> Is thy good sense hidden?
> Am I a canoe to be put about again,
> To go and be remade from some land
> That then you may wish to embark,
> You girls who have but lately grown?
> But is it not the manner of Tonga
> That after uncounted moons one is old?
> Is that a thing to be cause of remark?
> For is there but one man so dated?
> Believe rather 'tis our common weakness
> That was brought to earth . . . .

All one needs to know to appreciate this lament is that the lover makes a palpable hit in referring to the "Whisper-in-Manuka"—the fishhook of Maui, which in the mythology was used to dredge up

* Recall, for an impressive example, the Samoan proverbs in Chapter Two.

Tonga from the sea. He thus says that though he is old, so was Maui, so is every man in his time; and the fisherman's trade, that of Maui also, is traditionally one of the most revered in mythology, and certainly not to be despised by even the chiefly mat (the high-born spurning girl).

Cante Fable

Everywhere among folk and primitive narrators the *cante fable* (narrative interspersed with song) is an effective means to enliven a performance. It is very common among American folksingers, white and Negro, though on commercial recordings the spoken parts are edited out; among our professional folksingers, only Leadbelly (Huddie Ledbetter) was able to keep his *cante fable* performances intact on records. It is in fact so common a device that only among ourselves is it necessary to define it. Examples abound; here is a short one collected by Natalie Curtis from the Winnebago (253):

> Once there were some mice under a crooked log and they believed they were the only people in the world. One of them standing up and stretching his little arms could just touch the under side of the log. He thought that he was very tall and that he touched the sky. So he danced and sang this song:
>> Throughout the world
>> Who is there like little me!
>> Who is like me!
>> I can touch the sky,
>> I touch the sky indeed!*

Imagery

Imagery, since it is an evocation of beauty, is almost as artificial a concept as beauty itself. There are no absolutes. Probably no other natural product would be more widely accepted as a symbol of beauty than flowers, and yet the American Indians rarely alluded to flowers in their literature. Instead they turned their poetic eyes toward the heavens: "The Navaho myth is inconceivable without the stress laid on color, on rain streamers, rainbows, sky curtains, and sunbeams. It is difficult to think of Pawnee mythology without star-lore . . ." (Reichard, 1947: 34). Some Indians did not even look up

---

* A recent and convenient discussion of the *cante fable* is Herbert Halpert's "The Cante Fable in Decay," in Horace P. Beck, editor, *Folklore in Action: Essays for Discussion in Honor of MacEdward Leach*, pp. 139–150.

for beauty, or anywhere else. Reichard continues, saying the Coeur
d'Alêne myth is gray; there are no poetic allusions to clouds, stars,
mountains, flowers, or rivers; the only "dash of color in the grayness
of Coeur d'Alêne camas flat" is Mole's red dress. The Polynesians
were at the other end of the spectrum, finding beauty everywhere,
and they made a fetish of flowers (a pleasing survival is the lei given
to every tourist arriving in Hawaii). Eskimos live in a much more
colorful world than the ordinary citizen of the temperate zones im-
agines, but their literature sounds as if they had never seen any
environment but the realm of ice and snow that most people asso-
ciate with the extreme northern latitudes.

The gray world of the Coeur d'Alêne is relieved by their linguistic
imagery, which may not be economical, but which is certainly colorful
(Reichard, 1943: 98–100):

Card player: one whose business it is to bore himself arti-
ficially
Train: that which moves on all fours on but not attached to
a long object (tracks)
Deep voice: large cylindrical in the throat
Moonlight: light shines through in a wavy line
Be hopeful: fumble about in the heart
Relish food: cause something to be wholesome attached to the
heart

The Australian aborigines make good use of the few inspirations
their barren environment gives them. Taplin recorded a Narrinyeri's
impression of a locomotive (39):

> You see the smoke at Kapunda,
> The steam puffs regularly,
> Showing quickly, it looks like frost,
> It runs like running water,
> It blows like a spouting whale.

Parts of the Narrinyeri country of South Australia are no more
hospitable than the Hadhramaut, but the Narrinyeri had a more
poetic eye than the Bedouins, one of whom Thesiger (57) communed
with on this question in 1949:

> Sometimes, looking at a wonderful view, I have said to a
> Badui, 'Isn't that lovely?' and he has looked round for a
> bit and answered, 'No, it is rotten bad grazing.'

The mote was large in the Badu's beam; as Thesiger concluded, "if he had been a Persian he would have rhapsodized over it."

But there are souls dead to beauty in every society. My own mother was taken 2500 miles to see the Grand Canyon; she got out of the car and peered over the edge and said, "Yes. Lovely." And got back into the car.

Humor

Eskimos think it excruciatingly funny to ram a stick into a fish from head to tail and throw it to some begging sea bird. As the unsuspecting gull flies away, momentarily content, the Eskimos nearly fall out of their kayaks laughing about the gastric distress the bird is shortly going to have. The gull, if gulls were given to philosophy, might think "If it be not fun to me, what care I what fun it be?" It would not find much comfort in the fact that most if not all humor is based upon cruelty in one manifestation or other. When you look at it a bit, you find that humor is not very funny.

Humor is the most elusive, ephemeral, and ambiguous quality in literature. It is not timeless, as some humorists like to believe; no one can read Petroleum V. Nasby now and get many laughs out of him as his contemporaries allegedly did, and our own generation is beginning to wonder what we used to find so funny in Robert Benchley. Nor does humor cross the cultural barrier easily. Probably very little of the humor that primitive peoples see in their narratives is even suspected by collectors from our civilization unless a receptive audience gives some guidance to the meaning, and even then the ethnographer is more likely than not to miss the point. Acquaintance with the culture is not always a surety that humor will be recognized. A professor in a western university, a man who has taught the Bible as literature for years, thinks that the Hebrew authors were trying to be funny with such stories as Jonah and the whale. The makers of the Bible had many qualities, but humor is not one of them; anybody who finds funny stories in the Bible put them there himself. It helps if the collector has a sense of humor and it is certainly fatal to whatever comedy he finds if he does not. The least one could ask of an anthologist of humor is that he have a sense of humor himself, yet Oscar Williams puts into his "sparkling collection of . . . poems of wit, ribaldry, fun and foibles," his *Silver Treasury of Light Verse*, Sir Walter Raleigh's "The Lie," written in a harrowing time of bitterness and despair while he was waiting to be emasculated, hanged, drawn, quartered, and beheaded.

Judged by audience reaction, primitive peoples respond risibly to situations involving obscenity, scatology, anatomical deformity, ridiculous or incorrect behavior, discomfiture, ignorance, erroneous pronunciation, foreigners, transformations, practical jokes, satire, puns, sarcasm, irony, and minority opinion—or just about the same things we find funny. Important enough to be mentioned in its own sentence is recognition humor, in which the entire point lies in its being missed by members of the unsophisticated out-group. There is really nothing intrinsically funny about

> If you find your lonely bed at night as chilly as a tomb
> And you curl up in your blankets like a worm in a cocoon,
> It's not temperature that moves you, but a longing for the
> womb—
> As the id goes marching on

but it convulses people who know their Freud and those in such a group who pretend they do. The incongruity of the tune ("John Brown's Body") contributes a little to the humor, as incongruity always does. Similarly there is nothing intrinsically funny about the Chukchee tale which in its entirety goes

> Once a great raven performed the thanksgiving ceremonial
> in a narrow house and his tendons became cramped

except the allusions the Chukchee recognize.

Wherever sex is regulated, which is to say everywhere, allusions to sexual conduct whether licit or illicit are thought to be funny, regardless of whether the joke has anything else to recommend it. If sexual humor can be combined with some of the other sources of verbal amusement, such as recognition humor, it is that much better. The Dahomeans hide the sexual allusion under riddles whose official answers are painfully lame. Herskovits (1958: 56) mentions

> Hole within hole, hair all around, pleasure comes from inside.
> ANSWER: A flute being played by a bearded man.

If the present television popularity of Mitch Miller, the bearded community-singing oboist, lasts until the publication of this book, we can imagine this proverb entering our current joke domain with "Mitch Miller playing his oboe" being substituted for the Dahomean generalized answer, and thus attaining another level of recognition.

It is not strictly proper to go to the Africans for examples of good literature among the primitives, for they have attained the cultural level of cereal agriculture and are therefore in terms of our definition outside the scope of this study, but it is hard to find humor in societies lower on the subsistence scale that will go very well with sophisticated readers. Examining humorous literature around the world, one could almost parallel the evolution of culture from primitiveness to sophistication by the worth of a society's humor. By this scale the Africans would score high indeed. Consider this story collected by Courlander and Herzog among the Ashanti, entitled simply, "Talk":

> Once, not far from the city of Accra on the Gulf of Guinea, a country man went out to his garden to dig up some yams to take to market. While he was digging, one of the yams said to him, "Well, at last you're here. You never weeded me, but now you come around with your digging stick. Go away and leave me alone!"
>
> The farmer turned around and looked at his cow in amazement. The cow was chewing her cud and looking at him.
>
> "Did you say something?" he asked.
>
> The cow kept on chewing and said nothing, but the man's dog spoke up. "It wasn't the cow who spoke to you," the dog said, "It was the yam. The yam says leave him alone."
>
> The man became angry, because his dog had never talked before, and he didn't like his tone besides. So he took his knife and cut a branch from a palm tree to whip his dog. Just then the palm tree said, "Put that branch down!"
>
> The man was getting very upset about the way things were going, and he started to throw the palm branch away, but the palm branch said, "Man, put me down softly!"
>
> He put the branch down gently on a stone, and the stone said, "Hey, take that thing off me!"
>
> This was enough, and the frightened farmer started to run for his village. On the way he met a fisherman going the other way with a fish trap on his head.
>
> "What's the hurry?" the fisherman said.
>
> "My yam said, 'Leave me alone!' Then the dog said, 'Listen to what the yam says!' When I went to whip the dog with a palm branch the tree said, 'Put that branch down!' Then the palm branch said, 'Do it softly!' Then the stone said, 'Take that thing off me!' "
>
> "Is that all?" the man with the fish trap asked. "Is that so frightening?"
>
> "Well," the man's fish trap said, "did he take off the

stone?"

"Wah!" the fisherman shouted. He threw the fish trap on the ground and began to run with the farmer, and on the trail they met a weaver with a bundle of cloth on his head.

"Where are you going in such a rush?" he asked.

"My yam said, 'Leave me alone!' " the farmer said. "The dog said, 'Listen to what the yam says!' The tree said, 'Put that branch down!' The branch said, 'Do it softly!' And the stone said, 'Take that thing off me!' "

"And then," the fisherman continued, "the fish trap said, 'Did he take it off?' "

"That's nothing to get excited about," the weaver said, "No reason at all."

"Oh, yes it is," his bundle of cloth said. "If it happened to you you'd run too!"

"Wah!" the weaver shouted. He threw down his bundle on the trail and started running with the other men.

They came panting to the ford in the river and found a man bathing. "Are you chasing a gazelle?" he asked them.

The first man said breathlessly, "My yam talked at me, and it said, 'Leave me alone!' And my dog said, 'Listen to your yam.' And when I cut myself a branch the tree said, 'Put that branch down!' And the branch said, 'Do it softly!' And the stone said, 'Take that thing off me!' "

The fisherman panted, "And my trap said, 'Did he?' "

The weaver wheezed, "And my bundle of cloth said, 'You'd run too!' "

"Is that why you're running?" the man in the river asked.

"Well, wouldn't you run if you were in their position?" the river said.

The man jumped out of the water and began to run with the others. They ran down the main street of the village to the house of the chief. The chief's servant brought his stool out, and he came and sat on it to listen to their complaints. The men began to recite their troubles.

"I went out to my garden to dig yams," the farmer said, waving his arms. "Then everything began to talk! My yam said, 'Leave me alone!' My dog said, 'Pay attention to your yam!' The tree said, 'Put that branch down!' The branch said, 'Do it softly!' And the stone said, 'Take it off me!' "

"And my fish trap said, 'Well, did he take it off?' "

"And my cloth said, 'You'd run too!' " the weaver said.

"And the river said the same!" the bather said hoarsely, his eyes bulging.

The chief listened to them patiently, but he couldn't refrain from scowling. "Now this is really a wild story," he said at last. "You'd better all go back to your work before I punish you for disturbing the peace."

So the men went away, and the chief shook his head and mumbled to himself, "Nonsense like that upsets the community."

"Fantastic, isn't it?" his stool said. "Imagine, a talking yam!"

CULTURE AND QUALITY

Some literatures have greatness thrust upon them; others are condemned by their culture to sterility. There seems to be a certain limited amount of artistic energy available to each society, which can be concentrated on one form of endeavor or apportioned out more or less equally and thinly on many. The Pueblo tribes channelled their energy into ceremonialism, sparing little for their poetry, which beside the magnificent song texts of their Navaho neighbors is wretched stuff. England has a hundred writers for every composer or painter of note, a thousand writers for every sculptor—ratios that other European nations may reverse. How many Flemish authors can we put over against Flemish painters—the Brueghels, Rubens, Memling, van der Weyden, van Eyck, van Dyck, or van der Goes?

It is almost an anthropological truism that no aspect of a culture can be appreciably far in advance of the whole of the culture, but this principle breaks down in regard to art. Magdalenian culture generally was nearly as poor as any in the thousand-century history of *Homo sapiens*, yet Magdalenian painting is at least as good as anything turned out by modern artists. So too are myths of a high order among the Australian aborigines, whose material culture is scarcely superior to that of the Magdalenian Cro Magnons.

The Poor Cultures

In studying art it is nearly impossible to exclude value judgments, since one is dealing with an esthetic and therefore an estimable endeavor. However much we may sympathize with the "little elfmen" of the world—

> He slightly frowned, and with his eyes
> He looked me through and through—
> "I'm quite as big for me," said he,
> "As you are big for you"

—they must abide our question when we speak of literature.

No one attributes inferiorities in culture to racial differences any longer, and no substitute reason has yet been advanced to account for the unquestioned lacks that ethnographers have found in surveying peoples of the primitive world. For the ethnographers themselves, the very definition of their profession freed them from offering reasons for what they found; it was enough for them to record. Statements like the following are all too common in ethnographic summaries:

> This group [western Mixe Indians of Oaxaca] today lack virtually all types of tales—pre-Conquest, autochthonous post-Conquest, or European (Beals: 14).

> The folk tale quoted above, of which there are a number of variants, was about the only one I ever heard the Siriono tell. Although Moon is credited with having started everything in their culture, stories to account for these things were never told (Holmberg: 47).

> These few Samoyed Mohicans have only little folklore. I was able to record only a few dozen legends and puzzles, and to a large extent these are probably of Tatar origin. There are also few songs, since most Khamassin only sing Russian airs (Donner: 138).

> . . . the only resemblance to tales at all [among the Cayapa] is the alleged experiences that certain individuals, during intoxication or sleep, claim to have had in their encounters with strange spirits. There is nothing resembling a culture-hero cycle or any other cycle of myths. Animal stories, so common among aboriginal peoples, are almost unknown among the Cayapa (Barrett: 382).

> The Alacaluf have no musical instruments, and sing little or not at all except when the big house is erected (Bird: 78).

And so it goes. Some collectors prefer to let the literature condemn itself rather than to dismiss it with a brief judgment. As we have argued elsewhere, the literature of the Polar World is, beneath the façade of grandeur erected upon it by sympathetic collectors, poor stuff indeed. There are a few objective ethnographers who have put down literally what they heard among the people of the Far North. Rae did no façade-erecting on a Samoyed song (211):

O ya ya yo, very fine house, yaya yo yaya.
O strange men, yay o ay ya, no talkee our tongue, yaya.
Go ya Kanin Nos, ya yo, much cold, yo yo ya ya.
Angliski plenty money got, ya ya yee yaya.
Go Kanin Nos ya, never come back, ya yee, no more.
Lots reindeer on tundra ya, Kanin o, yee, ya.
Doktor o ya, very 'andsome man, ha hee ya yay ya.
Plenty vodka get, ya ya, good good o ay ya.

Before we go far in condemnation of the Eskimos, Chukchee, Yukaghir, Yakut, Tungus, Ostyak, Samoyed, and Lapps stretching a belt of poor literature around the world north of the 60th parallel, we would be well advised to learn a little humility by looking at some things Americans have been responsible for. Considering our origin, we are not nearly so bad at literature as we might be, if that is any excuse. American prose literature (and poetry apart from song) is poor not because the United States is a young country, the common plaint, but because its founding fathers who established the cultural pattern were men of barren imagination in these things.* The *Bay Psalm Book* is worth more in dollars and cents than any other book ever published in this country, but its contents are execrable as literature. Even worse is the great best seller of Puritan times, the book that probably sold more copies per capita than any other work written in America, Michael Wigglesworth's *The Day of Doom*. Little good can be said for Puritan literature, for there is little good in it. But for the world's marginal peoples, many of whom were near extinction and hardly in the mood to sing fine songs when white man decided it would do no particular harm to salvage at least a description of what he was destroying, it might well be that what appears to be poor literature is really the result of a poor collector working with a poor informant. This is true also for much folksong collecting; taking a tape recorder to a mountain cabin chosen more or less at random is not likely to produce any better example

---

* This estimation is made despite our earlier claim that literature is England's starriest crown. The Puritans, for all their virtues, were an atypical, almost folk group, whose discontent with English culture (rather than religious persecution) prompted their leaving the homeland. Anyone who thinks that Milton is an exception to this criticism of Puritan literature should read his less well known works.

of the genre at its best than would be obtained of modern popular rhythm if the Fuller Brush Man were to ask a random housewife to sing rock 'n' roll.

Poor literature too is often the result of the exhaustion of a culture pattern. Every trait that a society possesses, from making a poem to making an automobile, has a terminal limit within its pattern; evolution past that limit produces only grotesqueries. The automobile fender reached its terminal development within its functional pattern when it was made to stop mud from flying over the car's occupants; building it into enormous tailfins certainly went beyond the limit of function or art. So also in literature. In Shakespeare's time there were perhaps five million speakers of the English tongue, most of whom were illiterate, yet the age produced as many as a dozen playwrights of Shakespeare's calibre or near it. Some of us think that Marlowe was potentially better than Shakespeare, but he died with that promise unfulfilled at the age of 29. Today there are 300 million people speaking English, but what do we have in drama? Poetry too became moribund in England and America a century ago; the leading poetry journal in this country now has 5000 subscribers, some of whom are motivated by charity rather than love of literature, and the only kind of "poetry" that finds its way into general circulation is verse like "The Call":

America, arise!
The hour is over-late,
Red sickles scar the skies,
Red multitudes await
To hurl their hate.

Lay by the idle boast,
Omit the foolish word.
Allwheres from coast to coast
Let only this be heard:
For freedom gird!

Let all division end,
Set politics aside,
One object: to defend
Our word against the tide
Of right denied.

O, haste to heed the call:

Lest in some sudden hour
We weep to see the fall
Of all that yet might tower
To godly power.

We are not alone in this impotent conclusion.   Strehlow (1947: 6)
explains the sterility of Aranda tradition:

> . . . since every feature of the landscape, prominent or other-
> wise, in Central Australia is already associated with one or
> the other of these myths, we can readily understand the at-
> titude of utter apathy and the general mental stagnation that
> exist amongst the present generation of the natives as far
> as literary efforts of any kind are concerned. The thorough-
> ness of their forefathers has left to them not a single unoccu-
> pied scene which they could fill with the creatures of their
> own imagination. Tradition and the tyranny of the old men
> in the religious and cultural sphere have effectually stifled
> all creative impulse; and no external stimulus ever reached
> Central Australia which could have freed the natives from
> these insidious bonds. It is almost certain that native myths
> had ceased to be invented many centuries ago. The chants,
> the legends, and the ceremonies which we record today
> mark the consummation of the creative efforts of a distant,
> long-past age. The present-day natives are on the whole
> merely the painstaking, uninspired preservers of a great
> and interesting inheritance.

For many people besides ourselves it is true as the Eskimos sang,
that "all songs have been exhausted."

The Rich Cultures

Beauty is where beauty is found. The poorest culture may yield a
lofty thought exquisitely expressed. No one has ever successfully in-
dicted the Cheyenne as a poetic people, but even in this culture which
spent its energy killing off its young men, Natalie Curtis (153) found
a pathetic last song of a dying warrior trying to make the best of a
bad end:

Nay, I fear the aching tooth of age.

The Andamanese are too primitive to know how to make fire, according to some who have studied them at second hand, but they

felt deeply enough to join the sadness of nature and man in a lyric
too starkly translated by Edward Man (252):

> thou heart sad
> sky surface there look-at
> sky surface of ripple
> bamboo spear.

Only the frequency of beauty can be predicted. In the New
World, the most consistent high quality in cultures without writing
is found among the Navaho; in the Old World, among the Polynesians. Washington Matthews drew this passage from the Navaho
Mountain Chant (1884: 459):

> Where my kindred dwell, there I wander.
> Child of the White Corn am I, there I wander.
> At the Red Rock House, there I wander.
> Where the dark kethawns are at the doorway, there I
> wander.
> With the pollen of dawn upon my trail, there I wander.
> At the yuni the striped cotton hangs with pollen, there I
> wander.
> Going around with it, there I wander.
> Taking another, I depart with it, with it I wander.
> In the house of long life, there I wander.
> In the house of happiness, there I wander.
> Beauty before me, with it I wander.
> Beauty behind me, with it I wander.
> Beauty below me, with it I wander.
> Beauty above me, with it I wander.
> In old age traveling, with it I wander.
> On the beautiful trail I am, with it I wander.*

The Mountain Chant shows also that classic simplicity (as in the
poetry of A. E. Housman) is gem-like. The mythical figure Dsilyi
Neyani, homesick for the land he had left, is overcome by the sight
of the San Juan River, and expresses his nostalgia characteristically
in the Navaho terms of motion (Astrov: 48).

> That flowing water!
> My mind wanders across it.
> That broad water! That flowing water!

---

*How far a translator can go in destroying literary beauty can be seen in Walton's
translation of this song (1930: 108–109).

My mind wanders across it.
That old age water! That flowing water!
My mind wanders across it.

In comparing the two superlative literatures of the Navaho and
the Polynesians we should consider the environment that inspired
them.   The San Juan River is a poor stream running through poor
country, but the Polynesian islands might have evoked lyricism even
in Michael Wigglesworth. The Polynesians, too, may have retained
some of the poetic sensitivity of their Indonesian ancestors who even
now, as Odin Meeker said of the Laotians, are "far more interested
in decorating things with curlicues than getting ahead in the world."*
Brodrick (79–80) caught a magnificent piece of imagery in an *im-
provised* Cambodian festive song:

> Sorrow is born at the setting sun
> The kingfishers dart away
> To perch by the torrents' bed.
> Sadness at sunset
> While playing the air of Angkor-Reach
> The hymn that lulls the king to sleep.
> Sorrow of the evening sun.
> The birds fly off in couples
> To be hidden in the tree-tops
> Only my beloved and I meet never
> I plunge into the forest thickets
> Searching my beloved
> And then suddenly I see her
> Drawing water from the spring
> But it is not she, it is not she,
> It is the morning star
> Drinking on the edge of the misty sky.

Everywhere one looks in Polynesian literature there is mastery of
the art.   Katherine Luomala (1949: 90–91) gives the most unlikely
example one can imagine—a lullaby composed by a mad woman for
a wooden doll she had made and dressed with albatross feathers in
her hopeless longing for a child of her own.   In this Paumoto *oriori*
(which Luomala accompanies by an explanatory commentary), the

---

* The literature of the marginal Oriental lands has not been considered in this
study since nearly all of it is either sophisticated or folk; that is, Malaysia and In-
donesia are a generally literate area.   The Cambodian selection quoted here from
Brodrick is from a primitive ("non-literate") group.

old woman croons to her manikin child its ancestry:

> My little child,
> Thou camest from the peak at Hawaiki.
> On thy arriving, on thy coming ashore,
> To the country Maui fished up
> And made dry land
> Trees brought a child for me.

Then, to exhibit her knowledge and teach the child its genealogy, she told how the sea god Tangaroa went to the lower world Rua-ki-pouri in pursuit of knowledge. The child's ancestor is Chief Puhikai, god of sea monsters, who ordered his tribal brothers, Te Ninihi, Te Wiwi, and Te Wawa to leave their lairs and assist Ruamano who had been attacked by magicians.

> Tangaroa sought below in Rua-ki-pouri.
> Thy ancestor is Puhi, chief of the sea,
> Who caused Te Ninihi, Te Wiwi, and Te Wawa
> To rise and float from their lairs,
> When Ruamano was driven ashore—
> Such was his fate due to powerful magicians.
> Now I have taken this story as a lullaby for my child.

She returns for a moment to the myth about Maui. Several obscure lines are omitted.

> Forth from the depths appears the land
> With Tongariro, mountain of the gods . . .
> We are of high born rank, O child!

She pretends that the child cries for food. To divert its attention, she tells it a little more family history:

> O little one! Thou criest for food.
> There is no food for thee,
> From me, your mother, O little one!
> Te Rahiri ate the shell of the moon,
> Called Te Wai-tokihi-rangi.
> Often I have heard, O little one,
> The story told in many lands,
> That we came hither with Tamatea.

Tamatea was the captain of the Takitumu canoe, from whose crew and passengers the Takitumu tribe claim descent. The

mother tells the child the names of her schools and her
teachers.   Then if the child is ever questioned about its
genealogy or the reliability of its learning, it will tell where
its mother, who taught it, received her education.

> Lest thou be questioned at Te Mania,
> At Te Hora-a-Moehau,
> Enter straight the house, Rupe-o-Huriwaka,
> The house of the ancestors of the Pokai-akatea,
> Whence I gained the Tokaru from Pae-kawa.

Alas, for the mother's education, she was slightly deaf.

> I did not, O little one,
> Distinctly hear the whole,
> For one ear is deaf.
> But one thing I did grasp—
> The strong desire, the ardent wish for Tane-mata.

Tanemata is the god associated with learning.   The mother
ends her *oriori* with an invocation:

> Offer up the sacrificial fern-root.
> Utter the inciting invocation
> Utter the invocation of memory . . . .

Edward Tregear cites a shorter lullaby from New Zealand (75):

> Here is little Rangi Tumua, reclining with me
> Under the lofty pine tree of Hine-rahi.
> And here am I, my little fellow,
> Seeking, searching sadly through the thoughts that rise.
> In these days, my child,
> For us two no lofty chiefs are left.
> Passed are the times of thy far-famed uncles,
> Who from the storms of war and witchcraft
> Gave shelter to the multitude, the thousands.

No "Rock-a-bye-Baby" doggerel for the Polynesians!
The Polynesians thus literally had their poetic lessons at their
mothers' breasts; before they were able to understand the lesson,
they absorbed the feeling for elegant expression which in adulthood
they perfected in the formal schools.   Buck, thinking only of the
remarkable navigational accomplishments of the Polynesians, called
them the Vikings of the Sunrise; he could have called them the

Greeks of the Pacific with more aptness. Like Homer, the Polynesians were capable of sustained literary mastery—whole cycles of narrative hold a plateau of quality. Here are two illustrative songs from the tragic cycle of Toga-te-huareva, a chief who lost a conflict with his family's enemy, Matakahi-te-ariki, and whose every possession, including his wife, were given to Te Ariki-huru-tara. In the first intricate song, Te Ariki-huru-tara is given the poetical name of Makahi-ragi, and Toga is given the name of Marahara (Buck, 1938: 344–350):

> (*Refrain*) Trouble, O trouble.
> Great is the love for the chiefly friend,
> Pehenua-kura.
> A lone land lies with
> Matakahi-te-ariki,
> The land of Matahara named Tutuira
> Now occupied by the chief Makahi-ragi.
>
> A people without a head is
> With Matakahi-te-ariki,
> A people belonging to Matahara
> Named Tuarau
> Of whom the head is now Makahi-ragi.
>
> A lonely house is with
> Matakahi-te-ariki,
> The house of Matahara
> Named Hapai-o-pua
> Now occupied by the chief
> Makahi-ragi.
>
> A deserted spring is with
> Matakahi-te-ariki,
> A pool belonging to Matahara
> Named Te Vai-raromea
> From which drinks the chief
> Makahi-ragi.
>
> A love-lorn wife is with
> Matakahi-te-ariki,
> The wife of Matahara

Named Ugaru-te-ganagana
Now espoused by the chief
Makahi-ragi.

Later in the cycle Toga-te-huareva magically charms his lost wife, Ugaru, to a pool at night, where they part forever:

(*Refrain*) Joy turns to sadness.
I stretch out my hand,
O my beloved,
It touched below your wrist
Ah! Joy will turn to sadness.

I stretched out my hand,
O my beloved,
It touched your sweetness,
Ah! Joy will turn to sadness.

I stretched out my hand
O my beloved,
It fell into empty space,
Ah! Joy has turned to sadness.

The Polynesian navigators touched on Australia in prehistoric times, leaving adze-caches along the Murray River. Had the contact been friendly—as it probably was not—the two peoples would have had mutual regard for each other's literature. Several illustrations have already been cited; in line with the cinema cliché, this summary view of the quality of primitive literature can close with the farewell of a Culture Hero in northern Australia, "Nagacork's Good-Bye" (Robinson, 1952: 47):

And the old man Nagacork went on a long walkabout to see all the blackfellows, the birds, animals, fish and reptiles.

And as Nagacork travelled through all the different countries of the tribes he sang.

"Allo, allo, allo, allo, allo, cha nallad, wirritt, burra burra, cubrimilla cubrimilla, bo, bo." This means, "Oh well, all you people who belong to me, you have changed into blackfellows, animals, birds, reptiles, fish, sun, moon, and stars.

I go now. I go forever. You will see me no more. But all the time I will watch about you."

And the blackfellows say that they can see the old man Nagacork lying among the stars. His lubra is lying near him with one arm behind her head. And the blackfellows say that the stream of stars that the white man calls the milky way is the smoke of Nagacork's camp-fire drifting across the night.

Chapter Five / THE MAKER AND THE GLEEMAN

The entertainer is an individual apart from his society. Often he is rewarded far above any logical valuation of his wares and he is permitted behavior that in other members of his community would be intolerable, but his rewards and his status are on sufferance, whether he is a Japanese *kabuki* actor intensively trained at his hereditary art or a Rotarian called to the head table to sing about his irregular attendance. Not many students of comparative literature have ever heard of Iadmon of Samos, but in Iadmon's household Aesop was only a slave. In Shakespeare's England actors escaped the severe punishments for vagabondage only by taking spurious employment as servants to some aristocrat. Shakespeare himself wrote his plays as a member of the domestic staff of the two Lords Hunsdon and the King, and one reason we know so little about him in connection with the theatre is that on acquiring modest wealth as a shareholder in his theatrical company he was probably anxious to dissociate himself from the sordid business of the stage, so, like members of the upper stratum of New York's underworld who move across the river to respectable homes in Plainfield, Shakespeare moved back to Stratford and bought New Place. The low life of less successful Elizabethan writers is well described in Robert Greene's *A Groatsworth of Wit Bought with a Million of Repentance*, written on his squalid deathbed. We have the term "legitimate theatre" because for most of the history of English drama there were only two playhouses exempted from the law against such places. In the primitive world the same ambivalence obtains toward professional entertainers; the shaman from Siberia to Australia has enviable status, yet his disabilities are so great that many shamans hold the office against their will. And the Polynesian *arioi* probably felt that their work as professional hedonists was badly rewarded when their children were put to death.

In many societies, too, the professional entertainer is driven by circumstances into his trade. The Eskimo born an epileptic is born a shaman, and blind men from Homer to the Reverend Gary Davis have had to go to begging or busking.

This may be too tragic a picture of the entertainer. Tears are not always cutting through the Pagliacci's grease paint. Though their gratification may be transitory, it is often intense. The pride of the Turkish *kemenche* player who boasted in his song

> The strings of my *kemenche* will make you jump wherever you are, because my name is Sadik from Rize. Do you understand who I am?   (Cowell)

is the pride of all competent performers. Charlie Chaplin took great if blasphemous satisfaction in knowing that in Lhasa he was better known than Jesus Christ.

We can distinguish in all societies two basic kinds of literary entertainers. To use the poetically apt Anglo-Saxon names, there is the man who sings, chants, or recites to an audience material he composed himself—the *scop*, or "maker"; and there is the man who uses the compositions of others—the *gliwman*, the "gleeman." In either case he is primarily a performer; few societies have any place for the man who makes without doing. Even Shakespeare made his money as an actor and a member of his stock company, not as a playwright.

COMPOSERS AND COMPOSITION

It is hard for us to understand how unimportant the individual is in most societies. In a practical sense the individual everywhere is the ultimate creator of literary material (*das Volk dichtet* only through individual representatives) but his identity is rarely preserved along with his creations. Quick oblivion is the fate of composers in societies without printing; their material is usurped by their listeners and becomes anonymous. Moreover, when the stabilizing force of print is absent, the material is further molded into the general cultural domain by what has been called the "folk process." Accordingly, when we read folk and primitive literature, we must keep in mind that quality is quality of a culture, not of an individual genius. A work of literature on these levels is more even in style and quality than a poem, a novel, or a play would be with us. And as Hartland cautioned in one of the first studies made of this material (3), "we must above all things beware of crediting the story teller with that degree of conscious art which is only possible in an advanced culture and under literary influences." All authors are children of their culture, but if they are members of folk or primitive groups, their parent is a tyrant.

But like every anthropological generalization this has its exceptions. One of the most impressive exceptions is the magnificent re-creation made of the European animal tale "The Cock and the Mouse" by a Zuni Indian. In the summer of 1866 Frank H. Cushing, the early collector of Zuni stories, took three Indian friends—Palo-whaita, Waihusiwa, and Heluta—over the "Ocean of Sunrise" to Europe. While at Manchester-by-the-Sea, they entertained their English friends with story telling, Cushing himself contributing the jejune tale of "The Cock and the Mouse" from T. F. Crane's *Italian Popular Tales:*

> Once upon a time there were a cock and a mouse. One day the mouse said to the cock, "Friend Cock, shall we go and eat some nuts on yonder tree?" "As you like." So they both went under the tree and the mouse climbed up at once and began to eat. The poor cock began to fly, and flew and flew, but could not come to where the mouse was. When it saw that there was no hope of getting there, it said: "Friend Mouse, do you know what I want you to do? Throw me a nut." The mouse went and threw one and hit the cock on the head. The poor cock, with its head all broken and covered with blood, went away to an old woman. "Old aunt, give me some rags to cure my head." "If you will give me two hairs I will give you the rags." The cock went away to a dog. "Dog, give me two hairs; the hairs I will give the old woman; the old woman will give me rags to cure my head." "If you will give me a little bread," said the dog, "I will give you the hairs." The cock went away to a baker. "Baker, give me bread; I will give bread to the dog; the dog will give hairs; the hairs I will carry to the old woman; the old woman will give me rags to cure my head." The baker answered: "I will not give you bread unless you give me some wood." The cock went away to the forest. "Forest, give me some wood; the wood I will carry to the baker; the baker will give me some bread; the bread I will give to the dog; the dog will give me hairs; the hairs I will carry to the old woman; the old woman will give me rags to cure my head." The forest answered: "If you will bring me a little water, I will give you some wood." The cock went away to a fountain. "Fountain, give me water; water I will carry to the forest; forest will give wood; wood I will carry to the baker; baker

will give bread; bread I will give dog; dog will give hairs;
hairs I will give old woman; old woman will give rags to
cure my head." The fountain gave him water; the water he
carried to the forest; the forest gave him wood; the wood he
carried to the baker; the baker gave him bread; the bread
he gave to the dog; the dog gave him the hairs; the hairs he
carried to the old woman; the old woman gave him the rags;
and the cock cured his head.

It is a good thing for us who have to read this tale that the fountain did not ask the cock to go any further with this thing, or we
would need some rags to cure *our* heads. The story is a poor one—
it seems almost contrived in its worthlessness. The basic incident
is unmotivated, the cumulative interdependent tasks are let run on
and on without reason, no tension or conflict is developed, and the
tale is completely without point. We can imagine the embarrassed
but polite reception of the story by the Englishmen present, who had
in any event no illusions about the quality of American story telling.
Nor could Cushing have expected such a poor effort to make any
impression upon his Indian companions; but a year later, back at
Zuni, at a similar tale competition he was astounded to hear Waihusiwa present this transfiguration:

Thus it was in the Town of the Floods Abounding [Venice]
long ago. There lived there an old woman, so they say, of the
Italia-kwe [Italy-people], who, in the land of their nativity,
are the parental brothers of the Mexicans, it is said. Now,
after the manner of that people, this old woman had a
Takaka Cock which she kept alone so that he would not
fight the others. He was very large, like a turkey, with a
fine sleek head and a bristle-brush on his breast like a
turkey-cock's too, for the *Takaka*-kind were at first the
younger brothers of the Turkeys, so it would seem.

Well, the old woman kept her Cock in a little corral of
tall close-stakes, sharp at the top and wattled together
with rawhide thongs, like an eagle-cage against a wall,
only it had a little wicket also fastened with thongs. Now,
try as he would, the old *Takaka* Cock could not fly out, for
he had no chance to run and make a start as turkeys do in
the wilds, yet he was ever trying and trying, because he
was meat-hungry—always anxious for worms;—for, although the people of that village had abundant food, this old

woman was poor and lived mainly on grain-foods, where-
fore, perforce, she fed the old *Takaka* Cock with the refuse of
her own eatings. In the morning the old woman would come
and throw this refuse food into the corral cage.

Under the wall near by there lived a Mouse. He had no
old grandmother to feed him, and he was particularly fond of
grain food. When, having eaten his fill, the old Cock would
settle down, stiff of neck and not looking this side or that,
but sitting in the sun *ka-ta-ka-toking* to himself, the little
Mouse would dodge out, steal a bit of torilla or a crumb, and
whist into his hole again. Being sleepy, the *Takaka* Cock
never saw him, and so, day after day the Mouse fared sump-
tuously and grew over bold. But one day, when corn was
ripe and the Cock had been well fed and was settling down
to his sitting nap, the Mouse came out and stole a particularly large piece of bread, so that in trying to push it into his
hole he made some noise, and, moreover, had to stop and
tunnel his doorway larger.

The Cock turned his head and looked just as the Mouse
was working his way slowly in, and espied the long, naked
tail lying there on the ground and wriggling as the Mouse
moved to and fro at his digging.

"Hah! By the Grandmother of Substance, it is a worm!"
cackled the Cock, and he made one peck at the Mouse's tail
and bit it so hard that he cut it entirely off and swallowed it
at one gulp.

The Mouse, squeaking "Murder!" scurried down into his
sleeping place, and fell to licking his tail until his chops
were all pink and his mouth was drawn down like a crying
woman's; for he loved his long tail as a young dancer loves
the glory of his long hair, and he cried continually: "Weh
tsu tsu, weh tsu tse, yam hok ti-i-i!" and thought, "Oh,
that shameless great beast! By the Demon of Slave-Crea-
tures, I'll have my payment of him! For he is worse than
an owl or a night-hawk. They eat us all up, but he has taken
away the very mark of my mousehood and left me to mourn
it. I'll take vengeance on him, will I!"

So, from that time the Mouse thought how he might com-
pass it, and this plan seemed best: He would creep out some
day, all maimed of tail as he was, and implore pity, and thus,
perchance, make friends for a while with the *Takaka* Cock.

So he took seed-down, and made a plaster of it with nut-resin, and applied it to the stump of his tail. Then, on a morning, holding his tail up as a dog does his foot when maimed by a cactus, he crawled to the edge of his hole and cried in a weak voice to the *Takaka:*

"*Ani, yoa yoa!   Ita-ak'ya Mosa,*
  Motcho wak'ya,
  Oshe wak'ya,
  Ethl ha asha ni ha.   Ha na, yoa, ha na!"

"Look, you, pity, pity! Master of Food Substance,
  Of my maiming,
  Of my hunger,
  I am all but dying, Ah me, pity, ah me."

Whereupon he held up his tail, which was a safe thing to do, you see, for it no longer looked like a worm or any other eatable.

Now, the *Takaka* was flattered to be called a master of plenty, so he said, quite haughtily (for he had eaten and could not bend his neck, and felt proud, withal), "Come in, you poor little thing, and eat all you want. As if I cared for what the like of you could eat!" So the Mouse went in and ate very little, as became a polite stranger, and thanking the Cock, bade him good-day and went back to his hole.

By-and-by he came again, and this time he brought part of a nutshell containing fine white meat. When he had shouted warning of his coming and entered the corral cage, he said: "Comrade father, let us eat together. Of this food I have plenty, gathered from yonder high nut-tree which I climb every autumn when the corn is ripe and cut the nuts therefrom. But of all food yours I most relish, since I can-not store such in my cellar. Now, it may be you will equally relish mine; so let us eat then together."

"It is well, comrade child," replied the Cock; so they began to eat.

But the Cock had no sooner tasted the nut than he fairly chuckled for joy, and having speedily made an end of the kernel, fell to lamenting his hard lot. "Alas, ah me!" he said. "My grandmother brings me, on rare days, something like to this, but picked all too clean. There is nought eat-

able so nice. Comrade little one, do you have plenty of
this kind, did you say?"

"Oh, yes," replied the Mouse; "but, you see, the season
is near to an end now, and when I want more nuts I must go
and gather them from the tree. Look, now! Why do you
not go there also? That is the tree, close by."

"Ah me, I cannot escape, woe to me! Look at my wings,"
said the Cock, "they are worn to bristles—and as to the
beard on my breast, my chief ornament, alas! it is all
crumpled and uneven, so much have I tried to fly out and
so hard have I pushed against the bars. As for the door,
my grandmother claps that shut and fastens it tightly with
thongs, be you sure, as soon as ever she finishes the feeding
of me!"

"Ha! ha!" exclaimed the Mouse. "If that's all, there's
nothing easier than to open that. Look at my teeth; I even
crack the hard nuts with these scrapers of mine! Wait!" He
ran nimbly up the wicket and soon gnawed through the hold-
ing-string. "There! comrade father; push open the door,
you are bigger than I, and we will go nutting."

"Thanks this day," cried the Cock, and shoving the
wicket open, he ran forth cackling and crowing for gladness.

Then the Mouse led the way to the tree. Up the trunk
he ran, and climbed and climbed until he came to the top-
most boughs. "Ha! the nuts are fine and ripe up here," he
shouted.

But the *Takaka* fluttered and flew all in vain; his wings
were so worn he could not win even to the lowermost
branches. "Oh! have pity on me, comrade child! Cut off
some of the nuts and throw them down to me, do! My wings
are so worn I cannot fly any better than the grandmother's
old dog, who is my neighbor over there."

"Be patient, be patient, father!" exclaimed the Mouse.
"I am cracking a big one for you as fast as I can. There,
catch it!" and he threw a fat nut close to the Cock, who
gleefully devoured the kernel and, without so much as
thanks, called for more.

"Wait, father," said the Mouse. "There! Stand right
under me, so. Now, catch it; this is a big one!" Saying
which the Mouse crawled out until he was straight over the
Cock. "Now, then," said he, "watch in front!" and he let
fall the nut. It hit the Cock on the head so hard that it

bruised the skin and stunned the old *Takaka* so that he fell over and died for a short time, utterly forgetting.

"*Te mi thlo ko thlo kwa!*" shouted the Mouse, as he hurried down the tree. "A little waiting, and lo! What my foe would do to me, I to him do, indeed!" Whereupon he ran across, before ever the Cock had opened an eye, and gnawed his bristles off so short that they never could grow again. "There, now!" said the Mouse. Lo! thus healed is my heart, and my enemy is even as he made me, bereft of distinction!" Then he ran back to his cellar, satisfied.

Finally the Cock opened his eyes. "Ah, me, my head!" he exclaimed. Then, moaning, he staggered to his feet, and in so doing he espied the nut. It was smooth and round, like a brown egg. When the Cock saw it he fell to lamenting more loudly than ever; "Oh, my head! *Ta-ka-ka-ka-a-a!*" But the top of his head kept bleeding and swelling until it was all covered over with welts of gore, and it grew so heavy, withal, that the *Takaka* thought he would surely die. So off to his grandmother he went, lamenting all the way.

Hearing him, the grandmother opened the door, and cried; "What now?"

"Oh, my grandmother, ah me! I am murdered!" he answered. "A great, round, hard seed was dropped on my head by a little creature with a short, one-feathered tail, who came and told me that it was good to eat and—oh! my head is all bleeding and swollen! By the light of your favor, bind my head for me lest, alas, I die!"

"Served you right! Why did you leave your place, knowing better?" cried the old woman. "I will not bind your head unless you give me your very bristles of manhood, that you may remember your lesson!"

"Oh! take them, grandmother!" cried the Cock; but when he looked down, alas! the beard of his breast, the glory of his kind, was all gone. "Ah me! ah me! What shall I do?" he again cried. But the old woman told him that unless he brought her at least four bristles she would not cure him, and forthwith she shut the door.

So the poor Cock slowly staggered back toward his corral, hoping to find some of the hairs that had been gnawed off. As he passed the little lodge of his neighbor, the Dog,

he caught sight of old Wahsita's fine muzzle-beard. "Ha!"
thought he. Then he told the Dog his tale, and begged of
him four hairs—"only four!"

"You great, pampered noise-maker, give me some bread,
then, fine bread, and I will give you the hairs." Whereupon the Cock thought, and went to the house of a Trader
of Foodstuffs; and he told him also the tale.

"Well, then, bring me some wood with which I may heat
the oven to bake the bread," said the Trader of Foodstuffs.

The Cock went to some Woods near by. "Oh, ye Beloved
of the Trees, drop me some branches!" And with this he
told the Trees his tale, but the Trees shook their leaves
and said: "No rain has fallen, and all our branches will
soon be dry. Beseech the Waters that they give us drink,
then we will gladly give you wood."

Then the Cock went to a Spring near by,—and when he
saw in it how his head was swollen and he found that it
was growing harder, he again began to lament.

"What matters?" murmured the Beloved of the Waters.

Then he told them the tale also.

"Listen!" said the Beings of Water. Long have men neglected their duties, and the Beloved of the Clouds need payment of due no less than ourselves, the Trees, the Food-
maker, the Dog, and the Old Woman. Behold! no plumes
are set about our border! Now, therefore, pay to them of
thy feathers—four floating plumes from under thy wings
—and set them close over us, that, seen in our depths from
the sky, they will lure the Beloved of the Clouds with their
rain-laden breaths. Thus will our streamway be replenished
and the Trees watered, and their Winds in the Trees will drop
three dead branches wherewith thou mayest make payment
and all will be well."

Forthwith the *Takaka* plucked four of his best plumes and
set them, one on the northern, one on the western, one on
the southern, and one on the eastern border of the pool. Then
the winds of the Four Quarters began to breathe upon the
four plumes, and with those breaths of the Beloved came
Clouds, and from the Clouds fell Rain, and the Trees threw
down dry branches, and the Wind placed among them Red-
top Grass, which is light and therefore lightens the load it is
among. And when the Cock returned and gathered a little

bundle of fagots, lo! the Red-top made it so light that he easily carried it to the Food-Maker, who gave him bread, for which the Dog gave him four bristles, and these he took to the old Grandmother.

"Ha!" exclaimed she. "Now, child, I will cure thee, but thou hast been so long that thy head will always be welted and covered with proud-flesh, even though healed. Still, it must ever be so. Doing right keeps right; doing wrong makes wrong, which, to make right, one must even pay as the sick pay those who cure them. Go now, and bide whither I bid thee."

When, after a time, the Cock became well, lo! there were great, flabby blood-red welts on his head and blue marks on his temples where they were bruised so sore. Now, listen:

It is for this reason that ever since that time the medicine masters of that people never give cure without pay; never, for there is no virtue in medicine of no value. Ever since then cocks have no bristles on their breasts—only little humps where they ought to be;—and they always have blood-red crests of meat on their heads. And even when a hen lays an egg and a *Takaka cock* sees it, he begins to *ta-ka-ka-a* as the ancient of them all did when he saw the brown nut. And sometimes they even pick at and eat these seeds of their own children, especially when they are cracked.

As for mice, we know how they went into the meal-bags in olden times and came out something else, and, getting smoked, became *tsthliko-ahai*, with long, bare tails. But that was before the Cock cut the tail of the *tsthliko* Mouse off. Ever since he cried in agony: *"Weh tsu yii weh tsu!"* like a child with a burnt finger, his children have been called *Wehtsutsukwe*, and wander wild in the fields; hence field-mice to this day have short tails, brown-stained and hairy; and their chops are all pink, and when you look them in the face they seem always to be crying.

Thus shortens my story.*

Waihusiwa performed a feat of imaginative re-composition that in another time and another place might have made him a major

---

* For a similarly fine example of re-creation on the folk level, see "Aunt Molly Jackson and Robin Hood, a Study in Folk Re-Creation," Greenway, 1956.

author; it is hard to over-praise him. Yet how much credit should go to him, and how much to his culture? Ruth Benedict, who worked intimately with the Zuni, wrote (1935: I, xxix) that the most usual stylistic device in their tales was

> . . . the endless incorporation of cultural details. In most mythologies the picture of cultural life that can be abstracted from the tales, as in the studies of the Tsimshian, Kwakiutl, and Crow . . . is a comparatively adequate description of most phases of social life, but in Zuni there is in addition a loving reiteration of detail that is over and above this faithful rendition.

The Polynesian culture, so rich in literary, religious, navigational, and cannibalistic endeavor, provided the perfect preliterate workshop for individuals as skilful as Waihusiwa. Experts in several aspects of the literary craft were recognized; on Mangareva, said Buck (1938: 305):

> The general term for being expert is *tu'uga*, but as applied to an expert in songs, it is *pou*. The term *pou* required a qualifying word to show in what field the person was skilled. The commonest form of song is the *kapa*, and the person expert in that form of song was therefore a *pou-kapa*. If he was expert in the type of song termed a *keko*, he was a *pou-keko*.

With the Polynesians as the usual exception, few primitive peoples have preserved the names of their *scopas* for us. The pre-Islamic Bedouin story-makers who displaced more sophisticated poets are representative of another class of exceptions, that of cultures which in a technical if not practical sense had written language or which were close enough to writing for their poets' names to be remembered. So Lebkicher can say, "Many of the early poets had thrilling careers, and some of them bore picturesque names such as Ta-abbata Sharran (He Carried Evil under His Armpit)." Another in this category is the great Aztec poet, ruler of Texcoco, Nezahualcoyotl, who died just before the Spaniards arrived. Some sixty chants and songs have been credited to him, including the best thanatopsis in Indian poetry.

The Ghost Dance, because of the lucky presence of James Mooney at its beginning, has left us the names of some composers and their songs. Most readers will judge the Ghost Dance songs to be slight things; they were not so to the Indians. One of the most important composers in this genre was the Arapaho apostle of the Dance, Sitting Bull (not to be confused with the Sioux Sitting Bull), several of whose songs are given by Mooney in his great study of this nativistic endeavor. Of these, perhaps the most interesting to us is the following (972):

> My father did not recognize me
> My father did not recognize me
> When again he saw me,
> When again he saw me,
> He said, "You are the offspring of a crow,"
> He said, "You are the offspring of a crow."

Mooney explains that "This song . . . relates his own experience in the trance, in which he met his father who had died years before. The expression, 'You are the child of a crow,' may refer to his own sacred character as an apostle, the crow being regarded as the messenger from the spirit world."

Sitting Bull—both Sitting Bulls, in fact—belonged to a class of religious practitioner who in the most primitive cultures combined the offices of minister, physician, and entertainer—the shaman. The usefulness of the spiritual dimension which we considered in Chapter Two lies in the fact that it is the treasury of spiritual energy, which mankind contrives in one way or other to tap. Since the possessors of the divine energy and its coveters are sentient creatures, the tapping to some extent must be done by verbal communication. Stretching again the definition of literature, the texts of these *mana*-drawing communications come into our purview. As there are two fundamental kinds of religious practitioner—the priest and the shaman— so there are two fundamental kinds of spiritual communication— prayer and magic. Higher cultures assume a humble position before their deities, and draw *mana* by supplication, usually by means of the priest, who gets his power because of his ordination. Prayer is so universally alike that we need no illustration of it; moreover, it is rare among the peoples whose literature we are studying. Primitive peoples, including folk groups, are less convinced of their spiritual insignificance than we are, and so their assault on the spiritual treasury is direct and forceful and their agents are shamans who, unlike priests, derive power from their personal qualifications. Shamans, wherever they are found, from the Siberian steppes to the American Bible Belt, are a confraternity of identical twins: neurotic, abnormally sensitive and suggestible, Dionysian, visionary, auto-

hypnotic, excitable, independent (none are members of widely organized cults or denominations except their own); they heal by laying
on of hands, terrorize by imprecation, and draw spiritual power into
themselves and their followers by coercing the spirits with magical
rites and incantations. Their incantations are taken by ourselves as
being within the realm of literature since we do not believe in their
religion, and to an extent are taken to be literature also by their own
people, for the shaman is an entertainer as well as a religious func-
tionary. He is apt to dress outlandishly, gyrate about like a dervish,
and utter the closest thing to literature that his people are likely to
hear. Of all primitive composers, the shaman is the most important
widespread kind.

Like *Kubla Khan*, composition among shamans takes place in
dreams induced by some unusual stimulus—usually empty stomachs,
which are easy to acquire in hunting-gathering and shamanistic societies. It seems unnecessary that continually hungry people like the
American Indians hastened the inevitable by deliberate fasting, but
this was common. There are many other dream stimuli on this level
of subsistence; we are told that there was little sleep on the Lewis
and Clark expedition, for some Indian was always waking up at
night with a bad dream that he had to sing out to the pounding of a
drum. Everything has a genius that may spring into a man's mind
and leave a dream song. On the far reaches of the Telon River in
the Malay Peninsula the Temiar have only one contact with civilization—the outboard motorboat that brings supplies and trade
goods. Thinking perhaps that a people could have a worse god, the
shamans are visited by the spirit of the "Bah Motoh" which gives
them commemorative songs.

The Polar World is the stronghold of shamanism as Oceania is the
stronghold of the *mana* concept, and therefore produces a greater
number and variety of these dream-composed songs than other
regions. Because of their incidence, Polar World shaman songs once
in a while manage to attain continuity and intelligibility, like this
example from the Eskimos of Southampton Island:

> Before they came to this religion
> They used to meet with strange things
> Not seen by ordinary people;
> The land moved, the rocks moved,
> They used to meet with strange, strange things.

Certain more restricted groups also found both religious and secular inspiration in dreams. Possibly no other society in the primitive world developed dreaming so fully as the Mohave and neighboring Yuman tribes. "Their whole civilization was dominated by dreams," wrote Wallace (252); "dreams were associated with everything religious—myths, songs, shamanism, dances—and with most secular happenings as well. Among the Mohave the most important event in a person's life was to have a *sumach ahot*—a mana-bestowing dream that came unsolicited and unstimulated by fasting and the like, and which gave permanent evidence of its occurrence by a song." Among the Bedouins, too, the shaman was the composer. Lebkicher says (152), "the poets were originally a type of seer or soothsayer (*sha'ir*, the Arabic word for poet, means 'one who knows,' that is, 'one who had magical knowledge'); they recited rhymed prose, which according to popular belief was inspired by jinn or demons." These men of course were pagans—organized religion cannot tolerate the subversive shaman, no matter how entertaining he is.

The masculine pronoun used in the preceding discussion of shamanistic composers is not just rhetorical. Several peoples have women shamans and therefore woman composers, but they are a rarity. In the higher religions women officiants are nearly non-existent; where they occur, one can argue strongly that the religion that employs them is breaking down. The ancient prejudice against women in religious and associated activities has been inherited by our own culture. The priest sings at the altar, but the women choristers must call down from the back loft—and in the Roman Catholic and English churches, they are not even permitted in that insulated and isolated area. The disability imposed upon women in religious literature evidently carries over into secular life, for there is a distressing minority of women in the A.S.C.A.P.

An area that has had almost no study in ethnoliterature is the effect upon composition of the unstable personality of the shaman, though "schizophrenic language" in our society has been well examined. There is no doubt that neuroticism, insanity, and other mental abnormalities cast their shadows upon the language of their victims—it is not entirely envy that leads uncreative people to call poets mad.* An extreme instance, though it has not produced any literature, is the "talking in tongues" that occurs at shamanistic meetings and evangelistic revivals.

---

* The greatest folk composer in the English language whose name we know, Woody Guthrie, may have come by his unique form of verbal expression through his inheritance of Huntington's Chorea, an extremely rare degenerative mental illness.

As a disgruntled member of the American hill folk once complained, the Devil seems to have all the good songs. But sometimes the pagans are robbed of their literature by the Christians—medieval English writers plundered the Sarsen treasury for stories and made little pretense at covering their deed. Luomala (1949: 14–15) tells us about the pirating process that went on in Polynesia when convert ministers and priests wanted a good story to illustrate their Christian sermons. An Aitutaki native missionary named Simeona ("Simon") thus used the motif of Maui of the eight heads to make a point of one:

> One day Maui noticed a ray of light above him. He became curious to know if there was a whole world full of light outside. He found a hole through which the light came, but his eight heads prevented him from squeezing through the narrow opening. He plucked off one head and tried again. But in vain. Off came a second head. No success. He jerked off a third. Still no luck. Then he tore off one head after another until at last he had only two left. Even yet he could not get through the hole! Finally he pulled off one of his last two heads. Then he crawled easily through the hole into the sunshine of the earth which he found so attractive that he made it his permanent home. Because of his deed, all mankind, his descendants, now have but one head apiece and live in the light.
>
> So it is with poor sinners living in darkness and the shadow of death. By the grace of God, some of them get a glimpse of the blessed light of the Gospel, and long for a full enjoyment of its saving truths. They fail, because of the eight heads, that is, a heart divided between a desire to serve Christ and an equally strong desire to go on enjoying their old heathen pleasures. There is no emerging into the light, peace, and life of the Gospel until the entire seven be plucked off; until with a single eye and a single heart, they agonize to enter the kingdom of heaven.

There are some inanities in Simeona's sermon, but we must concede that he did a better job with his pagan material than Robert Mannyng did with his witch story.

Religion, as we shall see further in Chapter Seven, has an inertial effect on literature. Secular compositions, therefore, are both more frequent and more varied than their sacred counterparts. The priest sings his Credo as Gregory laid it down a millenium and a half ago, but the Samoyed makes up a new song every time he gets drunk (Islavin: 131). The Toda compose songs chiefly at funerals and at dairy building, which seem to us inapposite occasions, but not so when it is known that the Todas are religiously immersed in milk, so to speak.

THE POSSESSION OF LITERATURE

Song and story in the primitive world are not always free as air, to be breathed in and sung out by anyone who likes their literary, spiritual, or rhythmic qualities. Until man achieved control of his food supply through the discovery of agriculture and invented wealth and its associated blessings (like war and theft), possessions were mainly incorporeal. A desert aboriginal of Australia, coming within five thousand years of a faint idea of conspicuous consumption, might carve himself an impractical eight-foot boomerang for prestige, but for most of mankind at this stage of cultural evolution possessions were immaterial, serving most of the functions of material wealth, but much easier to carry. In the immaterial treasury of primitive man one of the most nearly universal valuables is myth and its allied forms, such as ritual songs. The concept of literary ownership is among the few really inalienable rights of man, guaranteed to him by society, custom, religion, and copyright laws, his to have and to hold, to perform or to suppress, to inherit and even to sell.

There are some places where song and story are in the public domain, but at least as frequent and as widespread are the places where they are owned and sold. From Melanesia to the Great Lakes, from the African grasslands to the Arctic tundra, an owner of a song can sell it to another. Often there is a primeval form of entailment that restricts such disposition of a myth, but birthrights were sold for messes of pottage before the Bible first recorded the inequitable transaction. As we might suppose from their sharp behavior in other situations, the Dobu customarily cheat their children of their rightful inheritance of curses by selling the incantations to some covetous sorcerer. The Dobus' more pleasant neighbors in the Trobriand islands make an even better thing of their ownership by selling the usufruct of charms, which of course is inexhaustible. Moreover, selling a story is not the same thing as selling the ability to tell it competently, as the Trobrianders understand (Malinowski, 1926: 21). The Bedouins, like the Dobu, have commended themselves to ethnologists as a knavish people among whom "pillage and robbery rise practically to the level of professions. . . . He arises from his prone devotions to attack and murder if God provides the opportunity, praises the Almighty if successful, or accepts the result of failure as being ordained from on high" (Russell and Kniffen: 265). But there is no sanctimony like the sanctimony of thieves. Musil says of the Rwala Bedouins (283):

> The begging poets are not held in much esteem, being reproached for their insatiability, for their disregard of honesty in praising even scamps for a reward, and also because they lie and steal. They steal the ideas, sentences, and even whole verses of others. It often happens that the hearers assail such a poet with the words, "Thou liest. Thou stolest it from So-and-So!" The poet defends himself calling on others to be his witnesses, but the confidence of his hearers is gone, and they say: "A poet is a liar, *kassad kaddab*." When the poet learns that his composition or some of his verses are claimed by somebody else, he complains to the chiefs or even in the courts, but they refuse to listen on the ground that a poet cannot be trusted.

Happily, other peoples have more probity in these matters. Geronimo, the ferocious Chiricahua Apache shaman and war chief who was a nail in the white man's knee until his death in 1909 as a prisoner of war, told how long his family had owned his most powerful "medicine" (*mana*-conferring) song (Curtis, 1907: 324):

> The song that I will sing is an old song, so old that none knows who made it. It has been handed down through generations and was taught to me when I was but a little lad. It is now my own song. It belongs to me.
>
> This is a holy song and great is its power. The song tells how, as I sing, I go through the air to a holy place where Yusun will give me power to do wonderful things. I am surrounded by little clouds, and as I go through the air I change, becoming spirit only. He draws a symbolic illustration of the action of the song.

O ha le

O ha le

Through the air

I fly upon a cloud
Towards the sky, far, far, far,
O ha le
O ha le!
There to find the holy place,
Ah, now the change comes o'er me!
O ha le
O ha le!

Geronimo's song excites little cupidity in us, but in view of his amazing success against the white oppressors of the Indians, we can understand how envious his fellows were of his exclusive ownership of this powerful medicine song.

Where sodalities, cults, clans, and other organizations are important social groups, ownership might be vested in them rather than in the individual. The Kwakiutl recognized 658 titles or social positions in their tribe, and one prequisite of a rank was the use of certain myths (Driver: 226). Among the American Indians a rite or a ceremony could own a myth or song in the same sense that our Fourteenth Amendment allows a business corporation to be a "person" with rights of possession. When a highly integrated society breaks up under the destructive force of white contact, group ownership appears to revert to individuals, though it is the disintegration of the organization that makes a last member the heir of his group's literature.

THE EFFECTS OF LITERARY POSSESSION

As in biological evolution, the isolation of literary material through exclusive possession intensifies "genetic drift" in promoting variability, and danger of extinction in reducing the "gene pool." Variability through isolative ownership can reach almost unimaginable extremes in societies like the southern Ojibwa, in which parts of a totemic animal—the legs, the head, and the body fat—are in possession of different clans, each of which would accordingly have a different origin tale. As Landes concludes (32):

> . . . one can get as many origin tales of this kind as there
> are informants questioned, and no one person will recognize
> the tale told by another.

Furthermore, the same totems and their associated myths have an uneven distribution in these circumstances. Landes continues:

In some places there is a complete absence of some names that may be found more or less abundantly elsewhere. Thus, there is a large number of Ducks at Emo with none at all ninety miles to the south at Ponemah. Wolf appears at the latter place but not at Emo. Snake is at neither of these places, but appears north at Lake of the Woods around Kenora.

Similarly, in Australia, Elkin (1934: 171) noticed that during the performance of a series of historic totemic rites in the Musgrave Range,

> . . . different persons took the lead in chanting different sections of the same myth. Inquiry revealed the fact that a man could only lead that part of the chanting which referred to the doings of the hero in his own local country. He might know the part of the myth recording the same hero's deed in the next "country," but he is not the owner or custodian of that section, and therefore cannot normally lead the chanting.

It is possible that the situation Elkin describes shows a deterioration in the ownership concept, since he implies that in expedient circumstances a man could chant a myth of which he was not the custodian. Other collectors have found that a myth had to be assembled from bits and pieces held by individuals who simply did not know the parts to which their own fitted. Robinson (1956: 30–31) gives an example of this sort of fragmentation within a family, where two brothers have two segments of the same myth. As one of them, Mardinga, tells the story of "The Spirit Children, Ngarit-Ngarit,"

> In the place called Nimaluk where spring-water is bubbling up, the Rainbow-Snake Kunmanngur made a wide clear space. In this place Kunmanngur set lines of stones. He said, "These stones I put out in a dry place. These stones contain the spirits of my men-children. They are ngarit-ngarit, the spirit children. All my girl-children, the Murinbungo, I will keep with me in the water. I put the name Kooranimalik to this spring-water. And to this creek I put the name Kungunmalla. We cannot lose this country. We stop here. We watch this place called Nimaluk."

In another place the Rainbow-Snake made a big clear
space again. He set stones all around this place. And
Kunmanngur said, "In these stones are the spirits of my
fish-children, Wallamun the mullet." And in other places
Kunmanngur set stones for the spirit-children Pulangarr
the dingo, Ninno the tortoise and Kirick the goose.

One old-man camped near the place Nimaluk. He found
plenty of food there, fish, tortoise, goanna and yam. The
Rainbow-Snake sent out a big light from the bubbling
water. In the light from the water, Kunmanngur sent a
spirit-child to that old-man's wife. When the child was
born, it was a girl. Everyone said, "O, what a pretty girl!"
"O, what good hair this girl has!" "This is a good baby!"
The old-man said, "Kunmanngur has sent his child from the
water!"

The ngarit-ngarit, the spirit-child, may be in a fish,
goanna, tortoise, or a goose, or anything that is speared for
food. When this food is taken back to the camp the ngarit-
ngarit goes into a woman there. It goes in under her toe-
nail and goes up inside that woman.

Moitta was born with a crooked arm because his brother
had been out hunting and had speared a goose with a ngarit-
ngarit inside it. He broke the goose's wing and took it
back to the camp. And the spirit-child inside the goose
went into his mother and was born as Moitta with the
crooked arm.

Moitta's version of this Dreaming is, as Robinson points out, comparable to the allusion to Triton in Wordsworth's sonnet, "The
World Is Too Much with Us":

One day my father found a big billabong. He climbed a
tree to look out over the billabong. "O," he cried, "there
are plenty of geese here." Those geese did not fly away.
They went on feeding in the grass and in the billabong. As
my father was catching those geese, a rainbow came up in
the sky. The rainbow came right over his head. My father
took plenty of geese back to the camp.

When my father came back to the camp my mother asked
him: "What is the matter? Are you sick?" "O," said my
father, "I found a big water and caught plenty of geese.
Then something in the sky came right over my head."

Now the Rainbow-Snake had blown all those geese from
along his tongue. He had made that rainbow go right over
my father's head. After that my mother knew she had a
baby inside her. And my sister, too, she had a baby inside
her.

And Malandait the lightning makes ngarit-ngarit the
spirit-children. Malandait comes up. He kills trees. He
breaks them up. Everybody asks: "What is the matter?"
"Something is here!" Everyone gets frightened. Bye and
bye, one woman has a baby. The Rainbow-Snake makes
fish this way, he makes geese, anything.

One day my father stood on a hill and looked out a long
way over the salt water. He saw a long line of seaweed.
The tide was bringing it in. As my father stood on the hill
he heard the sound of the maluk, the bamboo drone-pipe of
the Rainbow-Snake in the salt-water: "Boom, boom, shsh,
shsh." The Rainbow-Snake was blowing the ngarit-ngarit
out of his bamboo: one line of fish, one line of sea-weed.
Plenty of fish were jumping out of the water and out of the
sea-weed. All right, this one finish. A big wind blew, blew
all day. My brother came up out of the salt-water.

No more Kunmanngur the Rainbow-Snake blows his
maluk from the dry country, always from water. Sometimes
he sends a pretty baby. When a rainbow is close up along
the camp and he sends a baby, it comes from water. The
rain falls straight down. The rainbow comes. Kunmanngur
makes those children the ngarit-ngarit.

Diamond Jenness has shown similarly extreme variations within
the same familial group of Copper Eskimos, but in Australia such
variations are often explainable by the degree of initiation of the
myth-teller. Mountford showed serious changes in graphic art re-
sulting from the artist's advancement in the annual initiation rites;
the same changes, but to a greater degree, occur in myth. Sex, too,
will affect tale and myth variations; the Routledges' analyses (200
ff) of the same story as told by men and women among the Kikuyu
show significant differences; Benedict (1935: I, xl) found the same
phenomenon among the Zuni.

Some aspects of human nature are the same the whole world over,
and certainly the ability to tell a story well is one of them. It is
a common error to think that primitive and folk societies are very

much more homogeneous than our own, that deviant behavior and differences in ability are suppressed.   Anyone who has collected folksongs in rural America knows that in any community one person is clearly the best "informant"—which means that he knows more songs and sings them better than anyone else.   Although the fact of variation in informant skill is well understood by the field worker, the restrictions of publication prevent its illustration.   No publisher and few authors care to print a series of feeble and insipid variants just to prove that there are feeble and insipid story tellers. Vapidity needs no demonstration, and therefore pairings like the following collected by Gladys Reichard among the Navaho (1944: 18) are exceptional.   In the story of which these passages are excerpts, the hero has disappeared and Talking God magically searches for him.   Reichard's first informant told the episode this way:

> . . . he reached for his cotton twine.   He took it out.   To the east he threw it, it would not move off, they say.   Also to the south he threw it again, it would not move off, they say.   Also to the west he threw it again, it would not move off, they say.   Downward, down into the earth he also threw it, it would not move off.   Upward he also threw it. That, then that twine being strung out upward, moved out through space.   The Hogan God also threw a blue cotton twine upward.   It became strung out upward.   "What is happening?   Upward our child must be.   Let's go after him.   The Wind Gods, it is they who have gone off with him!   Let's go after him."

Reichard's other informant goes well beyond this bare statement that a hero is lost and that a god has magical searching strings; he not only uses the characteristic Navaho repetition and color symbolism skilfully, but unobtrusively shows that one of the traits of Talking God is his playfulness even in serious situations:

> As they were travelling on a well known trail, the hero ahead of the gods, he suddenly disappeared.   They looked for him everywhere but could not find him.   Then one asked Talking God to help them.   He came, bringing his protective prayerstick and his six magic strings.   The strings were of different colors, each wound into a ball.   He took the white string, and holding one end of it, threw it to the east.   It flew like lightning far to the east, but returned swiftly to

his hand, and he knew that the one he sought was not in the east. He took out his blue string and threw it to the south. It came right back to him. He threw his yellow string to the west. It was the same. Then he threw his black string to the north. Again it was the same. The boy was not there. Then he took out his spotted string and threw it down. The end stuck. It did not return. "Does anyone live down there?" he asked Hunchback God. "Yes, down there is the dwelling of the Wind Gods," he said. The gods examined the ground and soon found a hole through which they descended to the home of the Wind Gods. There they found their child.

PAYING THE PIPER

Those impoverished cultures that offer so few enterprises for the talented men are likely to reward him almost prodigally. Elkin (1954) tells us that the songman of Arnhem Land is the only crafts-man who is paid for his work. Bascom (1953) describes the bands of professional drummers who walk about the town drumming the praises of important people who reward them with "dashes" or tips. Among the Mandan, payment was in tobacco mixed with red willow bark (Bowers: 93). The Ojibwa story teller was compensated by gifts and a feast (Densmore, 1929: 103). Tubatulabal stories were told to interested purchasers of the listening privilege in large houses where those who did not want to pay, considerately covered their heads with blankets—which may have disconcerted the performer as much as the deaf parishioner who turned off his hearing aid in the middle of a sermon disconcerted his minister.

The payment given to primitive gleemen is less than nothing com-pared to the practice of a country that gives even mediocre televi-sion comedians twenty times the salary of its President, but the in-centive is enough to make competition lively. Even in cultures as materially poor as that of the American Indian, jealousy, envy, and rivalry are at least as intense as among ourselves, and lead often to an individualism that the Protestant Ethic would not countenance. Among the Makolkol of New Guinea a singer arriving late for en-semble vocalizing "makes no effort to catch up with the main group, but just sings on, eventually to complete the song after all the others have finished" (Sheridan). Fletcher (quoted in Day, 12–13) de-scribes an even more cacophonic situation in American Indian singing:

When this society holds its formal meeting, a part of the closing exercises consists of the simultaneous singing by all the members present of their individual songs. The result is most distressing to a listener, but there are no listeners unless by chance an outsider is present, for each singer is absorbed in voicing his own special song which is strictly his own personal affair, so that he pays no attention to his neighbor; consequently the pandemonium to which he contributes does not exist for him.

THE GLEEMAN AT HIS CRAFT

In telling the prose versions of the myths, a narrator employs every dramatic device he knows to enliven his stories. He strains at an imaginary fishline as he tells how Maui hauled up the islands, some of them covered with houses, people, and plantations. He breathes heavily and huddles up to demonstrate how mankind wheezed and crawled about in the steaming, smoky blackness of the world before Maui separated sky and earth. He imitates Hina's shrill-voiced and staccato anxiety over her own possible fate and that of the loved one whom Maui has turned into a dog.

Katherine Luomala's description of the Polynesian narrator at his work (1949: 65) can be applied to any competent story teller anywhere in the world, for the craft of narration is not oratory but drama. When we read the tales of primitive people we owe it to ourselves as well as to the literature to piece out its imperfections with our thoughts, for it is our thoughts that must deck the kings and commoners of the preliterate societies. A great deal of terseness in this material is what Reichard (1947: 26) called "obscure simile," in which a line like "He did it" is accompanied by the narrator's acting out what the fictional character did. She describes such a simile, bare and insipid in text, requiring the narrator to leave the house and re-enter slithering across the floor on his stomach, like a snake. Firth said that on Tikopia "there is no such thing as a song per se . . . action of one kind or another accompanies the singing." Junod waxes as lyrical as a Broadway reviewer in appreciating the superb dramatic narration of a quartet of his best Thonga informants (215). Malinowski's Trobrianders played to the gallery with singing, gesticulating, voice-changing to indicate characters, and similar universal skills of the showman (1926: 21).

Good story tellers have good memories. Aunt Molly Jackson, the great Kentucky folk informant, launched into the 456 stanzas of "The Gest of Robin Hood" a few days after she saw the text for the first time; Junod's Shigiyane could recite tales for many nights without repeating herself (212); and the memories of the Polynesian *tohunga* who recited interminable genealogies allegedly without error, the Navaho priest who did the same with song cycles, and the Inca *quipucamaya* who could be turned on and off like a phonograph record, are only superior examples of the mnemonic equipment every gleeman must carry.

Some people are not impressed by these feats. Stanley D. Porteus, (who went to Australia to measure the intelligence of the aborigines, found his tests were thwarted by the cultural barrier, and concluded finally just by looking at them that they were not very smart), said,

> The evidence of any remarkable ability as regards memory is not particularly convincing when one takes into account the conditions of their life. It is true that the aborigine may know the words of many corroboree songs, but it must be remembered that he has a great deal of time in which to practice these songs and thus become familiar with them. In aboriginal camps singing goes on for many nights in succession, one song being sung sometimes for an entire evening. Apart from the legends of the tribe there is very little else that the aborigine needs to remember with any measure of exactitude except the words of these songs (294).

Porteus' psychology here lacks something in soundness, for the more one has to remember the easier it is to remember any part of it. Two centuries ago when Philidor played two games of chess simultaneously while blindfolded it was recorded as a phenomenon in the history of man, but today the record is up to fifty games. We have not become smarter, but we know better how to make use of our memories. Even in preliterate cultures mnemonic devices were known; the most elaborate of these was the *quipu* of pre-Conquest Peru, a tangle of knots and strings and colors that could keep a narrator going for days with letter-perfect renditions of myths, genealogies, poetry, and legends in the same way that a rosary is used to tally the 180 prayers in that garland of Catholic devotion.*

---

* The running-out of native Peruvian culture after Pizzaro's depredations is epitomized by the present use of the *quipu*—to count sheep.

Simpler memory aids are the sand scratching of the Aranda as he recites a *churinga* myth, and similar story accompaniments, of which the most beautiful is the Navaho sand painting. The Midewiwin priests used elaborate bark rolls, covered with esoteric pictographs, to help them remember the medicine songs of the eastern Indian tribes. Notched sticks are found for the same purpose from Canada to Australia. And evidently no people spoke better of their dead than the Sioux, whose elegiasts recited a dead man's deeds with the help of a great bundle of mnemonic sticks.

For the person who knows how to trick his memory into working well the physical mnemonic devices we have surveyed are as useless as canes to a sprinter. Many people besides blindfold chess masters carry their memory aids in the logical place for such things—inside their heads—and sing them out in lyrics that sometimes have no better purpose. Of these the most interesting to us is the medieval church chanting that gave birth to English drama.

THE GLEEMAN AND HIS AUDIENCE

Ever since the stinging criticism of Mrs. Frances Trollope a century and a half ago pulled our feet off the backs of the seat in front of us, quieted our guffaws, catcalls, and shouts of encouragement, and exhorted us to greater accuracy toward the theatrical spittoons, the empathic relationship of Americans to their entertainers has steadily weakened. In the days of the social frontier we had to be forcibly restrained from displacing the actors on their own stage; now even the elemental emotive responses have to be faked electronically with canned laughter and pickled groans. We have become so passively receptive to our poets, priests, and entertainers that the behavior of the primitives strikes us as unruly at best and unsanitary at worst.* Almost without exception primitive audiences share the mood set by the entertainer, though we might have better attentiveness if we used some of the expedients of other culture to assure mindfulness—like the Puritan practice of assigning a beadle to tap nappers on the head or the Mandan device of pinching them with a bird stick. Thonga poets handle their own beadling, throwing sand in the faces of those who do not clap vigorously enough as they perform (Junod: 187).

---

* An exception to the charge of unsanitariness is the Tubatulabal, who have to leave the room after hearing myth recitation and plunge several times into a pool of icy water (Voegelin: 48).

But such coercion is usually unnecessary among people who live close to their literature. The Salteaux keep up a steady flow of repartee with the actors (Hallowell, 1942: 45). Like the congregation of a Louisiana backwoods church with its "amens," the Barama River Caribs "continually supply exclamations, a high pitched 'ko-o?' or an 'ao-o' with rising and falling inflection. The pattern is for listeners continually to express surprise, astonishment, and amazement at the words of the speaker. It is also customary to repeat 'yao' and to grunt at frequent intervals as a means of encouraging the speaker and showing him that he is holding the listeners' attention" (Gillin: 70). At the recital of the Australian *alcheringa* myths, the clan members sit in a circle and beat the tempo of the narration with boomerangs in the sand.

Interchange between the entertainer and his audience is determined to some extent of course by the literary form. Riddles require dialogue just as charades require the absence of it. In Chaga riddling the challenger calls out "Orawe" ("Riddle"); the responder accepts with a shouted "Oyo" ("Set the trap"). If the answer is guessed, the challenger says "Now set yours"; if not, he says, "Give me a chieftainship: "I make So-and-So my slave" or "I make So-and-So my wife" (Raum: 220). The African call-and-response singing, the most characteristic feature of their music, demands multiple participation. Variant forms of antiphonal singing likewise need an active audience —among the Bard two singers exchange antistrophe for strophe, but the other choristers accompany the words by stamping and shouting in rhythm (Biddulph: 87).

The psychological significance of audience participation has not been studied to any productive extent, though Soviet folklorists— as one might expect from their sociopolitical orientation—are devoting some time to it. In the United States Alan Lomax has offered some stimulating hypotheses, though at present his suggestions are too tentative to allow any deductive application of them. For example, his belief that acephaly in singing correlates with well-integrated social organizations, such as the Australian; however, one can find among the Australian natives some of the most individualistic singing in the world. Norman Tindale recorded from the Bentinck Islanders songs chanted in a near-whisper with the singer's head on his chest and his hand cupping his mouth. Neither the Todas nor the Araucanians are poorly integrated socially, yet the same kind of extremely personal singing is found among them also (Rivers: 600; Cooper: 738).

While the Apollonian-Dionysian dichotomizing of cultures has much against it in ethnographic evidence, it is true that literature is one of the best gauges for determining the relative aggressiveness of a society. Dionysian literature means a Dionysian performer speaking to a Dionysian audience, and so the liveliest relations between an entertainer and his house are found among aggressive, competitive, and excitable people. Grinnell (II: 20–21) reconstructs a chaotic scene among the Cheyenne on the return of a victorious war party where the singers could hardly be heard above the shouting and howling of the village assembled. Though we have no good description of the situation, what we can infer from the archaeological and literary remains of our Anglo-Saxon forebears indicates a noisy time indeed in the meadhalls of Wessex as the gleeman shouted "Hwaet!" and shook his harp to quiet the drunken *geneatas*. Americans and Romans have often been likened in disposition and cultural psychology to the advantage of neither, and in entertainment there is much in common between the two peoples, even if an American orgy is on the whole more restrained than the Roman exhibitions of gracious living. The Polynesians were scarcely the most docile of people, and their *luaus* and *tangis* were scarcely the quietest of literary soirees. Among the Rwala Bedouins the strange delivery style of a poet—recitation in a nasal voice with blurted words half swallowed concluding with a falsetto whining (Musil: 283)—is clearly a reflection of the enormous difference in rank between a rich shiekh and a begging poet in that exceedingly Dionysian society. On the other hand, there are such people as the Dyak, who were uncommonly gentle folk for headhunters: the Dyak singer lies on a mat while performing to an equally otiose audience (Chadwick III: 480; Jacobs and Stern: 231).

THE ORGANIZATION OF ENTERTAINERS

Davenport in his survey of the lore of the Marshall Islanders makes an important point in observing that the absence of a cohesive professional organization of tale tellers in this region of Micronesia has prevented a systematization of myths (221). One of the chief functions of sodalities, from the local chapter of the Cootie Club to the West African Leopard Society, is the appropriation, organization, and systematization of literature and its attendant arts. The similarity between primitive secret societies and our own is inescapable: the Algonkin Midewiwin masters teaching myths, dogma, and songs to its terrified initiates by means of esoteric pictures and symbols invites comparison with the Masonic lodge (Driver: 420–422). Fletcher's remarks on American Indian sodalities could be applied with little alteration to Tuesday luncheon meetings all over the United States (1900: 115–116):

> In every tribe there were societies having a definite membership, with initiatory rites and reciprocal duties. Each society had its peculiar songs; and there were officials chosen from among the members because of their good voices and retentive memories, to lead the singing and to transmit with accuracy the stories and songs of the society, which frequently preserved bits of tribal history. Fines were imposed upon any member who sang incorrectly, while ridicule always and everywhere followed a faulty rendering of a song.

The American Legion's Forty-and-Eight organization is different only in equipment from the Pueblo *koshare* clowns, and before their vices abandoned the aging veterans of the first World War these delight-making legionnaires were at the point of developing into an American *arioi*, as Luomala describes it (1949: 70):

> The Society Archipelago formerly had a highly organized and graded society called the Arioi. The Arioi conducted dramatic performances, talent shows, and vaudevilles to entertain the populace. They travelled from island to island in grand style, in large canoes decorated with colored pennants. Images of Oro and his brothers, tutelary gods of the entertainers, had places of honor in the principal canoe. Captain Cook once saw about 70 canoes with 700 passengers in an Arioi expedition. Performances took place on the canoes while the audience watched from the shore, or in open-sided pavilions built on land to accomodate audience and performers. Every wedding of any importance had a band of Arioi to entertain guests, and traveling chiefs took a troupe with them to avoid boredom.

The *arioi* and its cognates elsewhere in Polynesia (*hura, hula*) provided and participated in less innocent amusements also, but here of course its resemblance to our veterans stops, and since these activities were hardly literary, they need not be described here.

Whereas the *arioi* was only a specialty organization in parts of the Pacific, formal literary and oratorical training was available everywhere in Polynesia to anyone with sufficient status to promise suc-

cess in the enterprise of communicative art. Handy, describing
the Marquesan form of literary education, says (1930b: 20):

> When a father desired to have his son or daughter taught
> legends (ha'akekai) and recitation of genealogy (mata tetau)
> he built in the neighborhood of his own dwelling a large
> special house (oho au) for the purpose, and employed a
> bard (tuhuna o'ono) to instruct the pupils. In this house
> as many as thirty men and women ranking from twenty to
> forty years in age would come to participate in the instruc-
> tion with the lad or girl for whom the oho au had been built.
> All lived at the oho au and were instructed in the bard's
> lore (tekao tuhuna). During the period of instruction,
> the pupils were tapu, being consecrated to the work, and
> sexual intercourse was prohibited.

In Tahiti and New Zealand literary education was more formal as
in the manner of the English public schools. Not given to wearing
shirts, the Polynesian Old Boy was unable to proclaim his alma mater
by an old school tie, but was voluble in later life on the subject of
his school, the curriculum, his teachers, and "very important, the
gifts he had given his teachers" (Luomala, 1949: 69–70). The pre-
senting of gifts to the faculty was not only the mark of serious students in Tahiti, but also could be called a commendable practice that
well could be emulated in allegedly more advanced cultures.

Africans were on the whole more subtle and insidious in their
training of children to literary, musical, and dramatic competence.
From the earliest days of his consciousness the African infant begins
to absorb the singing, dancing, drumming, and other rhythmic movement everywhere about him. No African child, Cudjoe says (281),
is likely to forget the pleasant rhythm associated with the grinding of
grain or the pounding of yams because "he feels the direct impact of
this rhythm" as he rests comfortably strapped to his mother's back.
Later, the Chaga have a special dance for the children—the *shiganu*
—whose aim is to recapitulate the songs and actions from the stories
and legends told around the fire by adults (Raum: 223–224). Participation is compulsory, and clumsy performers grow up virtually
disqualified as marriage partners, a consequence paralleled in Samoa,
where persons awkward at dancing are also doomed to single bless-
edness.

In most other societies bardic literature as well as myths is passed
down from generation to generation as Marshall describes the proc-

ess among the Burmese Karen (33–34), though the repertoire expected to be absorbed in letter-perfect manner by the initiates may
consist of hundreds of tales, legends, myths, and songs.

THE DECLINE OF THE STORY TELLER

Early observers of primitive literature like William Mariner in the
Pacific had a field of gold to harvest; we are like Ruth in the alien
corn, grubbing in the dust for a few overlooked grains.   The overwhelming of primitive cultures by Euramerican civilization brought
literal and figurative death to these societies.   Nearly every collector
now prefaces his published labors with the tacit or explicit apology
that he has worked in a dead literature.   Jochelson's remarks about
the Koryak are representative (1908: 343):

> At present there are no more story-tellers who are ready
> to present the current episodes in interesting combina-
> tions, and who weld the mythological stories into long
> tales.   The best proof of this is the fact that the art of
> story-telling has now passed over entirely to the women,
> while, until quite recently, the men were the best story-
> tellers.

Across the strait from the Koryak the Copper Eskimos are in
similar decline.   Jenness (1) wrote in 1924 that the professional story-
tellers are gone, and with them any notion of prestige for their art:
"Consequently, a man may live to old age and die without ever learning more than a half a dozen of the tales that have been handed
down by his forefathers."*

When Australian newspapers toward the end of the last century
reported with terrible regularity the death of a tribe's last man, it
was seldom noted that there died with each last survivor a body of
literature, sacred and secular.   Now some old men are not waiting
for their own deaths—they refuse to pass on the lore to the young
men who hang around the edges of the white man's civilization:
"They are not worthy of it," the old men say.   Fifty years ago Burton
was able to salvage Ojibwa songs and stories where a colleague who
had known the Ojibwa for nearly a half century insisted there were

---

* A happier trend is noticeable among some Arctic groups; contact with white
culture has helped their fight against the hard environment to the extent that societies that once used to kill their feeble aged now permit them to live and spend
their time telling stories.

neither among these degenerate Indians. One old man told Burton why they were so secretive about their lore (118):

> Sir, we do not understand it. We like you, but we do not understand what you are going. We ask what has the white man done to us? He has made us live in reservations, forbidden us to hunt in the forests, taken away our land. He has taken from us everything Indian that we possessed except our songs, and now you come and would take away those, too. You will have our songs sung all over the world where white men live, and when that has been done you will turn upon us, like the white men who came before you, and say, get out! I have no further use for you.

Chapter Six / MACRO-CHANGE IN LITERATURE

No matter what some folk say, good things do not come to a people by a Trickster fishing them out of the sea or a Culture Hero dropping them down from heaven on the sly. Whatever a society has comes to it either by independent invention or by borrowing from other cultures. Alphabets, wherever they appear, have migrated by diffusion from their ultimate origin among an eastern Mediterranean people; the zero, on the other hand, was invented independently by the Hindus, Maya, and Babylonians. Acting upon the cultural item after these two protogenic forces, are other anthropological processes of a lesser order—environmental determinism, acculturation, cultural inertia, cultural lag, transculturation, syncretism, metataxis—and these work upon literature exactly as they work upon pottery, in every culture. What Flinders Petrie saw happening to Egyptian vases we can see happening to coffee cups—and fairy tales. Anthropologists, who have been made aware of the tyranny of culture over man and who tend therefore to undervalue the individual artist, are familiar with these processes; literary people tend to overvalue the individual, to personalize for easier understanding as well as the retention of what little divinity man has left, the powerful forces over which he has really little or no control. For the latter readers some illustration of these processes will make the larger changes in literature meaningful.

Environmental Determination

There is a nice distinction between "environmental determination" and "environmental determinism," since the latter phrase implies an extreme philosophy of culture change. There are still some students who approach this matter mystically and say that similar environments always produce similar cultures; this monistic view has been rejected by most anthropologists. Nevertheless in similar environments similar problems, stimuli, and opportunities occur, and consequently similar responses. Where bamboo grows, people make panpipes; desert tribes are not apt to be overly inter-

ested in flood myths, or Arctic tribes with stories about how the
monkey got its tail. Environmental determination is clearest seen
in material culture, though some go so far as to attribute psychological responses to environment. The philosophy pervading the
literature of nuclear India—the mortification of the flesh, the deni-
gration of man as a material being, the quest for spiritual elevation,
the disregard for material possessions, the contempt for both comfort
and discomfort—has been blamed to the overpowering environment
of the Indian culture hearth with its cataclysmic sand and dust
storms, floods, cloudbursts, locust and rat plagues, and famines, as
well as the tremendous mountains to the north which constantly
remind man of his insignificance if his misfortunes do not. Many
will reject Gilbert's explanation for the self-humbling attitudes of
the Indians, but some attention must be paid to the force of environment on everything man has and does. Nomadic peoples living in hot desert regions where pork spoils quickly are not likely to
tell funny stories about the three little pigs.

Acculturation

Acculturation is a bloodless term for a bloody situation in which
a primitive people desperately tries to salvage some of its culture
by adapting it to Euramerican equivalents. This is an important
phenomenon, and will be treated at length toward the end of this
chapter.

Cultural Inertia

Cultural inertia describes the reluctance of a culture to change,
its preference to keep rolling in its accustomed grooves. The American ethos approbates change and abominates stagnation, and so we
are not sympathetic toward tradition, as other cultures euphemis-
tically call this retarding force. Several ancient cultures did very
well without looking about for new ways to do old things. If we
had been driving in black Model T Fords since the time of Henry
VIII we could better imagine the conservatism of the Indus Valley
civilization. In literature many things retard change. Hartland
said (5),

> . . . a people which requires its story-tellers to relate their
> stories in the very words in which they have been conveyed
> from time immemorial, and allows no deviation, will pre-
> serve its traditions with the least possible blemish and

the least possible change.   In proportion as latitude in repetition is permitted and invention is allowed to atone for want of memory, tradition will change and become uncertain.

Of all the forces which make this requisition of its story tellers, nothing is more tyrannical than religion.   The vestments of Roman Catholic priests are street clothes of Rome at the time of Christ with some symbolic additions; the habits of nuns are basically the ordinary wear of women in the medieval period when most of these holy orders were founded; the priest says his Mass in Latin, a language dead elsewhere for better than a thousand years; St. Patrick's Cathedral stands gothically among modern secular skyscrapers just as the Pueblo *kiva*, preserving the architecture of the early period of Anasazi development, nestles among the multi-storied secular buildings in Mesa Verde and Chaco Canyon.   The Protestant minister and the Polynesian *tohunga* pray with obsolete linguistic forms.   Myths, therefore, are everywhere the most stable form of literature, and in many places there are conscious, coercive efforts made to discourage individuals from changing them.   The inertial effect of religion means that everywhere there is greater freedom in composition and improvization in secular than in religious literature.   The religious song may be very good, but except in times of crisis, it resists improvement as it resists degeneration.   The *Kyrie Eleison, Agnus Dei*, and other missal usages of the Gregorian chant have not changed significantly in 1400 years.

Cultural Lag

"Cultural Lag" is a concept named by Ogburn in 1922 to describe the maladjustments that take place when one part of a culture moves more rapidly than others, thus producing frictional disruption with the correlated parts.   The collapse of Yir Yoront mythology, described later in this chapter, is only an especially tragic example that could be multiplied by the number of primitive societies that tried to accept white man's material goods and retain their own immaterial philosophies.

Transculturation

Herskovits invented the term "transculturation" for what might be more loosely called "cultural ping pong"—the bouncing back and forth of cultural items, the borrowing of something borrowed from the borrowers.   In mythology there is no better documented illus-

tration of this process than the development of early Christian belief, and in certain widespread motifs like the Tar Baby story, it is
very hard to tell where the borrowing began. Other motifs are
more easily traced. Before the introduction of tobacco and smoking into Europe, the word "pipe" was used metaphorically to describe any long, thin, tubular object, as the British Pipe Rolls;
in this sense it was first applied to the Omaha calumets, the "pipes
of peace," which are polygenetically found also in the Australian
"message sticks" (themselves erroneously named), and which were
not originally tobacco pipes. But through confusion of the two
meanings these later became tobacco pipes among the Indians,
who thus reborrowed the error. So also the misconception mentioned earlier about *mana* and the Great Spirit, which likewise got
over into the Indians' minds.

Syncretism

Mythology also gives the best examples of syncretism, which is
the convergence and amalgamation of different systems of belief.
The official Catholicism of Mexican Indians is a tangle of Christian
and native pagan elements, just as the holydays of the medieval
Christian church were a merging of Christian ideas and pagan festi-
vals. The section following on "Diffusion" has other examples of
this process.

Metataxis

"Metataxis" is a perceptive concept named by Marett to describe
the change in function of many items that are obsolescent in their
original context. When a trait or item is obsolescent it often does
not quietly vanish; if metataxis is operative, it may give up its
original subsistence function and survive as a sport for adults or a
toy for children until even the reason for its first invention is forgotten. Horses were once the greatest transportational discovery in
the history of man, but now they are used for sport, and are carried
about from place to place in automobile trailers, with hardly anyone
noticing the incongruity of the situation. The bow and arrow may
have been the means for the extermination of *Homo neanderthalensis*
by *Homo sapiens*, but it is now a metatactic toy for both adults and
children. The metatactic retrogression of the bow and arrow did
not occur only in our culture; in Polynesia and in ancient Greece it

was used only for sport—remember that Odysseus left his great bow at home when he was off fighting the Trojan war with more popular weapons. Proverbs are sometimes used by us, but as someone else said of them, they are now "the debased product of yesterday's wisdom." Fairy tales have gone entirely into the nursery, but according to one school of folklore they were once serious myths. Nursery rhymes in some if not many cases had their beginning in political allegories, and they too have taken refuge in the nursery.* Pirates at the beginning of our nation were an unfunny menace, but now they too are literary dolls for our children to amuse themselves with.

THE INDIVIDUAL IN ARTISTIC INVENTION

Inventions invent themselves, except in the minds of people who think that human beings have something to do with the process. As Kroeber stated the matter, given the boat and the steam engine, the steamboat is inevitable. Kroeber was a lax communicant in the theory of cultural determinism, an unpopular anthropological approach that sees culture as a "superorganic" entity with a mind and will of its own which operates through human beings. It is an approach as difficult to disprove as it is to prove, and so discussions of the subject end quickly in lost tempers, the opponents saying something like "cultures don't paint their fingernails, people do," and the proponents answering that if we have control over culture's movement, they wish devoutly that we would do something about the state of the world. The cultural determinists have the better of the dispute, seeing the way the world has gone; in Toynbee's phrase, creative geniuses are "no more than a leaven in the lump of ordinary humanity" (III: 243), and even Isaac Newton admitted that he stood on the shoulders of many precedent discoverers.

If there is any human activity in which man has some small

---

* The effort to find serious origins in the nursery rhyme has suffered because of the enthusiasm of its proponents, such as John Bellenden Ker (*An Essay on the Archaeology of Popular English Phrases and Nursery Rhymes*, 1834), James Orchard Halliwell-Phillips (*The Nursery Rhymes of England*, 1842), and Katherine Elwes Thomas (*The Real Personages of Mother Goose*, 1930). Presently there is an extreme reaction in folklore studies against historical interpretations of nursery rhymes, and the conservative view of the Opies so dominates this area that few will go so far as to suggest that they may be wrong. But the Opies are not omniscient (they write, [n, 29–30], ". . . the writers can only think of two songs about specific persons in recent years, 'Amy, wonderful Amy' [Amy Johnson] and 'Oh, Mr. Gable' [Clark Gable]") and the truth of the matter lies rather closer to poor maligned Katherine Thomas than to Peter and Iona Opie.

measure of will to exercise his imagination, it is in literary creation, and this for the reason that literature is comparatively free of utilitarian restrictions. But man is still bound as a member of his species, race, society, and culture to compose within the bounds and opportunities of his physical and intellectual environment. Xenophanes 2500 years ago pointed out the anthropocentricity of man's mythic creations:

> Yes, and if oxen and horses or lions had hands, and could paint with their hands and produce works of art as men do, horses would paint the forms of their gods like horses, and oxen like oxen, and make their bodies in the image of their several kinds. . . . The Ethiopians make their gods black and snub-nosed; the Thracians say theirs have blue eyes and red hair.

As for ethnocentricity, not many civilized men are quite so purblind as the Swedish philologist of the 17th century who said that in the Garden of Eden Adam spoke Danish, the Devil French, and God, of course, Swedish, but every tale maker is a child of his time and his place, the passive implement of his culture, which works its will through him. Coleridge is himself the best refutation of his statement that the poet puts two and two together and makes not four, but a star. He never understood how he made *Kubla Khan*, but John Livingstone Lowes in his brilliant retrograde analysis, *The Road to Xanadu*, showed how every line, every word, every thought of that poem had been put into Coleridge's subconscious by his environment. Boas showed the same process in the composition of myths of the Kwakiutl, among whom village communities combined to form tribes in which each village became a clan. Probably through the influence of northern tribes, totems and the necessity for clan mythology were adopted, and characteristically among this Dionysian people myths came to individuals through dreams stimulated by fasts and other mortifications of the flesh. So whatever the Kwakiutl mythmaker had in his mind came out subconsciously, as the opium dream composed Coleridge's poem; but since clans were exogamous, and since the husband acquired the myths of his wife's clan, the myths of adjoining tribes were appropriated.

For all that culture provides the material, the stimulus, the inspiration, and the style of every literary creation, it can work only through its human amanuenses, and fortunately for the healthy variation of story and song, the composer is never an accurate re-

corder of his culture. He makes mistakes. His individual personality, molded often by accidental family events, distorts the message,
as do also the imperfections of his understanding and senses. Stefansson (252–255) at the beginning of this century experienced
the culture of the Copper Eskimo working through an individual
narrator:

> We had here a striking example of how easy it is to be mis-
> led by native information. I had been led to believe in the
> spring that the Coronation Gulf people never had had any
> knowledge of the killing of bowhead whales, although they
> were familiar with the carcasses of those that had drifted up
> on their beaches. Neither had they apparently ever seen a
> live one, which is not strange, considering the two facts that
> bow-head whales are not only no doubt very rare in these
> waters, but the people themselves are always inland in the
> summer time and are therefore not in a position to see the
> whales even if they might come into these waters in July or
> August. But here at this village and now for the first time,
> after vain inquiries all summer, we heard various stories of
> whale killings, most of them, however, centering about a
> single man who they called Kaplavinna. They told how
> this person had a very large boat. This again was new in-
> formation, for up to that time we had heard nothing about
> anything but kayaks. In the spring, in fact, the people
> had seemed to be unfamiliar with the very name of kayak.

> I listened to several of these stories with great wonder
> and asked many questions which were readily answered,
> but which threw no great light on the subject, until it oc-
> curred to me to ask one of the narrators, "Who told you
> this story? Did you get it from your father?" The man
> said, "No, I got it from Natjinna." Now Natjinna had been
> a camp follower of ours all summer, and I had asked him
> specifically in the spring both about bow-head whales and
> umiaks and he knew nothing about either. It seemed
> strange to me that Natjinna should have misled me so in
> the summer, and I made up my mind to take him to task
> for it when I saw him. Two or three weeks later, when I
> happened to meet him, I asked how was it that in the spring
> he had been unwilling to tell me anything about whales or
> big boats and now he told long stories to others about them.

"Oh, but those were the stories that Natkusiak told me," he answered.

It turned out on investigation that my own man, Natkusiak, was the fountainhead of all these stories, and that the redoubtable whaler Kaplavinna was none other than Natkusiak's former employer, Captain Leavitt of the steamer whaler *Narwhal*. These were the local versions, changed to fit the circumstances and geography of Coronation Gulf, and translated into terms comprehensible to the Coppermine Eskimo. I had heard Natkusiak telling these stories the previous spring, but the versions that came to me a year later were so changed that they were not recognizable, and had been so thoroughly localized geographically that the narrators could tell me off just which Coronation Gulf headland the adventures had taken place.

When Natkusiak told these stories, as I noticed on many occasions, he never made any allowance for the fact that he was dealing with things entirely strange to the local people. He discussed davits, masts, sails, anchors, harpoon guns, dynamite bombs, the price of whalebone and the like, exactly as he would have done in his own home village at Port Clarence where these are all familiar topics and matters of everyday conversation. The very names of these things as well as the concepts behind them were absent from the vocabularies and the minds of the local people, and the ideas which they therefore got from Natkusiak's truthful stories were very far from those which have been gained from the same narratives by a people whose everyday experiences have made them comprehensible.

From the seeds sown here by Natkusiak there had grown up a local myth about Kaplavinna and his whaling adventures—a myth which Natkusiak himself would have fully as much trouble as I in recognizing—just as exactly as the discussion of the Christian religion by a missionary and of a strange social and political system by a school teacher gives rise to the most astounding ideas in the minds of the Alaskan Eskimo. . . .

Another story which we picked up at this time was that of the Imnait. These were vague and mysterious animals living in an unknown land to the west, which is also inhabited by the Kiligavait. This story did not give us nearly so much

trouble in identifying as did that of Kaplavinna, for the
name of the monster was a correct reproduction of that
used by my own Eskimo in the previous year in telling their
adventures in mountain sheep hunting. Mountain sheep, of
course, are found nowhere east of the Mackenzie River, and
could not, therefore, be directly known to the Coronation
Gulf Eskimo. These people were also unfamiliar with the
dangers involved in the possible snow-slides and other peculiar conditions of mountain hunting. They had received
from Natkusiak the general idea that mountain sheep hunting was dangerous, and being unable to ascribe any danger
to the mountains as such, they had transferred the danger-
ousness of the snow-slides and precipices to the sheep themselves; and the hairbreadth escapes from death in snow-
slides which Natkusiak had described became in their versions hairbreadth escapes from the teeth and claws of the
ferocious mountain sheep. The Kiligavait, which they had
associated with the mountain sheep in these narratives, were
nothing but the mammoth, known to all branches of Eskimo
race by name at least, and known here also, according to
what we were told, by the occasional finding of their bones.
Of course, Natkusiak had told nothing about mammoth
hunting, but the mysterious mountain sheep naturally allied
themselves in their minds with the also mysterious mammoth, and were therefore to be coupled together in recount-
ing the same adventures. Thus we had a side-light, not
only upon the origin of myths among primitive people, but
also upon the startling rapidity with which they grow
and change their form.*

Ruth Benedict was also close enough to the genesis of a tale with
mythic elements in Zuni to trace it to its factual basis (1935, II:
207-210, 306-307). The tale, told by a woman who was the daughter
of the chief character's wife, recounts three murders, the last of
which was the killing of a Navaho albino, a crime that was followed
by the birth of an albino child to the murderer's wife. The story
establishes a precedent for albinos in Zuni and the refusal of Hunter
society members to join other societies. The original occurrence was
a simple account of a single murder and the murderer's refusal to

---

* The lesson of this creation of "historical" fact should be kept in mind for the discussion of historical reliability in the next chapter.

join the bow society, an organization reserved for the purification of killers. It is easy to see how such an elemental event can gather irrelevant but specious accretions.

Those pioneer collectors who like Stefansson worked with native groups near the time of their contact with the white man were able to identify the origin of narrative elements that within a short time would presumably become syncretized. Bogoras, who led several expeditions among the Russianized Arctic tribes of Siberia at the turn of the century, showed the beginning of a blend of disparate elements:

> Although these people have lost their heritage, they obstinately cling to the remnants of their old traditions, blending them often with Russian elements, but more often keeping them in the unmutilated condition that they had before the coming of the Russians. These Russianized natives, moreover, have rescued from oblivion a large body of old Russian folklore, songs, tales, and epics, long ago forgotten by their neighbors of Russian blood; and so, in some very remote corner of that remote region, one may sometimes hear from the lips of a full-blooded Yukaghir or Yakut an epic song composed on the shores of the Dneiper in South Russia hundreds of years ago. All the sounds and words are preserved almost without distortion, though the meaning of the sentences remains quite obscure to the simple fisherman, who had never in his life seen a single rye-ear or fruit-tree, a town or village of more than thirty houses, kings or glorious knights with glistening armor, all of which the old epics continually treat in detail.

Religion, while it retards myth change, is often a prime mover in the making of myth and the adaptation of other myths to its peculiar philosophical bias. Dickson recounts from the Shammar Bedouin an eye-opening continuation of the Biblical Abraham-Hagar story by which the Bedouins justified their hatred of the Jews. Naively, his informant, very much involved in the ancient situation, revealed, "Your Book and the Jewish Taurat say nothing about this" (293). It has often been noticed that in Korea Buddhist stories prevail over Confucian tales; Homer Hulbert (379) convincingly attributes this to the fact that Buddhism was more imaginative while Confucianism was more reasonable; that Buddhism was the earlier intrusion, and therefore set the pattern for Korean thinking; that Confucianism gave an inferior place to the story-telling women, who understandably are more tenacious Buddhists; and that Buddhist stories have a localizing tendency.

The myriad cultural factors that affect, contaminate, confuse, and obscure the origin and development of literature are far more numerous than the preceding paragraphs suggest; they are so overwhelming that the worker in this difficult field shares with Isaac Newton the estimate he had of himself—"I seem to have been only like a boy playing on the seashore, and diverting myself in now and then finding a smoother pebble or a prettier shell than ordinary, whilst the great ocean of truth lay all undiscovered before me." Far from being able to perceive and trace all the permutations that literature undergoes even in the simplest societies, we are often not able even to assign to a story, myth, or song its protogenic beginning, to tell whether it came to a people through diffusion or independent invention. All too often even this basic question is decided by choosing the better of two impossible alternatives.

THE PROCESS OF POLYGENESIS

Polygenesis—the multiple independent origin of a trait found in different cultures—is a frequent occurrence when the item in question is simple in nature and a fairly predictable result of the interaction of the physical environment and the human perception. Jung's archetypes and his notion of the collective unconscious that ties men together in a mystical psychic unity are a metaphysical extension of this elementary situation. If the Tapirape Indians believe this world is the third, the first having been destroyed by flood and the second by fire, it is not really necessary to suppose that Central Brazil was in the dim past invaded by either Christian or Aztec missionaries; the idea is simple enough to have been invented independently by any number of people. So also the presence of religious pyramids in Polynesia, Central America, Egypt, and Mesopotamia ignites the imagination of lay archaeological theorists, who go to the back-breaking trouble of creating whole continents across the Atlantic and Pacific oceans to accomodate their diffusion. But if you have your gods in the sky (the most logical place for them), and your religion aspires to unity with the gods (as any good religion should), and you want to construct a practical path upward (which in spite of the Hebrews' opinion of the Tower of Babel, is a commendable aspiration), and your architectural technology is primitive (as, considering the previous ideas, it would be), what structure other than a pyramid could you possibly invent? The religious pyramid is so simple an invention that one can answer the skeptic's question, "Could many men have invented it?" with the same retort Dr. Johnson gave the champion of the Ossianic poems, "Yes, sir, many men, many women, and many children."

The Rainbow Serpent is a similar concept impressive in its distribution (all over Australia; among the Kumana of Eastern Bolivia, the Ashluslay of Gran Chaco, the Arawak, Jivaro, Vilela, and other South American Indians; the ancient Persians; and some African peoples) until one realizes that societies whose environment harbors polychromatic snakes and rainbows inevitably must see some resemblance between them.

But when the cultural item is a complex of several interrelated but not integral elements, or is not easily explained by the natural association of similar appearances, then polygenesis is a desperate expedient, the alternative explanation because it is the only alternative, when diffusion is so improbable as to boggle the imagination. One classical anthropological example is the case of the games parchisi and patolli. Patolli was a pre-Columbian Aztec game, played with flat dice, a scoreboard, a cross-shaped playing board, several men or counters, penalty and safety stations, and the idea of "killing" an opponent's man if your counter landed on a square it occupied. In ancient India the game parchisi was played, with the same six characteristics. Patolli and parchisi are so very complex in their six identities (each of which incorporates other elements) that the odds against polygenetic invention are astronomical—but so are the odds against diffusion of this single trait from India to Mexico.*

In literature there are many cases like the following pair of stories accounting for the origin of fire. It is inconceivable that the first fire-stealing fable, from the Jivaro of northwestern Peru (Karsten: 517), and the second, from the Djauan tribe of northern Australia (Robinson, 1952: 33–34), could have occurred independently to the minds of an unknown myth-maker in each of these places, but the complexities of the motifs are great enough to make the polygeneticist wish for many more differences:

> In ancient times the Jibaros did not know the use of
> fire. In those times, in preparing the food, they were in

---

* Discoveries made in the 1963 excavations at Teotihuacan in Mexico seem to establish a pre-Columbian contact between the Orient and Central America.

the habit of warming the flesh and making it tender by keeping it under the arms, and the manioc they made "ripe" by keeping it under the chin. Eggs were boiled by burying them in the sand and exposing them to the sun.

The only one who possessed fire was a Jibaro by the name Takkea. He had learned to make fire by rubbing two pieces of wood against each other. But he was an enemy of the other Jibaros and did not like to give it to them, nor teach them how to make it. Many Jibaros (who in those times had the shape of animals and birds) came flying and tried to steal fire from the house of Takkea, but they were not able to do it. Takkea kept the door of his house a little open, and when the birds came he killed them, squeezing them to death between the door and the post, and ate them.

Lastly the humming-bird, *himbui*, said to the rest: "All right, I will steal fire from Takkea's house." The humming-bird wet his wings and placed himself in the middle of the way, pretending to be unable to fly and trembling as if he felt cold. The wife of Takkea, returning from the fields, saw the humming-bird, and took him to her house with the intention of drying and taming him. After a while the humming-bird, having got half dry, shook his wings and tried to raise himself for flight but could not.

Takkea's wife again took him and placed him beside the fire. Soon the humming-bird was perfectly dry and prepared himself to steal some fire. Since he could not carry away a whole fire-brand he took the fire with his tail, allowing the feathers to catch fire and flew away from the house. He flew up into a high tree with very dry bark, which the Jibaros call *mukúna*. The bark caught fire and the humming-bird carried away a little of this bark, taking it to a house. "Here you have fire," he shouted to the rest, "light your fire from it at once, all of you may take of it, now you will be able to cook your food nicely. You need no longer make your food ripe by keeping it under the arms."

When Takkea saw that the humming-bird had fled with fire he got very angry and began to reproach his people. "Why have you allowed that bird to enter the house and steal fire? From now on everybody will have fire and that is your fault."

The Fire Bird. The legend of Wirritt-wirrit, who won for the blackfellows the secret of fire-making, as told in the Djauan tribe.

Among the trees growing along the rivers and billabongs you will see a glancing, swooping bird who had the colours of the sun and the leaves, the golden-brown grass and the sky. He has a straight, thin beak and two feathers stick out of the end of his tail like two thin sticks. This is Wirritt-wirritt who, in the dreamtime, stole for the black-fellows the secret of fire-making.

Before Wirritt-wirritt gained this secret, everyone had to eat their food raw, as a strong and sullen blackfellow named Koimul had the secret of fire-making and he closely guarded it against anyone who tried to take it from him.

And the secret of fire-making was contained in two sticks which Koimul carried about held closely and tightly in his armpit. And Koimul would not let anyone know the secret, as he wanted the blackfellows to stay along the rivers and billabongs. And so the blackfellows had to live on lily-bulbs and stems and seeds; and fish, goanna, tortoise or mussels they had to eat raw.

Many blackfellows had tried to get these two sticks from Koimul, but Koimul was quick to see anyone creeping up on him. And he was strong and cruel and kept to himself.

And one day Wirritt-wirritt came along and saw all the blackfellows eating their food raw.

"Why don't you get the fire from Koimul?" he asked.

"We have tried often, but no one has ever been able to get it," said the blackfellows.

"Yes," said others, "that Koimul never sleeps. He is too savage and quick."

"Why don't you try, Wirritt-wirritt?" called out other blackfellows.

"All right, then," said Wirritt-wirritt, "I'll try."

And Wirritt was light and flashing in his movements, and he came up on to the sullen Koimul and made no sound. And suddenly, in a brilliant swooping dive, he sped in on Koimul, snatched the two sticks from under his armpit and was off with them before Koimul knew what had happened.

It was useless for Koimul to follow the swooping and flashing Wirritt-wirritt through the trees.

And Wirritt-wirritt gave the old man Nagacork the two sticks he had taken from Koimul. Then Nagacork called the blackfellows out on to the plain away from the river and showed them the two sticks.

One of these sticks had a hole and a notch made in its side in the middle, and the other stick was sharpened slightly at one end.

And Nagacork sat down and held, with his feet, the holed and notched stick over a little pile of shredded bark. Then he took the other stick between the palms of his hands and twirled it rapidly backwards and forwards with its sharpened end in the hold of the notched stick. After a while the blackfellows saw the hole, where the stick was twirling, begin to smoke, and out of the notch ran a little stream of burning wood-dust which fell on to the shredded bark and set it alight.

And soon the blackfellows had many camp fires going and the smell of cooking was everywhere on the air.

And after Koimul had lost his firesticks he said, "I have no fire and I cannot make the blackfellows stay along the rivers and billabongs any more. None of those blackfellows are friends of mine. I'll go and live in the river."

And Koimul went down to the river and there he met a blackfellow to whom he said, "Well, I'm going to dive in the river now and that's where I'll always live."

"Why," said the blackfellow, you can't live in the river; you'll drown."

"No, I won't," said Koimul. "That's where I'll live and stay all the time."

And Koimul dived into the river and became a crocodile.

But always when the blackfellows see Wirritt-wirritt flashing and swooping through the air, they say, "There goes Wirritt-wirritt, who gave us the secret of making fire. See, there are the two fire-sticks sticking out of the end of his tail."

Another origin motif scattered over the world is the idea of death originating through the refusal of a mortal to perform an ablution for a god. Two examples follow, the first from the Atayal of Formosa (Norbeck: 31) and the second from the Djauan of Arnhem Land (Robinson, 1962: 38).

This place was originally not an evil place. This place where we now live became an evil place because the flood came. The reason that this place became evil is that at the time of the flood, eels crawled on the surface of the land and indented it (made the topography irregular). Although our ancient ancestors again returned to their former abode, they still preserved their millet seeds.

There was a god whose custom it was to enter excreta. Once this god spoke to the Atayal promising: "If you will wash me off, you will shed your skin successively like the crepe myrtle and never grow old, and you will never die." However, as they did not wash this god he said, crying, "If you show me no concern and consider washing me too much trouble, we will be averse to protecting even the small children and will take their lives. The people whom we are not averse to protecting will be left to their own courses, and when their span of life is completed, we will then take their lives." He spoke thus, and in actuality it was no lie. People died even if they were children. The people whom he had not ceased protecting grew old, and then their lives were taken. This is why our lives have come to be as they are.

———

When Koopoo, the red plain-kangaroo, was travelling from Arnhem Land towards the eastern sea, he met Jabbor the native-cat. Jabbor asked Koopoo to give him half of the big business which was all the secret rites, ceremonies and corroborees, called Jaboordoorawa, belonging to Koopoo.

And Koopoo said, "No! This big business is all mine."

Jabbor then said he would fight Koopoo for it, but Koopoo called up all the blackfellows. And the blackfellows speared Jabbor with a flight of many spears. And this is why Jabbor comes to have spots all over him, for these spots are the holes that the spears made.

And as Jabbor lay dying, Deert the Moon came along and said to him, "If you will drink this water of mine you will always be able to come back to life."

But there were many other native-cats there who heard Deert the Moon say this and they would not let Jabbor drink.

"Very well then," said Deert the Moon. "Now you must
all die. Animals, blackfellows, everybody must die for ever.
If you had drunk my water, you would all have been able to
come back to life. I shall die, but you will see me return
again. I am Deert the Moon."

Australian examples of these widespread motifs are more pertinent
than those of other people, since the cultural and biological evidence
for the nearly complete isolation of these aborigines for several thousand years is as overpowering as any such evidence can be, so that
diffusion seems improbable for the parallels that time and again appear in the stories of the isolated continent and the rest of the world.
But Australia is not a unique instance of this difficulty. Many
complex and imaginative motifs are found in wide but not continuous distribution; if they were continuous, there would be no
doubt at all of their having come to their owners by diffusion, but
this process requires a degree of contiguity. In Africa (Abraham:
179), North America (Boas, 1910: 694), and South America (La
Barre: 40) there are stories of a jealous animal inducing her rival to
destroy her own children. Contact between aboriginal Africa and
aboriginal America is hard enough to accept, but again in Australia
the motif appears, and in widely-separated tribes—the Mungkan
of Queensland (McConnel: 91) and the Euahlayi of New South
Wales (Parker: 1–5).

Br'er Rabbit's well known trickster ploy—"Don't throw me in
that briar patch"—has an analogue in the story of "The Buffalo,
the Ant, and the Tortoise," three companions in war. The tortoise
is captured in an attack on an enemy village, and

> To punish him for his presumption, the enemy resolved to
> put him to death in such a manner as would be most painful
> to him. They accordingly threatened him successively with
> a number of different forms of torture, such as baking in hot
> embers, boiling, etc., with each of which the captive artfully
> expressed his entire satisfaction. They finally proposed to
> drown him; and this mode of punishment being so earnestly
> protested against by the tortoise, they determined to carry
> it into immediate execution.

Had this story been recorded in Africa, the mother country of
Br'er Rabbit, diffusion would be established—but it comes from the
American Plains Indians at the time of first white contact (James in
Davidson: 115)! And what is one to make of the belief that a shrew

cannot cross a footpath and live, found anciently and independently in England and in Africa (Evans-Pritchard: 170)?

THE PROCESS OF DIFFUSION

Many of the instances offered for polygenesis are about as convincing as the small boy who, when his father asked him where he got the roller skates, answered, "I made 'em." Perhaps because of the ingrained human wish for the mystical to be true, or perhaps because of the tyrannical influence of Franz Boas, anthropologists are reluctant to admit the distribution of a culture trait by diffusion unless the situation conforms with the rules laid down by Boas in 1891 and 1914 for tale diffusion: that the tale be so complex that on probability grounds independent origin is eliminated, and that continuous distribution of the tale be proved. Boas, like so many other formulators of rules, was not so dogmatic about their applicability as some of his students who formed the second team of ethnolitterateurs and who also came under the intellectual dictatorship of Aleš Hrdlička, the Doubting Thomas of American anthropology. Other irrelevant factors make the case of diffusion less persuasive than it ought to be, such as the deception implanted in our minds by the map projection of Mercator which for 400 years has disguised the fact that the western coastline of the Western Hemisphere and the eastern coastline of the Eastern Hemisphere form one of the straightest lines in geography. The western coast of Canada and the United States is taken to be an ethnic continuum and the cultures resident along it are treated in ethnographies as if they were located on a commuter line, whereas the whole of the northern Pacific Ocean is obtruded between southern Alaska and northern China. Since this particular illusion is one of the most indestructible fallacies in ethnogeography, it would be useful to hear what some of the men who have collected stories in this remote region have to say on the subject:

WALDEMAR BOGORAS (1902: 579–580)—The mythology and folklore of northeastern Asia are essentially different from the Ural-Altaic mythology, and point to a group of conceptions and a mode of expression which have little relationship to those of the interior of Siberia; on the contrary, they possess affinities eastward along the shores of the Bering Sea to the northwestern part of America. The differences of both mythological cycles are so distinct and important that one may almost assume that, from an ethnographical point of view, the line dividing Asia and America lies far southwestward of Bering strait, extending from the lower part of Kolyma river to Gishiga bay. In the whole country east of this line, American ideas, or, more properly speaking, ideas characteristic of the North Pacific coast of America, prevail. . . . The second striking feature of the folklore of both shores of Bering Sea and of the adjoining parts of the Northwest coast of America are the numerous lewd and ribald stories, often without any apparent coherence with these. It is truly remarkable that even in this class of stories similar ones are quite frequently found on the east and the west coasts of Bering Sea. On account of their very incongruity they arrest the attention and suggest a common source; and as we go farther to the south, along the Pacific coast of Asia, the folklore of the Ainu, with its simple method of description, its numerous animal stories and obscene episodes, must be classed within the same group of ideas.

FRANZ BOAS (1938: 612)—A few complex stories consisting of a sequence of unrelated elements have an exceedingly wide distribution. Perhaps the most convincing one of these is that of the Magic Flight, the outstanding elements of which are the flight from an ogre, and objects thrown back over the shoulder forming obstacles—a stone which becomes a mountain; a comb which becomes a thicket; oil which becomes a body of water. The tale is known from the Atlantic border of Europe eastward over Asia and North America, reaching the Atlantic coast in Greenland.*

WALDEMAR JOCHELSON (1908: 358) [summarizing comparisons of Koryak myths with Eskimo, Indian, and Old World analogues] . . . out of 122 episodes, there occur in

1. Old World mythology   8
2. Eskimo mythology   12
3. Indian mythology   75
4. Indian and Eskimo mythology   10
5. Indian and Old World mythology   9
6. Indian, Eskimo, and Old World
       mythology   8

---

* Kroeber (1948: 545) reminds us that "In Japan it enters into official Shinto mythology, first put into writing in A.D. 712."

7. Eskimo and Old World mythology......   0
                                          ──
                                         122

Jochelson's concordance added more evidence to support the contention, based on similar studies, that the Eskimo were late comers to the area and in some cases caused a hiatus in distribution of tales and motifs that consequently obscured the connection of adjoining lores and invalidated Boas' thesis that diffusion had to be established by continuous distribution. Other scholars have shown the movement of recreational culture along this busy coastal highway: Tylor in 1896 demonstrated pre-Columbian intercourse between the Northwest Pacific coast story of "Raven's War on the South Wind" to the Asiatic "Wandering Animals and Objects" tale.

The truth of diffusion is stranger than the fiction of polygenesis. Tobacco smoking was taken by Raleigh to England, and England's expanding empire diffused the practice eastward where other peoples carried it onward and over the Bering Strait back again into the New World, so that some northern Indian tribes learned the noisome habit by a 20,000-mile bucket brigade, though the trait began only a few hundred miles to the south of them. Even among birds: Oakley cites how one or several geniuses among English tits learned to peck the tops off milk bottles, a discovery that quickly spread by diffusion through nearly the whole of this species in the British Isles (3). Unfortunately for our systematic knowledge of the process, the destructive effect of white contact has run the time out on tracing the diffusion of literary motifs among primitive peoples. We have few examples like that described by Elkin (1954: 260) of the spread of the *molonglo* ritual in eastern and central Australia:

> W. E. Roth reported that whatever its origin was, it spread from the Worgaia at the head of the Georgina to the Yaroinga by 1893, to the Pitta-Pitta of Boulia by 1895, and the Miorli of the Middle Diamantina in 1896. From there it passed on to the Dieri near Lake Eyre by about 1900, and Penong on the Great Australian Bight by 1915. At some point it turned north, for I saw it performed by Aranda and Loritja men at Horseshoe Bend, Central Australia, in 1930.

The *molonglo* diffusion involved about twenty tribes in its movement from the headwaters of the Georgina River in the extreme northwest of Queensland to Penong, on the eastern end of the Nullarbor Plain, which journey took 25 years to cover over a thousand miles; then upward another 500 miles in 15 more years. If this dissemination of an idea seems slow, one could compare the relationship in many parts of the world among tribes. The indigenous names of tribes, almost without exception, can be translated "the human beings," with the implication that persons outside the tribe are not human beings and are not to be treated as such. Tribes are genetic and cultural isolates. Members of one tribe do not ordinarily marry persons from another tribe nor do they permit such people to sit down in their restaurants. Even in Australia, where tribal concepts are weak and relations with strangers are much too friendly, "tribes" are 86 per cent endogamous (Birdsell: 200). Any communication in the circumstances is remarkable, and that there is not much cordial interchange is established by the great variety of languages in certain areas. The French Academy catalogued 783 different languages (not counting dialects) in South America and the Antilles, a situation that reflects the mutual unfriendliness of these tribes;* yet Metraux (114 *ff*) and others have shown the distribution throughout the continent of certain tales and motifs that could not have come about through any means other than diffusion. How do peoples who see their neighbors as walking entrées manage to communicate stories? The nearest thing yet to a practical One World is the internationalism of literature.

Diffusion need not depend on land routes or rapid transportation. There are no barriers on earth or in the waters under the earth to the transmission of a good story. The Sahara is latticed by trade routes, and the floor of the Pacific is carpeted with Polynesian canoes that sank before running aground on the American coasts. Anyone who has seen the carved houses of the Northwest Pacific Coast and those of New Zealand seven thousand watery miles away will not be convinced that there was no communication between these people, blood types and language notwithstanding. Some stories travelled comparable distances on camel back: Lattimore found the explanatory tale accounting for the unique genital organs of the camel among the Chinese, the Mongols, the Persians, and the Arabs (157–159)—

---

* Some readers will question both the number of languages in South America and the conclusion drawn from them. Probably the differences now seen in these languages will be lessened as further study is made, but now that glottochronology, which attempted to date separation of peoples by language change, is receiving increasing criticism, we need not assume that languages change at a universally constant rate.

peoples, by the way, who have a long history of restraining their passion for one another. And most moved of course on bare feet: Thomson discovered a hitherto unknown desert tribe in Australia, the Bindibu, using an uncommon word for a common animal— *pudjikat;* it took him a while to realize that somehow the familiar term "pussy cat" had preceded the white man into one of the most remote parts of the earth.

THE EFFECTS OF WHITE CONTACT

It took 75 years to exterminate the Tasmanian aborigines. The job could have been done in one-third the time if the settlers had persevered in the enthusiasm and efficiency with which they began, instead of indulging in such sentimentalities as slicing off ears for punishment and fingers for tobacco stoppers, and killing aborigines only when they needed dog meat or a Sunday's recreation at the hunt (Turnbull, *passim*). One certainly cannot blame Governor Arthur, for his proclamation of martial law in 1828 effected in one year the destruction of two thirds of the aborigines then alive. The real mistake was in establishing in 1830 an ethnic zoo with the few natives who were left, thus unnecessarily delaying the death of the last male until 1869 and the last female until 1876. Both the settlers and the aborigines had other things on their minds during the short period of their acquaintance, and so next to nothing remains of native Tasmanian literature. At the Flinders Island zoo the Great Pacificator, George Augustus Robinson, innovated a newspaper, *The Aboriginal, or Flinders Island Chronicle,* but so far as we know, no copies were ever printed. And the Reverend Thomas Wilkinson tried to prepare the inmates for their imminent destiny by translating the first three chapters of Genesis into what purported to be Tasmanian. Critics who did not appreciate the immense task Wilkinson took upon himself in so short a time to complete it found fault with lines like "Troteh Godneh pomleh heavenneh co-etanneh; lywerrah crackny," with which his translation began. "Lywerrah crackny" meant "And darkness was upon the face of the deep"— an economy, as Turnbull remarked, "which Homer or Pushkin might have envied."

Two thousand miles north, the Yir Yoront were shielded against the settlers by enlightened missionaries who premitted only two or three harmless artifacts to enter this Old Stone Age culture, like the steel axe. Yet the introduction of this simple tool into Yir Yoront society rotted away their entire culture—social organization, patterns of behavior, religion, and mythology (Sharp).

Unlike the Tasmanians, other primitive societies died lingeringly on the edges of frontier towns, trading their meagre culture for tobacco and firewater. White men who draw their judgments from drunken Indians sitting in the gutters of Gallup, New Mexico, impute to the people they destroyed a subhuman obtuseness about their situation and life in general, misinterpreting their

> . . . condition of parasitism, of hanging around the white man's station or settlement, getting what [they] can, and doing only what [they] must; together with a willingness to take punishment, kicks and punches, without hitting back . . . appearing stupid, funny, childlike, and pleased with the patronizing (Elkin: 1947).

Though it is a futile enough retaliation, these people get back at the white man in various ineffectual ways, some subtle, like "squandering their money on taxi rides" (which is the only means they have to put a white man in a position of subservience) and some blunt, like calling him opprobrious names among themselves and lampooning him in their songs and tales. The latter information is obviously hard for white collectors to obtain (Greenway, 1953: 67–120), but it exists in sufficiently wide distribution to establish anti-white satire and ridicule as a frequent literary form among primitive groups today. Rasmussen (240) outlines a Copper Eskimo tale of a woman who would not take a husband and who copulated instead with dogs, by which she became the mother of the first white men. Tracey (1948: 14) recorded a song from the Chopi about their Portuguese employers who came into much sung criticism for the deplorable conditions in the Rand mines:

> O-oh, listen to the orders,
> Listen to the orders of the Portuguese.
>
> O-oh, listen to the orders,
> Listen to the orders of the Portuguese.
> Men! The Portuguese say, "Pay your pound."
>
> Men! The Portuguese say, "Pay your pound."
> This is wonderful, father!
> Where shall I find the pound?
> This is wonderful, father!

Where shall I find the pound?
O-oh, listen to the orders,
Listen to the orders of the Portuguese.

In recent Coeur d'Alêne story the Grizzly Bear runs out and claws to death passersby directed past his lair by the traitorous Coyote, an uninteresting series of events until one learns that the Grizzly Bear is the United States Government and Coyote is the interpreter hired by the whites (Reichard, 1947: 32). An almost unbelievably sophisticated parable was reported from the Kikuyu by a native who after becoming an anthropologist (he studied under Malinowski and at the London School of Economics) went on to become the leader of the terrorist Mau Mau and ultimately prime minister of Kenya:

Once upon a time an elephant made a friendship with a man. One day a heavy thunderstorm broke out, the elephant went to his friend, who had a little hut at the edge of the forest, and said to him: "My dear good man, will you please let me put my trunk inside your hut to keep it out of this torrential rain?" The man, seeing what situation his friend was in, replied, "My dear good elephant, my hut is very small, but there is room for your trunk and myself. Please put your trunk in gently." The elephant thanked his friend, saying, "You have done me a good deed and one day I shall return your kindness." But what followed? As soon as the elephant put his trunk inside the hut, slowly he pushed his head inside, and finally flung the man out in the rain, and then lay down comfortably inside his friend's hut, saying, "My dear good friend, your skin is harder than mine, and as there is not enough room for both of us, you can afford to remain in the rain while I am protecting my delicate skin from the hailstorm."

The man, seeing what his friend had done to him, started to grumble, the animals in the nearby forest heard the noise and came to see what was the matter. All stood around listening to the heated argument between the man and his friend the elephant. In this turmoil the lion came along roaring, and said in a loud voice: "Don't you all know that I am King of the Jungle! How dare anyone disturb the peace of my kingdom?" On hearing this the elephant, who was one of the high ministers in the jungle kingdom, replied in a

soothing voice, and said: "My lord, there is no disturbance
of the peace in your kingdom. I have only been having a
little discussion with my friend here as to the possession of
this little hut which your lordship sees me occupying."
The lion, who wanted to have "peace and tranquility" in
his kingdom, replied in a noble voice, saying, "I command
my ministers to appoint a Commission of Enquiry to go
thoroughly into this matter and report accordingly." He
then turned to the man and said: "You have done well by
establishing friendship with my people, especially with the
elephant who is one of my honourable ministers of state.
Do not grumble any more, your hut is not lost to you. Wait
until the sitting of my Imperial Commission, and there you
will be given plenty of opportunity to state your case. I am
sure that you will be pleased with the findings of the Commission." The man was very pleased by these sweet words from
the King of the Jungle, and innocently waited for his opportunity, in the belief, that naturally, the hut would be returned to him.

The elephant, obeying the command of his master, got
busy with other ministers to appoint the Commission of
Enquiry. The following elders of the jungle were appointed
to sit in the Commission: (1) Mr. Rhinoceros; (2) Mr. Buffalo; (3) Mr. Alligator; (4) the Rt. Hon. Mr. Fox to act as
chairman; and (5) Mr. Leopard to act as Secretary to the
Commission. On seeing the personnel, the man protested
and asked if it was not necessary to include in this Commission a member from his side. But he was told that it was
impossible, since no one from his side was well enough educated to understand the intricacy of jungle law. Further,
that there was nothing to fear, for the members of the Commission were all men of repute for their impartiality in justice, and as they were gentlemen chosen by God to look after
the interests of races less adequately endowed with teeth
and claws, he might rest assured that they would investigate
the matter with the greatest care and report impartially.

The Commission sat to take the evidence. The Rt. Hon.
Mr. Elephant was first called. He came along with a su-
perior air, brushing his tusks with a sapling which Mrs.
Elephant had provided, and in an authoritative voice said,
"Gentlemen of the Jungle, there is no need for me to waste

your valuable time in relating a story which I am sure you all know. I have always regarded it as my duty to protect the interests of my friends, and this appears to have caused the misunderstanding between myself and my friend here. He invited me in to save his hut from being blown away by a hurricane. As the hurricane had gained access owing to the unoccupied space in the hut, I considered it necessary, in my friend's own interests, to turn the undeveloped space to a more economic use by sitting in it myself; a duty which any of you would undoubtedly have performed with equal readiness in similar circumstances."

After hearing the Rt. Hon. Mr. Elephant's conclusive evidence, the Commission called Mr. Hyena and other elders of the Jungle, who all supported what Mr. Elephant had said. They then called the man, who began to give his own account of the dispute. But the Commission cut him short, saying: "My good man, please confine yourself to relevant issues. We have already heard the circumstances from various unbiased sources; all we wish you to tell us is whether the undeveloped space in your hut was occupied by anyone else before Mr. Elephant assumed his position?" The man began to say; "No, but . . ." But at this point the Commission declared that they had heard sufficient evidence from both sides and retired to consider their decision. After enjoying a delicious meal at the expense of the Rt. Hon. Mr. Elephant, they reached their verdict, called the man, and declared as follows: "In our opinion this dispute has arisen through a regrettable misunderstanding due to the backwardness of your ideas. We consider that Mr. Elephant has fulfilled his sacred duty of protecting your interests. As it is clearly for your good that the space should be put to its most economic use, and as you yourself have not yet reached the stage of expansion which would enable you to fill it, we consider it necessary to arrange a compromise to suit both parties. Mr. Elephant shall continue his occupation of your hut, but we give you permission to look for a site where you can build another hut more suited to your needs, and we will see that you are well protected."

The man, having no alternative, and fearing that his refusal might expose him to the teeth and the claws of members of the Commission, did as they suggested. But no sooner had he built another hut than Mr. Rhinoceros charged in with his horn lowered and ordered the man to quit. A Royal Commission was again appointed to look into the matter, and the same finding was given. This procedure was repeated until Mr. Buffalo, Mr. Leopard, Mr. Hyena, and the rest were all accommodated with new huts. Then the man decided that he must adopt an effective method of protection, since Commissions of Enquiry did not seem to be of any use to him. He sat down and said: "*Ng'enda thi ndeagaga motegi,*" which literally means, "there is nothing that treads on the earth that cannot be trapped," or in other words, you can fool people for a time, but not forever.

Early one morning, when the huts already occupied by the jungle lords were all beginning to decay and fall to pieces, he went out and built a bigger and better hut a little distance away. No sooner had Mr. Rhinoceros seen it than he came rushing in, only to find that Mr. Elephant was already inside, sound asleep. Mr. Leopard came in at the window, Mr. Lion, Mr. Fox, and Mr. Buffalo entered the doors, while Mr. Hyena howled for a place in the shade and Mr. Alligator basked on the roof. Presently they all began disputing about their rights of penetration, and from disputing they came to fighting, and while they were all embroiled together the man set the hut on fire and burnt it to the ground, jungle lords and all. Then he went home, saying, "Peace is costly, but it's worth the expense," and lived happily ever after.

One wishes that some collector other than Jomo Kenyatta had printed this story, but there are corroborating tales among other Negroes of the world. In the American South they tell the satirical tale of Old Sis Goose, who was captured by a fox, and to whom she appealed for a fair trial. The trial was duly held, but Old Sis Goose was dismayed to find that the judge, the jury, the prosecuting and defense attorneys, and the spectators were all foxes, "like a cat down the cellar with a no-hole mouse."

Making full allowances for retaliations of this nature, we must admit that a majority of the primitive oppressed are willing to accept oppression and the deserving of it. For every story like Kenyatta's, there are dozens like that printed by Stirling (123), which tells of the completion of Creation, when the newly-made men washed in a large jar of water: "the first to wash, while the water was clean, became white men; those who followed, after the water had become dirty, are the Indians; those who were last of all are the negroes."

Contamination

Until acculturation studies were accepted as a proper field of inquiry, collectors were uninterested in picking up Europeanized tales, though the amount of borrowing and the adaptation of it are clearly of great importance in understanding both the society in question and culture change in general. Persons who, like Burton, actually tried to contaminate aboriginal culture, are still held guilty of inexcusable offense. Burton innocently describes a typical situation (119) that used to drive anthropologists mad:

> The confidence of those Indians who were concerned in the play was won by a rather hazardous experiment. I made a four-part arrangement of "My Bark Canoe" and gave it to a quartette of white singers who chanced our way. This was in the afternoon. In the evening the Indians were called together and I told them that I would show them what I was doing with their music. I said that if they would sing "Chekabay tebik" in their way, my friends would sing it in the white-man way. After characteristic hesitation the Indians complied. The quartette, taking the pitch from the Indians, immediately repeated the song in English. The excitement of the Indians knew no bounds. They yelled as if they were engaged in fierce combat and, surrounding the startled quartette, demanded a repetition of the piece. Several repetitions were given before the Indians were satisfied, and then they crowded about me, asking eagerly if they could learn to sing like that—meaning in parts.

The end result of this contamination among the American Indians is like the love songs Willard Rhodes recorded among Plains youths. In text these are typical Indian songs, except that the vocables surround an English rather than an Indian thematic phrase:

> We-a he-a, We-a he-a,
> We-a he-a, We-a he-a,

> We-a he-a, We-a he-a he yo ha,
> We-a he-a, ya ya, We-a he-a ya ya,
> When the dance is over, sweetheart,
> I will take you home in my one-eye Ford,
> We-a, he-a, he yo ha,
> We-a, he-a, We-a he-a ya yaaa.

And,

> We ne ya he-a he-a, we ne ya he-a,
> We ne ya he-a he-a, we ne ya he-a,
> We ne ya he-a he-a, we ne ya he-a,
> We ne ya he-a he-a, we ne ya he-a,
> We-a he-a eee, eee-e,
> My sweetheart he ne ya he ya,
> She got mad at me because I said hallo to my old timer,
> But it's just okay with me ya ho we-a eee-e.

The worldwide lust for the automobile displaces the camel in this nightmare travesty of the *Song of Songs* from the Kuwait Bedouins (Dickson: 228).

> I hope and long to ride her in a car
> In the car of the Saiyid which hoots its horn.
>
> I wish to steal her away, whose breasts are not too large,
> And I wish to flee with her to the countries of the North.
>
> What indeed would take a camel a month, can be done in
>   one short day,
> I'll make him haste his way, along the desert track.
>
> She stopped me and met me, with her golden hair all loose,
> My heart was afire for her, for the tattoo marks on her face.
>
> And were I to possess her now, I'd become one of the mer-
>   chant class,
> Though she beat me and lamed me, happiness would be
>   mine for ever.

Motifs and tale types have always been the most willing part of literary culture to migrate and to be accepted as immigrants. A

Solomon story (well known as the plot of Chrétien de Troyes' *Cliges*) about an adulterous wife of a chief who pretends to be dead and has herself buried in an accessible coffin with ventilation holes so that she can carry on her affair with the chief's nephew, is found in the Pacific Northwest, and, moreover, has been incorporated into the religious Raven cycle (Krappe: 313–314).   There are many such examples, and Krappe suggests the possibility which we know to be a certainty, that analagous processes helped in the making of the Christian mythology.   The Roman Catholic Church has been working for many years clearing apocryphal saints out of the roster of the blessed, and the end is not yet in sight.

War has, so far, been always the greatest stimulus to cultural changes and progress; the passage of millions of soldiers and sailors through the western Pacific in World War II had an incalculable effect on the culture of the peoples of Oceania, including their literature.   Davenport (235) found the Marshall Islanders singing "The Song of the Bombs":

> The powerful heat of the bombs
> The sound of the machine guns scare me
> The sound of the machine guns scare me
> The sound of the machine guns scare me.

> On the towers of the people
> Looking with binoculars, saw the dipping wings of the
>   airplanes
> Diving down dipping their wings, way on top of the clouds
> The many droning planes, racing to the target.

> Cause the bullets
> But there is no way to escape
> But there is no way to escape
> But there is no way to escape.

> I am counted with the dead and injured
> Dead before the gun and sword
> The enemy surrounds us
> Now we stand for our lives.

> For me, I would like to win the bravery medal for which
>   the military compete

For now, I am between life and death
For now, I am between life and death
For now, I am between life and death.

—sung to a Japanese melody! And Elkin was able to trace a new
step in the Djedbangari dance song of the Yirkalla (Riredjingo) of
Arnhem Land to the natives' imitation of the soldiers' "marking
time" after stopping a march (1953). In World War I Peter Buck
(Te Rangi Hiroa) said his Maori Regiment warmed up in the French
morning cold by performing a *haka* (posture dance), to the con-
sternation of the other allies. This sort of thing was in the severest
sense of the word a contamination to the early collectors. Dorsey
confesses his gullibility in publishing some riddles he collected among
the Omaha (232-233):

> When the writer was revising his material before pre-
> paring his article on "Omaha Sociology," he was furnished
> by one of the tribe (a prominent ex-chief, now dead) with
> several riddles, that appeared in "Omaha Sociology" as
> genuine Omaha riddles. Not until 1888 did he learn by
> accident that the riddles in question were versions of some
> that the children of his informant had read in "The Youth's
> Companion" (!). The informant was not a man to tell a
> wilful lie.

Götterdämmerung

Though they fall in the end, the heathen gods do not give in easily
to the deities of the white man. Often they are driven out into the
bush, but they linger on at the edge of the village, waiting for a
chance to get back into the minds of their old worshippers. Sometimes it is the white man's god who carries the old god's luggage.
The Melanesians of the New Hebrides identify the grandson of
Maui, Tamakaia, with Jehovah, and say that England was a fish
caught by Tamakaia that flew off the line when his hook broke (Luomala, 1949: 15). Gladys Reichard's best informant—Klah, whom we
met earlier chiding those who made mistakes in Navaho myth recital—took a little known deity, Begochiddy, a spoiled son of the
Sun, who spent his time in obscenities (his name meant "One-Who-
Grabs-Breasts") and taking care of the insects, whose god he was,
and made him into the Christian Jesus (1944). The Samoyed have
one of their deities, Itte, carry on a titanic struggle with Christ, who

defeats Itte only by joining forces with the Devil (Indiana University: 97).

Some of the most interesting adaptations of Christian minor deities are those of the Negroes of Haiti, who merge their old Dahomean gods with the appropriate patron saints (Herskovits: 1937, 1958). Legba, the Dahomean Trickster, becomes St. Anthony, because the chromolithographs of St. Anthony show him as an old man in rags, supporting himself with a stick; in this guise he looks like Legba in his role of path-opener. For the same reason Legba sometimes becomes St. Peter (the carrier of keys). The Christian missionaries, in return, made Legba into the Devil. One of the most important *vodun* gods, Damballa (the Rainbow Serpent!) becomes St. Patrick, whom the pictures show with serpents. Moses comes in from the Old Testament to take the place of Damballa's father, again because of his association with snakes. St. John the Baptist undergoes a change because he is represented holding a lamb. The ram is the Dahomean symbol of the thunder god, and John becomes the raging thunderer. Herskovits gives the myth which explains John's new role:

> On a given day of the year, God permits each saint to have control over the universe. St. John the Baptist, however, is so irresponsible and his rage is so violent, that God fears for the consequences were he allowed to exert his power on this day. Plying him with drink the day before, he is therefore made so drunk that when he is told his day is already passed, his rage is terrible, and he causes great storms to flay the earth; and it is a commonplace in Mirebalais that this day is marked by tempests of almost hurricane proportions, with great displays of thunder and lightning. Though he can do some damage, his power is now limited, however, to his own sphere.

If this seems outrageous treatment of the baptizer of Jesus, consider what the Yaqui do to St. Peter and Christ himself in this story collected by Giddings (46):

> One time San Pedro and Jesucristo were walking along, Jesucristo sent San Pedro up to a near-by house to get a cooked chicken. On the way back Pedro ate one leg of the chicken.

When Jesucristo saw what San Pedro had brought back, he asked, "Why has this chicken but one leg?"

"It never had another leg," answered Pedro. "All of the chickens around this part of the country have but one leg, Sir."

The two proceeded and came to a big tree under which were sleeping many chickens. All of the chickens had one leg tucked up out of sight under their feathers.

Pedro pointed to them and said, "You see! All of the chickens have but one leg apiece."

Jesucristo took a rock and threw it at one of the chickens. It woke up and stood on both feet.

"Oh," said Pedro, "a miracle!" He then took up a rock and threw it at the rest of the chickens. "You see," he said, "I can perform miracles, too."

Since religious stories and myths are taken up by religious people, it is not hard to catch those rare uses of Christian material as satire and blasphemy. Nearly always when an Old or New Testament story is adapted by a primitive society, the adaptation is a serious addition to the native canon, and often the integration is very good indeed. Perhaps the most famous adaptation of this kind in aboriginal America is the Nativity Tale that Parsons discovered among the Zuni, in which the infant Jesus becomes twin girls:

In the West there lived a Mexican girl (*ellashtoki sipaloa*) who never went out. She staid all the time in her own house. She would sit where the sun shone in. The sun impregnated her ("gave her a child"). At this time soldiers were guarding her. One of the soldiers saw her, and said to the others, "The one we are guarding is pregnant. If she does such things, what is the use of guarding her? Let us kill her!" The next day in the morning she was to die. That evening the Sun by his knowledge (*yam anikwana*) came into her room, and said, "Tomorrow you are to die." "Well, if it is to be, I must die," she said. He said, "No, I won't let you die, I will get you out." The next morning early by his knowledge he lifted her up out of the window. "Now go to where you are to live." So she went on till she came to a *sipaloa* planting. She said, "What are you planting?" He said, "Round stones (*akyamowe*)." Because he

did not answer right, she did something to the seed, and his
corn did not come up. She went on a little ways, and she
came to another one planting. She asked him what he was
planting. He said, "I am planting corn and wheat."
Because he answered her right, she did nothing to his seed,
and they all came up. Then the soldiers found she was gone,
and they came on after her. They asked the first man if he
had seen a girl coming. He said, "Yes, she has just gone
over the hill." They said, "Well, we must be nearly up with
her, we will hurry on." So they went over the hill, and they
saw no one. They came to another little hill, and they could
not see her. They came to a river, and it was very deep.
They cut some poles, and they said, "We'll see how deep it
is." They stuck the poles down, and they said, "It is too
deep. There is no use in hunting any more for her." So
they turned back. But the girl had crossed the river, and
went on until she came to Koluwela, and there she lay in
(*chawasha*). She had twins. The pigs and the dogs kissed
(*tsulpe*) her. That is why the pigs and the dogs have children. The mules would not kiss her. That is why the mules
have no children. They came on to Itiwonna (middle, i.e.,
Zuni). At Koluwela they all (the mother and twins) became *topo'hi* (another sort of person), they became stone.
When they had the dances (at Zuni), she did not care to see
them. She did not like their dances. They had the *hematatsi*. She liked that dance. So she went on to Hakuk
(Acoma), because *hematatsi* was a dance of Hakuk. She
lives there today. The elder sister (*an kyauu*), i.e., of the
twins, is here. The younger (*an hani*) went south to where
the other Zuni (*ashiwi*) live. *Lewi*.

This is a notable example of syncretism in myth, and accords well
with the opinion of Kroeber (quoted in Redfield: 258) that "although
fifty per cent of Zuni culture may be borrowed from white culture,
the Zuni have so cast what they have taken over into their own
patterns, that ninety-nine per cent of their culture may be called
indigenous."*

The merging of Christian and pagan mythology by Mexican and

---

* Many Bible stories integrate well. Bushnell quotes a Tower of Babel story from
the Choctaw, which differs essentially from the original story only in the change of
nationality of the builders to Choctaw-speaking people—a lovely bit of Indian ethnocentricity.

Central American Indians is too well known to need much illustration, but it is one of the best examples of literary and religious syncretism known. Margaret Redfield collected an impressive literature in the Yucatecan village of Dzitas, which she was able later to separate into four categories: the *cuentos* (fanciful tales told for amusement), *historia* (legends), *adivinanzas* (riddles), and *ejemplos* (Bible stories with a moral, or secular morality tales in which Christian mythological figures act). A short but typical *ejemplo* is "Jesu Cristo and the Cha-Chaac" (16):

> Once some men were making *cha-chaac* and they saw a man coming. It was Jesu Cristo but they did not recognize him. Then they thought to themselves, "We don't want to give any of the breads away to this man." So they covered the breads with a pot, so that Jesu Cristo would not see them. After God had gone on, they looked under the pot and there they saw that all the breads had turned into gophers. The *cha-chaac* was the work of God, and the men should not have tried to keep him from sharing in the breads.

Redfield explains,

> On its face this *ejemplo* is one of those stigmatizing the vice of greediness. But there is more significance to the story than that. The *cha-chaac* is the rain ceremony offered to the pagan gods, still performed by many of the men of Dzitas. The ceremony takes two or three days, and during this period the men participating are withdrawn, tabooed to the things of this world. The sacred breads are given only to those who have participated in the preparations, not to any casual passer-by. When Jesu Cristo passed by he was not recognized and so was not given any of the divine breads to which, as a divine being, he had a right. Here is an illustration of the complete reconciliation in the minds of the people between Catholic belief and pagan practice.
>
> The changing of the breads into gophers probably has some reference, not understood by the writer, to some old Indian ritual element, since one of the breads at the *cha-chaac* is called in Maya "ba" (gopher).

Of all the books of the Old Testament none is so popular among primitive converts as Genesis. Anyone who is interested in anything is interested in origins, and whatever else may be said about it, Genesis is an eventful treasury of origin motifs and tales that are taken in by almost every group missionaries have labored among and many in which they have not. Since experience, reason, and environment suggested the same simple kinds of explanation to the ancient Semites as to their counterparts today, some tales have been reinforced by Biblical versions—the Flood story, for an example, is so widespread that it is usually impossible to tell when it is native and when it is the result of a Sunday school class, unless some clearly alien element is present, like the concept of Flooding for punishment. Primitive peoples are easier on themselves so far as the wages of sin is concerned. They will permit the existence of malignant spirits, for things do go wrong even in their world, but the demons' evil doing is generally unmotivated. However, if a people want to include the Sodom and Gomorrah story in their mythos, it is hard to fit in without the motivation of retribution (e.g., Latcham: 349), though some folk could do it easily enough. The Gullah, for instance, use the Bible as a starting block—one glance and they are off and running. In the Gullah creation God is there, but only barely. He occupies a detached position in regard to his work, and in fact he seems a bit bewildered and annoyed by the whole business, like T. H. White's Merlin or Paul Green's De Lawd. "In de beginnin' God been jus' a-projeckin' 'roun' in de element"; he makes the earth out of a mud pie, hoes himself a garden as any good African horticulturalist would do in the circumstances, appoints Br' Dog to be guardian and demiurge, and retires into his hut. As a surrogate creator, Br' Dog is new at his trade. He makes mouths in animals, but presuming upon his limited abilities, he makes rather a mess of Br' Alligator's physiognomy, incurring thereby his enmity and that of his fellow reptilian, Br' Sarpint. It was really none of Sarpint's business, the way Br' Dog looked at it, and so he punishes Sarpint's officiousness by fixing his mouth so that he can do nothing but hiss. The Gullah Genesis becomes an explanatory animal tale that, given a century to ripen, would have been indistinguishable from an African story; indeed, as the tale goes on, Br' Rabbit, the African Trickster, becomes the chief character (Stoney-Shelby: 3–21).

Few primitive literatures are as vital as the Gullah. The result of the clash of the gods has been in most cases the destruction of the old and the rejection of the new, the change of believers in falsehood to believers in nothing. The patriotic Peter Buck laments that in

Tahiti there is "an extreme reluctance on the part of most of the people, to admit knowledge of any such un-Christian things as myths or folk-tales" (1930: 102). Nearly everywhere it is as Jochelson says of the Koryak, they "have entirely forgotten their ancient myths, and have not created any new ones." Much of this passing is tragic. An anthropologist working among the moribund Yir Yoront noticed his toothpaste disappearing unaccountably; he watched, and discovered the old men stealing it for a new toothpaste cult—the old myth and magic and *mana* having failed them, they thought the mysterious substance was the source of the white man's power (Sharp). The old gods canot save their people; they cannot save themselves. In Cambodia

> There used to be on the hill near Kompong-Speu a black stone, and inside it a powerful Neak-Ta who had never seen an automobile. One night, it was perhaps about nine o'clock, a truck climbed up the hill. The motor made a lot of noise and the headlights gave off a great deal of light. Then the Neak-Ta was afraid. He said, "I cannot remain here, for it is dangerous." To hide himself he changed himself into an old man, but some people recognized him; he said, "I'm afraid of the big-eyed spirit, I'm afraid of the Truck spirit, I prefer to leave with my stone." The next morning the black stone was gone (Porée and Maspero: 168).

Nativistic Endeavors—The Last Battle

When the gods and their stones have gone and their people are left to suffer alone the onslaught of the white man, a curious thing often happens. Rather than give up to the inevitable, the oppressed people may make one last strenuous attempt to save themselves by embarking upon what is known as a messianic movement or nativistic endeavor. This phenomenon is a fascinating one for the anthropologist who can look upon it objectively without being overwhelmed by its tragedy, for it is probably the most complex polygenetic of all cultural traits. Whenever and wherever it is found, it usually takes the same form: a shaman arises in the area of greatest suffering and tells his people that he has been carried into the supernatural dimension where he has talked with the spirits (there is no acknowledged contradiction in the fact that these spirits may often be the gods of the oppressing invaders; in historical times Christ

often appears to the prophets of a new chosen people). The deities
tell him that they have not been disinterested in what has been
happening, and in fact they called him to announce a drastic change
they will institute. The oppressors (for contemporary primitive
groups this means the white man) are to be destroyed and the shaman's people chosen to inherit the earth. They need not do anything to assist in the millennium; all they are asked is to indicate
their acceptance of the mantle by performing some ritualistic act
and abandonng the corrupt ways that led to the white man's coming. Since the prophetic shaman is usually a mystical rather than a
practical person, quite convinced of the reality of his vision and his
message, his people seldom pay him any attention. But if something happens to substantiate the prophecy—like Tenskwatawa's
predicting an eclipse with the secret help of an almanac—or, most
importantly, if he gets the alliance of an organizing apostle who is
less interested in the prophet's revelation than what can be done
with it, a genuine nativistic endeavor may follow. The apostle
usually takes the movement away from the prophet after elevating
him to an impotent divinity and changes the peaceful mythology to
one of violence. His faith is as strong as the prophet's, but it is in
the people rather than the spirits. Both faiths are equally useless,
for the oppressors use the revolt as an excuse to put an end to it and
the people who carry it. Even so, faith might continue in the sur-
vivors if the prophet has not made one or both of the fatal mistakes
such prophets usually make: to set an unequivocal date for the
millenium and to die without arranging for a Second Coming. Those
very few messianic prophets who were far-seeing enough to provide
against these errors may, if other circumstances are right (for example, if the oppressors continue with a policy of steady persecution
rather than extermination or complete toleration), establish religions lasting for centuries. Judaism is the chronological leader,
with every promise of reaching three thousand years. There are
always within these long-lived messianic movements derivatory nativistic endeavors, if the original movement enters a time of com-
placency or if new oppressions occur; thus Judaism produced Christianity and Islam and these in turn produced lesser flare-ups, like
Protestantism, and each of these brought into existence countless
smaller socio-religious revolts—such as most of the several hundred
denominations listed annually by the *Yearbook of American Churches*.
Each of these of course has its mythology and its literature.

Inevitably messianic movements intrude into politics; there was

Joan of Arc (who was both her own prophetic shaman and organizing apostle), and in our own history, Tenskwatawa, who made three
American presidents.   Tenskwatawa—the Shawnee Prophet—used
his ferocious brother Tecumseh as his apostle, who patterned his
campaign on that of an earlier apostle of a nativistic endeavor,
Pontiac, and united the Indians intertribally against the encroaching
Americans.   As a brigadier general in the British army Tecumseh
had it out at Tippecanoe with Governor William Henry Harrison
(who also was created a general for the occasion) and was killed.
The Whigs a few years later discovered Harrison while looking for a
popular candidate, and largely on the basis of his lack of ambition
to do anything more than sit on the porch of his cabin drinking cider,
elected him president.   Harrison died quickly, and Tyler became the
second president to take office indirectly because of the Indian movement; later in the century, Harrison's great-grandson, running on his
genealogy, became the third.

In the western Pacific nativistic endeavors are known as "cargo
cults" from the pidgin word for trade goods.   Concerned observers of
the Melanesian situation who do not understand the larger underlying stimulus blame most of the 76 examples given by Worsley on
Second-Coming Christian missionaries whose ancestors sat around in
laundry baskets waiting to be hauled up to heaven in their own
nativistic endeavors, on Communists who likewise have been hunting souls in this region, and on American Army integration that
gave Oceanic Negroes a sight of the millennium in the thousands of
Negro soldiers in apparent equality with their white comrades who
swarmed by the millions through the islands in World War II.
Worsley drew nine common denominators from these cargo cults,
and these could serve well enough as the characteristic elements of
the nativistic endeavor anywhere:

1. Myth of the return of the dead
2. Revival or modification of paganism
3. Introduction of Christian elements
4. Cargo myths
5. Belief that the Negroes will become white man and vice versa
6. Belief in a coming messiah
7. Attempts to restore native political and economic control
8. Threats and violence against white men
9. Union of traditionally separate and unfriendly groups.

Violent and tragic as they were, the cargo cults had elements of amusement for Europeans; in the Great Pigs* cult of New Guinea in 1946 the natives built pitiful "radio antennae" of bamboo and rope to receive the news of the millennium; some of the natives were just a bit more realistic in naming as their messiah the "friendly king of America, Roosevelt."

Of all nativistic endeavors among primitive peoples, the one most interesting to readers of primitive literature was the second Ghost Dance. The first Ghost Dance began with a ragged band of Paiutes in western Nevada in 1869 or 1870, when a mysterious figure variously named Waughzeewaughber, Tavibo, and Wodziwob went up like Moses into the mountains and spoke with God, who gave him the wonderful news that the white men would be swallowed up by holes that would open in the earth and all their possessions would pass to the Indians. After the usual initial difficulty of convincing the people of the reliability of the prophecy, this first Ghost Dance (so named because a primary tenet promised the return of all Indians who had died since the coming of the whites if the Indians would dance a sacred dance) found an apostle who got the movement started on its spread over much of the western United States. Wodziwob assured the collapse of the first Ghost Dance by dying, and on the west coast the movement ended in the disastrous Modoc War of 1873.

Twenty years later in the same small area of impoverished western Nevada it began again under the prophet Wovoka, also known as Wevokar, Wopokahte, Kwohitsauq, Cowejo, Koitsow, Big Rumbling Belly, Jack Wilson, Jackson Wilson, and John Johnson, reputed to have been the son either of Wodziwob or of Wodziwob's organizing apostle. During an eclipse Wovoka fell into the usual shaman's trance in which he was carried up to heaven where God showed him paradisiacal Indians and gave him much the same message Wodziwob had received. Wovoka made the error of giving a precise date to the millennium—July 4, 1891, but the immediacy of the date probably did much to set off the explosion that followed. Wovoka did not lack for apostles, who came to receive his blessing, a rub of magical ochre, and the message—and who went off to convert their own tribespeople with hysterical enthusiasm. Among the Dakota alone he had Red Cloud, Short Bull, Crow Dog, Weasel Bear, Kicking Bear, and the great and implacable enemy of the whites, Sitting Bull.

The events that followed are fascinating to layman and anthro-

---

* The names of specific cargo cults are colorful: Great Pigs, Hau-Hau, Ghost Wind, Lazarus Movement, and the Chair and Rule Cult are typical.

pologist alike, but only relevant here is the literature that came out in a spate from Wovoka and his disciples. The most authentic gospel is contained in "The Messiah Letter," written by an Arapahoe apostle (who had learned English of a sort at the Carlisle Indian School in Pennsylvania) from the lips of Wovoka himself (Mooney: 780–781):

> When you get home you make dance, and will give you the same. when you dance four days and in night one day, dance day time, five days and they fift, will wash five for every body. He like you fick you give him good many things, he heart been satting feel good. After you get home, will give good cloud, and give you chance to make you feel good and he give you good spirit. and he give you al a good paint.
>
> You folks want you to come in three [months] here, any tribes from there. There will be a good bit snow this year. Sometimes rain's, in fall, this year some rain, never give you any thing like that. grandfather said when he die never no cry. no hurt anybody, no fight, good behave always, it will give you satisfaction, this young man, he is a good Father and mother, dont tell no white man. Jueses was on ground, he just like cloud. Every body is alive again, I dont know when they will [be] here, may be this fall or in spring.
>
> Every body never get sick, be young again, (if young fellow no sick any more) work for white men never trouble with him until you leave, when it shake the earth dont be afraid no harm any body.
>
> You make dance for six weeks night, and put you foot [food] in dance to eat for every body and wash in the water. that is all to tell, I am in to you. and you will received a good words from him some time, Dont tell lie.

What followed is an epitome of the growth of many religions, though telescoped by an insane speed in which one month equalled a century in the Christian myth and religion. Porcupine heard the message from Wovoka, but added some important elements—that Wovoka was Jesus Christ, that he had the stigmatic wounds of crucifixion on his hands, that he could speak in all languages,* that

---

* This was also one of the claims of a recent Negro American prophet, Daddy Grace of 125th Street and Eighth Avenue in New York, now deceased and, so far as we know, unresurrected. In point of fact, Wovoka could speak only Paiute and a few words of broken English.

he would himself bring the dead back to life. The Dakota under the
leadership of such malcontents as Short Bull and Sitting Bull
quickly added the uncanonical doctrine that the Indians were to be
used militarily in getting rid of the whites, and the tragic belief that
Indians who danced the Ghost Dance would be invulnerable—a
belief that Short Bull elaborated into the mechanism of the Ghost
Shirt (possibly suggested by the Mormons' endowment robe; the
Mormons, seeing in the 1870 Ghost Dance a fulfillment of their own
prophecies, were to their later embarrassment involved in this movement) that would ward off bullets. The Dakota also worked in their
sweathouse purification ceremony. The method by which the earth
was to open and engulf the whites was elaborated differently by
almost every tribe. None of these additions was approved by
Wovoka; he disclaimed all responsibility for the Ghost Shirt, and not
only repudiated the policy of hostility against the whites, but advised his Indians to follow the white man's ways. Like Jesus,
Wovoka was a gentle man whose religion was taken away from him
by his disciples. And like a less religious latter day prophet, Karl
Marx, he might have said in effect what Marx said in fact—"I am
not a Marxist."

The instability of these myths caused them to disappear almost as
fast as the Ghost Dance itself, but many of the songs of the Ghost
Dance are still alive today, and many more are known to us through
the collection of James Mooney, the Indian ethnologist and agent
who was on the spot when Wovoka issued his message. It is easy to
recognize a Ghost Dance song, since all follow a unique pattern
among Indian songs—the repetition of each line and their heavy
allusion to both old Indian mythic beliefs and the new doctrine of
the Ghost Dance. Densmore (1936: 66) with fine insight said of
them:

> The words of both the Ghost dance and hand-game songs
> indicate hypnotic influence, and to the present writer it
> seems possible that the paired phrases tend to promote the
> hypnosis. Peculiar rhythms are found in the songs of many
> tribes used in the treatment of the sick, and these are,
> in general, supposed to exert an influence that can best
> be described as hypnotic.

Herzog made a close study of all the available Ghost Dance songs
—texts and melodies—and agreed, adding (1935: 403):

The melodic range is usually narrow, essentially a fifth. As a rule there is no accompaniment. Many of the phrases end on the tonic. They fall into sections so symmetrical as to be startling in primitive material. This symmetry is achieved by the most essential feature of the style, a simple structural device, every *phrase* is rendered twice.

Drawn from Mooney's collection, the following selection of Ghost Dance songs (with Mooney's comments) illustrates the likeness and the uniqueness of the form:

SIOUX (DAKOTA):

> The whole world is coming,
> A nation is coming, a nation is coming,
> The Eagle has brought the message to the tribe.
> The father says so, the father says so.
> Over the whole earth they are coming.
> The buffalo are coming, the buffalo are coming.
> The Crow has brought the message to the tribe.
> The father says so, the father says so.

This fine song summarizes the whole hope of the Ghost Dance—the return of the buffalo and the departed dead, the message being brought to the people by the sacred birds, the Eagle and the Crow. The eagle known as wan'bali is the war eagle, from which feathers are procured for war bonnets (1072).

PAIUTE:

> The whirlwind! The whirlwind!
> The whirlwind! The whirlwind!
> The snowy earth comes gliding; the snowy earth comes
>   gliding;
> The snowy earth comes gliding, the snowy earth comes
>   gliding.

This song may possibly refer to the doctrine of the new earth, here represented as white with snow, advancing swiftly, driven by a whirlwind. Such an idea occurs several times in the Arapahoe songs (1054).

KIOWA:

> God has had pity on us,
> God has had pity on us.
> Jesus has taken pity on us,
> Jesus has taken pity on us.
> He teaches me a song,
> He teaches me a song.
> My song is a good one,
> My song is a good one.

In their confusing of aboriginal and Christian ideas the Kiowa frequently call the Indian messiah "Jesus," having learned the latter as a sacred name through the whites (1088).

ARAPAHOE:

> Father, have pity on me,
> Father, have pity on me;
> I am crying for thirst,
> I am crying for thirst;
> All is gone—I have nothing to eat,
> All is gone—I have nothing to eat.

This is the most pathetic of the Ghost-dance songs. It is sung to a plaintive tune, sometimes with tears rolling down the cheeks of the dancers as the words would bring up thoughts of their present miserable and dependent condition. It may be considered the Indian paraphrase of the Lord's Prayer (977).

The story of the Wounded Knee Massacre that put the quietus on the Ghost Dance has been told too often for our comfort. We prefer to remember instead the Indians as they were at Custer's Last Stand. But even more pitiable as a conclusion to this greatest of American nativistic endeavors is what happened to the prophet Wovoka: the last that was heard of him was that he was exhibiting himself as an attraction at a San Francisco carnival.

Through the Doors of Perception: Peyote

The Indians are learning. One of the most brilliant coups ever contrived by nativists anywhere was the chartering in 1910 of the peyote cult as the Native American Church.* Since then, various Societies for the Prevention of Things have been stamping on their collective hat in impotent rage, unable to campaign righteously against what is obviously a narcotic and Vice ring without simultaneously denying Freedom of American Religion. Our culture more than most is intolerant of the narcotics of others, though we refuse to recognize that tobacco (to say nothing of liquor) is rather high up on the list of habituating sotweeds. Other people's indulgences we classify indiscriminately and erroneously as aphrodisiacal, and in spite of the official religious nature of the peyote cult, several widely printed articles described the unspeakable orgies that these Indians indulge in. In actual fact peyote like all true narcotics (though peyote has so far resisted official definition as such) is to outward appearances stupefying. Inwardly, however, the peyotist is intensely stimulated, but the stimulation is confined to his visual, auditory, and olfactory senses; he has color visions, hears the music of the spheres, and smells strange odors, and as many decent Americans who have grown fond of Demarol know, when one is in a state of euphoria, one is not interested in the coarser pleasures of the flesh. What really annoys critics of peyote is that its effect on many is simply to make them sick.

Now that the Indians are no longer in a position to be difficult and tiresome, we can afford to be kindly toward them. Their peyote chewing and drinking is harmless at worst, and at best is in no sense anti-white but on the contrary encourages individual morality, brotherhood, good will, and docility—qualities that are officially acknowledged as part of the peyote ethic, the "Peyote Road" that has four lanes: Brotherly Love, Care of Family, Self-Reliance, and Avoidance of Alcohol.

The ritual of peyote is elaborate, as one might predict in an Apollonian rite, and is too complex to be described here. The literature of peyote is simple, probably because of the effect on the intellect (when the peyotist's attention is on the phantasmagoria of his imagings, he cannot be expected to compose or appreciate meaningful literature), and it is this simplicity that identifies the peyote songs of the American Indians north of Mexico as easily as a different sort

---

* James Mooney was the chartering agent.

of simplicity identifies the Ghost Dance songs.* The peyote songs of our aborigines, Nettl (16) says, are

> . . . characterized by the use of two note values in each song, by relatively quick tempo, relaxed vocal technique, and a closing formula on the tonic that consists of four even notes.

Densmore gives us a further musicological analysis (1936: 93):

> The rhythm of the peyote songs is simple, and the count-divisions consist chiefly of quarter and eighth notes. A dotted eighth and sixteenth note occurs occasionally, but no values smaller than a sixteenth are found in these songs. A rhythmic unit occurs in three of the five songs [here examined], but these units are short and simple. The trend of the melody is simple, but the songs have a compass of eleven tones, one has thirteen, and one nine tones, while one song has a compass of an octave. Four of the songs are major in tonality, and two of these are on the fourth five-toned scale. We have, therefore, a simplicity of rhythm and melodic progression with a very wide range. It may be this unusual structure that causes the melodies to seem elusive and unsatisfactory.

For those who cannot tell the Lydian mode from the Phrygian, this is to say that the peyote song is a series of ranging "yips" with a drum accompaniment that is roughly double the tempo of the singing. If Densmore and Nettl seem to pay too much attention to the musical features of the songs, it is because most peyote songs consist entirely of meaningless syllables. Here is a sampling of peyote songs, transcribed from Willard Rhodes' records; it will be understood that these will be repeated four or more times in accordance with traditional Indian practice:

KIOWA:

> He ya na-i na-i
> He ya na-i nau
> He ya no

---

* Mexican peyote songs are considerably different from those of the North American Indians.

SIOUX:

> Ha-i na he ya na
> Ha we ne yo

DELAWARE (LENNI LENAPE):

> Ha ya ke to eyona we
> He ya na ne ne ne

NAVAHO:

> He yeoi yo yanawana
> He ne yo

CHEYENNE:

> Hi na ha wi ni
> Nu he na yu

A Happy Ending

The road taken by the primitives after the Europeans burst upon them is not all downhill. Some few societies came to terms with the culture forced on them, and by selecting, changing, and syncretizing elements, have done remarkable things with stories that in white literature had stagnated through pattern exhaustion. The tale of Cinderella was selected by Malcolmson as one of the ten important themes in man's imagination; others have called it the best known folktale in the world; it was the first folktale to be studied in a detailed and scholarly manner (Cox: 1893). Five hundred versions at least are known in Europe, and in Chinese literature it is found in writing as early as the ninth century. But its pattern was long ago exhausted in the culture of its origin,[*] so when the tale diffused to the Zuni (who, as we have seen, have a genius for making tales borrowed from others their own), it became as Benedict said, "easily a better story than its original; it has been thoroughly adapted to its new cultural setting by the incorporation of all sorts of observations of Zuni life, motivation has been skilfully built up, and well known Zuni incidents have been appropriately introduced in a thoroughly workmanlike manner" (1935, I: xxxiii). This is the tale that

---

[*] An exception is the superb motion picture re-creation, "Sabrina."

Benedict praises, as collected among the Zuni by F. H. Cushing at
the end of the last century (54–64):

THE POOR TURKEY GIRL

Long, long ago, our ancients had neither sheep nor horses
nor cattle; yet they had domestic animals of various kinds,
amongst them Turkeys.

In Matsaki, or the Salt City, there dwelt at this time
many very wealthy families, who possessed large flocks of
these birds, which it was their custom to have their slaves
or the poor people of the town herd in the plains round
about Thunder Mountain, below which their town stood, and
on the mesas beyond.

Now, in Matsaki at this time there stood, away out near
the border of the town, a little tumble-down, single-room
house, wherein there lived alone a very poor girl,—so poor
that her clothes were patched and tattered and dirty, and
her person, on account of long neglect and ill-fare, shameful
to look upon, though she herself was not ugly, but had a
winning face and bright eyes; that is, if the face had been
more oval and the eyes less oppressed with care. So poor was
she that she herded Turkeys for a living; and little was given
to her except the food she subsisted on from day to day, and
perhaps now and then a piece of old, worn-out clothing.

Like the extremely poor everywhere and at all times, she
was humble and by her longing for kindness, which she never
received, she was made kind even to the creatures that depended upon her, and lavished this kindness upon the Turkeys she drove to and from the plains every day. Thus, the
Turkeys, appreciating this, were very obedient. They loved
their mistress so much that at her call they would unhesi-
tatingly come, or at her behest go withersoever and when-
soever she wished.

One day this poor girl, driving her Turkeys down into
the plains, passed near old Zuni,—the Middle Ant Hill of the
World, as our ancients have taught us to call our home,—
and as she went along, she heard the herald-priest proclaim-
ing from the house-top that the Dance of the Sacred Bird
(which is a very blessed and welcome festival to our people,
especially to the youths and maidens who are permitted to
join in the dance) would take place in four days.

Now, this poor girl had never been permitted to join in or even to watch the great festivities of our people or the people in the neighboring towns, and naturally she longed very much to see this dance. But she put aside her longing, because she reflected, "It is impossible that I should watch, much less join in the Dance of the Sacred Bird, ugly and ill-clad as I am." And thus musing to herself, and talking to her Turkeys, as was her custom, she drove them on, and at night returned them to their cages round the edges and in the plazas of the town.

Every day after that, until the day named for the dance, this poor girl, as she drove her Turkeys out in the morning, saw the people busy in cleaning and preparing their garments, cooking delicacies, and otherwise making ready for the festival to which they had been duly invited by the other villagers, and heard them talking and laughing merrily at the prospect of the coming holiday. So, as she went about with her Turkeys through the day, she would talk to them, though she never dreamed that they understood a word of what she was saying.

It seems that they did understand even more than she said to them for on the fourth day, after the people of Matsaki had all departed toward Zuni and the girl was wandering around the plains alone with her Turkeys, one of the big Gobblers strutted up to her, and making a fan of his tail, and skirts, as it were, of his wings, blushed with pride and puffed with importance, stretched out his neck and said: "Maiden mother, we know what your thoughts are, and truly we pity you, and wish that, like the other people of Matsaki, you might enjoy this holiday in the town below. We have said to ourselves at night, after you have placed us safely and comfortable in our cages: 'Truly our maiden mother is as worthy to enjoy these things as any one in Matsaki, or even Zuni.' Now, listen well, for I speak the speech of all the elders of my people: If you will drive us in early this afternoon, when the dance is most gay and the people are most happy, we will help you to make yourself so handsome and so prettily dressed that never a man, woman, or child amongst all those who are assembled at the dance will know you; but rather, especially the young men, will wonder whence you came, and long to lay hold of your

hand in the circle that forms round the altar to dance.
Maiden mother, would you like to go to see this dance, and
even to join in it, and be merry with the best of your people?"

The poor girl was at first surprised. Then it seemed all
so natural that the Turkeys should talk to her as she did to
them, that she sat down on a little mound, and, leaning
over, looked at them and said: "My beloved Turkeys, how
glad I am that we may speak together! But why should
you tell me of things that you full well know I so long to,
but cannot by any possible means, do?"

"Trust in us," said the old Gobbler, "for I speak the
speech of my people, and when we begin to call and call and
gobble and gobble, and turn toward our home in Matsaki,
do you follow us, and we will show you what we can do for
you. Only let me tell you one thing: No one knows how
much happiness and good fortune may come to you if you
but enjoy temperately the pleasures we enable you to participate in. But if, in the excess of your enjoyment, you
should forget us, who are your friends, yet so much depend
upon you, then we will think: "Behold, this our maiden
mother, though so humble and poor, deserves, forsooth, her
hard life, because, were she more prosperous, she would be
unto others as others now are unto her."

"Never fear, O my Turkeys," cried the maiden,—only
half trusting that they could do so much for her, yet longing
to try,—"never fear. In everything you direct me to do I
will be obedient as you have always been to me."

The sun had scarce begun to decline, when the Turkeys of
their own accord turned homeward, and the maiden followed them, light of heart. They knew their places well,
and immediately ran to them. When all had entered, even
their bare-legged children, the old Gobbler called to the
maiden, saying, "Now maiden, sit down," said he, "and
give to me and my companions, one by one, your articles
of clothing. We will see if we cannot renew them."

The maiden obediently drew off the ragged old mantle
that covered her shoulders and cast it to the ground before
the speaker. He seized it in his beak, and spread it out,
and picked and picked at it; then he trod upon it, and
lowering his wings, began to strut back and forth over it.
Then taking it up in his beak, and continuing to strut, he

puffed and puffed, and laid it down at the feet of the maiden, a beautiful white embroidered cotton mantle. Then another Gobbler came forth, and she gave him another article of dress, and then another and another, until each garment the maiden had worn was new and beautiful as any possessed by her mistresses in Matsaki.

Before the maiden donned all these garments, the Turkeys circled about her, singing and singing, and clucking and clucking, and brushing her with their wings, until her person was as clean and her skin as smooth and bright as that of the fairest maiden of the wealthiest home in Matsaki. Her hair was soft and wavy, instead of being an ugly, sunburnt shock; her cheeks were full and dimpled, and her eyes dancing with smiles,—for she now saw how true had been the words of the Turkeys.

Finally, one old Turkey came forward and said: "Only the rich ornaments worn by those who have many possessions are lacking to thee, O maiden mother. Wait a moment. We have keen eyes, and have gathered many valuable things,—as such things, being small, though precious, are apt to be lost from time to time by men and maidens."

Spreading his wings, he trod round and round upon the ground, throwing his head back, and laying his wattled beard on his neck; and, presently beginning to cough, he produced in his beak a beautiful necklace; another Turkey brought forth earrings, and so on, until all the proper ornaments appeared, befitting a well-clad maiden of the olden days, and were laid at the feet of the poor Turkey girl.

With these beautiful things she decorated herself, and, thanking the Turkeys over and over, she started to go, and they called out: "O maiden mother, leave open the wicket, for who knows whether you will remember your Turkeys or not when your fortunes are changed, and if you will not grow ashamed that you have been the maiden mother of Turkeys? But we love you, and would bring you to good fortune. Therefore, remember our words of advice, and do not tarry too long."

"I will surely remember, O my Turkeys!" answered the maiden.

Hastily she sped away down the river path toward Zuni. When she arrived there, she went in at the western side of

the town and through one of the long covered ways that
lead into the dance court. When she came just inside of the
court, behold, every one began to look at her, and many
murmurs ran through the crowd,—murmurs of astonishment at her beauty and the richness of her dress,—and the
people were all asking one another, "Whence comes this
beautiful maiden?"

Not long did she stand there neglected. The chiefs of
the dance, all gorgeous in their holiday attire, hastily came
to her, and, with apologies for the incompleteness of their
arrangements,—though these arrangements were as complete as they possibly could be,—invited her to join the
youths and maidens dancing round the musicians and the
altar in the center of the plaza.

With a blush and a smile and a toss of her hair over her
eyes, the maiden stepped into the circle, and the finest
youths among the dancers vied with one another for her
hand. Her heart became light and her feet merry, and the
music sped her breath to rapid coming and going, and the
warmth swept over her face, and she danced and danced
until the sun sank low in the west.

But, alas! in the excess of her enjoyment, she thought not
of her Turkeys, or, if she thought of them, she said to
herself, "How is this, that I should go away from the most
precious consideration to my flock of gobbling Turkeys? I
will stay a while longer, and just before the sun sets I will
run back to them, that these people may not see who I am,
and that I may have the joy of hearing them talk day after
day and wonder who the girl was who joined in their dance."

So the time sped on, and another dance was called, and
another, and never a moment did the people let her rest; but
they would have her in every dance and they moved round
the musicians and the altar in the center of the plaza.

At last the sun set, and the dance was well-nigh over,
when, suddenly breaking away, the girl ran out, and, being
swift of foot,—more so than most of the people of her village,—she sped up the river path before any one could
follow the course she had taken.

Meantime, as it grew late, the Turkeys began to wonder
and wonder that their maiden mother did not return to
them. At last a gray old Gobbler mournfully exclaimed,

"It is as we might have expected. She has forgotten us; therefore she is not worthy of better things than those she has been accustomed to. Let us go forth to the mountains and endure no more of this irksome captivity, inasmuch as we may no longer think our maiden mother as good and true as once we thought her."

So, calling and calling to one another in loud voices, they trooped out of their cages and ran up toward the Cañon of the Cottonwoods, and then round behind Thunder Mountain, through the Gateway of Zuni, and so up the valley.

All breathless, the maiden arrived at the open wicket and looked in. Behold, not a Turkey was there! Trailing them, she ran and she ran up the valley to overtake them; but they were far ahead, and it was only after a long time that she came within the sound of their voices, and then, redoubling her speed, well-nigh overtook them, when she heard them singing this song:

> Up the river, *to! to!*
> Up the river, *to! to!*
> Sing *ye ye!*
> Up the river, *to! to!*
> Up the river, *to! to!*
> Sing *yee huli huli!*
>
> Oh, our maiden mother
> To the Middle Place
> To dance went away;
> Therefore as she lingers,
> To the Cañon Mesa
> And the plains above it
> We all run away!
>
> Sing *ye yee huli huli,*
> *Tot-tot, tot-tot, tot-tot,*
> *Huli huli!*
> *Tot-tot, tot-tot, tot-tot,*
> *Huli huli!*

Hearing this, the maiden called to her Turkeys; called and called in vain. They only quickened their steps, spreading their wings to help them along, singing the song over and over until, indeed, they came to the base of the Cañon Mesa, at the borders of the Zuni Mountains. Then singing once more their song in full chorus, they spread wide their wings, and *thlakwa-a-a thlakwa-a-a-*, they fluttered away over the plains above.

The poor Turkey girl threw her hands up and looked down at her dress. With dust and sweat, behold! it was changed to what it had been, and she was the same poor Turkey girl that she was before. Weary, grieving, and despairing, she returned to Matsaki.

Thus it was in the days of the ancients. Therefore, where you see the rocks leading up the top of Cañon Mesa (*Shoya-k' oskwi*), there are the tracks of Turkeys and other figures to be seen. The latter are the song that the Turkeys sang, graven in the rocks; and all over the plains along the borders of Zuni Mountains since that day turkeys have been more abundant than in any other place.

After all, the gods dispose of men according as men are fitten; and if the poor be poor in heart and spirit as well as in appearance, how will they be aught but poor to the end of their days?

Thus shortens my story.

Chapter Seven / THE USES OF LITERATURE

In 1623 a Dutch expedition sailed into the mouth of what two centuries later would be named the Coleman River on the northern extremity of the world's last unknown continent. During the two days that the crew spent on the alluvial flats of this tropical Australian wilderness, they were approached by a hundred men of the Yir Yoront tribe. The Dutchmen shot one and captured another (for caged savages were popular attractions in the large cities of Europe), and then set sail, to leave this region untouched again by white men for another 241 years.

The shock to the minds of these Paleolithic peoples of seeing European culture for the first time is beyond our imagination, unless we can conceive how Neanderthal man might have felt emerging from his cave shelter to see an airplane land. No matter what our astronauts encounter on the first extraterrestrial landing, no matter how green the inhabitants or how numerous their legs and tentacles and antennae, the earthmen will not be so stunned as the aborigines must have been at the sight of the great sea vehicle of the bearded creatures with the colored flapping skin and magical sticks that made fire and smoke and deafening noises and caused men to fall dead with holes through them. If anything should have engraved itself in the minds, myths, dreams, legends, genealogies, and lore of these people, it would be an event like this. Yet all memory of the meeting has been lost to the natives.

The next contact of whites with the Yir Yoront came in 1864, when a party of overlanders driving a small herd of cattle to the new government station on the northern point of the Cape York Peninsula was attacked by the natives, precipitating the "Battle of the Mitchell River," in which at least thirty of the aborigines were killed and more wounded and drowned. This clash was incomparably more traumatic than the other, but when the first anthropologist probed into the Yir Yoront subconscious only seventy years later, he could not find a shred of remembrance of the battle (Sharp).

Of course the Yir Yoront are Old Stone Age savages, and one cannot expect too much from them. But van Gennep said "within fifty years of Napoleon's death the French peasantry had completely forgotten the facts of his career, and ten years earlier it was difficult to find anything surviving of the songs about him which had once such a widespread popularity" (Raglan: 10). And the British are no better; they have Napoleon meeting St. George in the same ballad—without the dragon, however.

Yet some romantic people insist that despite an occasional lapse, the collective mind of man is an infallible repository that transforms everything that enters it into historically reliable literature. "Do not be put off by people who say that traditions cannot be transmitted orally for hundreds of years," advises Glyn Daniel; "that is an ignorant assumption by those who have not studied the oral literature of tales. The best example that comes to my mind is from India. The Rig Vedas first written down in the 18th century A.D. preserve a most accurate picture of the cities which the Aryan invaders met in India when they invaded it in, let us say, the 18th century B.C. And nobody believed it until excavation in the last thirty years revealed these cities." Daniel (here the writer of mystery novels rather than the archaeologist) goes on to suggest that Lyonesse and the Lost Lands of England in the Arthurian legend, the stories of the siege of Troy, the Holy Grail, Glastonbury, the Flood, Theseus and the Minotaur, Tristan and Isolt, and even the connection of those old frauds, the Druids, with Stonehenge are based on fact. Yes, remarked E. K. Chambers in his *Arthur of Britain* (193–194), "when I passed Athelney last year a Glastonbury car-driver called my attention to a farmhouse in which 'Arthur' burned the cakes."

Since people want romantic things to be true, Daniel has no lack of supporters in this matter of folklore and history. Some accompany him out of patriotism, like Kyagambiddwa, who upholds the claim of an aged Baganda as a descendant of Rameses II of Egypt on the basis of genealogical chants which the ancient fellow could recite (15). Others, like Densmore, Bascom, and Herskovits, are good scholars who have mellowed away from youth's cynicism and who would never think of checking the validity of the process in a replicable way—like asking their students when and how the Second World War began or what the Maginot Line was or who was president of the United States in 1926 or what they were doing Tuesday afternoon three weeks ago. The human memory unsustained by history books has about as firm a grasp of what happened in the past as the folksinging mountaineer who explained to the collecting professor that his next song was going to be about a son of Queen Elizabeth

named King Napoleon, who led an army south by boat across the
Alps to capture a group of towns near Moscow called the "Bonny
Bunch of Roses-O."

Actually this folksinging mountaineer was unusually valuable as a
preliterate historian. Most people—primitive, folk, and sophisticated—have not the faintest suspicion at the time of its occurrence
of what is significant in contemporary history. As Lowie said of his
Indians and their traditions (1917: 164):

> . . . nothing is more striking than the extraordinary impor-
> tance assigned to trivial incidents. Such things may be
> absolutely true, but from none of them is the fabric of
> history made. On the other hand, if we turn to occurrences
> of tremendous cultural and historical significance, the
> natives ignore them or present us with a wholly misleading
> picture of them.

Lowie continued to show that the two most important events in
Indian history, the coming of the white man and the introduction of
the horse, are either ignored or fantastically distorted,* and concluded that "Indian tradition is historically worthless." Galbraith,
no anthropologist, independently says the same thing about modern
Americans, and sums up (92), "Where great events are concerned,
there is every evidence that the moving finger sticks."

The arguments that have been advanced to support the historical
reliability of tradition rarely stand more than casual scrutiny.
Many of them fall into the See-There-Is-the-Very-Spot-Where-It-
Happened category, like Olive Pink's Just So story:

> An old altjeringa headman ordered away a number of travel-
> ling altjeringa men of another totem from his "home water"
> and offered to lead them to another place where water could
> be obtained from a soakage, but it was only a camouflaged
> offer of assistance; for he soon pretended to find a prickle
> in his foot, which he made the excuse for turning back to
> his own "water." This incident is immortalized in a ritual
> song and one can be taken to the locality where the event
> is believed to have occurred. Moreover, "prickles" do still
> grow in that area, which is not so all over the estate.

---

* In his earlier monograph on the Assiniboine Lowie gave an example of the wild
ideas that got into the mind of the Indians on the fairly recent introduction of the
horse (1909: 101).

Beyond the immediate obvious objection, there is the possibility that someone who got a prickle in his foot made up the story with no other motivation; furthermore, it would be interesting to know what kind of "prickle" this was—if it was cactus, we cannot take the tale back to the Dreaming, for this was a recent importation from America. And speaking of cactus, ask any cowboy sitting on the rail at a dude ranch how old that ole cowboy song, "The Strawberry Roan" is; he will put it back at least as far as the Alamo, though it was written in the 1920's.

Frances Densmore illustrates another kind of fallacy, that which overloads a word with historical significance (1950: 453).

> A certain Chippewa song also refers to an event with a known date. This song refers to a treaty known as the "Salt Treaty," which was concluded at Leech Lake, Minnesota, August 21, 1847, between the United States Government and the Pillager band of that tribe. In the early days the Minnesota Chippewa had no salt and by the terms of that treaty they were to receive five barrels of salt annually for five years. In this song the Pillagers taunt the other Chippewa, who were not included in the treaty:
>
> "Let them despise us, salt we have, beyond the belt of timber we live."

The crucial phrase in the Pillagers' song may mean many things that do not call for the mental preservation of a century-old treaty which after five years meant nothing at all in the salt economy of any of the Chippewa. On this point Raglan's dictum bears hard: "Matter that is . . . not part of the group tradition . . . dies out in the second generation" (1937: 14).

Herskovits published an example of the mnemonic process by which historical events could have been remembered that, as a process, is convincing to anyone who has had experience in this branch of memory study. The remembrance of a Dahomean informant whom he was plying for legendary song lapsed momentarily, he recalls (1938, II: 321), but

> . . . under his breath, to the accompaniment of clicking finger-nails, he began to sing, continuing his song for some moments. When he stopped he had the names clearly once more, and in explanation of his song stated that this was the Dahomean method of remembering facts.

Facts? The mnemonic by no means establishes the implication that what went into the Dahomean record-keepers' mind was accurate to begin with, and indeed in the same discussion Herskovits refers to another song-legend in which the Haya of Tanganyika tell how they had their watery origin in Lake Victoria.

It is true, as Bascom insists it is (1957: 103), that the "fact that verbal tradition is not an accurate historical account does not mean that it cannot have its basis in historical events." Nothing comes from nothing, but the transmutations the human mind can and does make of the simplest reality utterly destroy tradition as a reliable guide to what happened in history. It is not hard to agree with Raglan (1937: 8) when he says that to peoples without writing, not only writing but the purpose of writing is totally inconceivable, "and since the purpose of writing is inconceivable, the idea of any form of knowledge which might be preserved is also inconceivable." Oral literature has a real importance to history—not to tell us what happened, but rather what people felt about what happened.

The Unreliability of Informants

There are several faulty links in the chain that runs from an historical event of the undocumented past to the present legendary account of it, and the weakest of all is the chronicler. The bad informant—that is, the member of the folk or primitive community who is only a passive recipient of his heritage—rarely gets to be an informant at all, since the collector quickly finds and concentrates his attention on the community's best spokesman. This good informant is above all things else an imaginative creator who molds the traditional material into a unique expression of the best things in himself and his people, and in so doing is willing to sacrifice a small fact for a great truth. A good informant is an unreliable informant.

We read in the cursory surveys of primitive literature in anthropology school texts and in more extensive sources as well (e.g., Bascom, 1957, and Dixon, 1916), that Polynesian genealogies and exploration traditions, African *Shahnamehs*, and Indian migratory legends are good evidence for the historical accuracy of legend. The society, we are further told, enforces accuracy in recitation, and it is almost axiomatic that a priest in certain narrative rites would be torn limb from limb if he committed a spoonerism. "A single mistake in a single song of many hundred that form an essential part of

Navaho Indian curing rituals," repeats Herzog (1936: 568), "invalidates the whole performance so that it has to be repeated, from the beginning, after due purification." It is theoretically correct that careful proofreading has eliminated all the typographical errors in this book and that the Sherman Anti-Trust Act prevents monopolies in business enterprise; but as Mr. Dooley remarked about the latter legislation, what looks to the public like a solid wall is a triumphal arch to the corporation lawyer—and to the preliterate informant. The inviolability of Navaho and Polynesian traditional narrative is the foundation upon which all lesser canons stand, yet even these classic examples are often honored in the breach. Reichard, speaking of her best Navaho informant, Klah, said (1944: 23):

> I have seen him provoked by one of the few things which could annoy him, error in ceremonial procedure and the stubborn resistance of a singer to correction. Klah did what he could but did not succeed in making the chanter correct the error, for he would not acknowledge it.

As for the Polynesians, one of the earliest native commentators on the accuracy of the genealogies upon which whole ethnologies are built admitted that after all the genealogist was the chief's employee. If a usurping chief (and most fell into this category) had horse thieves hanging in his family tree, it was the genealogist's job to cut them down and out. We have historical evidence of an impressive genealogical chant composed in just such a manner at the beginning of the 18th century in Hawaii. A royal family, needing a pedigree to support its *de facto* status, had a 2,102-line genealogy composed to account not only for the family, but by tracing its ancestors back, the rest of creation besides (Beckwith). This chant, the *Kumulipo*, had in it one of those old reliable, ambiguously prophetic passages about the coming of the white man; in this case, Captain Cook, who becomes the fabricated god "Lono."

Mead reminds us of a second source of error as she observed it on Manua. Of the *solo*, a loose poetical form that was the ultimate verification of mythical history, she wrote (148):

> The *solo* was anything but a really faithful repository of mythological truth. Its form was so indeterminate that it could be broken up into half a dozen pieces and each piece would seem equally coherent to those who heard it. Similarly, new parts could be added, separate *solos* com-

bined, fragments of old *solos* patched together into a new
solo. The allusiveness was so vague, the most cursory reference stood for such an involved event, that the auditor
could not check the veracity of any given version. Powell
speaks of the custom of demanding from a narrator, "*Ta mai
le soifua*," which is a demand to demonstrate the life or
power of the tale by reciting the *solo*. But this type of
request usually only taxes the quick wits of the narrator,
for the short *solo* can be bent to a dozen uses.

Mead makes the concession that things are looser on Manua than
in New Zealand, and it is the Maori mythological histories that are
taken to be the most sacrosanct in the preliterate world. But Emory,
who knew these people well, said (112):

In New Zealand tribal members trace their descent from
ancestors who came from the ancient homeland, Hawaiki, in
the fleet of the 14th century, A.D. Native experts still
argue fiercely over accounts of these migrations, which
ended with the colonizing of New Zealand. In a post-Euro-
pean dispute between two men of different tribes over which
canoe brought the *kumara*, a sweet potato which was a
staple in Maori diet, one of the men finally said in weary
compromise, "You have your *kumara* and your ancestor, I
have my *kumara* and my ancestor."

Let us permit a few other field collectors to comment in this
symposium. Grimble found in the Gilbert Islands a clan elder
named Taakeuta who was regarded as infallible when he spoke on
Gilbertese myths *ex cathedra* in the *maneaba*, or "speak house."
Taakeuta had wisdom as well as infallibility (153):

Every elder of every clan, of course, claimed that his
particular rendering of the creation story was the one and
only truth. They argued together about their pet cosmogon-
ies as earnestly (shall I say?) as the physicists of civilization talk about their cosmologies. But when they took
their differences to Taakeuta sitting by his Sun stone, he
never failed to send them away friends. He would listen to
each side's story in total silence and whisper at the end
(Karongoa-of-the-Kings always whispered its judgments):
"Sirs, there was Naareau the Elder, there was Naareau the

Younger. They did what they did. They were great; we
are little; no man among us knows all their works. Enough!
Let each clan turn away content with its own knowledge."
Having said which, he would treat them to an account radi-
cally different from either of theirs, and, usually, quite
unlike the last one I had heard from him.

The African historical narratives have impressed credulous visitors
who come with a glowing wish to believe in their reliability. Junod
spent nine years among the Thonga, long enough for reality to
overcome romanticism, and his final estimation of the historical
worth of these stories was that

> The antiquity of the tales is beyond any doubt; they
> are certainly very old. This antiquity, however, is only
> relative; that is to say they are constantly transformed
> by the narrators, and these transformations go much further
> than is generally supposed, further even than the Natives
> themselves are aware of. After having heard the same
> stories told by different story-tellers, I must confess that I
> never met twice with exactly the same version. First of all
> *words* differ. Each narrator has his own style, speaks freely
> and does not feel in any way bound by the expressions used
> by the person who taught him the tale. It would be a
> great error to think that, writing a story at the direction
> of a Native, we possess the recognized standard form of the
> tale. There is no standard at all!

> . . . with regard to the sequence of the episodes; although
> these often follow definite cycles, it is rare to hear two
> narrators follow exactly the same order. They arrange
> their material as they like, sometimes in a very awkward
> fashion. The tricks of the Hare are sometimes attributed
> to the Small Toad. In Zulu folklore they are all given as
> the deeds of a dwarf, called Hlakanyana. I have heard
> Natives mixing up elements of totally different styles. . . .
> New combinations thus constantly take place, sometimes
> absurd when the literary sense is lacking.

> I will go further: new elements are also introduced, owing
> to the tendency of Native story-tellers always to apply the
> circumstances of their environment to the narrative. This
> is one of the charms of Native tales. They are living, viz.,
> they are not told as if they were past and remote events, in

an abstract manner, but considered as happening among the hearers themselves, the names of listeners being often given to the heroes of the story, which is, so to speak, forced into the frame of everyday life. So all the new objects brought in by civilization are, without the slightest difficulty, made use of by the narrator. . . . There is not the remotest shadow of historic or ethnographic criticism in the minds of Bantu story-tellers; hence the changes which are constantly deforming old traditions. Lastly, my experience leads me to think that, in certain cases, the contents of the stories themselves are changed by oral transmission, thus giving birth to numerous versions of a tale, often very different from each other and sometimes hardly recognizable (218–219).

Tale telling is an art, sometimes the only art a people has, and the teller of tales is his own authority for their authenticity. Anyone who has collected folktales or folksongs from a good informant has come into touch with supreme arrogance, for such a person tolerates no criticism, literary or historical, from anybody. As Radin affirms (1956: 122):

It can be safely asserted that there exists no aboriginal tribe in the world where the narrating of myths is not confined to a small number of specially gifted individuals. These individuals are always highly respected by the community, and they are permitted to take liberties with a given text denied to people at large. In fact they are sometimes admired for so doing.

"It was not one man alone who was awake in the dark ages," says an old Maori proverb, yet some of our own scholars insist that it was so, and that, moreover, he passed on his lore to a distant posterity that retained it in its pristine form. How this idea is equated with the studies that have been done on the changes that are worked by the "folk processes"—studies such as that of Kenneth S. Goldstein which showed an Irish broadside becoming such diverse things as "The Streets of Laredo" and "St. James' Infirmary"—are rather puzzling. As for anyone's infallibility, the storytellers in primitive societies have the grace at least to claim none for themselves. Emory tells of a Tuamotuan tribal scholar caught out in an inconsistency (107); he stopped, and sighed,

Correct is the explanation, wrong is the lore.
Correct is the lore, wrong is the explanation.
Correct, correct is the lore.
Ah, no!
It is wrong, it is wrong, alas!

Culture as a Censor of History

If men were the free agents that some philosophers claim them to be, the reliability of legend would be better, but there is a greater force working upon composition than the composer's psychological drives, abilities, and incapacities. Culture has the large say in what is being said. Covertly in myth, overtly in folktales and other secular forms, culture tells the composer what to say and his people what to do. Probably few of the writers of the ludicrous atrocity stories that inflamed Americans against Germans in the First World War were deliberately falsifying history; they were only holding the pen of their culture, which needed to protect itself in every possible way. If it were not a fact quickly admitted and quickly ignored, one might insist on man as a *tabula rasa* on which he himself writes the information at the dictation of his culture. Where this cannot be seen in a literature, where critics and collectors see only the artist working with his art, the observer simply is not looking very hard. Sometimes the culture prevents observers from seeing its hand. Only in an irreligious age could one look so objectively at the hidden forces directing the formation of the legend of Jesus, as Charles Francis Potter did (1950b: 548–549):

> It is of interest to students of folklore that when the synoptic gospels are arranged chronologically in the order of their composition, the first, *Mark*, written about a generation after the death of Jesus, has no infancy narratives, no mention of a virgin birth, and no record of post-resurrection appearances of Jesus. But these stories all appear in *Luke* and *Matthew*, written barely another generation later. ... The accretionary process of constant expansion and addition of legend and lore continues when we pass to the later Christian apocrypha and pseudepigrapha, on through the church fathers, ante-Nicene, Nicene, and post-Nicene. The stories about Jesus and Mary become more and more miraculous and wildly incredible in the apocrypha of the Eastern Church, especially in Ethiopian Geez and Coptic manuscripts.

If this can happen to a true religion, what can we expect in a false one? Yet many scholars attribute to heathens what they will not attribute to ourselves, and the experience of field workers who have lived among other peoples and who have had the scales fall from their eyes is ignored when the summing up of historical authenticity is made. Malinowski (1926) saw clearly enough that myth

> . . . cannot bear sober dispassionate history, since it is always made *ad hoc* to fulfil a certain sociological function, to glorify a certain group, or to justify an anomalous status. These considerations show us also that to the native mind immediate history, semi-historical legend, and unmixed myth flow into one another, form a continuous sequence, and fulfil really the same sociological function.

Furthermore, he continues, myth is adjusted to later events:

> One of the most interesting phenomena is the adjustment of myth to cases in which the very foundation of such mythology is flagrantly violated. This violation always takes place when the local claims of an autochthonous clan, i.e., a clan which has emerged on the spot in question, are overridden by an immigrant clan. A conflict of principles is created, for obviously the principle that land and authority belong to those who are literally born out of it does not leave room for any newcomers. On the other hand, business is business. So, the result is that a special class of mythological stories that justify and account for the anomalous state of affairs comes into existence.

This adjustment can be made if sufficient time is available for the absorption of the new concepts. If the first shock is followed by others, the entire system may break down. One of the causes of the Yir Yoront collapse was the agnosticism and ultimately the atheism that followed the inability of their mythology to absorb the steel axe. Before the coming of white man Yir Yoront mythology was a lame thing that denied its people several comforts enjoyed by their neighbors since these things had no precedent in the cosmogony, but it worked well enough until the missionaries gave them the axe. In the Yir Yoront totemic system the soul of the stone axe was owned by the Sunlit Cloud Goanna clan, and was accounted for by its mythology. The Head-to-the-East Corpse clan, appropriately, was the owner of ghosts, and since ghosts were thought of as white, the white man and his axe logically fell into this clan's possession. A theological dispute ensued, and as Lauriston Sharp summed it up, with the deluge of white influence, conflicting myths do not have time to adjust themselves and doubt seeps into the minds of the people—doubt that is made negative certainty as other shocks quickly follow.

What Malinowski saw in the Trobriand Islands other anthropologists see in the tribes they study. Radin's classic analysis of culture making a myth (1926) shows that the main point of this story about the spirit contention is that the action is underlain by the real-life conflict between the Tunderbird and Waterspirit clans. The Waterspirit clan, once very strong, is now small and weak, while the Thunderbird clan, once weak, has prospered and has presumed upon its good fortune in a manner much resented by the other clans. The tale of the Traveller, therefore, shows the Thunderbird defeated, but through treachery; thus the will of the people to see the Thunderbirds discomfited is done, but in a way that acknowledges the ascendency of the Thunderbird clan.

Dozier in 1956 offered the thesis that the chief function of the Hopi-Tewa migration myth is to reinforce the hostility between this tribe and their neighbors, the Hopi:

> The major and most crucial part of the tale . . . deals with the reception accorded their ancestors at Hopi. It is a vituperative indictment against their neighbors, condemning their behavior toward the original Tewa migrants as inhumane and ungracious. The legend has become a rationalizing mechanism for hostile feelings against the Hopi neighbors and an important accommodating device for the maintenance of cultural distinction (176).

Less purposeful, less devious cultural direction of myth change is commoner among primitive societies than this deliberate manipulation of stories and their tellers. Peter Buck shows how localization, one of these casual processes, molded story in Polynesia (1938: 303–304):

> The tendency throughout Polynesia to localize the scene in which the actors moved is very marked in Mangareva, and this localization has caused complications undreamed of by the local historians. Thus the local version of the widely spread legend of Apakura necessitates six voyages between

Mangareva and Raiatea, a distance of over 900 miles. Voyages between neighboring islands of a group, such as that in which the original story occurred, were readily made, but flitting to and fro over journeys of almost 1000 miles makes what was a historical incident assume the nature of a myth.

Once localization was adopted as a literary technique, the early authors did not hesitate to add details to give the story a full local significance. The actual sites where ancient characters lived and the scenes of their activities were included in local story, so that later generations have come to believe that the tales did occur in Mangareva. The local details are so convincing that it is only the existence of similar tales with identical characters and similar incidents in other parts of Polynesia that enables one to distinguish what tales occurred in far-off islands and what are truly local.

Even less purposeful are changes that come about through the defects of language, though these are potent destroyers of historicity. Mooney in his great work on the Ghost Dance illustrated nearly all the processes that change myth and consequently change history also, including the meaning lost in linguistic passage (777). On Mangareva too Buck saw language creating a god (1938: 317):

Te tumu (source, cause) occurs in the cosmogony, myths, and genealogies of central, northern, and southern Polynesia, but in Mangareva he becomes a mythical person dwelling at the bottom of the sea in a coral house ('are naika). His local name in full is Te Tumu-he, but it is probable that the particle he has been tacked onto the original name in singing. Thus in the first line of the refrain of the above song "E Te Tumu-he" it would not have been euphonious to end on Te Tumu, and it is probable that the original composers added e in singing so that the line ran "E Te Tumu e" (O Te Tumu O).

Even the innocent punning of Samoa weakens the historical reliability of these legends; Mead says that puns generated five different tales about the origin of Manono and Apolina, two islands in western Samoa (156).

Myth and legend not only deceive us into accepting a fictitious history, but they affect the minds of their owners with the same disease; in this case, however, we can see the symptoms if they cannot. "So extraordinary," says Downes of the Tiv (44),

> is the power of suggestion, or the ability to completely divorce the occult from the actual, that things which are but figments of his imagination are real to the Tiv, and he had been known to swear to events which have eventually been entirely and absolutely disproved. Even in proof being established, it is found, that he is often of the same opinion.
>
> The following rather illustrates this,—A story reached me that an elder had raised a girl from the dead; my informants were convinced of the truth of this; in fact everyone in that area seemed convinced of it. I endeavored to trace the story to its source and found that the girl had been away with her mother for some two years, during which time the rumour had got about amongst her father's people that she had died. The father, visiting the mother's people, was surprised to find her alive and took her home, and the elder announced that he had raised her from the dead; a statement which no one doubted.
>
> In spite of having heard this evidence, my informants were as convinced as ever that a miracle had been performed, and rather annoyed with me for not believing what, I gathered, was to them a certainty which no proof to the contrary could alter.

More pathetic and more destructive to the historical accuracy of legend is this insistent self-deception when it is shared by the entire society. Hawes (240) learned from the only Sakhalin Gilyak who at that time (1903) had been reared and educated by the Russians, his people's excuse for their lack of a written language:

> The legend current among my tribe . . . tells how a Gilyak and a Chinaman were talking together one day on the shore. The former was showing his books and letters (characters) to the latter, when most unfortunately a great wind arose, and blew away all the letters save five; and to complete this great catastrophe, when the Gilyak's back was turned the Chinaman meanly made off with the small remnant.

As feeble an excuse for illiteracy as this tale is, it seemed good enough to the downtrodden Ainu, who maintain that their letters and records were stolen by a Japanese guest while they were occupied with post-prandial distress.

History, even if it is made out of whole cloth, is the story of the past, and some peoples retreat to it from the same circumstances that prompted the Gilyak and the Ainu to invent absurd legends of their deficiencies. Hulbert (1906: 377) showed how the Koreans gave themselves solace for their inferiority in cultural possessions:

> When asked why his people do not try to emulate the example of the West in industrial achievements, the Korean points to the distant past and cites the case of Yi Sun-Sin, who made the first iron-clad warship mentioned in history; and he actually believes Korea has beaten the world, though Korea today does not possess even a single fourth-class gunboat. Even so they point to these fantastic tales to illustrate the tone of Korean society, when, in truth, their principles are as obsolete as the once famous tortoise boat.

The latest examples of history being written to order are emerging from the new African nations, at least one of which now lays claim to having taught mathematics to the ancient Greeks.

THE PURPOSEFUL USES OF LITERATURE

Literature as Charter

In the preceding excerpts from the literature of primitive peoples and the statements of its collectors it is clear that what purports to be history is only what people want to be history. So universal is this manipulation of what happened in the past that many people have felt with Napoleon that history is a fable agreed upon. No society, regardless of its material poverty, is without a houseful of closets packed with skeletons that must be rationalized away, and myth is the best detergent for a dirty history. Americans have scrubbed Abraham Lincoln so clean that no one of his contemporaries would have recognized the Civil War politician as the man with the same name sitting in humble majesty in the Lincoln Memorial and in the minds of his people. The Navahos came into the Anasazi country with little more to their name than ambition and envy, yet their myth has erased the true story of how they acquired their present culture. The Navaho is no more reticent than ourselves in inventing mythological justification for what he wants to be true; in this process myth and legend become charters of possession and warrants of behavior. Honigmann (364), approaching the conduct of Americans as a sociologist, recognized these uses of literature:

> Enduring groups over time adopt a charter, that is, a set of basic values and beliefs by which the relations of members may be ordered and in terms of which the group relates itself to other groups. . . .

> The charter of a group may include scriptures, myths, and beliefs which, regardless of whether they rest on sound empirical evidence or not, govern the social relations of members. Thus in a factory, a former plant manager may be idealized despite the fact that quite contrary feelings existed toward him while he was around. The myth functions to compensate workers for the unhappiness they are experiencing under the current plant manager.

Australian mythology has been well demonstrated as a charter of land occupancy but it goes further than this, becoming in addition a mnemonic to culture, as Ursula McConnel described it for the Mungkan of Cape York Peninsula (162):

> . . . these stories are a fund of information, which it is important for people with no written record to keep in mind, if they are to maintain the necessary standards of knowledge and behaviour. For the stories record, in detail, where the best food supplies and materials are to be found; the route one must travel to find them; the best camping grounds *en route;* and the distances between them.

The Australians more than most people let their mythology direct their lives. If, says Lauriston Sharp, a Yir Yoront man was named Dog-Chases-Goanna-up-a-Tree-and-Barks-at-Him-All-Night, was left handed and had a broken wrist and was married to three wives, one of whom had a lame leg, it was because his mythical ancestor was named Dog-Chases-Goanna-up-a-Tree-and-Barks-at-Him-All-Night, was left handed and had a broken wrist and was married to three wives, one of whom had a lame leg. But the faith of the aboriginal Australians was great; other peoples are less naive about the true nature of their mythology. Malinowski's Trobrianders were very nearly casuistical about it; anything they had a mind to do they found sanction for in the mythology, and if the necessary sanction was not there, then they put it there. Often societies, it must be conceded, are not so sophistical about their charter myths; to the Yoruba of Nigeria, myths "are regarded as historically true and are quoted by the old men to settle a difficult point in a serious discussion of ritual or political matters" (Bascom, 1943: 129). Even societies that have lost their pristine beliefs, like the Tallensi (Fortes: 128) and the Lovedu (Krige and Krige: 60), will rummage them out when the occasion makes it expedient to do so.

Attitudes demand warrants as possession demands charters, so people construct mythologies to substantiate images that never had corporeal existence. It is interesting to trace the twining of attitude and image in the literatures of peoples with long and contiguous relationships. To the mind of the medieval European, the Chinese were a Yellow Horde, swarming on the borders, ready to pour down upon the civilized world. During the westward expansion of the United States, the image of the Chinese in the American's mind was the Chinky Chinky Chinaman stuffing his hands into his cuffs and grinning an idiotic grin when he finished ironing your shirt. Then the missionary's image of the simple peasant bearing the weight of the world on his thin shoulders and with barely enough soul to be saved. Somehow the missionary's Chinese metamorphosed into Rohmer's Fu Manchu, the insidious and inscrutable Oriental, who had a counter in Charlie Chan, still inscrutable but on Our Side. With the Japanese invasion of the mainland, the Chinese lost his insidiousness and became a Victim. And now once again the Yellow Horde. One can thus date American literature, folk and sophisticated, dealing with the Chinese by the image its author has conjured out of the prevailing attitude. What is here suggested for American literature Olmsted did for Korean literature. Analyzing two hundred tales of the Korean folk, he found the number of references to China overwhelmingly greater than those to other countries, which in itself is a significant commentary on Korean attitudes toward their dangerous neighbor. These references he was able to place into five repeated themes:

1. The use of China as a yardstick of virtue or fame.
2. The idea that China's development came from Korea.
3. The belief that Koreans are better Confucians than Chinese

4. The belief that Koreans are more clever than Chinese
5. The motif of Buddhist monks opposing by self-sacrifice Chinese designs on Korea

"All of these except the first," Olmsted concluded (52), "are of an anti-Chinese nature, and it may be significant that the first appears generally as an almost perfunctory allusion, and plays little if any role in the development of the plot or story. The others, in contrast, are usually the central part." How profitable an approach to literary analysis this searching for embedded and largely unconscious images and attitudes can be is well shown by Olmsted's work, for his findings refute the protestations of educated Koreans that they cherish affection for the Chinese. If our armed services intelligence knew more about this depth analysis of Korean oral literature some psychological use might have been made of it in our conflict with the North Koreans.

Literature as Censor

Some ethnologists have discovered that among many people myth seems to have nothing to do with morality; Radin said (1926) that "myths signally fail to reflect the mores." Other anthropologists disagree; Kluckhohn (1942: 64) wrote that myth among the Navaho "acts as a justification, a rationale for ritual behavior and as a moral reinforcement for other customary behaviors." Hallowell, a psychologist with a broad knowledge of primitive mythology and its function, extends Kluckhohn's remarks (548): "the 'true' story," by which he means myth, "in any human society, is to reinforce the existing system of beliefs about the nature of the universe, man and society. Such a function is particularly important in cultures like those of non-literate peoples, where there is no systematic intellectual and self-conscious articulation of a set of beliefs." Hewitt was equally sure of this (1905b: 967):

> The social and political bonds of every known tribe [of North American Indians] are founded essentially on real or fictitious blood kinship, and the religious bonds that hold a people to its gods are founded on faith in the truth of the teachings of their myths. No stronger bonds than these are known to savage men. The disruption of these, by whatever cause, results in the destruction of the people.

When scholars fall out in such general and assertive terms, there is sure to be a misunderstanding at the crux of the disagreement. In this instance the misunderstanding appears to be in the nebulous idea in the minds of most people of what constitutes morality. Morality is not absolute, and it is certainly not everywhere the same thing. In the Hebraic world morality once meant not boiling a young goat in its mother's milk. Among the Tikopia, Firth tells us, "in an ancient tale, the killing of Pu Kefy, a lad sides with his mother's brother against his father and so brings about the latter's death. The Tikopia display no horror at this indirect parricide; the boy's action seems to them an obvious corollary of his close association with the mother's brother." The only definition of morality that will work in every society, that will equate the "Thou shalt not kill" of the Hebrews and "Thou shalt kill" of the Polynesians, is that which says morality is what conduces to the preservation of the group. The Hermannsburg missionaries were sure the Aranda religion was deficient in omitting—even proscribing—the Christian virtue of thrift, and so they contrived to throw Albert Namatjira, the artist who alone in his race attained international recognition, into jail for "supplying an aboriginal with liquor." Namatjira died before the expiration of his sentence, another victim caught between the conflicting moralities of two worlds. His religion and mythology knew nothing about liquor or thrift, except to acknowledge the reality of extinction of the group where sharing was prohibited. Examples could be compounded to show that what the white man sees in primitive myth as amoral or immoral may be the sustaining moral foundation of its society. Whatever a society approves of, is good for that society and is moral; mythology as the charter of the society's relationship with itself and with nature is therefore the epitome of morality. It does not need to be explicit about what is good for its people; simple explicitness is therefore frequently the function of the "secular" tale, which is often an illustration in story form of a precept inherent in the mythology. But here too the relativism of culture may hide to outside view the "morality" of a story. Consider this tale from the Ngonde (a Nyasa group of Tanganyika Bantu), as collected by Mackenzie (165–166):

Once upon a time, when there was a famine, the Tortoise went to a far country to buy food. He found it in abundance, and made up a load; but on his way home he came upon a tree which had fallen across the path. So he laid down his load on the path, and followed the tree to see how big it was. When he was satisfied, he returned to pick up his load, but found that the Hedgehog had carried it off. Then the Tortoise said, "My friend Hedgehog, why have you taken off my load?" "Your load!" said the Hedgehog. "Why did you leave your load on the path? No, I have beaten you." The Tortoise went at once to the judge, who summoned the Hedgehog; and when he heard the facts he gave judgment for the latter. The judge said to the Tortoise, "You have lost the case. Why did you leave your load on the path? You are a fool." So the Tortoise went home, and the Hedgehog went off with the load of food.

After a long time hunters went out to hunt the Hedgehog, who, to escape from them, backed into a hole in the ground. And in that hole who was there but the Tortoise, who when he saw the tail of the Hedgehog coming in, promptly bit it off close to the bone, and said, "Now I've got you!" The Hedgehog was terribly angry, and went off to the judge. The judge summoned the Tortoise, who said, "Why did he separate himself from his tail in that way? The rest of us are all of a piece." And the judge said, "You are a fool, Hedgehog. Why don't you go like other people? You have lost the case."

Aside from the obvious motif of the Biter Bit, this tale imparts advice that might seem out of place in a society more Apollonian than the Ngonde, which Mackenzie called "spirit-ridden," but here it is quite apropos to follow the general precept: Stay out of trouble. Indeed, in our own strongly Dionysian society, the man on whom misfortune repeatedly falls is thought somehow to be at fault, just as among the Ngonde.

Didacticism is sometimes so deeply rooted that overt statement of a precept would cause its denial. Our culture likes dogs and dislikes cats, a preference that infiltrates even the animated cartoons, yet most people will say that a general dislike of cats is un-American.

Probably every society has tales that in some way impart a lesson in proper behavior, though few are so crude as to precede the explication as we do with the maladroit label, "Moral." Examples of the moral tale are so common, even in our best literature, that no exemplification is needed. Songs as inculcators of virtue, however, are unfamiliar to us. Some of these have already been mentioned

("Songs of Contention and Ridicule," in Chapter Two) but their use among primitive peoples is extensive enough to justify reiteration. The Trinidad calypso is echoed in the *gunborg* singing of south-western Arnhem Land; the Polynesian *arioi* often was called upon to sing out the sinners in a community. In Africa Fortes recorded a rather blunt indictment of a man named Badiemaal who had se-duced his father's brother's wife, one Bakyelbanoya (112–113):

> Badiemaal, you who rape vaginas, Oh!
> Bakyelbanoya is a slut.
> Zimbil-Badiemaal is a dog.
>
> Badiemaal, is this how you behave?
> Zimbil-Badiemaal will never inherit the lineage;
> Why did you copulate with Naaho's wife?

This song has little artistic beauty, but it was effective enough for the purpose, which was to get Badiemaal to leave Taleland. He should have known better, for, as Tracey tells us (1954: 237), "from their earliest childhood the young are left in no doubt about their code of behavior." Beginning in infancy they are told stories, punc-tuated by song, in which correct conduct is unconsciously demon-strated in all kinds of circumstances. The awful fate of those who transgress is emphasized repeatedly. In Central Africa, Torrend says (5), these little melodramas, with their happy combination of narrative and melodies containing choruses in which the hearers take part, are such a power that, with a few of them, a competent story teller can keep a troop of boys and girls interested for hours without the least thought of mischief.

On the hazy border between myth and secular story is the tale that concerns mortals and their behavior but into which a mythical character intrudes officiously to enforce some rule by rewards or punishments. This pseudo-myth is typical of folk societies created out of the clash of white and aboriginal cultures, though there are examples from primitive groups, such as this fragment from the Ojibwa (Densmore, 1929: 98):

> Winabojo lived with his grandmother. His daughter had
> grown up and lived in another lodge. He told his daughter
> to bring wooden dishes and spoons. She came bringing the

dishes and spoons. She was very beautiful and wore a red sash. The men had their feast and took their kettle back to the camp. They had come to ask favors, but they decided to wait until the next day.

They went to Winabojo on the following day, and he said, "You have come to ask favors. I will do what I can for you."

One man said, "I have come to ask you to give me a life with no end." Winabojo twisted him around and threw him into a corner, and he turned into a black stone. Winabojo said, "You asked for a long life. You will last as long as the world stands."

Another man gave Winabojo a present and said, "I have come to ask for unfailing success and that I may never lack for anything." Winabojo turned him into a fox, saying, "Now you will always be cunning and successful."

The others saw what was happening to these men and they became frightened. They decided to ask for one thing together, so they asked that they might have healing power in their medicine.

Winabojo put some medicine in a little leather bag and gave it to each man. He said that the others had asked so much that they had failed, but that he had given these eight men the real success.

But even this smacks strongly of Christian morality.

The white genesis of Margaret Redfield's *ejemplos* is clear. The story "showing that sons should not be selfish toward their mothers" is characteristic of this important genre of the Yucatecan folk (15–16):

Once there was a *senora* who had only one son. In course of time he grew up and married. Soon after the woman's husband was dying. As she stood beside him weeping, he said, "Now your son has grown, he can take care of you when I am not here." And with that he passed away.

At this time corn was very scarce. But the son of the woman had a thousand loads in his granary. When she had come to the point where she had not one bit of corn left, and not a *centavo* to buy more, the woman came and asked her son to give her one measure out of his store. The

young man was sitting there with his wife, and he looked at
her and she said, "We can not give you any because we have
not taken even one *almud* out of the granary. For if we
take some, all the rest will spoil."

So the woman went away feeling very sad. As she was
walking she met a man. "What is the trouble?" said he,
seeing her sorrow. Then she told him how her son had
refused to give her even one measure of corn from his
store. "Never mind, daughter, tell your troubles to our
Lord," said the man. This man was Jesu Cristo, though
she did not know it. Early the next morning the young
man and his wife heard a terrible noise in the granary.
"What can it be?" they said, and got up to see. When
they looked into the granary they saw that all the corn had
turned into worms. Thus, for refusing one small measure
to his mother, the man lost a thousand loads.

Redfield's explication shows how this *ejemplo* supported the failing
mores of Dzitas:

This *ejemplo*, which was one of the few contributed by
Doña Ana, stigmatizes not merely greediness in general, but
particularly the wickedness of sons who are unwilling to
provide for their mothers. A generation or so ago, in
Dzitas, large family groups predominated with married
sons living actually in or at least nearby the homes of
their parents and joining with them in maintaining a
single household economy. Unmarried daughters and
daughters-in-law contributed their services for the common
good, but it was the mother who controlled expenditures
and controlled the household. Even now a young man may
mourn his mother who would have given his unruly wife "a
good beating." The custom of bringing one's wife home to
live in the home of one's parents still prevails to some extent, particularly in the first years of marriage. But family
organization has largely broken down and with it the
prestige of the mother. Married sons, even though living
in the same house with their parents to reduce expenses, are
apt to maintain a separate household economy. Daughters-
in-law are unwilling to "serve" their mothers-in-law. Doña
Ana bewails the loss of her first daughter-in-law, who washed
her clothes and did everything to help her. The second

daughter-in-law not only does nothing except look after her own affairs, she is even unwilling to sit and eat with Ana. The occasion of telling this *ejemplo* was as follows: Ana's sister, Demetria, who was in very straitened conditions, like Ana herself, went to ask her son Juan for some corn. Juan being away from home, his wife Anastacia said that she could not give Demetria any corn in her husband's absence. Ana, who heard what had happened from her sister, became extremely indignant, recollected this *ejemplo*, which had been told her by her mother, and went home and recounted it to her son and his wife as a lesson to them never to do likewise. Here was an occasion when the *ejemplo* could be seen in action, upholding the moral order.

LITERATURE AND GROUP PSYCHOLOGY

Why the natives of Australia persisted in an Old Stone Age phase of culture—that is, a hunting-gathering subsistence without agriculture or animal domestication—ten thousand years after other people progressed to spinach and taxes and theft and war is a question that has exercised the ingenuity of many theorists. The most distinguished anthropologist of our time, Alfred Kroeber, offered a most persuasive psychological explanation: The Australian aborigines ran about naked in sun and rain eating snakes and grubs and lizards and weeds because they like to. "A mode of life," said Kroeber, "engenders an attitude; the attitude fortifies custom; and the outcome is a culture kept by its society as materially meager as possible. . . . Their propertylessness is the result of habit forming attitudes and therefore voluntary in one sense . . ." (1948: 763). In simpler terms, their poverty was due to their psychology. But it is an ancient rule of logic that a simple theory accounting for all the facts must be preferred over one more complex, and the simple facts of the matter are that in Australia there are no indigenous animals that can be domesticated or plants that can be cultivated. And although at least a half-dozen independent tests have proved the ability of the aborigines to withstand greater extremes of climate than Europeans, this by no means proves that they like to sit stark naked in icy rains. There are only two or three genera of diurnal game animals in Australia, and these are hard to catch, so that when a man sees a kangaroo, he cannot afford the time to take off his coat, fold it over a rock with his hat neatly on top—he must always be instantly ready to hurl his spear. In this situation clothes are an encumbrance.

Similarly Freud gave a complex and ingenious psychological explanation for the immaterial culture of the aborigines—the extended incest prohibition, totemism, social cooperation and integration, and the like—but again Occam's Razor (our rule of logic) cuts it all away. The simple explanation is that in small ecological groups (the Australian aboriginal horde averages forty people) the two great destructive competitions, for food and women, must be eliminated or at least ameliorated, and the Australian system does this admirably. In these situations, then, psychological explanations fail.

But the alternative explanation for the peculiarities of human behavior—cultural or economic determination—also fail at times. The rejection by the Navaho of the Ghost Dance that swept through so many of their neighbors was explained on economic grounds, whereas in bare fact, as Hill said (1944: 524), "the Navaho were frightened out of their wits for fear the tenets of the movement were true"— that the ghosts of the dead would return. Navaho do not like ghosts. The Hopi too rejected the Ghost Dance for the same reason (Kennard). Although they are not quite so terrified of the dead as the Navaho, the Ojibwa did not take up the Ghost Dance because their psychological orientation led them to repress aggression through fear; their sense of impotence made it impossible for them to contend against the whites (Barnouw: 1950).

The point of these examples is that both cultural and psychological explanations must be applied with care. Sometimes neither works well. The Navaho and their Pueblo neighbors live in the same environment, but the Navaho myths and rituals are concerned with disease and healing while the Pueblo are concerned with rain and fertility—though the circumstances of their residence have made the Pueblo far more susceptible to endemic disease (Kluckhohn, 1942: 73). Both the Eskimo and the Chukchee are continuously threatened by famine, and so the literature of both peoples tend to develop the themes of cannibalism, individual strength and skill, and fear of dependency and incompetence. But the Eskimo stories do not emphasize cruelty and strong mutual hatred and distrust, as the Chukchee tales do (Kardiner: 125 ff). Kardiner goes on to say that in the Marquesas, food scarcity

leads to certain constellations of a hypochondriacal character within the personality structure of the individual.

It is from these constellations that the secondary institutions are derived. Thus fears of losing intactness and effectiveness lead to configurations of incompleteness, rage, fear of being eaten up, and the wish to eat others up. From these are derived multiple naming, myths of successive rebirths, embalming, cannibalism, and the establishment of being a good feeder as the measure of prestige, much feasting with emphasis on bulk, and a euphoria based on the prototype of a full stomach (226).

But these themes and preoccupations permeate the literature of other parts of Polynesia, where the plentifulness of food—which led to over-population—was the problem, not famine. And in Melanesia, where there is too much food to eat and to store, ogres are typically cannibalistic gluttons.

Without supporting evidence we can never be sure that the literature of a people reflects psychological reality. Often, as in the Trickster stories, quite the opposite is true. Benedict has shown that the abandonment of children at birth is a constantly recurring theme in Zuni tales, as are grandiose polygyny and savage vengeance, yet in real life these things are wholly absent (1935, I: xvi, xxviii). Mixed in with this fantasy are realistic themes, such as witch tales and stories of succubi, that are transformations of the masculine fear of women in Zuni.

Forms too, despite Jung's concept of archetypes, are unreliable. Answering his rhetorical question whether the primitive's reaction to music is the same as ours, Herzog said (1936: 567):

The little that has been done . . . yields findings which may seem chiefly negative. Music, it appears, is not a universal language. Features which in one style carry a certain emotional or symbolic value may have an entirely different significance in another style, or may function in an entirely different realm. The difference between formal and emotional or symbolic functioning must be kept in mind. As one example, we are apt to look upon accentuation and upon fluctuations in intensity (crescendo, diminuendo) and in time (accelerando, ritardando) as primarily expressive features. In many primitive styles, however, including American Indian styles, they are features dictated either by purely formal considerations, or by technic. For instance, in some Indian styles, practically every tone of a melody is strongly stressed; accent cannot here, as with us, serve the function of underscoring expressive peaks. For another example, the pleasing soft timbre of the flute or flageolet on which love-melodies were at first performed, and from which they were transferred to the voice.

Still another source of error in literary reflections of group psychology is the position of the deviant personality in literary composition. Psychologists tell us that Isaac Newton was a victim of masturbation phobia; that Shakespeare, Whitman, Tschaikowsky, and Proust sublimated homosexual yearnings in their work; that Bacon, Spinoza, Spencer, Schopenhauer, Rousseau, Nietzsche, Hume, Descartes, Marx, Wagner, Keats, Robespierre, Diderot, Napoleon, Hitler, Shelley, Coleridge, Pascal, and (God save the mark) Freud himself, were off their several chumps. Whatever truth there is in this, is present in primitive societies also. The excellent picture of the deviate that Barnett drew from Palauan society (65–71) could be made for any other society as well, and considering the amount of literature composed by shamans who are by definition deviant personalities, it might be said that the majority of literary works in primitive culture are made by unrepresentative people who thus reflect an unrepresentative psychology.

Yet there is much that literature can tell us about the group attitudes of the people from whom it emanates, for psychological inertia may be greater even than cultural inertia. As Homer Hulbert says of the Koreans (384):

Before he was a Confucianist, before he was a Buddhist, he was a nature worshipper. True enough, the monk can scare him with his pictures of a physical hell, but it is nothing to the fear that he has of the spirit which inhabits yonder tree on the hillside. The Confucianist can make the chills run up and down his back by an inventory of the evil passions of the heart; but it will not begin to compare with the horror which seizes him when in the middle of the night a weasel overturns a jar in the kitchen, and he feels sure that a *tokgabi* is at work among his lares and penates. The merchant will not be moved by a homily on the duty of fair dealing with one's fellow men, but he will spend all day spelling out from the calendar a lucky day on which to carry

out a plan for "doing" an unwary customer.   Countless
are the stories based upon these themes.

What we deeply feel about life, what we are often not conscious of in
our intellects, may be revealed by our literature.   McGranahan and
Wayne analyzed the 45 most popular plays in Germany and the
United States during the 1927–1928 season and found these basic
themes (112):

Theme	United States	Germany
Love	60%	31%
Morality	36%	9%
Idealism	4%	44%
Power	2%	33%
Outcast	0%	18%
Career	11%	9%

Characterization also followed the notorious stereotypes: "Frequently in the German plays the central character is a ruthless,
treacherous, or egotistical individual who wins success because of
these very qualities."   Ever since Cornelius Tacitus first laid eyes
and pen on the Germanic peoples we have been told that they are
carnivorous sheep, but in the field of national character these generalizations have been rejected because they are not replicable.
But if there is any place at all left for observational evidence in this
scientistic age, the analysis of literature is a valuable source of information about group thinking and feeling—even infra-literature,
like motion pictures, as Kracauer's *From Cagliari to Hitler* proved.

Often there is good correlation between what a people's literature
says about them and what they say about themselves.   "The first
reaction of the Coeur d'Alêne for even the most trivial offense is 'I
will kill (or injure) him,'" and expectedly Coeur d'Alêne myth is
full of punishment for offenses, inadvertent or deliberate (Reichard,
1947: 12).   Australian society places many devices, subtle and blunt,
in the way of anyone who is driven to exercise aggression, and Australian music is likewise peaceful, lacking savagery and hysteria
(Jones).   Their inability to control nature makes life for the aborigines of Australia a one-possibility affair, and fatalism is characteristic
of their literature (notice in the Australian tales cited in this book
the unprotesting resignation of victims to their fate).   The violence
and brutality of the sub-Arctic peoples of Eurasia written indelibly
upon their histories are written just as fast in their tales (Coxwell:

515). Aymara tales also express violence and hostility, but in their case the attitudes are due to a harsh environment and long subjugation by contemptuous masters, as LaBarre showed (40 *ff*). Sex rears its head in Polynesian tales just as often as it does in Polynesian life. And in considering the work in group psychology by Benedict, Hewes, and others, we have seen many examples of literature reflecting subconscious attitudes.

Occasionally, too, tales reveal more about a people than they are willing to admit. Anthropologists, possibly with a wistful thought to their own desires, maintain that in polygynous societies wives are not given to jealousy, and cite testimonials from multiple spouses (taken often in the presence of their husbands) to prove the case. Bogoras (1909: 612) thus quotes Chukchee women as saying of their crowded ménages, "We don't care, we don't think about those things," and "Good and clever women don't get angry over such matters," but they tell stories like this:

> There lived a man with two wives, an old one and a young one. When he took the young wife, he abandoned the old one, did not love her nor sleep with her any longer. He beat her all the time. In great grief she went out into the desert and came to a bear's haunt. She entered. The bear mother was angry at her for entering. The woman said, "Why don't you kill me? My husband always beats me. It is better that you kill me."
>
> The woman stays with the bears and lives with them. When spring comes, the bears let her go, with presents and incantations. She returns home, and by means of their incantations succeeds in driving her rival from the house. The latter perishes from hunger and cold.

Such stories are so common in polygynous societies that one is made very skeptical about protestations to the contrary. Ennis (50–52) repeats a hair-raising story of "A Junior Wife's Jealousy" from the Ovimbundu people of Angola, and Rosalie Sorrels has collected a folk-song from many different Mormon women in Utah, "Christine Leroy," that indicates that Deseret was not the Eden that the mythology of Brigham Young led us to believe it was.

This very familiar function of literature releasing consciously suppressed tensions sometimes is manifested in overt social action, as in the calypso-flyting-litigation forms discussed previously. Titiev gives still another form in his "Social Singing among the Mapuche" (6). In this Araucanian tribe the strong masculine dominance gives the women almost no opportunity for social protest except in songs that are so symbolic and allegorical that no one can be sure what is being protested. A typical example goes,

> tregul peuman
> kuifi meu kai
> welu fele pulai
> alka pülelen.

Free translation: I dreamed of a lapwing a long time ago, and now I am like a hen under the wing of a rooster.
Interpretation: In explaining this song my informant said that it is of the type sung by a young wife to call attention to the fact that her husband is sexually overactive. On hearing such a complaint, her relatives and friends try to advise her spouse to moderate his marital behavior. Sometimes a group of elderly men will arrange to meet the husband in private, without the wife's knowledge, in order to give him the benefit of their experience. Among other things they may tell the husband not to seek sexual satisfaction daily and to abstain from intercourse for at least twelve hours after a meal.

Indian doctors, said Frances Densmore, were primitive psychologists, and with several modern ideas, too, for she quotes Natawika, a Menominee doctor, who admitted, "The medicine will not work unless they pay for it" (1953: 446). Since few primitive peoples believe there is anything accidental about illness, and since the majority of all shocks that the flesh is heir to are psychogenic, ritual, singing, and TLC when accompanied by the proper dosage of belief, cure as well as penicillin. Sometimes better. As Howells remarks in his delightful book on primitive religion, *The Heathens,* "what help would it give the Melanesian to know about the microorganism? He can do something about the devil, but not about the bug." The pharmacopoeia of uncivilized peoples, therefore, is principally literary. If a Navaho goes to a hospital he is stuck with a needle and shoved out; but if he stays at home (and can afford it), his fellows will dance and sing around his *hogan* for nine days and nights, and he knows somebody down here cares about him. This is sound psychology in anybody's culture, and healing songs are universally one of the most important branches of literature, although the only vestige we have of the genre is the get-well card.

Because of the enormous amount of print that has been expended upon the Oedipus tale, it deserves a brief mention—but only that. Whatever clinical evidence the psychoanalysts adduce for its existence in Western psychology, the theme is not worth the theorizing. And what theorizing has been done about this famous story!* In Lessa's summary of explanations (1961: 193–214) he reminds us that Comparetti saw the tale as a reinforcement of incest prohibitions; that Breal, Constans, and Cox made a solar allegory out of it; that Robert defended the alternative vegetation allegory; that Lévi-Strauss read it as a problem of autochthony versus bisexual reproduction; that Thomson forced it into Marxist dialectic; that Jung substituted affection for Freud's lust; that Rank interpreted it in terms of his theory of the birth trauma; that Fromm made of it a device for expressing contention over parental authority; that Money-Kyrle agreed with Freud but said the disgraceful scene of father-killing and mother-marrying was enacted many times instead of a single Original Sin; that Róheim and Feldman said it was still going on; that Levin recast the situation in terms of infantile resentment against abandonment and the psychological drives of rejection instead of the obscenities of Freud; that Devereux intruded homosexual cathexes—and that is a good place to stop this summary, remembering, however, that Freud started it all by "keeping totemism, tabu, and exogamy in the air all at once, without dropping any of them, by using the Oedipus complex and a whiskery old conception, the 'primeval horde,' " as Howells unsympathetically put it. The reason the theme deserves no more than a mention is not so much that it is absurd, as that it is not found in the indigenous literatures of North America, South America, Negro Africa, Australia, Siberia, or China—and in Polynesia only one dubious example has been recorded in the Marquesas (Lessa, 1961: 204). The psychoanalysts require the story to be more nearly universal than this, and so Barnouw (1950) cites an example from the Ojibwa and Róheim from the Australians—but in Barnouw's tale the incestuous mother is a stepmother in a Trickster story where the object is to reinforce an avoidance in the method we have already observed, and in Róheim's story the parricided father is a "father-substitute." The uncommitted anthropologists and folklorists who have bothered to remark

---

* None of it by folklorists, a little by anthropologists, and nearly all of it by Freudian theologians, orthodox and heretic.

on the Oedipus story feebly try to point out that between all kinds of relatives there is both hatred and lust, and sometimes the two emotions trample down the incest fence, but they are not aware that they are arguing a religious dogma, though they find out quickly enough when the psychoanalysts get after them.*

LITERATURE AS A REFLECTOR OF CULTURE

When our culture deals with the western wind, it is likely to be in an atmosphere redolent of romance, the reciter a hollow-cheeked poet overcome by Love:

> Western wind, when wilt thou blow,
> The small rain down can rain?
> Christ, if my love were in my arms
> And I in my bed again.

But the Chukchee has different things on his mind:

> Western wind, look here!
> Look down on my buttocks.
> We are going to give you some fat.
> Cease blowing.

And as he pronounces "the incantation he lets his breeches fall down and bucks leeward, exposing his bare buttocks to the wind. At every word he claps his hands" (Bogoras, 1909: 498). The force that makes the one man take up his lute and the other take down his trousers is the same—culture—but its manifestations are different as the people and their environment are different. If the Aleuts tell watery tales, it is because

the most ubiquitous item in the Aleutian environment is water. Fog, rain, mud, lakes, oceans, bays, the water is everywhere. Except for the relatively slight amount of vegetal material garnered from the land for food and for making baskets, almost everything used by the pre-white Aleuts came from the water. And much still comes from this source. Even the heavy timbers used in house construction are brought to these people by the sea. It would

---

* And if anyone reads the classic Greek tale of Oedipus instead of taking it from Freud's Revelation, he will see that it is not an Oedipus story, for Oedipus did not know he was committing parricide and incest.

be difficult to imagine a more water-conscious, a more water-dependent people (Shade: 3).

If the Andamanese fire-origin myths do not incorporate any practicable methods of initiating combustion it is because the natives of the Andaman Islands did not know how to make fire. If the Plains Indians sang mostly war songs, it is because their culture was centered on war and raiding. If Chukchee and Eskimo tales are concerned with arrogant and tyrannous individuals and the Kwakiutl stories with chiefly contests of property destruction, it is because the peculiarities of their social organizations require them to deal with these things. Where else but among the calendar-obsessed Maya would the creation story have passages like this?

> Then there came great misery, when it came about that the sun in Katun 2 Ahau was moved from its place for three months. After three years it will come back into place in Katun 3 Ahau. Then another katun will be set [in its place]. The *ramon* fruit is their bread, the *ramon* fruit is their drink; what they eat and what they drink. The *ix-batun*, the *chim-chim-chay*, are what they eat. These things were present here when misery settled, father, in Tun 9. At that time there were the foreigners. The charge [of misery] was sought for all the years of [Katun] 13 Ahau.*

Or could any other than a cattle culture produce poetry like this Nuer lament?

> The wind blows *wirawira*
> Where does it blow to?
> It blows to the river.
> The shorthorn carries its full udder to the pastures;
> Let her be milked by Nyagaak;
> My belly will be filled with milk.
> Thou pride of Nyawal,
> Ever-quarrelling Rolnyang,
> This country is overrun by strangers;

---

* From Roys' edition of *The Book of Chilam Balam of Chumayel*. Written in our alphabet, but transliterated from Maya, the *Chilam Balam* ("Interpreter of the gods, Jaguar") were the sacred hieroglyphic books of the Maya, destroyed by the missionaries. "Katun," "Ahau," and "Tun" are time references.

They throw our ornaments into the river;
They draw their water from the bank.
Blackhair my sister,
I am bewildered.
Blackhair my sister,
I am bewildered.
We are perplexed;
We gaze at the stars of God (Evans-Pritchard: 46–47).

There are only two serious cautions to be exercised in making a cultural reading of literature: that the material has not been borrowed indiscriminately from a neighboring people, and that the material is not anachronistic—that is, reflective of a phase long past. Boas was able to reconstruct nearly the whole of Tsimshian culture from its mythology, but in an early moment of disillusion he warned (1897):

A great many other important legends prove to be of foreign origin, being grafted upon mythologies of various tribes. This being the case, I draw the conclusion that the mythologies of the various tribes as we find them now are not organic growths, but have gradually developed and obtained their present form by accretion of foreign material. Much of this material must have been adopted ready-made, and has been adapted and changed in form according to the genius of the people who borrowed it. The proofs of this process are so ample that there is no reason to doubt the fact. We are, therefore, led to the conclusion that they are mythological explanations of phenomena of nature observed by the people to whom the myths belong, but that many of them, at the place where we find them now, never had such a meaning. If we acknowledge this conclusion as correct, we must give up the attempts at off-hand explanation of myths as fanciful, and we must admit that, also, explanations given by the Indians themselves are often secondary, and do not reflect the true origin of the myths.

Of course one must use intelligence in any inductive process; we do not accept the present-day Pueblo's explanation of the keyhole-shaped kiva as deriving from the Indians' understanding that the underground ceremonial chamber was the "key to heaven." Boas thirteen years older and wiser in experience than when the foregoing passage was written, stated that myths "reflect in detail the cultures of which they form part" (1910: 616).

Anachronisms are easily detected. In Zuni folktales entrance to a house is by means of a ladder to the roof and a second ladder down the hatchway, but one would not have been able to enter the ordinary Zuni dwelling in that fashion since 1888 (Benedict, 1935, I: xiv). Among the Zuni and the Ashanti and indeed many peoples who came lately to agriculture, tales may mention only hunting as a means of subsistence. It used to be thought that anachronisms were entirely deplorable, that at best they indicated a stagnating culture, but now we find that such retentions of obsolete customs may tell us much that would otherwise be difficult to obtain. Our fairy tales give a good insight into medieval feudal attitudes and therefore provide a supplement to the bare facts that history gives us of this period. Spencer (1947) was able to write the whole of Navaho cultural evolution from details embedded in the myths: the progression from a hunting-gathering subsistence to agriculture learned from the Pueblos to herding learned from the Spanish to the contemporary economy of silver-working and pastoralism, as well as the attitudes toward women arising from the change in social organization and attitudes toward homosexuals arising from the imposition of white disapproval. Wittfogel and Goldfrank elicited from Pueblo mythology an ancient concern with irrigation that archaeology was slow to confirm. L. S. B. Leakey (1959) in compiling a grammar of the Kikuyu, resolved otherwise inexplicable discrepancies in the ten noun classifications of that people's language by referring to attitudes in the traditional stories. Human beings, for instance, are in the first classification, but misers are in an animal classification; lions should be in an animal classification but are instead in the human classification. The Kikuyu tales clarify these anomalies in the absence of Kikuyu grammarians by showing misers to be subhuman and lions to be human—the Kikuyu highly revere the king of beasts and are afraid of offending him by placing him with the other animals.

Culture may hide behind the scenes, as it does in the plays of Shakespeare or the dramatic poems of Chaucer, but what takes place on the stage is entirely its production and all the men and women merely players, singing songs and telling tales written for them by its ghostly hand.

Chapter Eight / THE SCHOLARS*

The Greeks had a theory for it, of course, as they had for everything else, and like Aristotle's pronouncements on the sexual difference in teeth and Plato's dicta on the origin of the state, the ancient Greeks' view of the beginning of myth was erected on a solid basis of intuition. Pythagoras may have been right when he said that myth was really didactic allegory, and Raglan may be right when he says that myth is the detritus of ritual, but so far as scientific verifiability is concerned, the only difference between these two theorists is that Raglan has 250 centuries of reiteration built into the foundation of his introspection.

Probably no area of intellectual speculation other than theology has encouraged so much diverse and contradictory theorizing than myth—which is only to be expected, since myth is part of religion. Even the Freudians, who condemned God to the subconscious, talk like theologians when they talk of myth; Róheim ends his controversial book on the psychoanalysis of Australian myth with the orison, "Like the Savior God of Christendom, Malpunga the phallic hero and all the eternal ones of the dream have a claim to the proud sentence, 'I am the Path, the Truth, and the Life.' " Only since the contention of evolution against Revelation (one could hardly call it the *triumph* of evolution over Revelation) has serious interest been shown in any area of primitive literature other than myth; therefore more than 99 per cent of the history of scholarship in this field of what we now can call art is a chronology of religious opinion, and since theology does not encourage dissidence, these opinions rigidly express the dominant intellectual bias of the time in which they were made. Euhemerus of Messana is often given credit for pro-

---

* This survey does not include folk scholarship—that is, study of the lore of the folk as defined in the Introduction—except as it has intruded upon the literature of primitive peoples, nor does it include scholarship that has not found expression in English language research. For this omitted material the best and most recent surveys are the special double issue of the *Journal of American Folklore*, October-December, 1961, "Folklore Research around the World," issued also as a separate publication by the Indiana University Press; and Richard M. Dorson's article, "Current Folklore Theories," in *Current Anthropology*, 1963, 4: 93–112.

pounding an original and sophisticated theory some three hundred years before Christ when he said that gods were only deified men and myth was only sanctified legend, but he was only echoing an earlier Semitic idea.

THE MEDIEVAL THEOLOGIANS

Discussion of myth was not a rarefied academic exercise in the early days of the Dark Ages. Christianity had a hard time becoming established in this world, however well it was established in the other world, and Christian mind and muscle were exerted to put an end to persistent paganism. While the muscular Christians were tearing pagans limb from limb in the marketplaces, the intellectual Christians contended less effectively against the reasonable protest that it was a strange coincidence that civilization in Europe began to die with the birth of Christianity. The fact of the matter could not be denied, but the Christian apologists had to offer a better refutation than *post hoc ergo propter hoc*, and they dredged out even Euhemerus to impugn pagan myth and pagan morality. There were centuries of literary polemics on the subject, beginning with Orosius' *Historiae adversum paganos*. How far we have come in this endeavor may be seen by Spengler's use of Orosius.

There were other strings to the medieval bow. Myth, from which was excepted the New Testament, was seen to have derived either from Hebrew myth, or, to the more credulous, from True Stories about real demons, offspring of human women and fallen angels. Pythagoras was cited, too, since polemicists never trouble themselves about consistency, and the Pythagorean theorem about didactic allegory is ideally topological, capable of being twisted into the most unlikely shapes. As allegory it appealed to the medieval mind, which was a morass of allegory.

The Renaissance provided an interregnum in the dominance of theological disputation. One of the earliest scholarly ideas in the best sense of that word was the suggestion of Johan Christoph Wagenseil in 1699 that the chain tale came from Hebrew liturgy; Wagenseil thus anticipated James O. Halliwell's attribution of one of the best known chain tales—"The House that Jack Built" to Jewish religious origin. The English Renaissance had a number of "maggoty-headed" eccentrics like Wagenseil whom we now thank for preserving, among other things, the bulk of surviving Anglo-Saxon manuscripts. John Aubrey was called by a contemporary "a

shiftless person . . . little better than crazed," because he was the
first archaeologist in England (who discovered and saved the Aubrey
Holes at Stonehenge), and one of the first folklorists (on the basis
of his manuscript notes to *Remaines of Gentilisme and Judaisme*,
written in 1687).

THE ENLIGHTENED ANTI-CHRISTIANS

The thousand-year battering that the heathens and their mythologies took from the militant Christians ended with the Age of
Reason, and the neo-pagans that Deism produced began some rather
vicious battering themselves. It is futile now to assign responsibility or credit for the inception of Deism, which was a point on the
road to atheism, but certainly the Reformers had most to do with it.
Though the intellectual development of Deism was strongest in
England, the British adherents of that philosophy are not those
best remembered today, for the often-overlooked reason that Deistic
controversialists flourished only where there was an anti-clerical
tradition to add fuel to their fuming—specifically, in France and in
Puritan America. The doors to criticism of Christian belief were
broken open by Bernard Fontenelle's *The Origin of Fables*, written
before the end of the 17th century but not published until 1724,
which made the fatal identification of pagan and Christian myth.
Fontenelle's thesis was that all myths, regardless of the religion from
which they depended, were useless survivals into an age of reason,
absurd meanderings of the primitive mind. Pierre Bayle's *Dictionary Historical and Critical* (1738) carried the argument further,
and also anticipated Raglan in denying myth any historical validity,
Frazer in analyzing the Adonis rite, and Müller in suggesting solar
origins for mythical figures. Of these anti-Christians Voltaire is by
far both best known and most skilful among the cut-and-slash men,
though if it had not been for the torturing of the Protestant Calas in
1761 and the beheading and burning of a 16-year-old boy in 1765
for mutilating crucifixes, Voltaire probably would have been content
to let the Deism he had picked up in England during his visit early
in the century lie quiet. At any rate, after these events the fat was
in the fire, and Voltaire and his friends Diderot, D'Alembert, and
others went about destroying the clergy by destroying the mythology
on which their authority rested. Incidentally Voltaire like Bayle
anticipated later mythologists—Benfey's Indianism, Müller's na-
turism, and Durkheim's sociogenesis. The Englishmen whose writings Voltaire built into a weapon against the Church were moderate

commentators in natural religion, which Deism purported to be: Locke, Hume, Tillotson, Lord Herbert of Cherbury, Matthew Tindal, Thomas Chubb, with only a few, like Woolston and Collins, attacking the Bible. Before leaving France to look in upon two or three of the American incendiaries we should mention Charles de Brosses, who made the first real anthropological approach to mythology in his *Du culte des Dieux fetiches* (1760) by actually comparing some beliefs of primitive peoples. It was his conclusion—a belief that still is held today—that myth had its inception in "fetishes," that is, *mana*-filled symbols of animism.

On the other side of the Atlantic the former Puritan settlements were showing subconscious resentment against the weakening theocrats by refusing to pay ministers' salaries, accusing them of witchcraft, and harrying them from their parishes on one pretext or another to the frontier, where the Indians could finish them off. The seeds of Deism which blossomed into a pale violet in England burgeoned into wild thistle under the ministrations of Thomas Paine, Constantin Volney, Ethan Allen, and Elihu Palmer. Others might have done more had they not been expending their energies on more practical pursuits, like good American Deists—Fitch with his steamboat; Franklin with his electricity, general store, post office, and other enterprises; and Jefferson with his politics. But Volney, Allen, Paine, and Palmer were quite enough for the orthodox.

Volney's *Ruins: or a Survey of the Revolution of Empires* (1791) revived the criticism that Augustine and Orosius tried to allay, that religion was not the best foundation for a civilization. Paine, having destroyed the power of kings, ambitiously carried his rebellion to higher quarters in his *Age of Reason*, which maintained that the Bible was the work of a pack of rogues; that Christ was not God, but a "blasphemously obscene" fable; that Christianity was not divine, but a mischievous invention "too absurd for belief, too impossible for conviction, and too inconsistent for practice." Paine had a sharp way of putting things; he wrote that Christianity was the "strangest system of religion ever set up," because it "committed a murder upon Jesus in order to redeem mankind for the sin of having eaten an apple." Ethan Allen was sharper yet. Allen, associated vaguely in most Americans' minds with Ticonderoga, the Green Mountain Boys, and pencils, is the classic example of what happens to theological tradition in a backwoods environment where any man's opinion is as good as any other man's. An itinerant English physician, one Thomas Young, told Allen about Deism; this was all the

introduction he needed to demolish Christian mythology. He reminds one of Raglan in the mordancy of his writing, though it is not
nearly so grammatical, and he knew nothing about ritualism—and
would not have liked it if he did. Anyone who is not infuriated by
what Allen has to say about the Bible will be delighted by it. He
has been criticized by those who take the Bible literally for taking
the Bible literally. He was a bit naive in thinking he could argue
people out of unreasonable beliefs, but his book is very funny nevertheless.

A more bitter and tragic commentator on Christian mythology
was Elihu Palmer. Palmer began his career auspiciously enough as
a Phi Beta Kappa at Dartmouth and as a divinity student later.
Though some hint of what was to become of him was apparent in
one of his first sermons after graduation, a Thanksgiving Day sermon
in which he scandalized his fellow clergymen by exhorting the congregation to make themselves as happy as possible, he was sufficiently orthodox at this point to satisfy if not elate his superiors.
But he kept on with such uncanonical texts as happiness and he
was eventually thrown out of the church. He took a job preaching
with Fitch's Universal Society, a proto-Unitarian group. It was
even then impossible to be too unorthodox for the Unitarians, but
he was too unorthodox for the owner of the building in which they
met, and he and his society were put out of the place. He went
West, studied law, returned to Philadelphia in 1793 and was admitted to the bar in that terrible year of the yellow fever, caught
the disease, and as a punishment for his sins, lost his eyesight. With
no other profession open, Palmer went back to preaching Deism with
less and less success until his death in 1806.

Palmer wanted to make people happy, and he saw Christianity
and its myths a device for making them miserable; therefore, he
attacked it and its tenets. His memorable work is *Principles of
Nature, or, a Development of the Moral Causes of Happiness and
Misery among the Human Species*, which like other Deistic books,
hit at Christianity through its mythology. The Bible, Palmer said,
lacked certain literary virtues:

> As a human composition, its merits have been greatly over-
> rated; it is exceeded in sentiment, invention, style, and
> every other literary qualification. The obscurity, incredi-
> bility, and obscenity, so conspicuous in many parts of it,
> would justly condemn the works of a modern writer. It

contains a mixture of inconsistency and contradiction; to call which the word of God, is the highest pitch of extravagance; it is to attribute to the Deity that which any person of common sense would blush to confess himself the author of.

In his specific criticisms it is easy to understand why the wrath of man if not of God fell hard upon his head:

> Sophistry and folly united cannot exhibit a greater specimen of nonsense and irrationality. This story of the virgin and the ghost, to say no more of it, does not wear the appearance of much religion; and it would not, it is presumed, be difficult in any age or country, to find a sufficient number of men who would pretend to be ghosts, if by such pretensions they could obtain similar favors, especially with the consoling reflection superadded, of becoming the progenitors of the pretended Saviour of a wicked and apostate world. How absurd and contradictory are the principles and doctrines of this religion! In vain do its advocates attempt to cover this transaction of ghosts and supernatural agents. The simple truth is, that their pretended Saviour is nothing more than an illegitimate Jew, and their hopes of salvation through him rest on no better foundation than that of fornication or adultery.

This passage is far from being the most offensive in his book as he leads to the conclusion that man-corrupted imagination is the source of evil through the religious fables it has created. Hell, he says, had to be invented to punish those who would not submit; and then it was necessary to create "inhabitants suited to the nature of the climate, and the unfortunate condition in which they were to reside. The idea of a Devil was accordingly formed, and the reality of his existence rendered an indubitable truth by the reiterated assertions of superstitions." For all his interest in making others happy, Palmer was himself a very unhappy man.

THE LINGUISTIC FOLKLORISTS

Happiness and a more sophisticated view of myth, pagan and Christian, came in with the Romantic period, which saw man and his works as they should be, not as they are. The important figure in this era was Johann Gottfried Herder, who set the pattern for

later romantics by saying myth was primitive poetry inspired by
awe and admiration of nature, imagination becoming human. To
prove his assertion that myth was "a philosophy of natural law,"
Herder relied less on surmise than a wide reading in primitive behavior, customs, ritual, and mythology, such as they were at that
time; he was in fact a comparative anthropologist as well as a literary
critic who made the first distinction between legend, tale, and myth.

But systematic investigation in the field of secular folklore did
not begin until a decade after Herder's death, with the publication of
Kinder- und Hausmärchen (Volume I, 1812; Volume II, 1815) by the
prodigious brothers Grimm, who by that time had put a quarter-
century of work into folktales. Jakob (1785–1863) and Wilhelm
(1786–1859) began their scholarly life as philologists and, indeed, are
revered for their pioneering work in that field by linguists who are
entirely innocent of folktale scholarship. Similarly folklorists have
not been properly appreciative of the great interest in Indo-European
linguistic studies stimulated by the discovery of Sanscrit and its relation to modern European language in the early 19th century; in a
real sense, folktale investigation was merely an offshoot of linguistic
investigation, providing documentary evidence of the larger processes.

Though the *Kinder- und Hausmärchen* was not translated into
English until 1884, it is still one of the great classics in folklore, joining in that position Jakob Grimm's *Deutsche Mythologie* (1835). The
Grimms' work crystallized two major theories—that European folk-
tales came from Indo-European origins and that *Märchen* are the
detritus of myth—and a minor suggestion, that motifs are more
likely to be polygenetic and complex elements diffusive. The major
theories held the stage of scholarship as long as any man could wish
for his ideas, but are now abandoned as all theories in an unscientific
field must be, replaced in the Grimms' case by the secondary pronouncements.

Careful and brilliant analysis removed the homeland of the Indo-
Europeans from India to the area of Lithuania, but the tremendous
contributions of India to western culture were still held to include the
folk literature of Europe. Theodor Benfey, German Sanscritist
(1809–1881), became the progenitor of the "Indianist Theory,"
though the first suggestion in a firm sense of this origin of European
folktales was made by Deslongchamps in his *Essai sur les fables
indiennes* in 1838. Benfey takes credit because of his great scholarly
reputation—he was the first substantial Sanscritist, editing the

Samaveda in 1848, the *Panchatantra* in 1859,* and a prodigious Sanscrit-English dictionary in 1866—and his development of the theory that all tales began in India and spread almost worldwide through oral tradition until the 10th century, then by literary tradition along with the spread of Islam, and finally to the Orient through Buddhist literature. The theory dominated folklore scholarship until enough collections were made to disprove the "all," and then the roof fell in upon the Indianists. Reinhold Köhler, for example, brought evidence to support Benfey's theory insofar as India was an important, but not the only source of European folktales. Emmanuel Cosquin also admitted the importance of India, but said that Egypt was important, too, and significantly earlier as the spring of literature. The mistake the Indianists made with their Indo-European linguistic evidence was simply allowing enthusiasm to becloud the subtleties, as Bender showed in his brilliant work, *The Home of the Indo-Europeans.* Bender proved that the oldest documents, the *Avesta* and the *Rig Veda*, in spite of their Indian provenance, are strikingly lacking in words for common faunas; the *Avesta* does not mention the lion, tiger, or elephant; the *Rig Veda* does know the elephant, but only by a phrase name, and has no knowledge of the tiger. An overpowering accumulation of evidence of this sort took culture and tales out of India, perhaps too insistently. The trouble with theories in myth and tales is that they have a tendency to be exclusively monistic in the arguments of their proponents.

Paralleling the linguistic approach was another that still has to achieve its greatest development: the contention that oral literature is most purposefully studied as sociohistorical documents. As stated by Otfried Müller in his *Introduction to a Scientific System of Mythology (Prolegomena zu einer wissenschaftlichen Mythologie,* (1825, English translation, 1845), the approach insisted that to understand a people's myths one had to know a great deal about their culture, and conversely, to understand a culture, one had to know the myths. Müller was too far in advance of his time; ethnographic knowledge would not be either plentiful or reliable enough for nearly a century, and his own evidence was drawn almost entirely from Greek myth and culture.

Otfried was submerged beneath a greater Müller—Friedrich Maxi-

---

* In view of the parallel development of anthropology, which was to displace the linguistic approach to mythology, the dates are significant: 1848, the year of discovery of the first Neanderthal skeleton, and 1859, the year of publication of *The Origin of Species.*

millian, born two years before Otfried's book was published. Young Max Müller of Dessau, Germany, demonstrated a precocity in music, but was dissuaded from exploiting his talent by his godfather, who convinced the boy that there was no money in music. Since the godfather was Jacob Mendelssohn, he was thought by Max's family to be an authority on this point, and so young Müller took up Sanscrit instead, which presumably appeared to have more future than music. At the University of Leipzig Müller came under influence of teachers whose names still are looming large in linguistics —Burnouf, Brockhaus, Bopp, and Schelling. Under the aegis of Burnouf and with a letter from Bunsen to the Prince Consort, Müller went to England in 1846 to edit the *Rig Veda*, and stayed at Oxford the rest of his life, writing great volumes of stuff, including *Chips from a German Workshop*, *History of Ancient Sanscrit Literature*, *Science of Language*, *Introduction to the Science of Religion*, *Comparative Mythology*, and *The Sacred Books of the East*. Some of these went beyond the covers of one book; *The Sacred Books of the East* ran to 51 volumes. While writing these things he incidentally founded the "Solarist" or "Comparative" school of mythology, which was to contend for the rest of the century (he died in 1900) with the "Anthropological" school as the dominant approach to myth scholarship. Müller's thesis was that myth began in a "mythopoeic" age, when noble ideas of sun gods were formed. As the Aryan* language disseminated, so did the mythopoeic ideas; but since language changes, the meanings progressively became distorted; this in turn required fresh interpretations based on nothing more substantial than folk etymology. This process was a "disease of language," but from it myths were created. Since to Müller the mythopoeic pantheon was set in the sky (he went so far as to say "every time we say 'Good Morning' we commit a solar myth"), his theory was unnecessarily tied to an untenable supernatural. It was his misfortune and that of his followers that his theories were propounded before anthropology was well enough developed to give him either help or hindrance; later he was so deeply committed by his personality and training** to an indefensible position that he could do little against such opponents as Andrew Lang but splutter.

---

* In view of the disrepute that this term has fallen into even with laymen since Hitler, it should be marked to Müller's credit that he insisted that the word was not a racial but a linguistic adjective, and that he would no more speak of an Aryan race than he would a dolichocephalic dictionary.

** Oxford in denying him the Chair of Sanscrit in 1860 because he was a foreigner probably recognized his inflexible Germanic academic obstinacy.

Müller had many companions in his solar theory, perhaps too many for his own comfort. Surely George William Cox, "Sir George" as he insisted on being addressed, was at times an embarrassment. Cox wrote several volumes impressive in size, the most important of which were *Mythology of the Aryan Nations* (1870) and *An Introduction to the Science of Comparative Mythology and Folklore* (1881) which carried the solar theory to such lengths that even Müller thought it advisable to restrain him. Cox anticipated the Freudian dialectic in turning refutations into corroborations, going so far, believe it or not, to interpret "black" as meaning "white." Though not a solarist, Georg Schwidetsky used the linguistic-archaeology method in taking language itself back to the literal dawn by translating the cry of the proto-primate lemur, *ururur*, as "aurora." Other solarists held to firmer ground. Robert Brown, though he instituted a small heresy in turning from the Indo-Europeans to the Semites in his *Semitic Influence in Hellenic Mythology* (1898) made a solid contribution to scholarship. Still readable if not still believable are the American solarists, Daniel Brinton (*Myths of the New World*, 1868) and John Fiske (*Myths and Myth Makers*, 1873). Müller saw Brinton as having arrived at the solar explanation independently, and used him as corroborative evidence; Brinton courteously did the same with Müller.

There is much to be said for the linguistic approach of Max Müller and his associates. If they had kept to the basic point that (most) myths (in Europe) were an Indo-European inheritance, and that some may have originated in the "disease of language," they would have been all right. Boas found what is rare in these theories—actual evidence of the process—but by then Müller and his approach were dead and beyond help. However, it is worth remembering in judging Müller's theory that homonymy can give rise to myth, as he said. Boas wrote (1911: 71):

> In America we find this tendency, for instance, among the Pawnee, who seem to have been led to several of their religious opinions by linguistic similarities. Incidentally such cases occur also in other languages, as, for instance, in Chinook mythology, where the Culture Hero discovers a man in a canoe who obtains fish by dancing, and tells him that he must not do so, but must catch fish with the net, a tale which is entirely based on the identity of the two words for *dancing* and *catching with a net*.

But, as Dorson put it in his excellent obituary of the solarists (21),

> In making their equations, Müller and other comparative
> philologists of his day filled their pages with a series of
> acrostic puzzles that inevitably arrived, after conjecture,
> surmise, and supposition, at a predestined goal. For
> Müller it was the sun, for Kühn the storm-clouds, for
> Schwartz the wind, for Preller the sky.

As evidence began to come in from the young academic discipline
of anthropology, it became ever more apparent that Müller's primitive mythopoeia was as unreal as his primitive peoples. Waterman's
analysis of 26 Indian mythologies found only 138 tales explaining
astronomical, meteorological, and hydrographic phenomena while the
number referring to earthly matters was 1053; in Melanesia the
Banks' Islanders prosaically believe the sun and moon to be rocks,
which brings the concept down to earth. Other cultures also keep
their eyes on the ground.

THE ANTHROPOLOGISTS

It was inevitable that Müller one day would be delivered into
somebody's hands, but he did not deserve to be delivered into the
hands of Andrew Lang. Lang was the archetypical surly Scot, born
in 1844 in Selkirk, feeding on oatmeal and becoming more learned
and irascible until arriving in London in 1875. He was one of the
last of the polymaths; he wrote learnedly on everything, from crystal
gazing to Scottish history. He even wrote novels and fairy tales.
Perhaps his chief interest was Jacobite history—he wrote a half-
dozen books, some multi-volumed, on this subject; but he also wrote
books on French history, folklore, anthropology, Greek literature,
ballads, Homeric studies, and Australian totemism. His bibliography contains fifty titles on the Australian aborigines alone. Though
his main function in life was to be the scourge of God, he propounded
a few noteworthy theories on myth: that myths in many cases were
invented for the etiology of totemism, that religion is essentially
different from myth, that myth comes from a pre-moral stage of
culture, that myths were made to satisfy an emotional lack. Lang
fought with everybody in every discipline he imagined himself
master of, and the most infuriating thing about him was that he was
usually right. Müller continually and with increasing futility
pointed out the absurdity of someone who knew no Sanscrit arguing

Sanscrit with the world's authority on Sanscrit, but Lang kept on scoring off Müller.

Lang has been called the leader of the "anthropological" school, but this term, as the quotation marks suggest, is a misnomer. The "anthropological" school of the end of the 19th century was actually the approach of comparativists who had a lot of knowledge, most of which was wrong. Nowadays the comparativists fail because there is too much knowledge for any one man to synthesize. In both cases a fallacy is generally committed by comparativists: that of assuming that every phenotype has the same genotype. In a way, this approach evolved from the comparative mythology school, extending the folk unity of mankind from Eurasia to the world at large, and maintaining that to find the ultimate meaning and function of the folktale, one had to distill out the *Urmären*, as Ehrenreich called it. The resemblance is shown by the retention of the solar (sometimes altered slightly to the lunar) hypothesis. Lang cannot therefore be fairly placed in the group, though he prepared the way for true anthropological investigation, that is, investigation based upon evidence rather than supposition. Moreover, it would not have been to Lang's liking to be placed in agreement with anybody.

Arnold van Gennep is also put into the "anthropological" group of this time, but since he abandoned the astronomical and cosmic explanations, he might better be called an early functionalist. His interests lay chiefly with the Australian aborigines, and in the field of primitive literature, with animal tales and thence to totemism, which interests he syncretized in his important book *La formation des legendes* (1910) in the summation that the function of folklore was to sustain and substantiate rules of behavior.

The founder of the anthropological school but standing far above it was Sir Edward Burnett Tylor. If the parentage of so faulty an approach as the comparativist can be charged to him, it is because he is the father of anthropology in every meaningful sense. He subscribed exclusively to none of the theories that contended in the last quarter of the 19th century, but took from each its essential validity; even in his approach to the concept which he first isolated, *culture*, he acknowledged the dangers of broad generalization; as Kroeber was to say of him, he took his approach from the data, framing no panaceas and cherishing no pet theories. His independence stemmed doubtlessly from his own origin as the son of prosperous Quakers who had by the time of his birth—1832—stopped shaking with religious enthusiasm and accepted the enlightened ideas

that distinguish that sect today. He suffered no great privation in
being denied the formal education of the English universities; privately educated and free to test his knowledge by travel, he was
under the dominance of none of the imposing names that surely
would have channeled his abilities into conventional grooves. The
fierce partisan tempests of the Müllers and Langs seem like clouds
swirling bodilessly around the mountain that is Tylor. Myth was
only part of culture to Tylor, and it is only because he took this
together with all other anthropological knowledge for his province
that we include him as a theorist on the subject, though the sections
on myth in his *Researches into the Early History of Mankind* (1865)
are very important in methodology. He first identified the concept
of animism, and saw it linked inseparably to myth, the two religious
elements that enabled primitive peoples to see intelligence in all
things and to draw upon that universal intelligence for the good that
was in it. He could not have lived when he did without having his
thinking influenced by evolution, and so he is often called an evolu-
tionist, again a narrow case for such a wide man; but he did classify
myths into a two-phase sequence, nature myths and philosophical
myths, the latter on a higher level of pseudo-science. Primitive
peoples evolved too, but because their culture had not developed
sufficiently to give them the facts they needed for true science, not
because their mental processes were different.

Directly or indirectly Tylor was the progenitor of all the English-
speaking anthropologists who followed him, and it was in recognition
of his influence and accomplishments rather than a hope of future
exploitation of his genius that he was made Professor of Anthropology at Oxford in 1896. He was chairman of the committee that
sent Franz Boas to the Northwest Pacific coast in 1888; it was his
book *Primitive Culture* that took Frazer out of a dull law career and
into anthropology. It is impossible to mention in this survey of
scholarship the many anthropologists after Tylor who worked with
the sacred and the secular literature of primitive peoples; nearly all
of the two hundred authors consciously drawn upon in this book owe
in some measure a debt to Tylor; nearly all made a contribution themselves that deserves recognition. But few of them propounded
theories and gathered disciples, theories and disciples that would
shortly die and leave memories only as curiosities in the intellectual
growth of their discipline. It is a sad fact of scholarship, nevertheless, that if a man wants to be remembered beyond his own lifetime,
he must issue a theory and assemble disciples, no matter how absurd

the theory or inept the disciples.

Franz Boas did it with disciples alone. Jacobs, in assessing his influence (1959b: 128), ruefully concluded,

> Twenty years after Boas penned his last statement on folklore (1938) the discipline remains almost exactly where he left it; an immature science which possesses a towering mass of essentially incomprehensible miscellanea, most of them ticketed according to geographical provenience. A modest shelf of diffusionist theses stands beside the descriptive items.

Yet Boas' work seems far more modern than that of his misty contemporaries, people whose names are ancient history to students now. A teacher affects eternity, and it was as a teacher that Boas made his greatest accomplishment; he made field work the internship of anthropologists, and sent such great students as Kroeber, Sapir, Parsons, Speck, Lowie, Benedict, Herskovits, Reichard, and Bunzel among the primitives and thence among another, larger, generation of students. If there is any serious attention at all being paid now to the literature of primitive cultures, it is because this was Boas' primary interest. His influence pervades this book; much of what is in it would have been allowed to die long ago had it not been for Boas and the people he trained to salvage as he did the vanishing lore of vanishing societies.

THE RITUALISTS

It is ironic that Boas' work—solid as the day he compiled it— should in the minds of most students of anthropology fade beside the tarnished brilliance of Sir James George Frazer. "No qualified anthropologist or culture historian today really accepts the fundamental thesis of *The Golden Bough*," said Radin, but in a dull and conformist age brilliance is admired more than dogged accuracy, and even those who are best aware of its confusion of fact and fancy regard *The Golden Bough* as one of the great productions not only of anthropology or of the English people, but of the human mind. Like Lang, Frazer was a Scot, born in Glasgow in 1854, educated at Glasgow and Cambridge Universities, made a Fellow of Cambridge in 1879 and called to the bar that same year. Then came his reading of Tylor's *Primitive Culture* and that first spark of interest in the curious rites of the priests of Aricia dealing with a golden bough.

With immense classical knowledge he forged into the woods at Nemi and found all the branches and roots intertwined; by the time he had brought some order to the tangled mass of myth, lore, religion, and superstition underlying European civilization, he had twelve volumes of some of the most densely-packed information ever written by one man—*The Golden Bough*, published first in 1890 and then fully in 1907–1912. Most people have read this work in the 1922 one-volume abridgement, now superseded by Gaster's edition which corrects the errors and guides the layman through material in which he must by himself become hopelessly mazed. *Totemism* (1887) preceded *The Golden Bough*, and following it were *Folklore in the Old Testament* (to write which he learned ancient Hebrew), and *Totemism and Exogamy*, among others.

The Golden Bough deals fundamentally with religion through its mythic expression. The theories reiterated through this monumental work are that magic evolved into religion, that the dying and reviving gods of ancient agricultural societies are vegetation gods, that homeopathy is one of the bases of magic, and that the king in primitive cultures is the surrogate of the vegetation god, the bringer of life. These ideas, it can well be supposed, did not get past Andrew Lang, who christened Frazer's approach the "Covent Garden School of Mythology," after London's famous vegetable market. Lang's almost instinctive doubts are well confirmed today (Gaster's edition of *The Golden Bough* contains as much refutation as abridgement), but Frazer's genius and personality created out of one observation —that myth was the detritus of ritual—a school of folklorists that overwhelmed Lang by sheer numbers, as it overwhelms by the same method more reasonable approaches today. Though Frazer was thus its creator, the Ritualist School was organized and propagated by Frazer's fellow classicist at Cambridge, Jane Ellen Harrison. As Frazer was inspired by a bough, Harrison was inspired by a clay seal from Knossos which persuaded her that the Minotaur was the King of Crete in a bull mask. She announced her discovery of the key to understanding all art in her book *Prolegomena to the Study of Greek Religion* (1903) and codified the theory in her greatest book, *Themis*, in 1912, which stated unequivocally that myth arises from ritual, of which it is the spoken correlative; that rites die, but myths continue in art, literature, religion, and other symbolic activities, with decreasing understanding of the progenitive rites and increasing folk explanation for the supplanting myths. How this theory fired the imagination of folklorists in the early years of this century one can appreciate by merely noting some of the titles and theses that emanated from the Ritualists:

Rite to philosophy: Cornford's *From Religion to Philosophy*
Rite to art: Harrison's *Ancient Art and Ritual*
Rite to drama: Murray's *Euripides and His Age*
Rite to Greek comedy: Cornford's *The Origin of Attic Comedy*
Rite to *Hamlet:* Murray's lecture, "Hamlet and Orestes"
Rite to ancient Scandinavian drama: Phillpotts' *The Elder Edda and Ancient Scandinavian Drama*
Rite to European witches: Murray's *The Witch Cult in Western Europe*
Rite to the Arthurian Legend: Weston's *From Ritual to Romance*
Rite to law: Goitein's *Primitive Ordeal and Modern Law*
Rite to science: Buchanan's *Poetry and Mathematics*
Rite to fairy tales: Saintyves' *Les contes de Perrault et les recits paralleles**

One flails the air in disputing with the Ritualists. Either they cut the ground away from argument by their premises—"myth . . . is simply a narrative associated with a rite" (Raglan, 1955: 76)—or they deny the applicability of reason altogether—"The pursuit of cognition in myth or folk literature has led to all the worst excesses of speculative research, whether the political slogans and events Katherine Elwes Thomas found hermetically concealed in nursery rhymes in *The Real Personages of Mother Goose* (1930), the wisdom, deliberately coded and jumbled, that Robert Graves uncoded in *The White Goddess* (1948), or most recently, the secret fire worship Flavia Anderson discovered hidden behind every myth in *The Ancient Secret* (1953)" (Hyman: 90). What possibly can be said in reply to Raglan's argument that the Trobrianders' story of the origin of death through refusal to slough off skin arose in ritual: "I know of no such rite, but it may safely be postulated as the prototype of the many rites in which a change of dress symbolized the beginning of a

---

* Though rite as the origin of fairy tales was recognized independently before Harrison and Saintyves in William Wells Newell's *Games and Songs of American Children* (1883), Henry C. Bolton's *The Counting-Out Rhymes of Children* (1888), Alice Gomme's *The Traditional Games of England, Scotland and Ireland* (1894), and Lina Eckenstein's *Comparative Studies in Nursery Rhymes* (1906). Also preceding the Ritualists proper are William Simpson's *The Jonah Legend* (1899) and John M. Robertson's series of books on the mythical Jesus, which are ritual studies of the Bible. The influence of the Ritualists is incalcuable. T. S. Eliot made *The Waste Land* out of a longing for church, a bad dream, and Jessie Weston's *From Ritual to Romance*, and that poem has had some influence of its own.

new life" (1955: 83)? Or to their contention that since myth cannot
be proved to be anything else, it must therefore be the remains of
ritual? Or to Hyman's admission that "the ritual approach is certainly compatible with varieties of mysticism" (89)? The Ritualists
write so well and reason so badly that any discussion of their theory
must be done behind their backs.

If we assume that the question can be resolved by examination of
what evidence is available—an assumption that the Ritualists probably would not accept—then the situation becomes even more confusing. As Kluckhohn summed up the relation of myth to ritual
(1942), the Todas have much ritual but very little myth; the classical
Greeks, a rich mythology but poor ritual; the early Romans, no
mythology; the Mohave Indians, a poor ritual but rich mythology;
the African Bushmen, many myths but few rituals; the Central
Eskimo, rich mythology and rich ritual; the American Indians in
general, good myth but poor ritual. In the short but important
history of the Ghost Dance, one of the few opportunities scholars
have had to watch a religion and a mythology being made, the myth
was clearly first everywhere, with ritual springing up later to reinforce it—a pattern that seems very likely in other religions from
Christianity to Murngin totemism. To the Ritualists this evidence
is irrelevant; theirs is a system of faith, not reason, and the only
eventuality that will destroy the school is the mortal enemy of faith
—heresy. Heresy among the Ritualists, some would be pleased to
note, is very recently beginning to appear with Flavia Anderson's
The Ancient Secret (1953)—attacked by the orthodox Hyman in the
quotation cited above—and Margaret Murray's fantastic book *The
Divine King in England* (1954).

THE FREUDIANS

When all faiths are under siege, contradictory faiths often unite
against the common enemy, reason. Frazer was perilously close to
Freud's position, though he refused to read Freud, and Freud drew
his anthropological method from Frazer and sulked when the anthropologists found error in his suppositions. But now Hyman can
open the door to ecumenical unity (88): "In regard to psychology,
the ritual approach can draw centrally on Freudian psychoanalysis,
informed by new knowledge and less circumscribed by ethnocentric
patterns." Freud is given credit, by those who believe it was a credi-
table action, for the intrusion of psychoanalysis into myth scholarship

with his indestructible book *Totem and Taboo* (1912), whose central thesis is much too well known. Among other things, Freud laid down the dogma that myths and dreams are basically the same, products of man's unconscious, reflecting the conflicts of the id, ego, and superego; both, therefore, are pure symbolism. The fact that no one consciously recognizes these as symbols has nothing to do with the case, and anyone who objects to the symbolic interpretation on this basis is, in Róheim's word, "naive." It is not generally known that Freud was not so promethean as some of his disciples think. Two other equally important books were published in 1912: Otto Rank's *Das Inzest Motiv in Dichtung und Sage* and Carl G. Jung's *The Psychology of the Unconscious*, but as in the case of Charles Darwin and Alfred Russel Wallace, we choose to simplify multiple invention. Even in Freud's theory the seed of the idea came from his reading Robertson Smith's *The Religion of the Semites*, in which Smith built the foundation of the whole dubious structure on a dubious incident of ritualistic killing and eating of the totem dubiously reported by a dubious St. Nilus less than five centuries after Christ.

Jung's theory, while dubious, offers a nice explanation for the curious similarity of motifs in widely separated parts of the primitive world. It was his idea that human beings possessed a psychic unity, a collective unconscious, in which were embedded "archetypes," instinctive, culture-free, tropismatic responses to situations and stimuli. Not only are the Colonel's Lady and Judy O'Grady sisters under their skins, but siblings also of the Hodmadods of Monomatapa, and it is no accident that in so many cultures myths, tales, and songs originate in dreams. Myths and their structural elements, motifs, are the best evidence for the past and present of these universal ideas, explaining the unknown and the unknowable. The unfortunate thing about Jung's theory is that nobody has found a way of using it or making it intelligible, and now that Jung himself, his principal champion, is dead, we can expect it to slide unobtrusively into history.*

---

* Since Lucien Lévy-Bruhl recanted before his death, it is worth only a footnote to describe his independent promulgation of a theory close to Jung's—the idea of "*participation mystique*" and "*representations collectives*," which saw the thinking of primitive people as fundamentally different from our own, an inability to separate what the semanticists call the Extensional and Intensional Worlds, an imperfect mentality that produced myths. This theory was stated in his *Les fonctions mentales dans les sociétés inferieures* (1910; translated into English as *How Natives Think* in 1926) and repudiated posthumously in *Les carnets de Lucien Lévy-Bruhl* in 1949. Ernst Cassirer, highly admired by those who admire him, came to much the same conclusions as Lévy-Bruhl through different materials, and did not recant.

Dead too is the last of the unreconstructed psychoanalytical anthropologists, Géza Róheim,* whose theories were aptly described by one critic as "weird." His writings are full of interpretations like "the foreskin is the child, which is put back into a mother symbol; at the same time that the child is separated from the mother, the foreskin is reintroduced into the mother" (1945: 68). But it is profitless to criticize Róheim or even to quote him to illustrate his reasoning. To the unbeliever no refutation is necessary; to the believer none is possible. Róheim himself said (1947: 32), "No one can really understand what it is all about without having been analyzed"—one is strongly tempted to say "without having been baptized."

Paul Radin understood what it was all about. Analyzing four Winnebago hero cycles, Radin produced such insights as this (1948: 8):

> These four cycles, within limits, lend themselves to a definite temporal sequence. The first, symbolized by Trickster, represents what might well be identified with the undifferentiated libido; the second, symbolized by Hare, the partially and imperfectly differentiated libido; the third, symbolized by Red Horn, the well differentiated libido, and the fourth, symbolized by the Twins, the integrated libido. Let us call these four periods the primordial, the primitive, the Olympian and the Promethean.

No one did call them that, and now that Radin, too, is gone, no one will. When they were alive and well, these notable Freudians made some anthropologists uneasy; Malinowski complained that

> . . . the psychoanalysts . . . have come at last to teach us that myth is a daydream of the race, and that we can only explain it by turning our backs on nature, history, and culture, and divine deep into the dark pools of the sub-conscious, where at the bottom there lie the usual paraphernalia and symbols of psychoanalytic exegesis.

But with their passing, conventional anthropology is willing to let the minor relicts persist in their harmless vagaries.

---

* Róheim claimed in 1947 (13): "As far as I know the present writer was (and perhaps still is) the only anthropologist who accepted psychoanalysis without any reservations."

THE FINNISH SCHOOL

It is not wholly ethnocentrism that limits this and most surveys of primitive literature scholarship to English-language researches, for dispassionate interest in exotic primitive peoples is characteristic of only a few segments of western civilization. In most other countries where "folklore" is studied, it is transparently an instrument of national purpose, a device to identify and preserve the distinguishing genius of the nation, especially if that nation has been dominated by oppressive alien peoples or if it needs some support from folklore in its totalitarian effort. Thus in Finland, a country whose history has largely been one of subjugation to Sweden and Russia, a surprising amount of effort has been exerted for more than 250 years on the collection and study of Finnish-language folklore, but the Swedish-speaking Finns have been treated like unwanted stepchildren (Richmond in Dorson, 1961: 328). Therefore, despite their possession of the world's best-known folk epic (the *Kalevala*), a long history of remarkably sophisticated folk scholarship, and their development of the Historic-Geographic Method, the Finns would scarcely warrant more than cursory mention in these restricted pages if it were not for the fact that one of the tools they fashioned to bring order to an enormous amount of collected material is becoming standard equipment for scholars in folk and primitive literature everywhere.

Henricus Matthiae Florinus began Finnish folk studies with his *Ordinary and Charming Proverbs of the Old Finns* in 1702 and was followed by a continuum of collectors and writers like Elias Lönnrot and Eero Salmelainen, but not until the last quarter of the 19th century (when the writings were put, surprisingly, into German rather than Finnish) did this activity begin to transcend a narrow patriotic purpose. In view of the direction Finnish folk studies have taken, the most important of the scholars of this period was Julius Krohn, whose *History of Finnish Literature* (1897) enunciated the principles that still guide the methodology not only of Finnish folklorists, but many other European and American workers as well.

Actually Julius Krohn was the eldest member of a triumvirate (including also his son Kaarle Krohn and Antti Aarne) that established by practice rather than principle the "Historic-Geographic Method,"—a patient and meticulous collection of all pertinent variants of a tale (pertinency would exclude versions clearly derived from earlier examples), separation of these into basic episodes or elements, and the analysis of these components in determining the "life history" of the story—its original form, source, and date of composition. Even before the definitive statement of the method was made by Kaarle Krohn in his *Die folkloristische Arbeitsmethode* in 1926, many scholars were assembling these narrative biographies and publishing them in the *Communications* of the Folklore Fellows, founded by Krohn, Bolte, Olrik, and von Sydow in 1907. The method still burgeons; the *FF Communications* has passed its 190th monograph, including such classic examples of the system as Holger Olof Nygard's *The Ballad of Heer Halewijn* (Number 169) and Kurt Ranke's study of the tale of "The Two Brothers and the Dragon Slayer" (Number 114).

It would be of only esoteric interest to describe the work and theories of other notable members of the Finnish school, such as Walter Anderson, Martti Haavio, Jouko Hautala, Lauir Hakulinen, Matti Kuusi, and Otto Anderson, or their non-Finnish opponents, like Friedrich von der Leyen, Jan de Vries, or the irascible Albert Wesselski, for nearly all the activity of these people in or out of agreement is restricted to the lore of Europe and therefore irrelevant in a summary of scholarship among primitive peoples. What is relevant is the concept and classification of tale-types and motifs that emanated from the Finnish method and consummated by the great American disciple of Krohn, Stith Thompson.

The earliest publication of a method of classifying folktales was J. G. von Hahn's *Griechische und albanesische Märchen* (1864), but his materials were too scanty and geographically restricted and his perception of the constituent elements of the narratives too superficial to be useful. Subsequent attempts at classification through the following half-century likewise made no impression on practical scholarship. In 1910 Antti Aarne published as the third volume of *FF Communications* his *Verzeichnis der Märchentypen*—the first work to distinguish clearly between a compound "type" or tale and its elemental components, "motifs."* Aarne realized the materials on which his work was based were far too incomplete to serve as a universally applicable system and tried to provide for expansion of types when other, non-European narratives were brought under scrutiny. Scholars began to use this classification, and slowly the corpus of narratives grew until in 1924 an alteration and expansion

---

* "A *type* is a traditional tale that has an independent existence. It may be told as a complete narrative and does not depend for its meaning on any other tale."

"A *motif* is the smallest element in a tale having a power to persist in tradition. In order to have this power it must have something unusual and striking about it" (Thompson, 1951: 415).

of the *Verzeichnis* was clearly necessary. Aarne planned this revision, but died before undertaking it. Thompson accepted Krohn's invitation to revise the index, and in 1928 the classification was pubpublished as *The Types of the Folk-Tale: A Classification and Bibliography (FFC* 74), ordering all known narratives into 2500 general types under three main divisions, Animal Tales, Ordinary Folk-Tales, and Jokes and Anecdotes. This classification is so obviously bound to the culture and psychology that produced it and the tales it analyzes that it can be applied to primitive, non-European material only by wrenching either the classification or the material beyond the point of usefulness. Many criticisms were made and suggestions were offered for revision, but Thompson soon realized that its basic fault was the complexity of the types it subsumed.* He turned his attention to the elements that the tales compounded, and began the work that led to his great 1955 edition of *The Motif Index of Folk Literature*, of which he says in his introduction (11):

> The purpose of the present study . . . has been to arrange in a single logical classification the elements which make up traditional narrative literature. Stories that have formed part of a tradition, whether oral or literary, find a place here. The folktale, the myth, the ballad, the fable, the mediaeval romance, the fabliau, the jest, the exemplum, and the local tradition have all been included, though inadequately recorded. . . . Certain aspects of folklore have been definitely omitted. I have not treated superstitions, customs, religious beliefs, or proverbs, except as they happen to form an organic part of a narrative. To have included these would have doubled the size of the index.

The work grew pragmatically, without a final plan in mind, out of an omnivorous collection of notes. In the process of the work the arrangement underwent several changes, evolving finally to a plan of 23 divisions, progressing generally from the mythological to the realistic. These divisions Thompson lettered from A to Z, omitting I, O, and Y, called Chapters. Within the Chapters organization continued by means of a rough decimal system (unlike a true decimal system the subdivisions may go beyond ten; for example, "Why Jackal Has Bare Tail" is A2317.12.2). Each Chapter has grand

---

* Another revision was made in 1962, but the objections remain.

divisions of a hundred numbers or some multiple of a hundred numbers. Within these grand divisions arrangement proceeds by tens or groups of tens. Provision for items not yet discovered is made by the open-end-method—the "decimal" places can be extended indefinitely. The grand division E501 has, for instance, more than 200 subdivisions. To list all the subdivisions would take at least one third the space of Thompson's six-volume, 5,550-page work.

The student of primitive literature without training in motif indexing will not find it very useful;* to index a tale "properly," there is no alternative to serving an internship with Thompson or one of his students. More serious is the inadequacy of the accompanying bibliography; merely naming or numbering motifs makes the literature in which they appear no more intelligible than naming or numbering stars makes astronomy intelligible. The value of an index of this kind therefore depends directly on the exhaustiveness of the bibliographic references, and these, unfortunately, are quite insufficient. Only about five hundred titles are listed altogether, some areas of the world are not covered at all, and some motifs have only one reference. Worst of all is the orientation of the work to Western themes, culture, psychology, and interpretation; most motifs of literatures like the native Australian or Melanesian would have to be thrust into the "Miscellaneous" categories. However, one does not condemn a shovel because it will not saw wood. The *Motif-Index* is a tool that was designed to facilitate the Historic-Geographic analysis of European tales; that it should work at all in the larger and in some ways fundamentally different area of primitive literature is surprising; that it works well enough to be used by most contemporary ethnological folklorists is a quietus to all criticism.**

A POSTSCRIPT ON ETHNOMUSICOLOGY

A few years ago on an Australian quiz show the master of ceremonies suspected a contestant knew little about serious music in the United States and consequently [asked him as his 64-guinea question, "Who had the greatest influence on the development of American music?" The competitor boomeranged him with the

---

* Should relations between parents and children go in T600 (Care of Children) or P200 (The Family)? Should extramarital intercourse go in K1500 (Deceptions Connected with Adultery) or T400 (Illicit Sexual Relations)?

** To see how tales are indexed, refer to any issue of *Western Folklore*.

answer "Thomas Edison." As American music would be inconceivable without the phonograph, so primitive music as a subject of study is inconceivable without the tape recorder. In its most tenuous definition, ethnomusicology can be traced back historically to the Renaissance, but as a province of literature and anthropology it did not exist in a practical way until acoustical recordings could be made easily in the field and reproduced cheaply and in quantity in the studio. Fifteen years ago no anthropologist was expected to know anything about the music of the people he chose to study, and if he did, he certainly was not expected to communicate his knowledge. Some very few ethnographers had enough musical training to write down the sounds their primitive informants made with voice and instrument; but what was reproduced from their notes in the laboratory had almost no resemblance to the original. Writing an Indian *swara* with European musical notation was like writing poetry with the Table of Atomic Weights. Now one commercial company alone has more than 800 records—400 listening hours—of music from the world's primitive and folk cultures for sale, and a number of American universities have purchased the entire stock for the use of their students and scholars. The 1961 meeting of the Society for Ethnomusicology heard a paper by Alan Lomax analyzing the styles of several hundred societies, all drawn from these Ethnic Folkways records, and most of the audience were able to understand and evaluate the conclusions from their own acquaintance with the same material. The field anthropologist of today finds that the portable recorder is a much more important tool than the cephalic calipers.

Modern ethnomusicology struggled into being with genius and energy as inadequate substitutes for electrical equipment. Toward the end of the 18th century several competent investigators followed the lead of Rousseau's *Dictionary of Music* in studying Chinese, Indian, and Arabic music, and a large amount of work was done after the Romantic period in the texts of folksongs, but the stranger musics of the remote parts of the world had to wait upon recording devices. Nettl in his short history of ethnomusicology speaks of the formation of two schools, the German and the American. The founders of the German school were Carl Stumpf, a psychologist who recorded songs from a group of visiting Bella Coola Indians in Berlin in 1882, and Alexander John Ellis, an English physicist who evolved a system of interval measurement for non-European scales that is still used. Because of the professional interests of Stumpf and Ellis, the German school took the path of acoustics and psychology. The

American school turned in another direction. Nettl suggests that the proximity of the American scholars to a rich body of primitive material, the American Indian, almost required them to concentrate on ethnographic studies, while the Germans with much less opportunity to collect, concerned themselves with analysis. Nevertheless the first serious work in the American field was done by a German, Theodore Baker, and the German collection of records was probably the greatest in the world until its destruction by bombing in World War II. The names of the American ethnomusicologists run all through this book—James Mooney, Alice Fletcher, Franz Boas, George Herzog (who emigrated from the German school), and Frances Densmore, to name only the leading members. Densmore died in 1957 at the age of ninety, having published more than two thousand Indian songs.

The German ethnomusicologists are not so familiar, since they dealt less with texts than with the music: Kurt Sachs and Erich von Hornbostel, who developed an irreplaceable system of classifying musical instruments; Robert Lach, the music historian; Bela Bartok, the composer who drew more heavily than any other of his art upon primitive sources; Marius Schneider; Miecsyslav Kolinski; and Otto Abraham are outstanding.

The German school has not recovered from the severe blow dealt it by the war; the American school has prospered even in general adversity—the Great Depression and the subsequent employment of scholars by the United States Government in collecting material began the huge holdings of the Library of Congress Archive of Folk Song, and the war stimulated the development of incomparably better recording equipment than the Germans knew.* In 1955 the Society for Ethnomusicology was founded in this country, and there is little doubt that it will soon gather into its burgeoning organization all the world's workers in primitive music to join Charles Seeger, Alan Lomax, Richard Waterman, Alan Merriam, Helen Roberts, George Herzog, Gertrude Kurath, George List, Bertrand Bronson, Gilbert Chase, Daniel Crowley, Melville Herskovits, Edward Lowinsky, William P. Malm, Frederick Ramsay, Gustave Reese, John Ward, Charles Haywood, Nadia Chilkovsky, Willard Rhodes, David McAllester, Johanna Spector, Vernon Taylor, Mantle Hood, Rose Brandel, Roxane McCollester, T. Gerald Dyar, and Bruno Nettl. But the man who has had the most influence on the discipline since

---

* Americans made almost all the significant inventions in acoustical recording.

Thomas Edison is, like Edison, never included in a list of important people in contemporary music. He is Moses Asch, who put into the hands of scholars the portable equipment that recorded the great collection of the Ethnic Folkways Library, and who in a practical way enabled technology to create an academic discipline.

Bibliography

Limited to References Cited in the Text

ABRAHAM, ROY CLIVE
    1933   The Tiv people. Lagos, the Government Printer.

ARBERRY, ARTHUR J.
    1952   Omar Khayyam. New Haven, Yale University
                 Press.

ASTROV, MARGOT
    1950   The concept of motion as the psychological leit-
                 motif of Navaho life and literature. Journal of
                 American Folklore 63:45–56.

AUSTIN, MARY
    1930   The American rhythm: studies and reexpressions
                 of Amerindian songs. Boston, Houghton Mifflin
                 Company.

BALDWIN, B.
    1945   Usituma! Song of heaven. Oceania 15:201–238.
    1950   Songs of the Trobriand sunset isles. Oceania
                 20:263–285.

BALKEN, EVA R. and JULES H. MASSERMAN
    1940   The language of phantasy. Journal of Psy-
                 chology 75–86.

BARNETT, H. G.
    1960   Being a Palauan. New York, Henry Holt and
                 Company.

BARNOUW, VICTOR
    1950   Acculturation and personality among the Wis-
                 consin Chippewa. Menasha, American Anthro-
                 pological Association Memoir 72.

1955   A psychological interpretation of a Chippewa
              origin legend. Journal of American Folklore
              68:73-85, 211-223, 341-355.

BARRETT, SAMUEL A.
1925   The Cayapa Indians of Ecuador. New York,
              Museum of the American Indian Notes and
              Monographs No. 40, Parts I and II.

BASCOM, WILLIAM R.
1943   The relationship of Yoruba folklore to divining.
              Journal of American Folklore 56:127-131.

1949   Literary style in Yoruba riddles. Journal of
              American Folklore 62:1-16.

1953   Drums of the Yoruba of Nigeria. New York,
              Ethnic Folkways record P 441.

1955   Verbal art. Journal of American Folklore
              68:245-252.

1957   The myth-ritual theory. Journal of American
              Folklore 70:103-114.

BASEDOW, HERBERT
1925   The Australian aboriginal. Adelaide, F. W.
              Preece and Son.

BEALS, RALPH L.
1943   Problems of Mexican Indian folklore. Journal
              of American Folklore 56:8-16.

BECK, HORACE P. Ed.
1962   Folklore in action: essays for discussion in honor
              of MacEdward Leach. Philadelphia, The Ameri-
              can Folklore Society, Inc.

BECKWITH, MARTHA A.
1951   The Kumulipo: a Hawaiian creation chant.
              Chicago, University of Chicago Press.

BENDER, HAROLD H.
1922   The home of the Indo-Europeans. Princeton,
              University of Princeton Press.

BENEDICT, RUTH
1933   Myth. *In* Encyclopedia of the social sciences.
               178–181.

1934   Patterns of culture. New York, Houghton
               Mifflin Company. Pelican Books edition, 1946.

1935   Zuni mythology. New York, Columbia Uni-
               versity Press, 2 volumes.

BENET, WILLIAM ROSE
1948   The reader's encyclopedia. New York, Thomas
               Y. Crowell Company.

BERNDT, RONALD M.
1953a   Djanggawul: an aboriginal religious cult of
               northeastern Arnhem Land. New York, Philo-
               sophical Library.

BERNDT, RONALD M. and CATHERINE BERNDT
1953b   A selection of children's songs from Ooldea,
               western South Australia. Mankind 4:423–434.

BIDDULPH, J.
1880   Tribes of the Hindoo Koosh. Calcutta, Office of
               the Superintendent of Government Printing.

BIRD, JUNIUS
1946   The Alacaluf. *In* Julian H. Steward, Ed., Hand-
               book of South American Indians. Washington,
               Bureau of American Ethnology Bulletin 143,
               Volume I.

BIRDSELL, JOSEPH B.
1958   On population structure in generalized hunting
               and collecting populations. Evolution 12:189–
               205.

BOAS, FRANZ
1891   Dissemination of tales among the natives of
               North America. Journal of American Folklore
               4:13–20.

1897   The growth of Indian mythologies. Journal of
               American Folklore 9:1–11.

1898   Introduction to James Teit, Traditions of the
              Thompson River Indians of British Columbia.
              Boston and New York, Houghton Mifflin Com-
              pany.

1910   Tsimshian mythology. Washington, Bureau of
              American Ethnology Annual Report 31.

1911   Introduction to Handbook of American Indian
              languages, Part I. Washington, Bureau of
              American Ethnology Bulletin 40:1–83.

1914   Mythology and folk-tales of the North American
              Indians. Journal of American Folklore 27:374–
              410.

1925   Stylistic aspects of primitive literature. Journal
              of American Folklore 38:329–339.

1938a   General anthropology. Boston, D. C. Heath
              and Company.

1938b   The mind of primitive man. New York, The
              Macmillan Company, rev. ed.

BOGORAS, WALDEMAR (BOGORAZ)

1902   The folklore of northeastern Asia, as compared
              with that of northwestern America. American
              Anthropologist 4:577–683.

1904–1909   The Chukchee. New York, American Museum
              of Natural History Memoirs Volume VII (The
              Jesup North Pacific Expedition).

BOULTON, LAURA

1954   The Eskimos of Hudson Bay and Alaska. New
              York, Ethnic Folkways record P 444.

BOWERS, ALFRED W.

1950   Mandan social and ceremonial organization.
              Chicago, University of Chicago Press.

BREEKS, JAMES WILKINSON

1873   An account of the primitive tribes and monu-
              ments of the Nilagiris. London, India Museum.

BRIGHT, WILLIAM

1961   Language and music: areas for cooperation. In press.

BRODRICK, ALAN H.

1948   Little vehicle: Cambodia and Laos. London, Hutchinson and Company.

BUCK, PETER H. (TE RANGI HIROA)

1930   Ethnology of Tongareva. Honolulu, Bernice P. Bishop Museum Bulletin 70.

1938   Ethnology of Mangareva. Honolulu, Bernice P. Bishop Museum Bulletin 157.

1949   The coming of the Maori. Wellington, Whitcombe and Tombs, Ltd.

BURTON, FREDERICK R.

1909   American primitive music with especial attention to the songs of the Ojibways. New York, Moffat, Yard and Company.

BUSHNELL, DAVIS I., JR.

1909   The Choctaw of Bayou Lacomb, St. Tammany Parish, Louisiana. Washington, Bureau of American Ethnology Bulletin 48.

CALAME-GRIAULE, GENEVIEVE and BLAISE CALAME

1957   Introduction a l'étude de la musique africaine. Supplement à la révue musicale No. 238.

CARROLL, JOHN B.

1956   Language, thought, and reality. New York, Wiley.

CHADWICK, H. MUNRO and N. KERSHAW CHADWICK

1940   The growth of literature. New York, The Macmillan Company, 3 volumes.

CHAMBERLAIN, ALEXANDER F.

1903   Primitive woman as poet. Journal of American Folklore 16:205–228.

CHAMBERS, E. K.

1927   Arthur of Britain. London, Sidgwick & Jackson, Ltd.

CHASE, RICHARD

1949   Quest for myth. Baton Rouge, Louisiana State University Press.

CHILD, FRANCIS JAMES

1932   English and Scottish popular ballads. Edited by G. L. Kittredge and Helen Child Sargent. Boston, Houghton Mifflin Company.

CODRINGTON, ROBERT H.

1891   The Melanesians: studies in their anthropology and folklore. London, Oxford University Press.

COLLOCOTT, E. E. V.

1928   Tales and poems of Tonga. Honolulu, Bernice P. Bishop Museum Bulletin 46.

CONNOLLY, R. M.

1897   Social life in Fanti-land. Journal of the Royal Anthropological Society of Great Britain and Ireland 26:128–153.

COOPER, JOHN M.

1946   The Araucanians. Washington, Bureau of American Ethnology Bulletin 143, 2:687–760.

COURLANDER, HAROLD and GEORGE HERZOG

1947   The cow-tail switch and other west African stories. New York, Henry Holt & Company.

COWELL, HENRY

1951   Music of southeast Asia. New York, Ethnic Folkways record P 423.

COX, MARIAN R.

1893   Cinderella. London, Publications of the Folk-Lore Society No. 31.

COXWELL, C. FILLINGHAM

1925   Siberian and other folk-tales. London, C. W. Daniel Company.

CRONYN, GEORGE W.

1918   The path on the rainbow. New York, Boni and Liveright.

CUDJOE, S. D.

1953   The techniques of Ewe drumming and the social importance of work in Africa. Phylon 14: number 3.

CURTIS, MARTHA E.

1952   The black bear and white tailed deer as potent factors in the folklore of the Menonimi Indians. Midwest Folklore 2:177–190.

CURTIS, NATALIE

1907   The Indians' book. New York, Harper and Brothers, Publishers.

CUSHING, FRANK HAMILTON

1901   Zuni folk tales. New York, G. P. Putnam's Sons.

DANIEL, GLYN *et al.*

1955   Myth or legend. London, G. Bell and Sons.

DAVENPORT, WILLIAM H.

1953   Marshallese folklore types. Journal of American Folklore 66:219–237.

DAVIDSON, LEVETTE J.

1948   White versions of Indian myths and legends. Western Folklore 7:115–128.

DAY, A. GROVE

1951   The sky clears; poetry of the American Indians. New York, The Macmillan Company.

DENSMORE, FRANCES

1929   Chippewa customs. Washington, Bureau of American Ethnology Bulletin 86.

1936   Cheyenne and Arapaho music. Los Angeles, Southwest Museum Papers No. 10.

1943   The use of meaningless syllables in Indian songs. American Anthropologist 45:160–162.

1950   The words of Indian songs as unwritten literature. Journal of American Folklore 63:450–458.

1953   The use of music in the treatment of the sick by American Indians. Washington, Smithsonian Report for 1952, Publication 4128.

DICKSON, H. R. P.

1951   The Arab of the desert. London, George Allen & Unwin.

DIXON, R. B.

1916   Oceanic mythology. Boston, Marshall Jones Company.

DONNER, KAI

1926   Bei den Samojeden in Sibirien. Stuttgart, Strecker und Strecker. Translated by Rinehart Kyler.

DORSEY, J. OWEN

1893   Modern additions to Indian myths, and Indian thunder superstitions. Journal of American Folklore 6:232–233

DORSON, RICHARD M

1955   The eclipse of solar mythology. *In* Sebeok, 1955, 15–38.

1961   (Ed.) Folklore research around the world. Journal of American Folklore 74:285–460. Special double issue.

DOWNES, R. M.

1933   The Tiv tribe. Kaduna, The Government Printer.

DOZIER, EDWARD P.
1956   The role of the Hopi-Tewa migration legend in
            reinforcing cultural patterns and prescribing
            social behavior. Journal of American Folklore
            69:176–180.

DRIVER, HAROLD E.
1961   Indians of North America. Chicago, University
            of Chicago Press.

DURKHEIM, ÉMILE
1947   The elementary forms of the religious life.
            London, George Allen & Unwin.

EARLE, JOHN
1892   Beowulf. Oxford, Clarendon Press.

EDWARDS, CHARLES L.
1895   Bahama songs and stories. New York, G. E.
            Stechert & Company.

ELKIN, ADOLPHUS PETER
1934   Cult totemism and mythology in northern South
            Australia. Oceania 5:171–192.

1947   Aboriginal evidence and justice in north Aus-
            tralia. Oceania 17:173–210.

1953   Tribal music of Australia. New York, Ethnic
            Folkways record P 439.

1954   The Australian aborigines: how to understand
            them. Sydney, Angus & Robertson, 3rd edition,

EMORY, KENNETH P.
1934   The legends of Maui and Takahi. Honolulu,
            Bernice P. Bishop Museum Bulletin 127.

ENNIS, MERLIN
1962   Umbundu. Folk tales from Angola. Boston,
            Beacon Press.

ESPINOSA, AURELIO
1930   Notes on the origin and history of the tar-baby
            story. Journal of American Folklore 43:129–209.

1938   More notes on the origin and history of the tar-
              baby story.   Folk-Lore 49:168–182.

1943   A new classification of the fundamental elements
              of the tar-baby story on the basis of two hundred
              and sixty-seven versions.   Journal of American
              Folklore 56:31–37.

EVANS-PRITCHARD, E. E.
1940   The Nuer.   Oxford, Clarendon Press.

FINCK, HENRY I.
1899   Primitive love and love-stories.   New York,
              Charles Scribner's Sons.

FINLAYSON, H. H.
1945   The red centre: man and beast in the heart of
              Australia.   Sydney, Angus & Robertson.

FIRTH, RAYMOND
1936   We, the Tikopia.   New York, American Book
              Company.

FLETCHER, ALICE C.
1900   Indian story and song from North America.
              Boston, Small Maynard & Co.

1915   The study of Indian music.   Proceedings of the
              National Academy of Science, I:231–235.   Quoted
              in Day, 1951, 12–13.

FLETCHER, ALICE C. and FRANCIS LA FLESCHE
1906 (1911)   The Omaha tribe.   Washington, Bureau of
              American Ethnology Annual Report 27.

FORTES, MEYER
1949   The web of kinship among the Tallensi.   Lon-
              don, Oxford University Press.

FRAZER, SIR JAMES GEORGE
1959   The new golden bough.   New York, Criterion
              Books.   Edited with notes and foreword by
              Theodor H. Gaster.   Abridged from the 12-
              volume edition (1907–1915).   This abridged edi-
              tion is more valuable to the student than either
              the original edition or the previous abridgement.

FROST, ROBERT
1939   Collected poems of Robert Frost.   New York,
            Henry Holt and Company.

FURNAS, JOSEPH CHAMBERLAIN
1948   Anatomy of paradise.   New York, William
            Sloane Associates.

FURNIVALL, FREDERICK J.
1901   Robert of Brunne's 'Handlyng Synne,' A. D.
            1303.   London, Early English Text Society,
            No. 119.

GALBRAITH, JOHN KENNETH
1960   The liberal hour.   Boston, Houghton Mifflin.

GARNETT, JAMES M.
1882   Beowulf.   Boston, Ginn & Co.

GASTER, THEODOR H.
1952   The oldest stories in the world.   Boston, Beacon
            Press.

GAYTON, ANN H.
1935   The Orpheus myth in North America.   Journal
            of American Folklore 48:262-286.

GEORGES, ROBERT A. and ALAN DUNDES
1963   Toward a structural definition of the riddle.
            Journal of American Folklore 76:111-118.

GIDDINGS, RUTH W.
1959   Yaqui myths and legends.   Tucson, Anthropo-
            logical Papers of the University of Arizona No. 2.

GIFFORD, EDWARD WINSLOW
1926   Yuma dreams and omens.   Journal of American
            Folklore 39:58-69.

GILLIN, JOHN
1936   The Barama River Caribs of British Guiana.
            Cambridge, Mass., Papers of the Peabody
            Museum XIV No. 2.

GOLDSTEIN, KENNETH S.
1960   The unfortunate rake: A study in the evolu-
              tion of a ballad. New York, Folkways Records
              FS 3805.

GORDON, R. K.
1926   Anglo-Saxon poetry. London, J. M. Dent &
              Sons, Ltd. Everyman's Library No. 794.

GREENBERG, JOSEPH H.
1947   Islam and clan organization among the Hausa.
              Southwestern Journal of Anthropology 3:193–
              211.

GREENWAY, JOHN
1953   American folksongs of protest. Philadelphia,
              University of Pennsylvania Press.

1956   Aunt Molly Jackson and Robin Hood: a study
              in folk re-creation. Journal of American Folk-
              lore 69:23–38.

GRENDON, FELIX
1909   The Anglo-Saxon charms. Journal of American
              Folklore 22:105–237

GRIMM, WILHELM
1884   Grimm's household tales. London, translation
              by Margaret Hunt of Kinder– und hausmärchen,
              Leipzig, 1856.

GRINNELL, GEORGE BIRD
1923   The Cheyenne Indians. New Haven, Yale
              University Press, 2 volumes.

GUMMERE, FRANCIS B.
1909   The oldest English epic. New York, Macmillan
              Company.

HAILEY, LORD, Ed.
1957   An African survey. London, Oxford University
              Press, revised edition.

HALL, JOHN LESSLIE
1896   Beowulf, an Anglo-Saxon epic poem. Boston,
              D. C. Heath.

HALLOWELL, A. IRVING

1942   The role of conjuring in Saulteaux society.
        Philadelphia, Publications of the Philadelphia
        Anthropological Society No. 2.

1947   Myth, culture and personality. American
        Anthropologist 49:544–556.

HAMBLY, WILFRED D.

1934   The Ovimbundu of Angola. Chicago, Field
        Museum of Natural History Publication 320,
        Anthropological Series XXI, No. 2.

HANDY, EDWARD SMITH CRAIGHILL

1927   Polynesian religion. Honolulu, Bernice P.
        Bishop Museum Bulletin 34.

1930a   History and culture of the Society Islands.
        Honolulu, Bernice P. Bishop Museum Bulletin
        79.

1930b   Marquesan legends. Honolulu, Bernice P.
        Bishop Museum Bulletin 69.

HARNEY, BILL and ALAN MARSHALL

1960   The two who went talkabout. Sydney, Score
        record POL 017.

HARTLAND, EDWIN SIDNEY

1890   The science of fairy tales. New York, Frederick
        A. Stokes Company.

HASSAN, MALAM and MALAM SHUAIBU

1952   A chronicle of Abuja. Translated by Frank L.
        Heath. Ibadan, Ibadan University Press.

HAWES, CHARLES H.

1903   In the uttermost East. London, Harper and
        Brothers.

HERSKOVITS, MELVILLE J.

1937   African gods and Catholic saints in New World
        religious belief. American Anthropologist 39:
        635–643.

1938   Dahomey. New York, J. J. Augustin, 2 volumes.

HERSKOVITS, MELVILLE J. and FRANCES S. HERSKOVITS
1958   Dahomean narrative. Evanston, Northwestern
            University Press.

HERZOG, GEORGE
1935   Plains ghost dance and Great Basin music.
            American Anthropologist 37:403–419.

1936   Research in primitive and folk music in the
            United States. Washington, American Council
            of Learned Societies Bulletin 24:561–656.

HEWES, GORDON W.
1954   Mexicans in search of the "Mexican." American
            Journal of Economics and Sociology 13:209–223.

HEWITT, J. W. B.
1905a   Nanabozho. In Hodge, 1905.
1905b   Mythology. In Hodge, 1905.

HILGER, M. INEZ
1957   Araucanian child life and its cultural back-
            ground. Washington, Smithsonian Institution
            Miscellaneous Collections, Volume 133.

HILL, W. W.
1944   The Navaho Indians and the ghost dance of
            1890. American Anthropologist 46:523–527.

HODGE, FREDERICK WEBB, Ed.
1905   Handbook of American Indians north of Mexico.
            Washington, Bureau of American Ethnology
            Bulletin 30, 2 volumes.

HOEBEL, E. ADAMSON
1941   The Asiatic origin of a myth of the northwest
            coast. Journal of American Folklore 55:1–9.

HOFFMAN, W. J.
1891   The Mide'wiwin or grand medicine society of the
            Ojibwa. Washington, Bureau of American
            Ethnology Annual Report 7:143–300.

HOLMBERG, ALLAN R.
   1950   Nomads of the long bow: the Siriono of eastern
                 Bolivia. Washington, Smithsonian Institution,
                 Institute of Social Anthropology Publication
                 No. 10.

HONIGMANN, JOHN J.
   1959   The world of man. New York, Harper &
                 Brothers.

HOWELLS, WILLIAM W.
   1950   The heathens: primitive man and his religions.
                 New York, Doubleday & Co., Inc.

HUFFMAN, RAY
   1931   Nuer customs and folk-lore. London (Oxford),
                 Humphrey Milford.

HULBERT, HOMER B.
   1906   The passing of Korea. New York, Doubleday,
                 Page & Co.

HULBERT, JAMES R., Ed.
   1935   Bright's Anglo-Saxon reader. New York, Henry
                 Holt and Company.

HUTSON, JAMES
   1921   Chinese life on the Tibetan foothills. Shanghai,
                 Far Eastern Geographical Establishment.

HYMAN, STANLEY EDGAR
   1955   The ritual view of myth and the mythic. *In*
                 Sebeok, 1955.

INDIANA UNIVERSITY
   1955   The Samoyed. Typescript prepared for the
                 Human Relations Area Files.

ISLAVIN, VLADIMIR
   1847   The Samoyed in their domestic and social life.
                 St. Petersburg, Ministerstva Gosudarstvennykh
                 Imushchestv. Translated by Sheldon Wise *et al.*,
                 Human Relations Area Files.

JABLONSKI, EDWARD
    1959   Notes to "The golden apple," Elektra record
                EKL 5000. New York, Elektra Records.

JACOBS, MELVILLE
    1947   Oral literature. *In* Melville Jacobs and Bern-
                hard J. Stern, Outline of anthropology, New
                York, Barnes & Noble, 216–229.

    1957   Titles in an oral literature. Journal of American
                Folklore 70:157–172.

    1959a   The content and style of an oral literature:
                Clackamas Chinook myths and tales. New
                York, Viking Fund Publications in Anthro-
                pology No. 26.

    1959b   The anthropology of Franz Boas: folklore.
                American Anthropologist 61:119–138.

JAMES, EDWIN
    1823   Account of an expedition . . . under the command
                of Major Stephen H. Long. *Quoted in* Davidson,
                1948, 115–116.

JENNESS, DIAMOND
    1924   Myths and traditions from Northern Canada,
                the Mackenzie delta and Coronation Gulf. Re-
                port of the Canadian Arctic Expedition, 1913–
                1919, XIII, Part A. Ottawa, F. A. Ackland.

JOCHELSON, WALDEMAR
    1908   The Koryak. Part I: Religion and myths of the
                Koryak. New York, G. E. Stechert and Co.
                (American Museum of Natural History Memoir
                10).

    1926   The Yukaghir and the Yukaghirized Tungus.
                New York, American Museum of Natural His-
                tory Memoir 9 (The Jesup North Pacific Expe-
                dition).

JONES, TREVOR A.
    1957   Arnhem Land music. Oceania 28:1–30.

JUNOD, HENRI
>1927   The life of a South African tribe. London, Macmillan and Co., 2nd ed.

KABERRY, PHYLLIS M.
>1939   Aboriginal woman, sacred and profane. London, George Routledge and Sons, Ltd.

KARDINER, ABRAM
>1939   The individual and his society. New York, Columbia University Press.

KARSTEN, RAFAEL
>1935   The head hunters of western Amazonia. Helsingfors, Centralryckeriet Societas Scientarum Fennica Communications Humanorum Litterarum VII, No. 1, translated for the Human Relations Area Files.

KENNARD, E. A.
>1937   Hopi reactions to death. American Anthropologist 39:491–496.

KENNEDY, CHARLES W.
>1940   Beowulf, the oldest English epic. New York Oxford University Press.

KENYATA, JOMO
>1953   Facing Mount Kenya: the tribal life of the Gikuyu. London, Martin Secker and Warburg.

KIEFER, EMMA E.
>1947   Albert Wesselski and recent folktale theories. Bloomington, Indiana University Publications Folklore Series No. 3.

KLAEBER, FRIEDRICH
>1936   Beowulf. New York, Heath, 3rd ed.

KLAPP, ORRIN E.
>1949   The folk hero. Journal of American Folklore 62:17–25.

KLUCKHOHN, CLYDE
    1942   Myths and rituals, a general theory. Harvard
                Theological Review 35:45-79.

KLUCKHOHN, CLYDE and DOROTHEA LEIGHTON
    1946   The Navaho. Cambridge, Harvard University
                Press.

KOLARZ, WALTER
    1954   The peoples of the Soviet Far East. New York,
                Frederick A. Praeger.

KRAPPE, ALEXANDER H.
    1946   A Solomon legend among the Indians of the
                North Pacific. Journal of American Folklore
                59:309-314.

KRIGE, E. JENSEN and J. D. KRIGE
    1954   African worlds. London, Oxford University
                Press.

KROEBER, ALFRED L.
    1948   Anthropology. New York, Harcourt, Brace and
                World Company.

    1957   Style and civilizations. Ithaca, Cornell Univer-
                sity Press.

KYAGAMBIDDWA, JOSEPH
    1955   African music from the source of the Nile. New
                York, Frederick A. Praeger.

LA BARRE, WESTON
    1950   Aymara folktales. International Journal of
                American Linguistics 16:40-45.

LANDES, RUTH
    1937   The Ojibwa of Canada. New York, McGraw-
                Hill Book Co.

    1938   The abnormal among the Ojibwa Indians.
                Journal of Abnormal and Social Psychology
                33:14-33.

LANG, ANDREW
>1898   The making of religion. New York, Longmans,
>   Green & Co.

LATCHAM, R. E.
>1909   Ethnology of the Araucanos. Journal of the
>   Royal Anthropological Society of Great Britain
>   and Ireland 39:334–370.

LATTIMORE, OWEN
>1941   Mongol journeys. New York, Doubleday & Co.

LEACH, MARIA, Ed.
>1949   Funk & Wagnalls standard dictionary of folklore
>   mythology and legend. New York, Funk &
>   Wagnalls Company, 2 volumes.

LEAKEY, L. S. B.
>1959   Personal communication.

LEBKICHER, ROY, GEORGE RENTZ, and MAX STEINEKE
>1952   The Arabia of Ibn Saud. New York, Russell F.
>   Moore and Co., Inc.

LEONARD, WILLIAM ELLERY
>1923   Beowulf: a new verse translation for fireside and
>   class room. New York, The Century Co.

>1929   Four footnotes to papers on Germanic metrics.
>   *In* Kemp Malone and Martin B. Ruud, Studies
>   in English philology, Minneapolis, University of
>   Minnesota Press.

LESLAU, WOLF
>1951   Music of south Arabia. New York, Ethnic
>   Folkways record P 421.

LESSA, WILLIAM A.
>1961   Tales from Ulithi atoll. Berkeley, University of
>   California Press, Folklore Studies No. 13.

LESSA, WILLIAM A. and EVON Z. VOGT
>1958   Reader in comparative religion. Evanston, Ill.,
>   Row, Peterson and Co.

LESSER, ALEXANDER
    1933   The Pawnee ghost dance and hand game. New York, Columbia University Contributions to Anthropology XVI.

LÉVI-STRAUSS, CLAUDE
    1955   The structural study of myth. *In* Sebeok, 1955, 50–56.

LIEDER, P. R., R. M. LOVETT, and R. K. ROOT
    1950   British poetry and prose. Boston, Houghton Mifflin Company.

LOMAX, ALAN
    1959   Folk song style. American Anthropologist 61:927–954.

LOWIE, ROBERT H.
    1909   The Assiniboine. New York, Anthropological Papers of the American Museum of Natural History IV, Part 1.

    1917   Oral tradition and history. Journal of American Folklore 30:161–167.

LUOMALA, KATHERINE
    1940   Oceanic, American Indian, and African myths of snaring the sun. Honolulu, Bernice P. Bishop Museum Bulletin 168.

    1949   Maui of a thousand tricks. Honolulu, Bernice P. Bishop Museum Bulletin 198.

MACKENZIE, D. R.
    1925   The spirit-ridden Ngonde. London, Seekyl Service & Co., Ltd.

MALCOLM, GEORGE A.
    1951   First Malayan republic. Boston, Cristopher Publishing House.

MALCOLMSON, DAVID, Ed.
    1941   Ten heroes. New York, Duell, Sloan and Pearce.

MALHERBE, W. A.
1934   Tiv-English dictionary. Lagos, Crown Agents for the Colonies.

MALINOWSKI, BRONISLAW
1926   Myth in primitive psychology. New York, W. W. Norton & Co.

1929   Sexual life of savages. London, George Routledge.

1935   Coral gardens and their magic. New York, American Book Co., 2 volumes.

MAN, EDWARD H.
1932   On the aboriginal inhabitants of the Andaman Islands. London, Royal Anthropological Institute of Great Britain and Ireland.

MARINER, WILLIAM
1817   An account of the natives of the Tonga Islands in the South Pacific Ocean. London, printed for the author.

MARSHALL, H. I.
1945   The Karens of Burma. Calcutta, Longmans, Green & Co.

MATTHEWS, WASHINGTON
1884   The mountain chant, a Navaho ceremony. Washington, Bureau of American Ethnology Annual Report 5.

1899   Navaho gambling songs. American Anthropologist 2:1–19.

McCANN, FRANCIS B.
1959   Medicine man. Sydney, Angus and Robertson.

McCONNELL, URSULA
1957   Myths of the Mungkan. Melbourne, Melbourne University Press.

OPIE, IONA and PETER OPIE
1951   The Oxford dictionary of nursery rhymes. Oxford, The Clarendon Press.

ORWELL, GEORGE
1949   1984. London, Secker and Warburg.

PARSONS, ELSIE CLEWS
1918   Nativity myth at Laguna and Zuni. Journal of American Folklore 31:256–263.

PARKER, MRS. K. LANGLOH
1953   Australian legendary tales. Edited by H. Drake-Brockman. Sydney, Angus & Robertson, Ltd.

PEI, MARIO
1949   The story of language. Philadelphia, J. B. Lippincott Company.

PINK, OLIVE
1936   The landowners in the northern division of the Aranda tribe. Oceania 6:275–308.

PORÉE, GUY and EVELINE MASPERO
1938   Moeurs et coutumes des Kmèrs. Paris, Peyot.

PORTEUS, STANLEY D.
1931   The psychology of a primitive people: a study of the Australian aborigines. New York, Longmans, Green & Co.

POTTER, CHARLES FRANCIS
1950a   Riddle. In Leach, 938–944.
1950b   Jesus. In Leach, 548–550.

RADCLIFFE-BROWN, A. R.
1922   The Andaman islanders: a study in social anthropology. London, Cambridge University Press.

RADIN, PAUL
1926   Literary aspects of Winnebago mythology. Journal of American Folklore 39:18–52.

1927   Primitive man as philosopher. New York, D. Appleton and Company.

1948   Winnebago hero cycles: a study in aboriginal literature. Baltimore, Waverly Press, Inc. Indiana University Publications in Anthropology and Linguistics Memoir 1. Supplement to International Journal of American Linguistics 14, No. 3.

1956   The trickster: a study in American Indian mythology. London, Routledge and Kegan Paul.

RAE, EDWARD
1875   The land of the north wind. London, John Murray.

RAGLAN, LORD
1937   The hero: a study in tradition, myth and drama. New York, Oxford University Press.

1955   Myth and ritual. *In* Sebeok, 1955, 76–83.

RASMUSSEN, KNUD
1932   Intellectual culture of the Copper Eskimo. Report of the Fifth Thule Expedition 1921–1924, Volume IX.

RATTRAY, R. S.
1923   Ashanti. Oxford, Clarendon Press.

RAUM, O. F.
1940   Chaga childhood: a description of indigenous education in an East African tribe. London, Oxford University Press.

REDFIELD, MARGARET PARK
1937   The folk literature of a Yucatecan town. Washington, Carnegie Institution of Washington Contributions to American Archaeology, III, 13, 1–50.

REICHARD, GLADYS A.
1943   Imagery in an Indian vocabulary. American Speech 18:96–102.

1944   Individualism and mythological style. Journal
              of American Folklore 57:16–26.

1947   An analysis of Coeur d'Alêne Indian myths.
              Philadelphia, American Folklore Society Memoir
              41.

RHODES, WILLARD
    1955   Music of the American Indian. Including: L34,
                  Northwest (Puget Sound); L35, Kiowa; L36,
                  Indian songs of today; L37, Delaware, Choctaw,
                  Creek, Cherokee; L38, Great Basin (Paiute,
                  Washo, Ute, Bannock, Shoshone); L39, Plains
                  (Comanche, Cheyenne, Kiowa, Caddo, Wichita,
                  Pawnee); L40, Sioux; L42, Apache; L43, Pueblo
                  (Taos, San Ildefonso, Zuni, Hopi). Washington,
                  Library of Congress, Archive of Folksong records.

RICHARDS, AUDREY I.
    1956   Chisingu, a girls' initiation ceremony among the
                  Bemba of Northern Rhodesia. London, Faber
                  and Faber.

RICHMOND, W. EDSON
    1955   Review of John Greenway, American folksongs
                  of protest. Journal of American Folklore
                  68:96–98.

RIVERS, W. H. R.
    1906   The Todas. London, The Macmillan Co.

ROBINSON, ROLAND
    1952   Legend and dreaming. Sydney, Edwards and
                  Shaw.

    1956   The feathered serpent. Sydney, Edwards and
                  Shaw.

RÓHEIM, GÉZA
    1945   The eternal ones of the dream; a psychoanalytic
                  interpretation of Australian myth and ritual.
                  New York, International Universities Press.

1947   Psychoanalysis and anthropology. *In* Géza Róheim, Ed., Psychoanalysis and the social sciences, New York, International Universities Press, 9–33.

ROUTLEDGE, W. SCORESBY and KATHERINE ROUTLEDGE
1910   With a prehistoric people: the Akikuyu of British East Africa. London, Edward Arnold.

ROYS, RALPH L.
1933   The book of Chilam Balam of Chumayel. Washington, Carnegie Institution Publication 438.

RUSSELL, R. J. and F. B. KNIFFEN
1951   Culture worlds. New York, The Macmillan Company.

SAPIR, EDWARD
1910   Song-recitative in Paiute mythology. Journal of American Folklore 23:455–472.

1921   Language: an introduction to the study of speech. New York, Harcourt, Brace and World Company.

SCHOOLCRAFT, HENRY ROWE
1853   Western scenes and reminiscences: together with thrilling legends and traditions of the red man of the forest. Buffalo, Derby, Orton & Mulligan.

SCHULTZ, E.
1949   Proverbial expressions of the Samoans. Journal of the Polynesian Society 58:139–184.

SCHULTZE, LEONHARD
1907   Aus Namaland und Kalahari. Jena, Gustav Fischer.

SCOTT, CHARLES T.
1963   New evidence of American Indian riddles. Journal of American Folklore 76:236–241.

SEBEOK, THOMAS A., Ed.

1955   Myth, a symposium. Philadelphia, American Folklore Society Bibliographical and Special Series Volume 5.

1958   Personal communication.

SERVICE, ELMAN W.

1958   A profile of primitive culture. New York, Harper & Brothers. 2nd ed., Profiles in ethnology, New York, Harper & Row, 1963.

SHADE, CHARLES

Ms   Ethnological notes on the Aleuts. Cambridge, Harvard University unpublished dissertation (1949).

SHARP, LAURISTON

1952   Steel axes for stone-age Australians. Human Organization 11:17–22.

SHERIDAN, RAY

1958   Music of New Guinea. Sydney, Wattle Archive Series record No. 2.

SIMPSON, COLIN

1951   Adam in ochre: inside aboriginal Australia. Sydney, Angus & Robertson.

SMITH, W. RAMSAY

1930   Myths and legends of the Australian aboriginals. New York, Farrar & Rinehart.

SORRELS, ROSALIE

1963   Personal communication.

SPAETH, J. DUNCAN

1921   Old English poetry. Princeton, Princeton University Press.

SPENCER, SIR BALDWIN and F. J. GILLEN

1927   The Arunta: A study of a stone age people. London, Macmillan, 2 volumes.

SPENCER, KATHERINE
  1947   Reflection of social life in the Navaho origin
              myth. Albuquerque, University of New Mexico
              Publications in Anthropology No. 3.

STANNER, W. E. H.
  1956   The dreaming. *In* T. A. G. Hungerford, Ed.,
              Australian signpost, Melbourne, F. W. Cheshire,
              51–65.

STEFANSSON, VALHJALMUR
  1913   My life with the Eskimo. New York, The
              Macmillan Company.

STEWARD, JULIAN H.
  1946–1959   Handbook of South American Indians. Wash-
              ington, Bureau of American Ethnology Bulletin
              143, 7 volumes.

STIRLING, MATHEW W.
  1938   Historical and ethnographical material on the
              Jivaro Indians. Washington, Bureau of Ameri-
              can Ethnology Bulletin 117.

STONEY, SAMUEL G. and GERTRUDE MATHEWS
  1930   Black genesis: a chronicle. New York, The
              Macmillan Company.

STREHLOW, T. G. H.
  1947   Aranda traditions. Carlton, University of Mel-
              bourne Press.

SWANTON, JOHN R.
  1905   Types of Haida and Tlingit myths. American
              Anthropologist 7:94–103.

  1910   Some practical aspects of the study of myths.
              Journal of American Folklore 23:1–7.

  1952   The Indian tribes of North America. Washing-
              ton, Bureau of American Ethnology Bulletin 145.

TAPLIN, GEORGE
  1873   The Narrinyeri. Adelaide, South Australia.

TAYLOR, ARCHER
1944   American Indian riddles. Journal of American
            Folklore 57:1–15.

1950   Proverb. *In* Leach, 902–905.

THESIGER, W. P.
1950   The Badu of southern Arabia. The Royal
            Central Asian Journal 27:53–61.

THOMPSON, STITH
1929   Tales of the North American Indians. Cam-
            bridge, Harvard University Press.

1951   The folktale. New York, The Dryden Press.

1955   Motif-index of folk-literature. Bloomington,
            Indiana University Press, 6 volumes.

(THOMSON, DONALD S.)
1957   Getting to know the nomadic Bindaboos. The
            Australian Women's Weekly, December 11.

THORKELIN, G. J.
1815   De Danorum rebus gestis secul. III & IV.
            Havniae Tippis, Th. E. Rangel.

TINDALE, NORMAN B.
1961   Personal communication.

TINKER, CHAUNCEY B.
1902   Beowulf. New York, Henry Holt and Company.

TITIEV, MISCHA
1949   Social singing among the Mapuche. Ann Arbor,
            University of Michigan Anthropological Papers
            No. 2.

TORREND, J.
1921   Specimens of Bantu folk-lore. New York, E. P.
            Dutton & Co.

TOYNBEE, ARNOLD J.
1934   A study of history. London, Oxford University
            Press, 6 volumes.

TRACEY, HUGH
    1948   Chopi musicians. London, Oxford University Press.

    1954   The social role of African music. African Affairs 53:No. 212.

TREGEAR, EDWARD
    1904   The Maori race. Wanganui, N. Z., Willis.

TSCHOPIK, HARRY S.
    1951   The Aymara of Chucuito, Peru. I. Magic. New York, American Museum of Natural History Anthropological Publications 44:133–308.

TURNBULL, CLIVE
    1948   Black war. The extermination of the Tasmanian aborigines. Melbourne, F. W. Cheshire.

TURNER, LUCIEN M.
    1894   Ethnology of the Ungava district, Hudson Bay Territory. Bureau of American Ethnology Annual Report 11.

TYLOR, EDWARD BURNETT
    1896   American lot games as evidence of Asiatic intercourse before the time of Columbus. Internationales Archiv für Ethnographie 9 (Supplement) 55–67.

VAN GENNEP, ARNOLD
    1910   La formation des legendes. Paris.

VENIAMINOV, IVAN E.
    1840   Notes on the islands of the Unalaska district. St. Petersburg, Russian American Co., translated by B. Keen for Human Relations Area Files.

VERWILGEN, LEO A.
    1952   Folk music of the western Congo. New York, Ethnic Folkways record P 427.

VOEGELIN, ERMINIE WHEELER
    1941   Tubatulabal ethnography. Berkeley, University
                of California Publications in Anthropological
                Records II, 1938–1941.

WAGLEY, CHARLES
    1940   World view of the Tapirape Indians. Journal of
                American Folklore 53:252–260.

WALLACE, W. J.
    1947   The dream in Mohave life. Journal of American
                Folklore 60:252–258.

WALTON, EDA LOU
    1930   Navaho song patterning. Journal of American
                Folklore 43:103–118.

WALTON, EDA LOU and T. T. WATERMAN
    1925   American Indian poetry. American Anthro-
                pologist 27:25–52.

WARMINGTON, B. H.
    1960   Carthage. New York, Frederick A. Praeger.

WARNER, W. LLOYD
    1937   A black civilization. New York, Harper & Bros.

WASSEN, HENRY
    1949   Contributions to Cuna ethnogeography. Re-
                sults of an expedition to Panama and Columbia
                in 1947. Göteborg, Etnologiska Studier 16:7–
                139.

WATERMAN, T. T.
    1914   The explanatory element in the folk-tales of the
                North American Indians. Journal of American
                Folklore 27:1–54.

WEYER, EDWARD, JR.
    (1958)   Primitive peoples today. New York, Doubleday
                & Company.

WHITING, B. J.
    1950   The college survey of English literature. New
                    York, Harcourt, Brace and Company, Volume I

WILGUS, D. K.
    1959   Anglo-American folksong scholarship since 1898.
                    New Brunswick, N. J., Rutgers University Press.

WILLIAMS, THOMAS RHYS
    1963   The form and function of Tambunan Dusan
                    riddles. Journal of American Folklore 76:95–
                    110.

WITTFOGEL, KARL A. and ESTHER S. GOLDFRANK
    1943   Some aspects of Pueblo mythology and society.
                    Journal of American Folklore 56:17–30.

WOOD, CLEMENT
    1943   Wood's unabridged rhyming dictionary. Cleve-
                    land, World Publishing Company.

WORSLEY, PETER M.
    1959   Cargo cults. Scientific American 200:117–128.

WRIGHT, ARTHUR F.
    1953   Studies in Chinese thought. Menasha, American
                    Anthropological Association Comparative Studies
                    of Cultures and Civilizations No. 1, Volume 53,
                    No. 5, Part 2, 286–303; The Chinese language
                    and foreign ideas.

Index

Book design by Kenneth S. Goldstein. Binding and end-paper designs by William B. Cechak, based on wood and metal sculptures of the Bakota peoples, Gabun, Africa. Text set in Scotch Roman in Monotype, composed and printed by Westbrook Publishing Co., Inc., Philadelphia, Pa. Bound by The Haddon Craftsmen, Inc., Scranton, Pennsylvania.